AF317026

THIS IS NOT A FAIRY TALE

THIS IS NOT A FAIRY TALE

SCIENCE MEETS ITS MAKER

SECOND EDITION

DR. KENNETH L. RYFKOGEL JR.

ISBN Paperback: 979-8986403700
ISBN Hardcover: 979-8986403793
ISBN eBook: 979-8986403748

Table of Contents

The Burning Question

As stated on the copyrights page, any unmarked Scripture citations are from the Holy Bible: King James Version.

The journey of discovery this book will take you on, begins with a very interesting story. This story is about a famous scientist named Dr. Anthony Flew who is a noted scientist, professor, and author. He was also an outspoken and confident atheist. Anthony Flew had been described as the world's most famous atheist of the second half of the twentieth century.[1] In an article titled, **"How the World's Most Notorious Atheist Changed His Mind,"** Anthony Flew was asked if he had heard a voice that made him suddenly stop being an atheist and start believing in God. Professor Anthony Flew replied:

> No, I did not hear a voice. It was the evidence itself that
> led me to this conclusion.[2]

Would anyone like to know what scientific evidence changed the mind of the world's most notorious and most outspoken atheist in modern history? You will read about it here. What changed the mind of Professor Flew constitutes one of the core reasons why this book had to be written.

Before we can get to that point, we need to cover a lot of ground as we embark on a scientific journey of discovery. In a nutshell, the intention of this book is to answer the burning question: Is there a God, or isn't there? In order to answer that question, I have formulated a detailed scientific argument for the existence of God. And what changed the mind of the world's most notorious and outspoken atheist is a critical aspect of the science that validates and proves the existence of a Creator.

A person may ask the question: How can science possibly prove the existence of God? In fact, there are only two real possibilities regarding two main genesis topics. The first topic concerns how our universe came into existence. Was it through self-creation or was it a Divine supernatural act of God? The second topic concerns how all of the species got here on the earth. The species either got here through a self-driven process of abiogenesis and evolution, or they are the product of Divine Creation. As a consequence, if it can be proven that self-creation is scientifically impossible for either the universe or living organisms, then only one possibility remains as being the truth. With that being said, let's begin.

To begin our journey of discovery, we first need to review the meaning of the word, *science*. Merriam-Webster defines science as knowledge or a system of knowledge covering general truths, or the operation of general laws especially as obtained and tested through **scientific method**.[3] You will recall from school that the Scientific Method is a problem-solving process that states something is only valid if it can be measured, tested, observed, and duplicated over and over again.[4] The Scientific Method is a definitive proving process.

In reality, we are all students of science because we have all been introduced to the various disciplines in science through years of education. Whether we realize it or not, many of us have a scientifically influenced view of reality. In mankind's quest for the truth, I believe many people have learned early in life that science can be relied upon as a guide because of its process of proving information through the Scientific Method.

This book's purpose is to take those people still searching for the truth on a scientific journey of discovery that will greatly broaden their horizons. The journey of discovery this book will take the reader on is the odyssey I experienced when I finally set out to find the truth. This is where I learned of Anthony Flew and his story. This book is the product of thousands of hours of my personal search for the facts. And being able to put into print what I discovered allows me to share all of this with you. This includes the pivotal scientific reason why Dr. Anthony Flew became a believer which constitutes a significant part of a later chapter.

As a healthcare professional in the fields of optics and ocular disease, I have been privileged to receive a tremendous amount of scientific education throughout my life. This background in science, coupled with decades of clinical experience, provide me with the tools to analyze scientific information, scientific data, and scientific claims.

While on the other hand, when it comes to the topic of religion, I had been baptized and served as an altar boy at a cathedral in a large midwestern city. I tried to balance science and the Bible as best I could, but over time, as I learned about evolution and the power of *science*, the scientist inside of me began to see the Bible and God as a 'feel good' fairy tale. It was my understanding that science could be proven, while God could not be proven. This mindset is present in some well-known scientists who believe God does not exist and have stated that we should instead place all of our confidence in the hard sciences. As I will discuss, comments from scientists like these are what swayed me into effectively functioning as a person who really did not believe in God.

It is here that I would like to draw the distinction between an unbeliever and a nonbeliever. An unbeliever is someone who is unsure and will remain that way until they witness definitive proof of God.[5] I am under the impression that people who are Agnostic fall into this category. These folks are said to be "on the fence" because they are not on one side or the other. On the other hand, nonbelievers do not believe in God which places them into the category of being an atheist.

Looking back in time on my own situation, and being quite honest with myself, I did not want to let go of my bedtime Bible stories and their magical fairy tale God. While at the same time, I was functioning on the level of a nonbeliever who really did not believe in God. Despite this, I never considered myself an atheist. If this sounds a bit confusing, it's because I had significant doubts and wasn't sure what to believe. I avoided this conundrum by simply ignoring the topic of God. However, if I ever got into a conversation with someone about the topic of God and I was experiencing a sense of hope at the time, I would optimistically agree with them. Looking back, I was doing this from a 'hope' perspective, not from a 'belief' perspective. I now feel these were attempts to convince myself that God was real.

Science is the reality that I believed in, while the story of God is what I held as a fairy tale dream. It was as if a spell had been cast where I saw God and the Bible as enchanted dreams. And like anyone with a dream, I wanted to keep it alive, but this was only a hope, not a settled belief. Because I never sat down and analyzed what I believed, I never realized that I was hoping in God instead of truly believing in God.

I was confused because I never really sat down to figure all of this out. But now, after really thinking this through, I realize there is a vast difference between hoping in something vs. truly believing in it. Let me give an example. Suppose that I buy a lottery ticket. Do I believed that I am going to win? No, I don't believe that I'm going to win, however, I hope that I'm going to win. If I bought a lottery ticket, my belief level of winning would be less than 1% even though my hope level would be high.

I now realize this is where I was when it came to believing in God. In the past, I hoped that God was real, but if someone had asked me what chance there was that God actually existed, my answer would have been, less than 1%. This is just like buying a lottery ticket. Do you see the huge difference between truly believing in something as compared to merely hoping for it?

In my case, I went from merely hoping that God is real, to knowing that God is real. This realization resulted from over four thousand hours of focused research. This book is the result of that research and represents what it took to convince me that God is 100% real. My belief level is now 100%.

I reasoned that if my epic journey of discovery allowed me to find God, then perhaps the research uncovered in this book will help someone else to find God. I believe there are some good people out there who really want to believe, but they just don't. Perhaps it doesn't seem realistic?

My research began several years ago when I had the T.V. on and heard Stephen Hawking proclaim there was no possibility that God existed.[6] He claimed this in an interview. As a result, I was convinced that Stephen Hawking had discovered evidence that made him an atheist and caused him to make this statement. I needed to know what evidence that he found? And I was shocked by the answer. You will read about it here.

As I was in the process of investigating Hawking's comments, I learned that 75-80 percent of the world's population believes in evolution. This statistic did not surprise me because I also believed in evolution. What did surprise me was the research that revealed the science of paleontology proves evolution theory never actually occurred. This revelation changed everything. I was shocked to find that sound science and historical facts point to a Creator. This book presents these scientific facts, not what I wish, hope, or dream.

One of the reasons that I wrote this book was for the nonbelievers who have made up their minds that God is just a fairy tale. They have eliminated the possibility of God existing because of what they think they know about the universe, evolution, and history. What this book is intended to do, is present critical facts that I have recently learned which opened my eyes to the existence of God. My goal is to cause people to say to themselves:

- "I did not know that scores of physicists worldwide in 1992 began believing in a Creator when it was proven that our universe did have a beginning. This means that it could not have brought itself into existence because there was no universe in existence to do so."
- "I did not know that a universe could not bring itself into existence from nothing in the absence of time."
- "I did not know there aren't any fossilized evolutionary mutant skeletons in the Fossil Record which means that no Darwinian mutant skeletons have ever been found on Earth that connect any two species in an evolutionary chain. You can't have a mutant process without any mutants. As a result, many scientists state that Darwinian evolution is *dead*."

- "I did not know that Charles Darwin stated that the absence of mutant intermediates in the Fossil Record poses the most obvious and gravest objection that can be urged against his theory of evolution."
- "I did not know that Hebrew oral stories of their history existed long before the Mesopotamian myths were written which means Hebrew scribes did not embellish myths from other cultures in order to write the Bible."

Many of us have learned incomplete information and misinformation when it comes to certain areas in science and history. Not being in possession of all the facts prevents us from seeing the scientific realities and the complete picture. As a result, not being in touch with reality causes us to reach the wrong conclusions. Being misled like this serves to push us away from the truth, the truth of God.

The real problem with this misdirection is that it leaves the future of our eternal souls in dire straits. We need to remember one thing, **forever**, is a long time. In other words, making a wrong turn with our eternal soul is really the most devastating mistake that a person can make in their entire existence! We see evidence in the Bible of how many of us are going to make this mistake. In Matthew 7:13 (KJV), we read that the highway to Hell is broad with many people on it, while the gate to the Kingdom of God is narrow that only a few are going to find. These odds don't sound good! Therefore, we need to instill a sense of urgency in ourselves in order to find the narrow gate to the Kingdom of God and avoid winding up on the wrong side of these odds.

This book is designed to alert nonbelievers and unbelievers of this stark reality. This book is engineered to present one last detailed argument for the existence of God to those who have become convinced that God is just a fairy tale.

When we embark on a journey, we don't start off with half of the directions to our destination. We need all of the directions, not some of them. Not being in possession of all the scientific facts can be referred to as, *pseudoscience*. Pseudoscience is, 'sort-of-science.' This is in contrast to being in possession of all the scientific facts which is referred to as, *sound science*. We need all of the directions on our journey in life to ensure that our eternal souls reach the best destination and don't get swept into dire straits. My goal with this book is to refute the common falsehoods about science and history that have caused many people to doubt or conclude that God is just a fairy tale. I do this by exposing and presenting all of the scientific facts (sound science).

What enables me to write such a book is my experience and perspective of living as a nonbeliever. I know what thoughts went through my mind, and I know how I used to think about the subject of God. I feel that I should write this book because I spent most of my life not truly believing in God. I also have the unique perspective of knowing exactly what information it took to finally convince me that God is real, and God's Book is actual history. I admit that I was a skeptical doubting Thomas, and what I am sharing in this book is what it took to convince me of the truth. It took over four thousand hours of determined investigation to convince me.

Having two degrees in science along with decades of clinical experience, provides me with the scientific education and expertise to know how to analyze and evaluate scientific claims. I have a bachelor's degree with a major in Biology and a minor in Chemistry. In addition, I hold a professional doctorate in Optometry which includes the science of optics and ocular disease. This has exposed me to a lifetime of scientific and clinical problem-solving experience.

It is this scientific background that contributes to my ability to analyze and draw attention to the pseudoscience that fosters what I refer to as a *"science without a God"* belief structure. In my opinion, any *science* that claims to have created itself can be more appropriately defined as *"science without a God."* And it is this *"science without a God"* belief structure that entices many people away from the truth. It not only leads people away from the truth of God; it also contradicts the scientific facts which I discuss in this book.

We need to demonstrate that God is real, and His Word is sound. Establishing this will only be possible by first exposing the pseudoscientific falsehoods that undermine our acceptance of a Creator. Like renovating a house, the flawed foundation must be replaced with a sound and true foundation. In this same way, the pseudoscience foundation that false belief structures have been built upon, needs to be torn out and replaced with the factual foundation of sound science.

It is my goal to demonstrate that once we are in possession of all the facts, it becomes apparent that the logical conclusion is to embrace a *"science with a God"* belief structure. In order for me to accomplish this, I need to present the reader with all of the scientific facts along with demonstrating how the book of science can be brought into agreement with the Book of God. As a consequence, this book presents all the scientific facts as I understand them (sound science), coupled with my attempt to bring the book of science into agreement with the Holy Bible.

The prime audience for this book includes anyone seeking the scientific truths that would aid them in answering hard questions in their quest to firmly establish their belief structure. This book is useful for those who don't know what to believe. This book is useful for believers with just a bit of doubt in one area. And I definitely feel this book could be useful for people who have decided they don't believe in God.

In addition, I also feel this book can be useful to the believer who has no doubt at all but is faced with hard scientific questions from nonbelievers. It is my impression that most of the atheistic arguments are based on their understanding of what *science* tells them to believe. Therefore, if believers are discussing God with nonbelievers and they find that everything they have tried has failed to convince the nonbeliever, then as a last measure, the factual information in this book can be presented as a strong scientific case for God.

This area of focus is referred to as Scientific Apologetics which is essentially using science to support Scripture and establish the existence of God. For all intents and purposes, if it could be demonstrated how self-creation has been proven to be scientifically impossible, this would establish that the only possibility left, must be true. In other words, in order to prove that God is real, all that has to be accomplished is proving that self-creation has been scientifically established to be impossible, and therefore, false.

The famous detective Sherlock Holmes is quoted as stating:

> When you have excluded the impossible, whatever remains, however improbable, must be the truth.[7]

Sherlock Holmes is designed to be a brilliant fictional character. As a result, I believe we can all see how intelligent and true this statement is. In this book, I will demonstrate how self-creation has been scientifically proven to be impossible which leaves the existence of God as the only possibility left. This is how the existence of God can be proven through science.

In closing out this introduction chapter, I wish to state this book has two main objectives:

1) This book attempts to reconcile science and the Fossil Record with the Bible.

2) This book essentially represents a legal case establishing that self-creation has been proven to be scientifically impossible.

Anyone serious about science and getting to the truth is not going to be able to disregard the numerous scientific facts presented in this book.

With that being said, I wish to prepare you for the fact there is some repetition that exists in this book. This is by design. The repetition is necessary as an attempt to correct several false impressions that many of us have been living under for our entire lives. Just reading about a fact once is typically not going to be enough to counter a lifetime of being exposed to half-truths which have led us to the wrong conclusions. Half-truths will have a negative influence that causes some people to quietly and slowly solidify a *"science without a God"* mindset. This process is so slow and subtle that it goes unnoticed, however, the effect is profound and is usually permanent. This is why it's critically important for people to be informed of all the scientific facts.

Here's a list of some of the *"science without a God"* half-truths that I'm referring to:

1) The explanation for the origin of the universe (did it create itself?)

2) The explanation for the origin of the first life on Earth (did it create itself?)

3) The explanation for the origin of all the species on Earth (did they create themselves?)

4) The explanation for the origin of the stories found in the Bible (do they have their origins in Sumerian works?)

Once we are fully informed with all of the facts, only then is the opportunity created for us to re-evaluate our lifetime belief structures. And on that note, let's begin our journey of discovery!

CHAPTER ONE

Why People Find It Difficult to Believe

We all want to know the truth. And there seems to be two camps of belief that people rely on for the truth, traditional science and religion.

Traditional science has long given the impression that the universe and life brought themselves into existence. This is the case because the explanations of traditional science make no mention of God. As a consequence, we are left with the impression that nature created itself. While on the other hand, the Bible declares that God created the universe and all life on the earth. This appears to put science and theology at odds with each other.

Many people have grown accustomed to the mindset that they can trust science as something provable, reliable, predictable, and tangible. However, when it comes to God, there are people who don't feel they can fully comprehend God because of the apparent lack of undeniable proof. In addition, most of us don't experience an observable physical presence of God. As a result, I'm sure there are many people who have the impression that God is something of a wonderful and mysterious fairy tale. This results in many people placing all of their faith in science, and no real faith in religion.

To many people, there appears to be an enormous divide between science and religion. I believe this causes many people to feel that they need to choose one side or the other. We feel as if science is pulling us in one direction while theology is pulling us in the opposite direction. As I have stated, we all want to know the truth. Many people believe the truth is either found in science or it is found in the Bible. This gives many of us the impression that a choice has to be made. This need to choose can be seen in a quote by a famous scientist named Stephen Hawking. I'm sure most of us are familiar with him as a well-known theoretical physicist. In an interview with Diane Sawyer, Hawking stated:

> There is a fundamental difference between religion, which is based on authority, and science, which is based on observation and reason. Science will win because it works.[8]

Hawking is declaring science is predicated on facts while religion is merely founded on obedience to an authority. Hawking is essentially stating there is a battle for the truth; and that battle is between the facts of hard science vs. the miracles of a fairy story. Notice how he states that science will win this contest.

In my opinion, I believe it could be said that Hawking is practicing *science* as his religion. I say this because he has clearly put all of his faith into the science that he thinks he knows. This is a classic example of the mindset that I believe many people have adopted over their lifetime. I am convinced that many people have chosen science over religion in their pursuit of the truth because they have become persuaded that science and the Bible can't both be correct. These folks felt that they had to make a choice, and according to people like Stephen Hawking, choosing science is the winning choice.

I used to think like this, but now I firmly believe that science and the Bible are both correct. This is the case because God created everything, this includes science. You are being misled if you come across anyone who makes you feel that you have to choose one over the other. You can have science and God; you don't have to choose. The way this can be demonstrated is by proving that self-creating science is impossible. Once self-creating science is proven to be impossible, it becomes evident that there has to be a Creator.

This situation directly relates to the Sherlock Holmes quote mentioned in the last chapter. Once self-creating science is proven to be impossible, only one possibility remains. In other words, we don't have to directly prove the existence of God; we only need to prove that the other possibility is false. Once the fantasy of self-creation is discarded, we will no longer feel that we have to choose between science and God. I firmly believe that it is possible to bring into agreement the truths of the book of science and the truths of the Book of God. In doing so, one factual reconciliation will become evident. Mankind needs the entire truth in order to see the complete picture. Once these two books are brought into agreement, it will become clear that we no longer have to choose one over the other.

That being said, my journey for knowledge and the truth started when I was younger. I gravitated toward science in high school, and as mentioned, I went on to earn two degrees in science. Throughout my education, I discovered that students are required to study the concept of evolution in depth. Because of this deliberate focus, many students develop the misconception that evolution must be a fact, even if they are not explicitly told that evolution is a fact.[9] In reality, evolution is only a *theory*—a theory that many scientists believe to be false. Therefore, when referring to evolution, we should always remember to combine it with the word, *theory*. Evolution, which is more appropriately referred to as, *evolution theory*, is the idea that new species are eventually produced by mutations in offspring when the mutations are beneficial to survival.

As I was learning this in school, a wonderful nun who worked extensively in our community gave me my first Bible. Around my freshman year in high school, I began to read this Bible, having heard that it was the number one selling book in the world. At the same time that I was reading of the magnificent stories in the Bible, I was also learning in school that mankind eventually evolved from the life that emerged in the oceans of early Earth. These two realms seemed to be on opposite ends of the spectrum. The religious realm was rooted in faith while the scientific realm was rooted in evolution and the Scientific Method. You will recall that the Scientific Method is a problem-solving process that states something is only valid if it can be measured, tested, observed, and duplicated over and over again.[10] The Scientific Method is a definitive proving process.

This rigid protocol is quite different from the religious realm which called for me to have faith and believe in God. Science demanded proof while religion required faith. This seemed to imply that science could be analyzed, tested, and proven, while God could not be analyzed, tested, and proven. Since I was a student of science, this seeming incompatibility began to weigh on me.

Despite this, I was still trying to reconcile these two camps of belief. I reasoned that perhaps God had produced the first living cell and then created the process of evolution to proceed from there.

Therefore, I believed that if God existed, He made mankind through evolution. This was my compromise with science to keep God in the picture. At this point, I was fully convinced of evolution while doing my best to also believe in God. However, because I was led to believe evolution was self-driven, this represented the first significant factor that seriously challenged my belief in God.

As I progressed in high school, I attempted to apply the Scientific Method of proving to establish the existence of God. And since God cannot be analyzed, tested, and proven like science can, I became convinced that God did not seem to pass the Scientific Method of proving. Because I was under the impression that evolution did pass the Scientific Method (which it doesn't), this caused me to believe in evolution and doubt the existence of God. This was the result of my false impression at the time, that evolution passed the Scientific Method. In my mind, in the battle for the truth, religion was losing this battle. This is what Stephen Hawking claimed would happen in a duel between science and religion. This was the second significant factor that challenged my belief in God.

The third challenging factor occurred when I learned that many epic myths written by other cultures were very similar to the stories found in the Bible. The point was being made to us that these myths had existed in written form before the Bible stories were written. When I heard this, I immediately had the profound impression this meant the Bible was not the original source.

I can't remember if the teacher specifically said this or not, but at the end of that day, because our attention was being drawn to the fact that the publication dates of the myths occurred before the Bible stories were written, I came away with the definite impression that the Bible was merely a collection of recycled myths from other cultures.

I'm pretty sure that I was not the only one to come away with that impression after hearing this. This resulted from the teacher focusing on the dates when these documents were physically written.

As a consequence, I began to ask myself why I still believed in the Bible? Why did I still believe in God? I reasoned, if the Bible's stories are not real, then maybe evolution did not need a God after all. Perhaps evolution was self-driven just as it seemed to be presented in school. As a result, I wound up looking to the Bible only for the morals of the stories it contained as I wondered whether life had made itself and did not need a God. All of this was driving a wedge between me and the topic of God.

By that point, my belief in God was fading into only a faint hope. But I kept reading the Bible because it somehow brought me comfort and made me feel happy before I went to sleep. I found the stories to be hopeful and filled with profound wisdom. There was something magical that I experienced when I read the passages in the Bible. Regardless, at the end of the day, I had demoted God and the Bible to the status of a dream and a hope. And based on that, it was my impression that the Bible was essentially a collection of bedtime stories that I enjoyed reading before falling asleep. What is worse, I did not consciously realize how all of this was slowly solidifying my belief structure.

I had been baptized, gone to church, read the Bible, and been an altar boy in a cathedral. I even talked about God to others. I had gone for decades thinking that I *believed* in God. However, once I was finished with school and got into the real world, my experiences caused me to slowly lose track of God. As each decade of my life went by, I became more convinced that God was just a fairy tale. To be quite frank, I wanted to believe in God, but I just didn't.

The turning point came one day several years ago. As mentioned in the last chapter, I heard Stephen Hawking state there was no possibility that God exists, in a nationally televised interview discussing his book, *The Grand Design*.[11] I knew how clever Stephen Hawking was and I feared he had discovered irrefutable scientific evidence that ended the argument for God. I had never wanted to delve into whether God existed because I was afraid of what I might find. I didn't want to lose my bedtime fairy tale dream.

I had actually heard Hawking make this claim many years prior, but I ignored it because I did not want to hear what he had to say. However, by the time I heard Hawking's quote for the second time, I was at the point in my life where I finally needed to know the truth, whatever it was. The time for dreaming, hoping, and avoiding the critics was over. I now realize there is a vital difference between truly believing in God and only hoping in God.

This is when I mustered up the courage to investigate what Hawking was saying. I was afraid but I pressed on. I started to visit websites to read highly educated critics of religion and Christianity. The inspiration for this book actually started as a rebuttal to one online critic, but I soon realized, instead of a rebuttal, I was writing a book. That rebuttal wound up being the inspiration for my chapter about Jesus.

I soon discovered that even the most educated critics had flawed arguments that failed to account for all the facts. I did not find a single critic who could prove that God did not exist or that Christianity was a false religion. I found the critics were either stating an opinion that was not a fact, making an unprovable argument, or making an issue out of something that had a solid and logical explanation. In addition, I found significant documented evidence that supports the Bible, God, and Christianity. After several thousand hours of intensive research, I realized that God and Christianity must be true. That was literally an epiphany moment for me! All the facts I had uncovered fit logically and perfectly together. This book is the result of that extensive research. This book exposes all the facts and brings them all together.

This research book is not only my rebuttal to critics of God and Christianity; it is also a tool that can be used by Christians to defend the truth. What we have been told throughout our lives about the universe and life creating themselves has been proven impossible. This book contains the sound science that reveals these falsehoods and demonstrates the truth of God.

Throughout my research I have found God to be supremely logical. God is the Father of all science and He is the Master Engineer. To properly demonstrate this connection between God and His Science, we must bring into agreement the book of nature and the Holy Writ of God.

Bringing science and God into agreement is exactly what 717 scientists from the Victoria Institute in London wished to do when they signed a manifesto in England in 1864. This manifesto, "The Declaration of Students of the Natural and Physical Sciences," informed the world that the signatories disagreed with Darwin's theory of evolution. This manifesto declares:

> We conceive that it is impossible for the word of God, as it is written in the book of nature, and God's Word written in Holy Scripture, to contradict one another, however much they appear to differ. We are not forgetful that Physical Science is not complete, but is only in a condition of progress, and that at present our finite

reason enables us only to see as through a glass darkly; and we confidently believe that a time will come when the two records will be seen to agree in every particular. We cannot but deplore that Natural Science should be looked upon with suspicion by many who do not make a study of it, merely on account of the unadvised manner in which some are placing it in opposition to Holy Writ.[12]

These scientists considered Darwin's idea that new species were spun off from existing species to be pseudoscience, not real science. As a result, these esteemed scientists did not want people to think that science is irreconcilable with God. On the contrary, they were wholly confident the book of nature and Holy Scripture would one day be found to be in agreement. Finding this agreement is one of the reasons why I wrote this book. I am convinced that many people who don't believe in God will change their minds once the false foundation of Darwin's evolution theory is exposed.

With that said, people need to see all the details starting with the beginning of the universe and then progress forward until they experience the life of Jesus. If people want to understand how the book of nature relates to the Word of God, they need to see the complete picture in order to come to a logical conclusion. And why is this so important? To begin to answer this question, let's hear from the esteemed scientist Dr. Francis Crick. He is one of the four people who received the Nobel Prize for their work in discovering DNA, which is the genetic code essential to all life. Crick stated:

> I realized early on that it is detailed scientific knowledge which makes certain religious beliefs untenable. A knowledge of the true age of the earth and of the fossil record makes it impossible for any balanced intellect to

believe in the literal truth of every part of the Bible in the way that fundamentalists do. And if some of the Bible is manifestly wrong, why should any of the rest of it be accepted automatically?[13]

In this single blunt statement, one of the world's discoverers of DNA states he has rejected God because he has rejected the Bible. And he rejected the Bible because the accepted scientific timeline used in geology to date the Fossil Record contradicted the traditionally interpreted timeline for the Bible. Crick believes this part of the Bible to be wrong, and if he can't believe that part of the Bible, why would he believe any other part? When Francis Crick rejects the entire Bible, he also rejects God. Francis Crick, you see, came to his nonbelief because he couldn't reconcile the book of science with the Book of God.

He made a choice, and he chose poorly. Francis Crick, despite his brilliance, didn't grasp the fact that we are indeed able to bring the book of science into agreement with the Word of God. Crick was knowledgeable enough to have found the bridges that would have connected the scientific ages with the Word of God, but he never did. Perhaps he never tried.

Unlike Francis Crick, I know that I can believe in an *Old Earth* and the Bible at the same time. In order to do this, we have to find the bridges that connect an *Old Earth* with the Bible. When I say, *Old Earth*, I mean the earth is billions of years old, not thousands of years old. Finding those bridges is what this book is all about. I believe in the Bible *and* in an *Old Earth*. And this book will show you why. Those who believe in an *Old Earth* need to see what Francis Crick did not. People who believe in an *Old Earth* need to realize that we can embrace the Bible and an *Old Earth* at the same time. This really needs to be done because we can't believe in a science that says one thing and God's Word that seems to say something different.

Another famous scientist who chose poorly is George Wald, a Harvard professor who won the Nobel Prize in Physiology in 1967. Wald stated:

> When it comes to the origin of life, we have only two possibilities as to how life arose. One is spontaneous generation arising to evolution. The other is a super-natural creative act of God. There is no third possibility. Spontaneous generation was scientifically disproved 100 years ago by Louis Pasteur, Spallanzani, Reddy, and others. That leads us scientifically to only one possible conclusion—that life arose as a supernatural creative act of God . . . . I will not accept that philosophically because I do not want to believe in God. Therefore, I choose to believe in that which I know is scientifically impossible, spontaneous generation arising to evolution.[14]

According to George Wald, the theory of spontaneous generation of life claimed that simple atoms and chemicals combine into complex compounds that would arrange themselves into basic living organisms.[15]

Before I proceed, I need to clarify the difference between spontaneous generation and abiogenesis. As you recall form biology class, spontaneous generation claimed that life (maggots) could arise from non-living organic matter (rotting meat) within 7 days. This was a 'life, from non-life' idea. Now, if we analyze George Wald's description of spontaneous generation in the previous paragraph, it is very similar to the description of abiogenesis.

Essentially, the difference is that *spontaneous generation* was thought to produce a complex organism like a maggot, flea, or mouse within the span of 7 days, while *abiogenesis* is thought to have produced a simple organism like a bacterium over the course of millions of years.[16] Both of these proposals are 'life, from non-life' ideas. It seems obvious to me that abiogenesis is a modern, modified version of spontaneous generation. Abiogenesis is not to be confused with, *biogenesis*, which is a 'life, from life' concept that is essentially the same as evolution theory, which I thoroughly explain in Chapter Five.

With that said, let's take a look at George Wald's significant quote. When we carefully analyze what he had to say, right at the beginning he declares there are only two possibilities for the origin of life. One possibility is spontaneous generation, and the only remaining possibility is a supernatural creative act of God. As George Wald proceeds in his statement, he describes how spontaneous generation had been scientifically proven to be false over 100 years ago. This brings George Wald to the sobering realization and conclusion that the existence of God was scientifically proven once spontaneous generation was proven to be false. I wish to stress that George Wald admits that it is a scientific fact that God not only exists, but that God was the one who is responsible for the origin of life on the earth.

Notice that when George Wald states spontaneous generation had been proven false, that he does not attempt to replace spontaneous generation with abiogenesis as the first possibility. I'm sure George Wald was fully aware of the hypothesis of abiogenesis when he made this statement in 1957. The hypothesis of abiogenesis is essentially the same principle as put forth by the Oparin-Haldane experiments from the 1920s and the Miller-Urey experiment in 1953.[17] As a consequence, abiogenesis became officially recognized as a circulated hypothesis in 1953. George Wald, who would go on to win the Nobel Prize in science (Biology), would have been quite familiar with these experiments and the hypothesis of abiogenesis by the time that he made his origin of life statement in 1957.

I wish to stress that Dr. Wald admits science has proven that a Divine supernatural act created the first life. Since Wald did not make mention of the hypothesis of abiogenesis, this tells me George Wald realized that spontaneous generation and abiogenesis are both 'life, from non-life' ideas, as a result, they can be grouped together. In other words, once spontaneous generation was proven to be false, it is my impression George Wald conceded that this likewise sealed the fate of abiogenesis, at least scientifically. It appears, from a scientific proving standpoint, mentioning abiogenesis was not going to change the conclusion. I believe this is the reason why he does not also mention abiogenesis in his statement of scientific fact.

From a **scientific standpoint**, Professor Wald tells us the correct conclusion has been established to be a supernatural act of God. However, from his personal **philosophical standpoint**, he insists there is no God and life created itself. What we see from George Wald's statement regarding spontaneous generation is that we are actually dealing with the two faces of George Wald. On the one hand, we are listening to George Wald the scientist, while on the other hand, we have George Wald the alleged philosopher.

The scientist admits the 'life, from non-life' hypothesis of spontaneous generation has been proven false and the origin of life has been scientifically established to be the result of a supernatural act of God. While at the same time, we have George Wald the alleged philosopher who refuses to believe in God and chooses to believe what he knows has been scientifically proven to be false. These two positions completely contradict each other. Let's breakdown this quote into its two component parts:

George Wald the scientist:

1) He admits the 'life, from non-life' idea of spontaneous generation has been proven false.
2) He admits the origin of life has been scientifically established to be a supernatural creative act of God.

George Wald the alleged philosopher:

1) He refuses to believe that God exists and is the originator of life.
2) He chooses to ignore the scientific facts.
3) He chooses to believe what he knows is scientifically false in order to maintain that atoms can bring themselves to life as living organisms.

Essentially, George Wald admits that God has been established, **scientifically**, to be the originator of life. However, **philosophically**, he thinks that he is free to believe whatever he wants. In reality, science and philosophy are always in agreement. George Wald's interpretation of 'philosophy' is clearly off the mark.

The most surprising news here is that George Wald admits that God has been scientifically proven to be the originator of life. On the other hand, the most shocking news is how a prominent scientist admits he will ignore the scientific facts and embrace what he knows has been proven false in order to continue to deny the existence of a Creator and believe what he wants to believe. I feel this demonstrates that we all need to analyze the factual data for ourselves in order to reach our own conclusions. Professor George Wald demonstrates to us that we should not rely on anyone else to create our belief structures.

That said, I'm not trying to tell you what to believe. My goal is to provide you with informed consent by showing you all the facts and then stand back and let you do the rest. You are entitled to know all of the science, not some of it. Once you are fully informed, what you do with these facts is up to you.

So, where did this leave George Wald? Well, he did not give up on the 'life, from non-life' idea. George Wald is quoted as confidently proclaiming that life would one day appear because of the existence of protons, neutrons, and electricity.[18] This sounds very similar to the hypothesis of chemical evolution which is included in the hypothesis of abiogenesis. This quote confirms to me that George Wald was aware of the abiogenesis hypothesis when he was making these statements.

This means to me, that this quote about protons, neutrons, and electricity is coming from George Wald the 'philosopher' (alleged philosopher). I will discuss the chemical evolution and abiogenesis ideas in greater detail in Chapter Four.

In George Wald's statement, we see that he admits the idea of spontaneous generation was proven to be scientifically false in 1858 by the French chemist Louis Pasteur and others.[19] Right after declaring this, he openly, and without apology, admits he embraces this well-known scientific falsehood for the simple reason that he refuses to believe in God. I must say, this is not science and it raises grave concerns.

Remember that Wald said there are only two possibilities. One is that spontaneous generation gave rise to evolution; the other possibility is that our scientific reality is the product of a supernatural creative act of God; "There is no third possibility." Putting this situation into perspective, consider that flipping a coin leads to only two possibilities—'Heads' or 'Tails.' There is no third possibility. Now, let's say that 'Tails' is spontaneous generation (abiogenesis) initiating the process of populating the earth through evolution, while 'Heads' represents a supernatural creative act of God. Dr. Wald has stated that spontaneous generation was scientifically disproved in the nineteenth century. This means that when we flip this coin, 'Tails' did not come up. In fact, it is impossible for 'Tails' to ever come up because it has been proven to be false.

What then? If the coin cannot come up with 'Tails,' then it has to come up with 'Heads,' a supernatural act of creation by God. Notice that Dr. Wald states by default the research scientifically concludes life arose as a supernatural creative act of God. Therefore, Wald admits to the entire world that the scientific evidence leads to God as the Creator. Notice that George Wald admits this once 'Tails' had been proven to be false. Remember the Sherlock Holmes quote? You see, once 'Tails' was proven false to George Wald, he knew this meant the only other possibility left, had to be true! This is exactly like the Sherlock Holmes quote.

Did George Wald follow the science and become a believer? No, he did not. He states that he is going to follow his *'philosophy'* instead which urges him to refuse to believe in God. George Wald's *'philosophy'* also compels him to embrace an idea that he knows has already been scientifically proven false! George Wald's flawed position results from him not following the science but instead yielding to his personal *'philosophy.'* In effect, George Wald has replaced the truth with what he wants the truth to be. The fact George Wald refused to believe in God does not change the truth. George Wald's position is the result of him contaminating sound scientific reasoning with his personal religious doubts and feelings.[20]

In the end, Wald's personal feelings ultimately caused him to choose to embrace what he knows to be scientifically false. It's shocking that George Wald admits this which makes me wonder how many others, who don't believe in God, are doing the same thing?

George Wald stubbornly refused to believe in God despite the compelling scientific evidence. As a result, he was never going to try to reconcile the book of science with the Book of God. Instead, his personal feelings are what caused him to embrace a known scientific falsehood in order for him to maintain a refusal to believe in God. The bottom line is that George Wald polluted what he knew to be the truth with what he wanted the truth to be. I believe George Wald made this grave mistake because he failed to see the entire picture, the big picture. This was a grave error for his eternal soul.

George Wald was not an expert in religion nor an expert on God; he was a scientist. Dr. Wald received his Nobel Prize in the field of science, not in the field of philosophy or in the field of theology. I don't mean to be disrespectful to Dr. Wald, but for the sake of his eternal soul, he should have stuck with what he was good at and followed the science. The purpose of this book is to expose and present the scientific facts that people are entitled to know. As a consequence, this will allow them to *follow the science*!

Despite this, science is currently confronted with the 'life, from non-life' hypothesis of abiogenesis. As I have already mentioned, abiogenesis has replaced spontaneous generation, however, I demonstrate in Chapter Four how abiogenesis also fails the Scientific Method. As a result, abiogenesis joins spontaneous generation as yet another failed scientific idea. As stated, Dr. Wald would have been fully aware of the abiogenesis hypothesis which existed before he made his significant quoted statement regarding spontaneous generation. This is evidenced in the next George Wald quote:

> If you start with a universe containing protons, neutrons, and electricity (electrons), life will eventually appear.[21]

What I find extremely interesting regarding Wald's statement about protons, neutrons, and electricity (electrons) spawning life, is that George Wald believed in the magic of inanimate objects bringing themselves to life. What we see here is that Wald had no problem believing in a supernatural creative event bringing dead objects to life, but he was somehow unable to believe in a supernatural creative God bringing dead objects to life. Wald also stated:

> Our life has a place as part of the order of nature. Life
> is a part of the physics of our universe.[22]

Let me take a moment here to clarify that a "supernatural" event is any occurrence that is beyond the explanation of science. As a result, because science cannot explain how lifeless atoms and dead molecules just made life appear in the form of a living mechanized organism, the idea of a universe magically creating life, from non-life, very clearly qualifies as a supernatural event! Wald definitely believed in a supernatural life-creating universe, but at the same time he refused to believe in a supernatural life-creating God. Now, if he can believe in a magical universe that creates life and supreme order, then why can't he believe in a Creator that creates life and supreme order? The practice of logic is clearly missing here. In addition, since Wald's universe creates life this means that George Wald's universe has *godly* powers.

In essence, George Wald is declaring that we live in a *godly* universe. This raises the question: If George Wald can accept living in a *godly* universe then why can't he accept living in a universe with a God? Where is the rationale that prevents him from believing in a universe with a God, if he is easily able to believe he is living in a *godly* universe?? The Nobel Prize winning George Wald is easily able to believe that he lives in a universe that has the magical ability to create life from dead molecules formed from lifeless atoms. From a logical standpoint, George Wald's refusal to believe in God makes no logical sense. George Wald does not have the logical footing to eliminate the possibility of God because he has no evidence to suggest or prove this.

Here is the decision that George Wald faced, he knew either the universe had godly creative powers or there was a Divine Creator with Godly powers. This means it should have been a 50/50 coin-toss chance where it could have gone either way for Professor Wald. On top of this, George Wald also had the additional information that spontaneous generation had been scientifically proven to be false. As a consequence, this shifts the 50/50 coin-toss chance very clearly in the direction of a Divinely created universe, which he admits.

I believe the added information of spontaneous generation being proven to be impossible, which proved to George Wald the existence and participation of a supernatural Creator, should have logically caused George Wald to completely agree with his scientific conclusion. Did George Wald logically follow the scientific evidence? No, instead, he went in the opposite direction simply because he did not want to believe in God. This is **not** the practice of scientific observation and reason.

In addition, I ask the question: How does Wald know that God didn't create the protons, neutrons, and the electricity (electrons)? He doesn't. In effect, Dr. Wald doesn't have scientific proof of anything regarding where protons, neutrons, electricity, electrons, or life came from. Wald has no evidence at all for his position and he never found what he was looking for. The only thing George Wald knew for sure, and with no good reason, was that he refused to believe in God.

The science of logic dictates that until a possibility has been proven to be false, it continues to remain a possibility. George Wald cannot prove that a Creator does not exist, yet he has eliminated the existence of a Creator as a possibility. This runs counter to logical reasoning. Happiness is found in the truth; the truth is never going to be found by disrespecting logic.

I don't have any objections to George Wald continuing to search for scientific discoveries, but I do see a problem with Wald eliminating God as a possibility without first proving that God does not exist. This is a breakdown in scientific reasoning, especially in light of the fact that he knows the 'life, from non-life' idea of spontaneous generation has been proven scientifically impossible.

Wald is throwing all of his belief into a 'life, from non-life' concept that has all of the cards stacked against it, while he rejects the only remaining possibility for which there is no proof against it. Once again, this is not logical, and this is not science.

Now, I'm sure there are a few people who may argue that George Wald apparently believed spontaneous generation (abiogenesis) occurred because he *'philosophically'* believed it could have happened at least one time. These people would argue that if something could happen just once, no matter how remote that probability is, then *'philosophically,'* that is all that is necessary. However, this argument is flawed because in order for an event to occur just once, it has to be physically possible (scientifically possible). George Wald admits spontaneous generation is not scientifically possible. I fully demonstrate later in this book how abiogenesis (and spontaneous generation) was not scientifically possible to occur, not even just one time.

I don't mean to be rough on George Wald here, but one of the reasons I went into detail analyzing his statements is because I wish to let people know that we need to learn all of the scientific facts so that we can refine our belief structures accordingly, for ourselves.

With all of this being said, the situation with George Wald is not unique. I believe that almost all skeptics (atheists), whether they realize this or not, have come to the same conclusion that they live in a universe with the magical power to create life from dead molecules and lifeless atoms. In effect, skeptics believe they live in a godly universe. This begs the question: How can all of those people believe they live in a magical universe with godly powers, but then at the same time, completely refuse to believe in the possibility of a universe with a God? That does not make any logical sense.

Before we get into the scientific facts listed in this book, it should appear that two logical possibilities exist, not one. Either science created itself from nothing, or God is the Creator. As you will see in Chapters Three, Four, and Five, the atheistic proposal of self-creation has already been scientifically eliminated. People on the fence regarding God need to realize that I'm trying to show them the truth. For the nonbeliever who follows the science, like Professor Anthony Flew did, the truth will set them free. The people who change their minds and wind up in the Kingdom of God because someone prodded them to think twice about how they established their belief structures, will one day admit that it was the best thing that ever happened to them.

The nonbelievers and unbelievers out there need to remember that if they are wrong about this, and they really do have eternal souls, then having your eternal soul exist forever in the wrong place will be the biggest mistake they ever made about anything in their entire existence. We need to be mindful that, **forever**, is a very long time. Don't spend forever in the wrong place because you didn't have all the facts when you established your belief structure.

This book is about getting to the truth. It is like a large box filled with intricate puzzle pieces. Every single piece fits-in and integrates with the elements around it. When completed, it forms a solid and comprehensive picture. I will show you how all the details fit perfectly together as they display one magnificent revelation. So be patient as you go through this detailed book at your own pace, remembering that all its puzzle pieces will fit seamlessly together at the end.

Now, if this book seems to go into detail that seems excessive, it is because I am attempting to deliver as many facts to you as I can. You are entitled to know all of the facts. In this way, perhaps you will see how it is possible to comprehensively reconcile the book of science with the Book of God.

CHAPTER TWO

The Trouble with Time

This entire chapter is dedicated to a disagreement regarding the topic of time. A timeline dispute exists that has caused a distinction where most religious people are either *Young Earth* believers or they are *Old Earth* believers. A *Young Earth* believer is convinced the universe and the earth are only about 6,000-10,000 years old. While an *Old Earth* believer is convinced the universe and the earth are billions of years old and animal life goes back hundreds of millions of years.

The *Young Earth* position is based upon the typical impression one gets from reading about *Creation Week* as it is presented in the Book of Genesis. *Young Earth* believers interpret Chapter One of the Book of Genesis to mean that *Creation Week* occurred over the short span of a seven-day workweek. These believers then add thousands of years of mankind's genealogies which leads them to conclude that less than 10,000 years has elapsed since the universe was first created by God. This is the traditional fundamental interpretation of the Book of Genesis along with parts of the Old Testament as they relate to the creation of the universe, the earth, all living things, and mankind's ancestral bloodlines leading up to today. This constitutes the *Young Earth* position.

On the other hand, scientific research indicates that the universe and the earth are billions of years old. While animals and marine life have existed for hundreds of millions of years. In fact, scientific research indicates the universe is 13.77 billion years old.[23] This constitutes the *Old Earth* position.

The *Young Earth* vs. *Old Earth* disagreement comes down to the scientific timeline of when the universe, the earth, and living organisms first came into existence and how it vastly differs from the traditional timeline interpretation of *Creation Week* in the Book of Genesis.

It is at this point that I wish to say I have faith in Scripture, and I believe the events listed in the Bible actually occurred. Therefore, one of the objectives of this book is to explain how these events were not only possible, but actually occurred. In doing so, this will allow us to visualize how the book of science and the Book of God are able to be brought into agreement. We need to find solutions to all of the challenges that are preventing the reconciliation of the scientific findings and the Holy Bible.

One such challenge is the timeline dispute between the Fossil Record evidence and the way that *Creation Week*, as it is recorded in the Book of Genesis, is typically interpreted because of how it is worded. The Fossil Record indicates species appeared over a long period of time. On the other hand, the Bible is traditionally interpreted to imply that species were introduced over a short period of time.

Before I go any further, I would like to acknowledge my deep respect for traditional fundamentalists. These believers are strict, highly disciplined, and make every effort to defend their position that the Bible speaks the truth, and that no errors exist in Scripture. I fully respect this high level of dedication and commitment to defending the Word of God. I fully agree with them. Even so, in rare instances things are not what they appear at first glance. For example, I call attention to Matthew 13:3-9 (KJV), we read:

> Behold, a sower went forth to sow; And when he sowed, some of the seeds fell by the wayside, and the fowls came and devoured them up: Some fell upon stony places, where they had not much earth: and forthwith they sprung up, because they had no deepness of earth: And when the sun was up, they were scorched; and because they had no root, they withered away. And some fell among thorns; and the thorns sprung up, and choked them: But other fell into good ground, and brought forth fruit, some an hundredfold, some sixtyfold, some thirty fold. Who hath ears to hear, let him hear.

This is Jesus telling the *Parable of the Farmer Scattering Seed*. This passage is not to be interpreted literally. This is not a message from God on how to cultivate plant seeds in order to be a successful farmer, even though Jesus is speaking about planting seeds and harvesting. Farming is not the intended purpose of this discussion. The seed is God's message while the different types of soil are represented by the different types of people who listen. Good people produce fruit while those who are not good are lost and do not produce fruit. It is clear to us that we are not supposed to literally interpret this passage. The words that are used in this passage are intended to serve the purpose of delivering a message that has nothing to do with actual farming.

I mention this because there is one pivotal statement found in the Book of Genesis that represents the main reason why the book of nature and the Book of God do not reconcile. This statement is made in Genesis Chapter One during *Creation Week*. The first mention of this statement is, "And the evening and the morning were the first day." This statement is repeated for each of the first six *Creation Days* of *Creation Week* (Genesis 1:5; Genesis 1:8; Genesis 1:13; Genesis 1:19; Genesis 1:23; and Genesis 1:31).

This critical statement has been interpreted to mean that all of the species listed for their particular *Creation Day* must have appeared in one, 24-hour period. This interpretation claims that 6,000 years ago, all the species that have ever lived, appeared at the same time over the course of a single week. To put this into perspective, these folks believe that all of the dinosaurs that have ever lived, began roaming the earth just 6,000 years ago. These people are referred to as *Young Earth* believers.

The Fossil Record demonstrates this was clearly not the case. This presents the most important challenge that prevents the Fossil Record from being brought into agreement with the Holy Bible. This single statement has caused over a billion believers worldwide to assert one common belief. They believe that all the creatures that have ever lived on the earth, appeared over the course of just seven days about 6,000 years ago. This is the traditional fundamental interpretation of the Book of Genesis.

As stated, I highly respect the traditional fundamentalists for their commitment to defending the Word of God. With this being said, I am convinced there is more than one way to interpret, "And the evening and the morning were the first day." I say this because I know the earth is much older than 6,000 years, and most of the world agrees with me. We are the *Old Earth* believers. Because of the reality of how old our Earth really is, there must be another explanation.

To address this challenge, I offer an explanation which may be a solution. If we look at the farmer parable used by Jesus, the words He used were intended to get a message across in an indirect manner. This means that Jesus was not talking about the intended topic. In this parable, the words chosen by Jesus are discussing the task of farming, but the words chosen were not intended to convey a message about actual farming.

This means that words used in Scripture should not always be taken at face value. This seed parable is an example of God using words that are intended to make another point. This is the reason why we can't automatically, literally interpret every word in Scripture. We can literally interpret Scripture most of the time, but not all of the time.

In John 16:25 (KJV) we read:

These things I have spoken unto you in proverbs: but the time cometh, when I shall no more speak to you in proverbs, but I shall shew you plainly of the Father.

Here we can see Jesus admitting that sometimes He does not speak plainly to mankind. This is referred to as speaking in proverbs. A proverb is a concise statement that communicates simple insight about a general truth.[24] A Proverb usually employs figurative language to deliver its intended message. This is what we observe in Genesis with regard to the verse, "And the evening and the morning were the first day." God is not really talking about creation occurring within the span of 24-hour days. No, God is using these words for another intended purpose. I am convinced this purpose is to introduce to mankind the construct of the seven-day workweek. I believe it's as simple as that.

In the same way that Jesus used farming words that were unrelated to the true message in His seed parable, God the Father used a reference that is typically related to a 24-hour period that was not exactly how He caused His creations to appear. God was accomplishing two goals here. God wished for mankind to get a general idea of the creation story (communicating a general truth-hence, a proverb). Then at the same time, God also wished to take this as an opportunity to introduce the concept of the seven-day workweek scheduling strategy. God wanted mankind to adopt this schedule model because it would pace mankind's work efforts and establish the weekly Sabbath celebration. Therefore, the verse, "And the evening and the morning were the fifth day," is an example of how God sometimes uses words in an indirect and nonliteral manner for the intended purpose of delivering His true message, just like we observe in His parables and proverbs.

This brings up another challenge presented by *Creation Week* where it groups similar species into specific *Creation Days* that follow in sequence. In other words, we get the impression from reading Genesis that all of the species from Day Five had to appear before any of the species of Day Six could appear. The Fossil Record indicates this was not the case. For example, the fossil evidence indicates that marine life (Day Five) and land animals (Day Six) appeared over the same period of time.

Once again, I believe this is an example of God putting the complex process of creation into a simple to understand story. By neatly grouping similar creations into their own *Creation Days*, it greatly simplified creation which allowed mankind to wrap their heads around this complex process. In this case, we have an example of how God uses words in an indirect and nonliteral manner for the intended purpose of facilitating mankind's absorption and digestion of a simplified version of God's creation story. While at the same time, mankind was also introduced to the seven-day workweek model.

You see, mankind is going to have to pass this creation story down to their offspring, generation to generation. In order for mankind to consistently do this, a simple creation story that is basic and easy to understand has to be presented to them.

That being said, the case I am making here is that God said what He needed to say in Genesis in order to get mankind into a mindset of basic understanding. This established a foundation for more advanced comprehension in the future. In other words (in the beginning) God decided to keep it simple. When matters are simplified, it necessarily causes many complex details to be left out. I would like to stress that God said what He needed to say to get His messages across. Therefore, this is not a matter of changing what is written in Scripture about what God said. This is a matter of understanding that **God said what He needed to say** in order to serve His intended purpose.

At this point, I wish to clarify that it should be noted that most marine creatures are classified as aquatic animals. Even fish are classified by modern science as animals. Algae and microorganisms that live in the water are not animals. As a result, regarding *Creation Week*, when we speak of marine life (Day Five), it lives in the water. If we are referring to animals (Day Six), it lives on land.

The next comment I will make regarding *Creation Week* is that I believe there are many people who look at *Creation Week* as it is written in Genesis and they think it is unreasonable to expect them to believe this actually happened. This stems from the fact that many people believe in evolution which claims to have occurred over a very long period of time. As a consequence, they don't believe the short timeframe of the traditional interpretation of *Creation Week* is accurate.

This is why I find the need to focus on *Creation Week* in order to present a demonstration of how it is possible to bring *Creation Week* into agreement with science and the Fossil Record. What I have already discussed constitutes a foundation of explanations that lay the groundwork for reconciling science and the Bible.

With that said, I feel that I can further demonstrate how *Creation Week* and the Fossil Record can both be correct. Once it is seen how *Creation Week* can be brought into agreement with the fossil evidence, it is only then that we can visualize how *Creation Week* could have actually occurred in the general manner that it is recorded in the Book of Genesis. Once it is seen how *Creation Week* could have possibly happened, it cannot merely be dismissed as an impossible fairy tale.

Now, it is true that many people feel that *Creation Week* could not have happened exactly the way it is depicted in Genesis because of one single statement that I have already discussed. This is the statement that is repeated six times: "And the evening and the morning were the …. day." As stated, this statement seems to imply that all creations occurred in the span of a standard seven-day week. However, the majority of people in the world are convinced that all of this creation could not have possibly occurred over the course of a seven-day workweek and the fossil evidence supports their position. As a consequence, the traditional interpretation of this verse does not represent the majority of popular opinion.

It is here that we will take a deep dive into Genesis Chapter One. This is the point where I will describe how I believe that God may have carried out *Creation Week*. In order to do this, I need to introduce several of my own conclusions and a few problem-solving concepts. Quite frankly, I believe that *Creation Week* is far more complex than it appears at first glance. To get started, I wish to present a brief introduction of several components involved in this rather complex issue. This brief introduction is intended to help you get oriented to what I am about to present. The significance of these components and how they relate to each other will become more evident as I go into detail explaining them throughout this chapter.

First of all, I believe *Creation Week* started billions of years ago, as soon as the earth was fully formed. There were obviously seven *Creation Days,* and because of this, they represent the first example of a seven-day workweek. *Creation Days* were actually *Divine Days* that were not 24 hours in duration, they were not standard (literal) days. Once the first six *Creation Days* got started, they all ran concurrently. The first six *Creation Days* actually lasted for billions of years until they all ended 10,000 years ago when Day Seven began right after the creation of Adam and Eve. This means the first six *Creation Days* ended at the same time, just as Day Seven was beginning. For reasons that I will discuss shortly, I believe Day Seven is still in progress which means *Creation Week* is not over yet.

In addition to *Creation Days* actually being *Divine Days,* I feel they also included the use of what I refer to as, *creation seeds.* A *creation seed* is a small encapsulated embryo that possesses DNA that is loaded with the genetic code that was unique for each particular species. There was a unique *creation seed* for each and every species. A *creation seed* functioned just like a common plant seed. There was a seed for the male and a seed for the female that opened together at their prescribed times. Once they germinated, God would have needed to have nurtured each couple to adulthood.

Then those adults would have taken care of the rest.

Now that I have introduced the concept of a *creation seed,* I can discuss that I believe each *Creation Day* had two phases, Phase 1 and Phase 2. Phase 1 of each *Creation Day* was the 'design and creation' portion where the *creation seeds* for that particular *Day* were formulated and produced. Phase 2 represents the 'germination and appearance' portion of each *Creation Day* where living species slowly emerged from their *creation seeds* over an extended period of time.

Therefore, each and every species either came forth at their designed appearance time by way of planted seeds, or God spoke each species into existence when their time arrived. I prefer this *creation seeds* proposal because it agrees with the traditional fundamental interpretation that something creative (Phase 1) occurred over the course of a seven-day workweek. What I mean by this is that the production of all the *creation seeds* could have taken less than a seven-day workweek. However, this was only the creation phase (Phase 1), not the germination phase (Phase 2) of *Creation Week.*

Let me give a seed planting example to demonstrate what I am proposing. Let's say that I wish to start a garden and I want four kinds of plants to germinate at different times and in a specific order. Plant seed #1 blooms first, preparing the way for seed #2. Then plant seed #2 blooms and prepares the way for seed # 3, and so on. But how do I get them to open at different times and in the correct order while planting them all in the same day?

One way is to coat each seed type with a resin that will delay its germination. Here's the idea. The thicker the resin coating is, the longer it takes for it to erode which finally allows that seed to germinate. The first seed gets no coating because it will germinate first. The second seed gets a 3 mm coating. The third seed gets a 7 mm coating, and the fourth seed gets a 10 mm coating. In this way, I can orchestrate the exact sequence and approximate times that they all open.

This is an example of how it is possible to plant many different seeds at exactly the same time (Phase 1), but they don't all open at the same time (Phase 2). I feel that some sort of a seed technique was utilized by God that only took one week to formulate which resulted in the appearance of billions of species over the course of a very long period of time. However, in the case of *Creation Week*, I don't believe a resin was used to delay germination. A more sophisticated timing mechanism would have been involved that could delay germinations for an extended period of time. This example helps to explain how the genetic profiles for all the species that have ever lived on the earth could have been formulated in the span of one standard week (Phase 1).

Next, I wish to explain why we get the feeling that an evolutionary process occurred because more and more complex species appeared over time. Because the complexity of species increased over time, it gives the impression of an evolutionary process. However, as I am about to explain, an evolutionary process did not occur, it just seems that way. Here's an example. Let's say that a brand-new car company is being formed, but it needs financial backing from a large bank. For the bank to approve the needed loan, this company must submit a business plan. This new car company draws up the necessary proposal as required, but in addition, they also wish to show the bank what their cars will be like over the next seven years.

Their engineers are given seven days to draw up designs for the first seven years of car models, one model will be released each year. The engineers designed seven cars in seven days with each subsequent model being a bit more advanced than the last. The design for the first car will serve as the starting template for designing the second car, while the design for the second car will serve as the working template for designing the third car, and so on (either the 'starting template' term or the 'working template' term can be used; they both mean the same thing). That said, once the cars are released, it will appear to the public that the car model is evolving over time. However, an evolutionary process based on performance, customer feedback, and suggestions will not be responsible for the changes witnessed over the years.

These cars were entirely designed in advance and slowly released at their predetermined times leaving the public with the impression this model is evolving over time. This impression would be false. Likewise, the slow introduction of more advanced species over time also gives the impression of an evolutionary process, but it only looks that way. In reality, simple species were activated first in order to prepare the way. Then over time, the more advanced species got their turn once the earth had been prepared for them.

In this scenario, earlier species are not mutating into later species because God had already formulated all the DNA profiles at the very beginning, just like the car model example. In other words, a progressive creative process did occur, but it was not evolution. I fully explain this in a later chapter. My objective up to this point is to state that God could have created the genetic profiles for all the species as seeds in the span of a standard week. Then, they germinated over long ages like we observe in the Fossil Record. We need to understand that the theory of Darwinian evolution is not the only long ages explanation for how species appeared.

When we consider that *Creation Week* was probably done in "God's Time" (long ages) and not in our time (one standard literal week), the Book of Genesis and the Fossil Record can be reconciled. I believe this is how God populated the earth because it agrees with the Fossil Record. Since I know that God is the Father of science, any bridge that connects God and His Science must be strongly considered as a possibility.

As mentioned, it is clear to me that the entirety of *Creation Week* (Phase 1 and Phase 2) took place over long ages. And if we are going to insist that any part of *Creation Week* took place over the span of a standard, seven-day week, this can be done by only looking at Phase

1 of each *Creation Day*. In other words, if we add up the time that it took for Phase 1 of all seven days, this could have amounted to a standard, seven-day week. In this way, the traditional fundamental interpretation of the timeline of *Creation Week* can be retained as being partially correct.

Since Phase 1 was the creating aspect of each *Creation Day*, we could agree that creations (*creation seeds*) only took seven standard (literal) days to produce. This would agree with the traditional fundamental interpretation of *Creation Week* in the Book of Genesis. I am proposing that "creations" (the genetic coded seeds) occurred over the course of a seven-day, standard workweek, however, this is **not** how long it took for these creations to appear as living creatures.

By contrast, the "germinations" (species appearances) occurred over the course of a seven-day, Divine Workweek (long ages), which is still in progress.

Creation seeds are a logical problem-solving concept that appears to be the most logical way to populate the earth with billions of species over the course of the earth's lifespan. This ties in with the two phases that I mentioned earlier. On *Creation Days* with living organisms (which included plants because they also have DNA), Phase 1 is where God generated the genetic code that would be necessary for each encapsulated embryo seed. For God, this would have been done quickly on each *Creation Day*. You will recall from high school biology class that plant seeds are considered embryos. Therefore, seeds are an embryo concept. I believe embryo *creation seeds* for vegetation and living creatures were created for Day Two, Day Three, Day Five, and Day Six.

As stated earlier, I feel *Creation Week* is presented the way that it is in Genesis because it was intended to teach mankind the concept of a seven-day schedule as a time management strategy. The first, time management gift from God was the night/day cycle. The second, time management gift from God was the construct of a seven-day work-week. I believe the way in which *Creation Week* is worded in Genesis caused mankind to interpret the creation event as taking place over the course of seven, 24-hour days. In reality, I believe this epic creative event actually took place over the course of seven *Divine Days* that lasted a very long time.

Regardless, mankind's interpretation that *Creation Week* was composed of seven typical days, drew their attention to the advantages of organizing 24-hour cycles into the framework of a seven-day week. The seven-day workweek functioned as a guide on how to best manage mankind's time.

The reason I am compelled to propose a *creation seeds* concept is because this is the only way I can see to reconcile the Fossil Record with the Book of Genesis. Except for Adam and Eve, I believe every species started as created seeds, just like the trees, plants, and grasses. This means that Adam and Eve were the only couple that were created as fully formed. They were different from all the other species because they were special. Even so, it is also possible that God only planted vegetation creations as seeds. Then, when it came to marine life, birds, and land animals, God could have spoken the initial male and female couples into existence as fully formed. The scenario that you prefer is up to you. Either way, God created each species individually.

God hand-crafted Adam from the dust of the earth into the likeness of Himself. Then, God hand-crafted Eve from one of Adam's ribs in order to establish the deep connection between Adam and Eve (husband and wife). I am not under the impression that God went through this very special process with any of His other creations.

Therefore, I feel the argument can be made that only mankind appeared as fully formed because Adam and Eve were created in God's image and likeness.

This seed concept may appear odd at first, however, support for a *creation seeds* concept can be seen in Genesis 2:8-9 (KJV), where God plants the Garden of Eden. This Scripture reads as follows, "And God planted a garden Eastward in Eden and there He put the man whom He had formed. And out of the ground, made God to grow every tree that is pleasant..." Notice how God plants this special garden which then resulted in various trees growing out of the ground. This proves that God utilized seeds that first needed to be planted which then germinated into trees. In other words, God did not just snap His fingers to make the Garden of Eden suddenly appear.

As I have mentioned, a plant seed is considered by science to be an embryo that germinates into a living organism. Forms of vegetation are considered by science to be living organisms. And if you think about it, an animal embryo starts off in the same way as being tiny, which then germinates into a fully grown creature. Even the birth of our universe (which I fully discuss in Chapter Three) was started with a very tiny seed we call the *Singularity*.[25] It was the smallest seed to ever exist, and yet, it germinated into the largest creation of them all.

From what we can observe, our expansive universe is two trillion galaxies in magnitude.[26] We see an example of this on Earth where the tiny mustard seed will germinate into one of the largest trees in the garden. It's clear to me that we live in a universe created by an intelligence who focuses on the utilization of seeds as a universal creation method.

To review, I believe each *Creation Day* had two phases and the *Creation Days* that involved living organisms accomplished this with *creation seeds* that germinated over a very long period of time. That said, I believe each *Creation Day* was actually a *Divine Day*, and *Creation Week* was a workweek composed of seven *Divine Days*. The first six *Divine Creation Days* were billions of years long, and we are presently in Day Seven.

You may ask: How could this be, if each *Creation Day* is composed of a night and day cycle? We need to consider that perhaps we are making an incorrect assumption about the statement, "And the evening and the morning were the sixth day." We are assuming this statement is referring to only one evening and only one morning, which equals one standard day. What if this assumption is false? What if there is more than one evening and more than one morning? What if there were many evenings and many mornings?

This possibility is supported by the fact these were Divine Days, not typical days. And if this is the case, what if the morning being referred to is not 12 hours later, but is a much longer period of time later? In this case, we could be talking about the first evening and a morning that could have occurred a long time later. This reasoning is supported by the fact that God does not state, "And the evening and the morning were the seventh day." Is the reason that God did not make this statement because Day Seven started, but is not over yet? I believe God does not make this statement because we are still living in Day Seven right now.

Day Seven is not over; it will end once there are no human souls on Earth any longer. At that point, all of mankind's souls will either be in Heaven or in the other place. This will bring *Creation Week* to a close. Remember, *Creation Week's* purpose was to support God's most prized creation, mankind, who God created because He wanted a family.

When God states, "And the evening and the morning were the sixth day," I believe what God is really saying is, **"And the (first) evening and the (last) morning were the sixth day."** This would amount to a *Divine Creation Day* that was extended in its duration. However, I feel that if God had said this, it would not accomplish God's intended purpose of delivering to mankind the construct of the seven-day workweek. This is why God said, what He said.

If someone believes that I have just added to Scripture what was not in Scripture, I have a simple response. When we traditionally interpret, "And the evening and the morning were the sixth day," we are subconsciously adding in an extra word, in two places. When we do this, it creates the statement, "And the (first) evening and the (first) morning were the sixth day." We subconsciously do this because of our assumption that God is only talking about a standard 24-hour day. I can assure you, there was nothing standard about any of these momentous and epic *Creation Days*.

Therefore, it can be argued that when we interpret this statement in a traditionally fundamental manner, we are adding in a word that was not present in Scripture to begin with. I believe we subconsciously add in this word because of how we traditionally think about time. However, as I will soon discuss further, God thinks about time differently than mankind thinks about time. This is because mankind's time is not God's Time. In an effort to discuss what is meant by "God's Time," I present 2 Peter 3:8 (KJV):

> But, beloved, be not ignorant of this one thing, that one day is with the Lord as a thousand years, and a thousand years as one day.

In looking at 2 Peter 3:8 (KJV), we can see that our construct of time cannot be applied to God. One day in the presence of the Lord is like a thousand years to us. But then we read that a thousand years in the presence of the Lord is as one day to us. This is clearly difficult to understand. However, because God has stated this, there must be a way for it to be true. How is this possible?

My short answer to this question is, I believe that God's Time has multiple dimensions, multiple gears, and multiple speeds. By contrast, mankind's time has one gear with one speed.

God's Time is so complex and variable that an equation can never be formulated to establish a consistent relationship between our time with God's Time. 2 Peter 3:8, is God's way of drawing our attention to the realization that we are not going to understand His Time. Notice how our concept of time is worthless when it comes to understanding God's Time. One day of God's Time does not equal one day of mankind's time.

In the case of *Creation Week*, it appears that God's Time for a *Creation Day* equals an even longer period of time. 2 Peter 3:8 confirms that a day mentioned in the Book of Genesis regarding *Creation Week* cannot be simply assumed by mankind to equal 24 hours. Why? Because the *Days* mentioned in *Creation Week* could be as "…one day is with the Lord…." 2 Peter 3:8, tells us this does not equate to one of our days, instead, we are told "…that one day is with the Lord as a thousand years…." This is a very important point that highlights the fact we have been making false assumptions regarding God's use of the word, *Day*.

With that being said, someone may try to make the argument that during *Creation Week*, a *Day* has been defined as a night and day cycle. But wait, not so fast. Let's look at the statement that I generated earlier, "And the (only) evening and the (only) morning were the sixth day." Now look at the first part of 2 Peter 3:8, where God states "…that one day is with the Lord as a thousand years…" This means that one evening and one morning with the Lord (one day) is as a thousand evenings and a thousand mornings of mankind's time. This means that when God states, "And the evening and the morning were the sixth day," **2 Peter 3:8 is telling us that this could be any number of mankind evenings and mornings!**

We need to realize these were epic and unique *Creation Days* of the Lord. As a consequence, I believe they required an exclusive version of God's Time. These were not typical *Days with the Lord* (which are special in their own right), instead, these were epic momentous *Creation Days with the Lord*. Because they were supremely special and unique *Creation Days*. They could have started with an initial evening period, ran their due course over an extended length of time, and then ended with a morning period that was long ages after that *Creation Day* initially began. Hence, "And the (first) evening and the (last) morning were the sixth day."

These *Divine Creation Days with the Lord* were supremely unique and set a precedent. There were no other *Days* like them. This is why no assumptions about them can be made. As 2 Peter 3:8 points out, we don't understand God's Time, it's as simple as that. Mankind has been missing something with regards to the timeline of *Creation Week* because mankind will never understand:

> But, beloved, be not ignorant of this one thing, that one
> day is with the Lord as a thousand years, and a thousand
> years as one day.

We need to stop being ignorant of the fact that we will never comprehend God's Time. This means that any assumptions regarding time, especially God's Time, may be completely off the mark. Here is a comment regarding mankind's misunderstanding of time that comes from theoretical physicist Carlo Rovelli who states:

Time is an illusion: our native perception of its flow does
not correspond to physical reality.[27]

We can clearly see that physicist Carlo Rovelli is telling us that mankind's impression of how time operates is way off the mark. In other words, mankind is actually clueless when it comes to the topic of time.

One of the aspects included in Einstein's theory of Relativity is that time is not constant.[28] Einstein's theory states time is relative to the perspective of the observer. The theory of Relativity points out that time is not as constant as most of us have grown accustomed to believe. This means the passage of God's Time during *Creation Week* may be far more complicated than traditionally thought.

It is also important for us to realize that Einstein's Special theory of Relativity predicts that time does not progress at a steady pace, and it can be altered by acceleration.[29] This means that if acceleration and speed are altered, then time is altered. We must remember that *God's Speed* is not mankind's speed. In addition, Einstein's General theory of Relativity predicts gravity has the consequence of slowing down time. As you can see, the theories of Relativity give us other reasons why God's Time is not mankind's time.

Based on these scientific observations, it is safe to say the dimension of time is far more complex than what we have traditionally assumed it to be. This is why I feel our simple assumptions of time regarding *Creation Week* are missing the more complex reality of what actually occurred. This is the reason why traditional interpretations of the timeline of *Creation Week* cannot be assumed to be correct. In fact, the Fossil Record tells us the traditional timeline interpretation of creation is completely off the mark.

The famous theologian R. C. Sproul is the person who formulated the original Chicago Statement of Biblical Inerrancy. R. C. Sproul once stated:

> When people ask me how old the earth is, I tell them I
> don't know—because I don't.[30]

Here is a scholar who wisely admits he does not know what the earth's timeline is. This means that he is fully aware of the message that God is sending to mankind with 2 Peter 3:8.

With all of this being said, by leaving out the words, "first evening" and "last morning," God eliminates confusion and delivers the message of the seven-day workweek schedule that simple mankind can easily absorb and adopt. Think of *Creation Week* as containing a few parable aspects.

This is supported by the fact that God does not state that a *Creation Day's* creations were good unless the entire *Creation Day* was already over. This is why I feel we have strong evidence to support a long ages interpretation as being correct because of the simple fact that God does not state, "And the evening and the morning were the seventh day." I believe the reason why God does not have Moses record this, is because the Seventh Day is not over yet.

If the statement, "And the evening and the morning were the sixth day," really referred to a 24-hour, literal day, then God would have also had Moses record, "And the evening and the morning were the seventh day." The fact that God does not have Moses record this about Day Seven proves that *Creation Week* is composed of very long *Divine Days*, not what we know as typical 24-hour days. This is the only logical explanation for why God does not have Moses record, "And the evening and the morning were the seventh day." This supports my assertion that *Creation Days* are *Divine Days* of extended periods of time. In this case, they are billions of years long.

Let me give an example of my *Divine Days* explanation. The first evening and the last morning are like bookends on a very long library shelf. The very first evening is the first book all the way to the left, while the last morning is the very last book all the way to the right. This means there were billions of years of time in-between these two bookends. In this scenario, instead of these bookends (evening and morning) being 12 hours apart, the bookends are billions of years apart (which is over a trillion, 24-hour days apart).

In this library example, the curator of this library would first point to the book on the far left of the shelf and say, "And the evening." Then the curator would walk all the way down to the last book on the far right of the shelf and point to it saying, "and the morning, were the sixth day." If we don't watch the curator do this, and just heard them say this, we would naturally assume the two books were right next to each other.

The first book would be the only seed *creation* book (Phase 1), while all the rest of the books would be the seed *germination* books (Phase 2). I believe this scenario brings Genesis Chapter One into alignment with the Fossil Record. This thoroughly explains what could have happened during *Creation Week* and how each *Creation Day* was a *Divine Day*, not a standard solar day. We know these were not solar days because Day One, Day Two, and Day Three, all took place before the Sun's light was mentioned in Day Four. If we are not dealing with light from the Sun in Genesis 1:3, then this light must be coming from God himself. I find it interesting to realize that *Creation Week* had two different light sources.

It seems logical to me that if the first three *Creation Days* were illuminated by God's Light, then all six *Creation Days* were illuminated by God's Light. I say this because I also believe *Creation Week* ran on God's Time. I feel safe stating this because mankind did not even exist until the end of Day Six. Once mankind appeared on the scene, this marked the end of the first six *Creation Days* that were used to prepare the earth for mankind. Because Adam and Eve appeared at the very end of Day Six which started Day Seven, I believe this marked when God's Time ended for *Creation Week* and mankind's time began.

This seems like the logical time for solar days to begin. I believe this means it's possible that only Day Seven has been illuminated by the Sun (I will further explain why I believe this). Since Divine Day Seven has been going on for about 10,000 years so far, that would be 10,000 years of solar days. Therefore, *Creation Week* occurred with God's Light and over God's Time.

The reason why I am discussing solar days is because, if God's Light is not the sunlight that we are accustomed to, then God's Time is not something that we are accustomed to either. What I'm saying here is that God's mention of an evening and a morning may not be what we would naturally assume. We assume the morning in question, came right after the evening. We assume a quick succession of the evening and the morning. However, if God is working over a much longer timeframe, then the morning He is referring to is not going to follow in quick succession after the first evening.

At this point, I wish to clarify that I believe we are dealing with four types of *Days* in the Bible:

    1) A *Day Period*—is a night/day cycle produced from the illumination of God's Light that resulted in a cycle period that was

about 24 hours in length. God's Light is definitely what illuminated Day One, Day Two, and Day Three, because the Sun is not mentioned until Day Four. That said, it seems logical to me that the first six *Days* of *Creation Week* were all lit by God's light in what amounts to billions of years of *Day Periods*.

2) A Solar Day—is a night/day cycle produced from the illumination of the Sun resulting in a 24-hour period of time.

3) A *Divine Day*—is any number of *Day Periods* or solar days. A *Divine Day* can vary in length and lasts for as long as God's intended use requires. For example, in 2 Peter 3:8 (KJV): we read, "But, beloved, be not ignorant of this one thing, that one day is with the Lord as a thousand years, and a thousand years as one day." In the first part of this verse, we see that a *Divine Day*, in this instance, is equal to 1,000 of our years. But then in the last part of this verse, 1,000 years of *Divine Days* with the Lord are equal to one of our solar days. This is a perfect example of how the length of time for a *Divine Day* can vary greatly and can't be predicted.

4) A *Creation Day*— Each *Creation Day* is an extra-special *Divine Day* that is specifically dedicated to creation. There are seven *Divine Days* that make up *Creation Week*. In the case of Creation Days One through Six, they are all composed of billions of years of *Day Periods* because they were illuminated by God's Light. In the case of Creation Day Seven, up to this point, it is composed of 10,000 years of solar days.

Here is my detailed breakdown of *Creation Days* that gives us a better mental picture:

- Creation Day One is on God's Time, lit by God's Light which unfolded inside the construct of Divine Day One.

– Creation Day Two is on God's Time, lit by God's Light which unfolded inside the construct of Divine Day Two.

– Creation Day Three is on God's Time, lit by God's Light which unfolded inside the construct of Divine Day Three.

I believe this continued to be the case for Creation Days Four, Five, and Six. However, Creation Day Seven is different, Creation Day Seven is on mankind's time, lit by the Sun's light which is currently unfolding inside the construct of Divine Day Seven.

I believe we are only scratching the surface as to how complex God's Time really is. My efforts to analyze *Creation Week* may seem complex, however, I believe that detailed efforts are necessary in order to establish that what is written in the Holy Bible could have actually happened. I am attempting to establish that the Bible speaks the truth. If my suggestions are possible, this means that what I am proposing cannot be proven false. And, of course, if something cannot be proven false, then it could be true. As a consequence, logic dictates that if something is possible, then it could be true. This is why the reconciliation of the Bible with the scientific findings is so critical. Once it is established how science can coexist with the Bible, the Bible can no longer be viewed by some people as a book of fairy tales.

Now, let's get back to *Creation Week*. Because God is telling Moses this, thousands of years after the first six *Creation Days* have already been completed, this allows God to assemble the *Creation Days* in a sequenced order. But in reality, I believe that all of the first six *Creation Days* ran concurrently. Phase 2 of each *Creation Day* ended at the same time when mankind appeared. As a consequence, we have been in Day Seven ever since.

In a nutshell, I interpret, "And the evening and the morning were the sixth day," to actually mean, "And the first evening and the last morning bracket and include all of the creations of God's Divine Day Six." This statement simplifies to, "And the first evening and the last morning were the sixth day." This is the best explanation I have as to how the *Creation Days* recorded in Genesis can reconcile with the Fossil Record. When we read, "And the evening and the morning were the sixth day," this actually means the first hours of Day Six marked the creation phase (Phase 1) which was the very beginning of the entire Day Six creation project. However, this entire Day Six creation project would wind up lasting for billions of years during its Phase 2.

This distinctive interpretation makes perfect sense because this crucial statement is not made about Day Seven. God did not have Moses record that the evening and the morning were the seventh day because we are still in Day Seven. This means *Creation Week* is referring to *Divine Days* of extended periods of time. This must be the reason why Genesis does not proclaim, "And the evening and the morning were the seventh day."

As stated, because of the way in which *Creation Week* is worded, we get the impression that previous *Creation Days* had to be completed and come to an end before the next *Creation Day* was started. We are under the impression that each *Creation Day* only lasted for 24 hours. I don't believe this is what actually occurred because the Fossil Record tells us this is not what happened.

For example, Day Five did not have to come to an end before Day Six started. It is true that Day Five started 24 hours before Day Six started, but Day Five did not have to end in order for Day Six to begin.

Clearly, God did not find the need to mention the long ages (Phase 2) timeframe information. God is in possession of all knowledge and it should be evident that everything that God knows is not recorded in the Bible. This is why we don't know everything that God knows. Therefore, the duration of Phase 2 for each *Creation Day* is an example of information that is not recorded in Genesis

In summary, Genesis could be worded like it is in order to keep creation simple to understand. In reality, I believe that God was discussing seven *Divine Days* of creation in Genesis. The manner in which God presented the seven *Creation Days* in Genesis Chapter One introduced the construct of the seven-day workweek which allowed mankind to quickly adopt and utilize it to manage time.

When we consider that Genesis 1:31, could mean, "And the first evening and the last morning were the sixth day," this would represent a *Divine Day* where the evening of the first 24-hour period and the morning of the last 24-hour period function to bracket the entire creative event. I feel the *Creation Days* in *Creation Week* represent examples of how God's Time is not mankind's time (2 Peter 3:8). A *Divine Day* is not a standard solar day that mankind is accustomed to.

Personally, I prefer this scenario as an explanation because the time that is bracketed in-between the first evening and the last morning of each *Creation Day* (billions of years) would be considered a demonstration of God's Time regarding a *Divine Day* as it relates to *Creation Week*. I say this because God's Time regarding another event could be a different length of time.

I would also like to point out that no one can prove that *Creation Week* did not occur. Therefore, because the scientific evidence indicates the earth is old, I'm going to agree that the earth has existed 4.5 billion years. As a consequence, *Creation Week* occurred over the course of a very long period of time, not within the span of a seven-day workweek.

The next thing I would like to say about *Creation Week* is this. Because this event is described as being a 'week,' it means *Creation*

Week is being associated with a measure of time, in this case, a week of some sort. The measure of time did not begin until the first clock was created by God in Genesis 1:5. In my view, anything that occurred before the night/day clock existed, is separate from any kind of event that is associated with a measure of time. In the original Hebrew language, the word, *heaven* (*heavens*), represents the universe. As we study these verses, we witness God giving mankind the gift of a night and day cycle which will function as a clock.

Note that a clock is different from time. Time began at the moment the universe was created. Time is defined as the continued progress of existence in the past, present, and future.[31] While on the other hand, a clock measures the amount of progress. This is why we are familiar with the logic that a clock measures the amount of time.[32] Even though time began at the beginning of the universe (Genesis 1:1), a clock was not established until Genesis 1:5, with the inception of the first night/day cycle. This suggests that after the creation of the universe, any amount of time could have passed between the beginning of verse 1 and verse 5. Why? This is because a clock did not exist to measure the amount of time that passed until verse 5. Regardless, there was no human in existence to perceive time until the end of Creation Day Six.

This means that the inception of the clock in Genesis 1:5 would not have been running on mankind's time. The clock was created by God for mankind. Please note that whenever God mentions any of His Days, they would have nothing to do with mankind's days because God's Time is not associated with the rotation of planet Earth. "God's Time" existed before the universe and the earth were created and existed. Therefore, even though the first clock was created in Genesis 1:5, it was not ticking until mankind existed.

Here is an example, if we bought a wind-up clock from the store, it obviously exists, but it is not running until we wind it up. When Adam was created, this wound the clock up and it began to tick. This is why there were no recorded clock measurements until Adam was created and began experiencing the passage of time once his brain started recording this data. Adam was not created until Genesis 1:26-27.

Because *Creation Week* is referenced as a timed event, it relates to everything that occurred on the earth from the moment that the first clock was created by God on Day One. Even though mankind did not exist to track time until the end of *Creation Week*, it is still referenced as a timed event from the moment that a clock existed (even though it was not ticking yet). As a result, *Creation Week* does not include the creation of the universe and the earth (Genesis 1:1) because they already existed before the time-measuring clock was created in Genesis 1:5. Remember, even when the first clock existed, it was not ticking and recording mankind's time until Adam arrived.

When discussing Creation Day One, a measure of time for Phase 1 is only going to start once a

clock exists. In other words, once the night/day cycle was established in Genesis 1:5, the first evening comprised Phase 1 of Day One. As a result, Phase 2 began after the *Day Period* of Phase 1 ended. Phase 2 of Day One simply consists of all the 24-hour days that occurred while God's Light was still on. As mentioned, I refer to these as, *Day Periods*. Once the Sun took over (which I explain later in this chapter), God was able to turn His Light off. This marked the end of Creation Day One, 10,000 years ago.

Now, it has come to my recent attention that when I carefully review the original Hebrew text in Chapter One of the Book of Genesis, it seems that we can date when *Creation Week* started. I say this because *Creation Week* started when God shined His Light on the earth and then divided the light from the darkness to create the first night/day cycle. This is recorded in Genesis 1:5 (KJV).

We can date this event because God divided the light from the darkness by causing the earth to spin. If the earth was not spinning, there would not be a night/day cycle.

As we all know, the earth's rotation around its axis is a necessary condition for our day and night cycle. And we know when the earth's spin began, because we know when the planet Theia collided with Earth. This was 4.5 billion years ago.[33] Earth began to spin because Theia slammed into Earth with a glancing collision.

Therefore, sometime after the earth was created, God refined and perfected its construction with somewhat of a glancing collision with Theia where Earth's iron core was significantly enlarged, and Earth's crust was significantly thinned out. Both of these alterations were beneficial to the earth which I discuss in a later chapter. Not only did the collision with Theia perfect Earth's design, but that collision also put Earth into its spin. Earth's spin is how God divided the light from the darkness and created the night/day cycle.

As a result, we know that *Creation Week* started just after the earth's design was perfected by God with the planet Theia. This is completely separate from the universe existing over 9 billion years before the earth was fully formed. This means the creation of the universe and the beginning of the earth's *Creation Week* were about 9 billion years apart. I believe *Creation Week*, was Earth's *Creation Week*. If some people insist that *Creation Week* started when the universe was created, then it started over 13 billion years ago resulting in a 9-billion-year timeframe between the creation of the universe in Genesis 1:1, and when the earth's form was fully completed in Genesis 1:5.

Either way, it took billions of years from the beginning of Genesis 1:1 (universe), to the end of Genesis 1:1 (when the earth was without form, dark, and void). This is when the earth was in its raw condition. Thus, the very first verse in the Bible lasted for billions of years. Why did it take so long? Well, maybe this is how long it takes for a new universe to settle down to the extent it created the element materials that coalesced to form the earth. In addition, it seems the universe has to be as old as it is and as big as it is to optimally support life on the earth, especially when it comes to the earth accumulating critical trace elements.[34]

In addition to what I have already proposed, I am about to present more information regarding *Creation Week* which will hopefully allow us to better visualize how it is possible to begin the process of bringing the book of science into agreement with the Word of God. All we have to do is find the ways that makes it possible for both books to be correct. Demonstrating how science and the Bible can be brought into agreement would be of interest to nonbelievers who seek the truth. This would also be of interest to those people who are trying to believe in God but have some doubts about what they are reading in the Bible.

Because *Creation Week* is so crucial, I feel that an in-depth discussion is necessary. As a result, I am going to state and clarify several important points regarding *Creation Week* that I believe are true. There are many important points, however, it is here that I wish to present 7 main points or conditions that I have listed and need to be presented so that you will be able to orient yourself. These points and conditions are as follows:

1) The main reason the book of science and the Book of God don't appear to be in agreement can be found in the Book of

Genesis. This is true because many traditional fundamentalists have interpreted Genesis to declare that *Creation Week* occurred over the course of a seven-day period which beheld the inception of the universe, the earth, and every single species that has ever lived on the earth. By contrast, science declares the universe and the earth are billions of years old. In addition, the Fossil Record demonstrates species appeared over the course of hundreds of millions of years, not over the course of 7 days. Hence, the book of science and the Book of God don't appear to be in agreement because of a timeline dispute.

2) Each *Day* in *Creation Week* is an organized section. Regarding *Creation Days* with living organisms, similar organisms have been neatly grouped together and placed into the same *Creation Day*. As a result, there are 7 sections of accomplishments in *Creation Week,* corresponding to the 7 *Creation Days*. This simplifies creation which allows mankind to easily absorb, understand, and teach their children and others about this momentous event.

3) The establishment of the night/day cycle on Day One was the start of *Creation Week*. That event coincides with the collision of planet Theia and Earth, 4.5 billion years ago.[35] This caused the earth to spin which allowed God's Light to create the first night/day cycle. Therefore, *Creation Week* started 4.5 billion years ago.

4) It is a fact that early Earth did not have an oxygen atmosphere and was instead plagued with toxic gases like methane and sulfur dioxide. The very first organisms on the earth were special bacteria that were apparently introduced in order to start the long process of terraforming the earth into an oxygen

environment that would eventually support complex life. This activity pertains to Day Two of *Creation Week*. Before 2017, scientists believed the very first fossil dated back to 3.5 billion years ago. However, in 2017, scientists have now found what they consider to be the oldest bacterium fossil which dates back to 3.7 billion years ago.[36] As a result, be advised that the oldest fossil will either be listed as 3.5 billion years old or 3.7 billion years old depending on the source that you reference. This information is important because it answers the question: Why would God's first created species be bacteria?

5) All the species for any particular *Creation Day* were created (at the same time) by using seeds that contained the genetic code for each specie. I refer to these seeds as, *creation seeds*. There was a unique *creation seed* for each species. *Creation seeds* of similarly grouped species did not all open at the same time, despite the fact they were all created and planted at the same time. Hence, *creation seeds* were timed to open at their predetermined times. A *creation seeds* concept solves the problem of how all the species could be created in the span of a seven-day workweek without them all living on the earth at the same time. A seed can sit dormant for a very long period of time before it finally germinated. The Fossil Record demonstrates the various species that have existed and how they were not all alive at the same time. This *creation seeds* proposal is an effort to find a way that traditional interpretations and the Fossil Record can find some measure of common ground. Traditional interpretations are correct about Phase 1 and the Fossil Record is correct about Phase 2. Personally, I find it easier to visualize seeds germinating over time as opposed to God speaking the

species into existence over time. For example, if we look at Genesis 1:11 (KJV), where vegetation is created, God states, "Let the earth bring forth grass…," This seems to be as seeds germinating out of the ground. Then in Genesis 1:24 (KJV), where animals are created, God states, "Let the earth bring forth the living creature…" This is how the plants, trees, and grasses emerged out of the earth. Since seeds brought forth vegetation out of the earth (soil), it's possible that animals were brought forth in the same manner, as germinating embryo seeds. Considering seeds, or God speaking species into existence, either way works.

6) Because the Sun was not mentioned until Day Four, this means that God used His own light on Day One, Day Two, and Day Three. This means there were two light sources involved in *Creation Week*. I believe there were two light sources in *Creation Week* because the Sun's light was blocked out by orbiting debris for most of *Creation Week*. This is because the orbiting debris was in-between the Sun and the surface of the earth. Orbiting debris existed because of Theia's collision with Earth and the multiple meteor collisions throughout Earth's history. Even though Day Four finally made the Sun visible, this process of clearing the orbiting atmospheric debris was very long. I believe Day Four did not fully accomplish this process until the end of Day Five and Day Six. This means that the clearing of this orbiting debris took billions of years to complete. This also means God probably used His Light for the entirety of *Creation Week*. God turned His Light on for billions of years. This was possibly done in a manner that simulated the solar night/day cycle that living organisms and mankind are best

suited for. Now, in order for this to work, God's Light must have been in-between the orbiting debris and the surface of the earth. This means *Creation Week* was composed of *Divine Days*, not solar days. As a consequence, *Creation Week* unfolded over God's Time, not over mankind's time.

7) As mentioned previously, the *Days* in *Creation Week* were billions of years long, where each *Creation Day* was composed of two parts or phases. Each *Creation Day* started with the first evening period (this constitutes the **creation phase** when the genetic codes for *Creation Days* with living organisms were formulated and placed into *creation seeds*). This first brief period was followed by billions of years of 24-hour periods that slowly introduced all the species for that particular *Creation Day*. This occurred over an extended length of time and constitutes the **germination phase** of the *creation seeds*. Here are the equations that apply to the *Creation Days*:

Each *Creation Day* = the first 24-hour period
+ billions of years (of 24-hour periods).
Phase 1 = the first 24-hour period
which is the creation phase
Phase 2 = billions of years of 24-hour
periods which is the germination phase
Therefore, each *Creation Day* = Phase 1 + Phase 2

I believe that once God initially supplied His Light and separated the light from the darkness with the earth's spin, all the subsequent *Creation Days* started within the span of a seven-day workweek (except for Day Seven). The key word here is, **started.** Phase 1 of Creation Days

One through Six occurred over the course of six, 'first evenings,' which means, six nights in a row.

For example, at the beginning of Day Two, Phase 1 of Day Two occurred where all the creation seeds were created for the various types of terraforming bacterial species. Before any of those *creation seeds* could open, Day Three started 24 hours later where all the *creation seeds* were created for the various types of vegetation (plants, trees, and grasses). Before any of those *creation seeds* could open, Day Four started 24 hours later where God commanded that the phenomenon described as gravity, would slowly clear the atmosphere of debris. This would be a very long process that would make the Sun, the Moon, and the stars finally visible. Then Day Five started 24 hours after Day Four started. Day Five is where all the *creation seeds* were created for marine life and birds. Before any of those *creation seeds* could open, Day Six started 24 hours later where all the *creation seeds* for the various types of land animals were created. In other words, 144 hours after the beginning of Day One, all of the first six *Creation Days* were running concurrently.

For example, Day Five did not have to come to an end with all of its species coming into existence before Day Six started. During *Creation Week*, all the *Creation Days* were running at the same time even though all their starts were staggered by a single 24-hour period. Once a *Creation Day* started, it did not have to run its full course and end (completing both Phase 1 and Phase 2) in order for the next *Creation Day* to begin. However, there is one exception to this and that would be Day Seven. I believe that we are currently in Phase 2 of Day Seven right now and this means that Creation Days One through Six all ended once the creation of Adam and Eve occurred. This ushered in Day Seven.

Therefore, Day Seven only began once all the other *Creation Days* were completed which was timed to occur at the very moment that mankind was created. God initially turned on His Light and created the first night/day cycle. The very 'first evening' marked Phase 1 of Day One and marked the beginning of *Creation Week*. Every day after the first night/day cycle marked Phase 2 of Day One. Phase 1 for Creation Days One through Six were completed within the span of a seven-day work-week. However, on Days with *creation seeds*, they did not germinate and introduce their species into existence until much later over the course of long ages during each *Creation Day's* Phase 2. The end of Day Six would mark when God turned off His Light. The end of Day Six was marked by three events:

— Adam and Eve were created 10,000 years ago.

— The ticking of mankind's clock began.

— Phase 2 ended for Creation Days One through Six. This included Day Four which ended with the Sun's light finally being able to reach the earth's surface which is when God turned off His Light.

There are two events that occurred within the 'first evening' of Day Seven which constitute Phase 1 of Day Seven:

- The Sabbath Day was established in the beginning of Phase 1 of Day Seven.
- God formed a covenant relationship with mankind in Day Seven.

As a consequence, the 'creations' that occurred in Day Seven include the creation of the Sabbath Day and the creation of the Covenant between God and mankind. As I have stated, I believe we are presently in Phase 2 of Day Seven which is composed of mankind's history. Once again, and just to clarify, Day Seven began 10,000 years ago, just as Day Six was ending. *Creation Week* unfolded over God's Time, this is why each *Creation Day* in its entirety (Phase 1 and Phase 2) was not a 24-hour period. Likewise, *Creation Week* in its entirety was not equal to 7 solar days in duration because the Sun was not even mentioned until after Day One, Day Two, and Day Three, were already started.

As stated, God created all the *creation seeds* for each particular *Creation Day* within the very first evening of that particular *Creation Day*. This means that for each *Creation Day*, it took less than twenty-four hours for God to formulate the *creation seeds* for each *Creation Day*. This is vastly different from how long it took the individual seeds to germinate (Phase 2) and cause the species to appear over long ages.

For example, on Day Five, God did create all the marine life and bird species *creation seeds* in the span of the first evening (Phase 1). However, those species did not all come into existence at once in the span of a single 24-hour day (Phase 2). Phase 2 would unfold over billions of years. Take notice that God also mentions that each *Creation Day* was successful, meaning the germination phase worked as planned. God apparently does not find the need to include and explain how long it took for the germination phases to unfold. Moses is able to record the success of each *Creation Day* because this history is being given to him after these *Creation Days* have ended and the results are evident.

I believe *Creation Week*'s timeline was far more complex than it appears. This causes confusion because of the simple fashion in which it was presented to mankind in the Book of Genesis. I believe this is the main reason why the book of science and the Book of God are not found to be in agreement. Traditional fundamentalists believe each *Creation Day* had only one phase that lasted 24 hours, while the Fossil Record reveals that each *Creation Day* lasted for much, much longer. It's no wonder why the book of science and the Book of God are not seen to reconcile. Mankind needs to find the bridges that connect these two books.

That being said, I believe we can all see that if each *Creation Day* had two phases (that involved *creation seeds*), then this would allow for an agreement to be found between the Fossil Record and the Bible. **In addition, this *creation seeds* explanation also demonstrates how species could have slowly appeared in a progressively advancing fashion giving the false impression that an evolutionary process occurred. In other words, evolution is not the only explanation for how species progressively appeared over an extended timeframe!**

Either evolution made all the species appear over time or they were made to appear over time by a Creator. These are the two possibilities for how all the species appeared over long ages. Chapter Five covers several critical facts about evolution that definitively eliminates one of these two possibilities.

With all of this being said, I feel the 7 important points that I mentioned are useful for two main reasons:

1) This list explains how *Creation Week* makes sense and allows the Fossil Record to be brought into agreement with the account of *Creation Week* listed in the Book of Genesis.

2) This list demonstrates how the theory of evolution is not the only *Old Earth* progressive process to be considered as being the possible reality of how all the species appeared when they did.

What I have described is a logical possibility for how species got here over a long timeframe. This demonstrates that *Creation Week* cannot be simply disregarded as an impossible fairy tale. We must also keep in mind that it cannot be proven by anyone that *Creation Week* never occurred.

Before I end my discussion of *Creation Week* in this chapter, I would like to present a very interesting example to help clarify what I have been trying to say up to this point. Hopefully this example will aid in visualizing what I believe occurred during *Creation Week*.

Let's say that we are at a racetrack watching a marathon car race that is going to last for 4.5 billion years. The track is very big, and it takes 24 hours to complete one lap. There are seven cars, just like there are seven *Creation Days*. This race starts 4.5 billion years ago as the first car takes off at 6:00 p.m. at night to mark the beginning of Day One. Since this race started at night, this first night phase is referred to as, *the first evening*. Twelve hours later, at 6:00 a.m., it reaches the half-way mark of its first lap. At this point, Phase 1 (which was 12 hours long) has been completed as the first evening. What has been accomplished by 6:00 a.m. (end of Phase 1, beginning of Phase 2), is that God's Light is shining, the earth is spinning, and the first night/ day cycle was in the process of being established (Phase 1 completed).

The beginning of this first morning at 6:00 a.m. is when Phase 2 begins. When this first car finally completes its first lap, it is 6:00

p.m. to start Day Two. Hence, it took 24 hours to complete one lap (one night/day cycle). As we continue, it's now 6:00 p.m., the beginning of Day Two, as the first car begins its second lap, this is when the second car starts its race. Twenty-four hours later, the second car crosses the start line as it completes its first lap at 6:00 p.m., it has completed its Phase 1 (first evening) and is 12 hours into its Phase 2. By this time, all the *creation seeds* have been made for bacteria and the other microorganisms responsible for creating the earth's atmosphere. This starts Day Three.

It's now 6:00 p.m., the beginning of Day Three, as the second car begins its second lap, and the first car begins its third lap. This is when the third car starts its race. Twenty-four hours later, the third car completes one lap and crosses the start line at 6:00 p.m., where it has completed its Phase 1 (first evening) and is 12 hours into its Phase 2. By this time, the land and waters have been separated and the *creation seeds* for vegetation have been made. This starts Day Four.

It's now 6:00 p.m., the beginning of Day Four, as the fourth car begins its race. The three other cars continue to race. Twenty-four hours later, the fourth car completes one lap and crosses the start line at 6:00 p.m., where it has completed its Phase 1 (first evening) and is 12 hours into its Phase 2. By this time, God's *Matter Converging Phenomenon* (described as gravity) begins the slow process of clearing the earth's atmosphere of orbiting rocky debris. This starts Day Five.

It's now 6:00 p.m., the beginning of Day Five, as the fifth car begins its race. The four other cars continue to race. Twenty-four hours later, the fifth car completes one lap and crosses the start line at 6:00 p.m., where it has completed its Phase 1 (first evening) and is 12 hours into its Phase 2. By this time the *creation seeds* for marine life and Birds have been made. This starts Day Six.

It's now 6:00 p.m., the beginning of Day Six, as the sixth car begins its race. The five other cars continue to race. Twenty-four hours later, the sixth car completes one lap and crosses the start line at 6:00 p.m., where it has completed its Phase 1 (first evening) and is 12 hours into its Phase 2. By this time the *creation seeds* for land animals have been made.

All of the activity up to this point includes the completion of Phase 1 (first evenings) for each of the first six *Creation Days* which could have occurred over the course of six, 24-hour periods of time. The duration of this designing and creating phase (Phase 1) agrees with the traditional interpretation of *Creation Week*. This means that God could have **created** all the seeds for each species within the span of the first evening of each *Creation Day*. This could have all happened within the span of a standard workweek

In addition, there is one more possibility to consider here. This explanation considers the scenario where the "evening and the morning" were back-to-back (only 12 hours apart). Let's look at Genesis 1:20-23 (KJV), on Day Five God states:

> And God said, Let the water bring forth abundantly the moving creatures that hath life, and fowl that may fly above the earth in the open firmament of Heaven. And God created great whales, and every living creature that moveth, which the waters brought forth abundantly, after their kind, and every winged fowl after his kind: and God saw that it was good. And God blessed them, saying, Be fruitful, and multiply, and fill the waters in the seas, and let fowl multiply in the earth. And the evening and the morning were the fifth day.

Since we know that God can see into the future, let's imagine that it's the first evening of Day Five of *Creation Week*, 4.5 billion years ago. God has just made all the creation seeds for marine life and birds. Then He gives the waters and the earth the command to bring forth His creatures when their time is due in the future (Phase 2). This could have all been easily done during the first evening of the 24-hour period which is Phase 1 of Day Five.

But now, imagine this, while it is still the first evening of Day Five, God looks into the future and sees that the waters and the earth bring forth all of His creatures just as planned, and God "saw that it was good. I believe it is reasonable to figure that God may have wanted to see the results right away. If you are God, and you can see into the future, why wait billions of years for the results when you can see the results right away?

Therefore, this is not a case of God seeing the results right away because all the species came to life right away. No, instead, God saw the results right away because He looked into the future. Remember that God can control time in ways we can't even imagine. Let's consider the scenario where God said what he meant to say in Genesis. If God looked into the future, then some people are going to assume that all the species came to life at once. The Fossil Record tells us this was not the case.

Please note that this viewing of the future could have taken place within the 12 hours of the first evening of Day Five. Now, fast forward to 1445-1440 BC when Moses is given this history while he is in the wilderness with the Israelites. Moses would have been told of God's actions, experiences, and visions (into the future) during the first evening of Day Five of *Creation Week*, 4.5 billion years ago. Therefore, it is possible that what is written in Genesis 1:20-23, could have occurred just as it was written. This explanation would be applied to all the *Creation Days*.

This means that within the first 24 hours of Day Five, God proclaimed His plan for Day Five, made the creation seeds, gave the waters and the earth the command to bring forth His creatures (at a later date in the future), then God looked into the future to witness that His plan worked perfectly. God could have stated all of this within the span of the first 24 hours of Day Five. And because of this, Moses would have been told that all of this happened within the daily cycle of Day Five. However, this would have given the impression to everyone reading this, that there was only one daily cycle of Day Five.

As stated, this caused mankind to recognize and adopt the seven-day workweek which was the result of not seeing the entire picture. And, of course, the next 4.5 billion years would have slowly seen the emergence of all these creatures just as the Fossil Record lists them. It would not be known to Moses that the species actually appeared over long ages of Phase 2 of Day Five. What Moses was told to write included Phase 1 and all of Phase 2 of Day Five, but this was only made possible by God looking into the future while He was in Phase 1 of Day Five.

Here is the breakdown:

1) During the first 12 hours of Creation Day Five (Phase 1), God states that He is going to create marine life and birds. God makes the *creation seeds*, and gives the command to the waters and the earth to bring forth His creations (at their prescribed times).

2) During the first 24 hours of Creation Day Five, God looked into the future and saw that the waters and the earth will indeed bring His creations to life (at their prescribed times) and that His creations look very good (visions of all of Phase 2). As the morning phase ends, Creation Day Five ends (Day

Six will follow next).

This means there is a way that God really did what He said that He did by the end of each *Creation Day's*, first night/day cycle. If God was looking into the future within the first 24-hour period of each *Creation Day*, this would have allowed God to make the statements that He made. Because we don't realize that God was looking into the future to see the results when He made His statements, and because we don't realize the appearances of these species took billions of years to unfold, we assume this all took place in one, 24-hour period.

If any of my three explanatory scenarios are correct, it would have accomplished three objectives:

1) God kept creation simple for mankind to understand and explain to future generations.

2) God ensured that mankind would adopt the seven-day work-week strategy.

3) God made sure that mankind would rest and honor Him on the Sabbath, every seventh day.

Therefore, regarding the statement, "And the evening and the morning were the fifth day," either God was using the parable technique where the words that He used had another intended purpose, mankind made an incorrect assumption, or God was looking into the future when He made His statements.

To re-cap:

1) If God was using a parable technique to keep creation simple and deliver other messages. This caused the words, "first" and "last" to be left out: "And the **first** evening and the **last** morning were the sixth day."

2) If "God's Time" was intended to serve a special purpose where the first evening and the last morning established a 4.5-billion-year

limit for each *Divine Creation Day*, then we are making an incorrect assumption that the "evening and the morning" were back-to-back and only 12 hours apart. In this scenario, words are not left out to create a parable, instead, we are simply making an incorrect assumption about what was stated. This is because we don't actually understand God's Time during *Creation Week*.

3) If God was looking into the future as He made His comments during the first 24 hours of each *Creation Day*, this would represent a clever way to neatly package what God's plans were, what the commands to the waters and the earth were, what results were seen in the future, and what God's responses were. This was all neatly packaged into a single day for each Creation Day, in order to keep the creation story simple, while at the same time, deliver other messages to mankind (work-week and weekly Sabbath).

I feel this provides a few reasonable explanations for the statement, "And the evening and the morning were the ... day." Once again, this statement is the main reason why the book of science and the Book of God do not agree.

Now, getting back to the marathon car race example. You will notice that I did not say that Day Seven began when the sixth car completed its first lap. This is because I believe that each *Creation Day* was a *Divine Day* that started with its first evening and ended billions of years later with its last morning. This means that all six cars continued to race for the next 4.5 billion years. As time went on, their *creation seeds* slowly opened. This caused the earth to be populated and prepared for the introduction of mankind. Notice how all the cars were running at the same time for most of the race.

Then, at 10,000 years ago, all six cars completed their races at the same time. Phase 2 for each car had just ended. All of their *creation seeds* had already germinated. Just as Day Six was drawing to a close, is when God created mankind. This ended Day Six and ushered in the start of the Seventh Day when the seventh car began its race. The passengers inside the seventh car were Adam and Eve. At 6:00 p.m. on that day (evening phase), they started their race as the other cars pulled off the track. Twenty-four hours later, the seventh car completes one lap and crosses the start line at 6:00 p.m. where it has completed its Phase 1 and is 12 hours into its Phase 2. By this time, the Seventh Day is established as a holy Sabbath and God has formed His Covenant with Adam and Eve.

Car seven has been making daily laps for the last 10,000 years as Phase 2 continues to unfold with the passing of mankind's history. As stated, I believe we are still in Day Seven right now because the Book of Genesis does not state that the evening and the morning were the Seventh Day!

I realize this example seems complex however, I believe *Creation Week* is a complex event that is really happening (most of it is over). The only way that I can envision this, is the manner in which I just described it. I firmly believe that if we combine everything that unfolded between all of the first evenings and all of the last mornings for the first six *Creation Days*, and then add in mankind's history, we wind up describing everything that we find in the Fossil Record.

Despite what I have already presented, I feel that more needs to be discussed regarding how the Book of Genesis has been traditionally interpreted which has put it at odds with science and the Fossil Record. This disagreement inspired the title of this chapter, "The Trouble With Time."

When I was in grade school back in the Seventies, I noticed the scissors never worked for some of us when we tried to cut paper. That was because we were left-handed, and almost all the scissors were designed for right-handers. Only a right hand could make the blades scrape past each other properly to cut the paper. The problem wasn't that there was something wrong with the tool we were using, it was just the wrong tool for us. Nowadays, of course, it is easy to find left-handed scissors, but they were something of a novelty back then. The solution to the problem was not to replace the right-handed scissors in the toolbox with a left-handed pair. Instead, it was to add a pair of left-handed scissors, so that both types were available.

What does this have to do with the reconciling science with the Book of God? Let's think of people who believe in a *Young Earth* as right-handers and those who are *Old Earth* as left-handers. Suppose we can somehow convince the many people in the world who believe the earth is ancient that the Bible allows for this. In that case, they will have access to the Bible and become comfortable with what they are reading because they understand how it could really be true.

At first glance, there does not appear to be any middle ground between *Old Earth* people and *Young Earth* people. How can both sides be right? If some people believe the earth and the universe are old, but the Bible supposedly teaches that they are young, will these people dismiss Scripture because it is supposedly a *Young Earth* book that doesn't seem to jive with the scientific findings?

It is safe to say that almost everyone who believes in a *Young Earth* also believes in God and the Bible since their ideas of a *Young Earth* are generally based on the traditional fundamental interpretation of the Bible. This way of interpreting the Bible has made many people define it as a *Young Earth* Book.

For anyone under the impression that the Bible is a *Young Earth* Book, it could serve as a disappointment to those who believe the earth is old. Some of those *Old Earth* people who are under this impression will never give the Bible a second thought because a *Young Earth* Bible does not agree with the Fossil Record timeline of an *Old Earth*.

Let's put some numbers on this divide. According to the Pew Research Center, about 80 percent of Americans believe that humans evolved. Four out of every five people believe in evolution, while about 20 percent of Americans do not believe in evolution theory but rather that mankind has always existed in our present form and that God created every species on the earth as distinct from every other species.[37]

In this same survey, we find that 33 percent of Americans believe evolution occurred independently, with no involvement from a higher power (God). This leads me to surmise these Americans are either Atheist or Agnostic. If someone believes that all the species made themselves, this leaves God out of the creation picture. This tells me the people in this category don't believe in God. What would be the purpose of a God if all the species can make themselves without a God?

On the other hand, about 47 percent of Americans believe that God created all the species on the earth through the process of evolution. Meanwhile, data from 32 European countries and Japan shows, on average, that around 75 percent of their people believe in evolution theory.[38] By combining all of this world survey data, we see that 75-80% of the Western world and Japan believes in evolution and an *Old Earth*. And if I estimate that the percentage of people who don't believe in God in the United States is essentially the same as the rest of the Western world, then at least 33% of the world does not believe in God. Therefore, there are billions of *Old Earth* people who do not believe in God. Despite this, there are fortunately more people who do appear to believe in God.

However, the group I wish to focus on are the skeptics who don't believe in God. Quite frankly, I personally estimate the actual number of people who don't believe in God to be **at least 40%.** That amounts to over three and a half billion people! Realistically, I think the number of nonbelievers and unbelievers is over four billion (a nonbeliever does not believe in God, while an unbeliever is unsure).

It appears the majority of these people reject God for one reason. It only stands to reason that people who believe that all the species made themselves are under the impression that science makes a God unnecessary. Specifically, they are convinced that **the science of evolution makes a God unnecessary.** This is why the topic of evolution is critically important and has created a sense of urgency. This is the reason why I concentrate on the theory of evolution in a later chapter.

In addition to the topic of evolution, the next question is this: How many of these people don't believe in God because they feel this would require them to believe that the earth is young? If a *Young Earth* is held to be the only possible interpretation of the Biblical text, then most of the people who believe in an *Old Earth* will be excluded. Consequently, the fate of their eternal souls will depend on whether they can figure out how to believe in God and an old Earth at the same time.

In looking at the major stumbling blocks that cause many people to reject the existence of a Creator, evolution is a stumbling block because many are convinced that it is a self-driven process that does not need a God. In addition, for many people, the topic of the age of the earth creates an impasse of irreconcilable differences. This can be solved if there was an *Old Earth* interpretation of Genesis that was acknowledged to be a reasonable option. Like Francis Crick, do any of these people refuse to believe in God because they are aware the Fossil Record, as interpreted by modern science, does not agree with a young Earth?

The Fossil Record is a vast collection of the many fossil remnants of organisms that have lived on the earth and have been arranged in chronologic and taxonomic order.[39] Because the ages calculated by science differ from those calculated by traditional fundamentalists, a conflict has arisen between the book of science and the manner in which the Word of God has been traditionally interpreted.

If someone refused to believe in a *Young Earth* because of their understanding of geology and paleontology, they would be faced with deciding how species appeared on the earth. Since *Old Earth* people believe in a longer timeline, they embrace the very old Fossil Record. This naturally causes many of these people to easily accept the theory of evolution because it is an *Old Earth* explanation. In other words, if billions of people believe the earth to be old, then they are going to gravitate to the theory of evolution because it agrees with an *Old Earth* timeline. If some of these people think the Bible is a *Young Earth* Book, this pushes many of them away from the Bible.

There appears to be a trend where *Young Earth* people embrace the Bible, while *Old Earth* people embrace evolution. This initiates the tragic decline for half of the evolution believers who will develop the mindset of rejecting God because they feel the science of evolution makes a God unnecessary.

Many *Old Earth* people have rejected the Bible because of its short timeline. This has caused them to instead embrace the concept of a self-driven evolution that doesn't need a God. First, they rejected the Bible which then caused them to reject God. It's like a vicious cycle that fosters nonbelief. This is what happened to Francis Crick, the Nobel Prize winner. As a consequence, I believe there are some people who believe the earth is old, who can't relate to the Bible because of the seven-day *Creation Week* listed in the Book of Genesis. *Creation Week* is seen by many people to represent the position of the Bible and God. This gives the impression that the Bible is a *Young Earth* Book that is not in touch with reality.

Now, I'm not blaming traditional fundamentalists for this. They are just trying to uphold the integrity of the Holy Bible. With this being said, what I have stated in the last paragraph is a reality for many people. Professor Anthony Flew, Professor Francis Crick, and I, were all in this mindset.

Unfortunately, Francis Crick did not escape this vicious cycle of nonbelief. By contrast, Anthony Flew and I did manage to follow the science and escape this cycle.

Perhaps another reason why traditional fundamentalists are so adherent to insisting on a *Young Earth* interpretation of the Bible is because it prevents acceptance of the long ages theory of evolution. Evolution theory causes many people to reject God because they become convinced that the science of evolution makes a God unnecessary. Because of this, I agree with traditional fundamentalists who don't wish to support the theory of evolution in any way. I consider anyone who rejects the failed theory of evolution to be an ally. I will discuss this more in Chapter Five.

With that being said, the main purpose of this chapter is threefold:

1) I will demonstrate how the *Old Earth* Fossil Record can find agreement with the Bible.

2) I will show *Old Earth* people who don't believe in God, that their belief in an *Old Earth* should not be the reason for their

rejection of God. Believing the earth is old does not mean separation from the Bible. Likewise, believing in the Bible does not require you to accept that the earth is young.

3) I explain how the *creation seeds* concept works which demonstrates how the theory of evolution is not the only *Old Earth* progressive process to be considered as being the reality for how all of the species got here.

If I had to sum up the message of this chapter in one brief statement, it would be as follows:

In the Book of Genesis, Chapter One, each of the first six *Creation Days* listed in *Creation Week* were *Divine Days* of creation that lasted for billions of years.

An *Old Earth* interpretation of Genesis enables us to reach a sizable group of people who will never be convinced of a *Young Earth*. I am one of those people who is convinced the earth is old.

This chapter demonstrates that an *Old Earth* is certainly compatible with the Holy Bible and no less acceptable than a *Young Earth* interpretation from a Christian perspective. It's important to note that I'm not suggesting that an *Old Earth* perspective should replace the *Young Earth* interpretation.

As the two kinds of scissors mentioned earlier, both should be available. I am not proposing that traditional fundamentalists change their interpretations. I am simply presenting another way in which Genesis could be interpreted. Logically, there is more than one way to interpret the timeline of creation in Genesis. This is so, because of the possibility that God could have used a parable technique to deliver His creation message. In addition, mankind could be making incorrect assumptions about what God stated. Or, God was looking into the future when He described *Creation Week*.

Suppose God—who is omnipotent (all powerful) and omniscient (all knowing)—wants us to know the exact age of something (including the earth). In that case, He is well able to tell us and will in fact do so. Look at Genesis 7:11 (KJV):

> In the six hundredth year of Noah's life, in the second month, the seventeenth day of the month, the same day were all the fountains of the great deep broken up, and the windows of heaven were opened.

God tells us precisely how old Noah was on the first day of the Great Flood. Notice that God not only tells us how many *years old* Noah was but how many *months old* and how many *days old*! This is much more accurate than merely counting years. Surely, if God had wanted us to know the exact age of the earth, He would have commanded Moses to record it with the same level of precision. Scripture like 2 Peter 3:8, is telling us to concern ourselves with God's *message*, not with God's Time.

Science tells us that our universe is 13.7 billion years old and the earth is 4.5 billion years old. Between the creation of the universe in Genesis 1:1, and the creation of the clock in Genesis 1:5, any amount of time could have elapsed. Remember, the lack of a clock means that we cannot measure how much time has passed from when the universe began (beginning of verse one) and when the *clock* began (verse five). Hours could have passed or billions of years, the Bible does not say. If God had wanted us to know this, He would have had Moses record it.

The universe was created in Genesis 1:1, while the clock of the day/night cycle was created in Genesis 1:5. This means there could have been a lot of time in-between verse 1 and verses 5 because a clock did not exist until Genesis 1:5. The universe could have been created long before the first clock was created. And, because the

Bible does not state the age of the *heavens*, a 13.7-billion-year gap is possible without contradicting what is written in the Book of Genesis. A 13.7-billion-year-old universe is not unscriptural. Therefore, based on this assessment, I agree with science that the universe is 13.7 billion years old.

One may ask: Why would a universe need to be 13.7 billion years old? Perhaps it takes billions of years for a new universe to settle down and allow time for God's star science to make the element materials that formed the planets and moons. Things of a galactic proportion take time, a lot of time. I discuss this more in Chapter Six.

There is even more evidence that agreements can be found between modern science and Genesis 1:1. Initially, when we read that God "created the heavens and the earth," many Christians are likely to assume by their close grouping in this verse that the universe and the earth were both created at the same time. However, science tells us there is roughly a 9.2-billion-year gap between the creation of the universe (13.7 billion years ago) and the formation of the earth (4.5 billion years ago). Therefore, science states the earth appeared about 9 billion years after the universe began.

What is a Christian to do with this massive divergence? First, we need to examine our reading of the Bible and our subsequent assumption that the heavens and the earth were both created at the same time. The heavens are mentioned in this verse first, and the earth is mentioned second. This reconciles perfectly with the order put forward by science. So far, so good.

For an important clue, let's turn our attention to Genesis 1:26-28 (KJV):

> And God said, let us make man (mankind) in our image,
> after our likeness… So God created man in His own

Image, in the Image of God created He him; male and female created He them. And God blessed them, and God said unto them, be fruitful and multiply.

It would be easy to assume that Adam and Eve were created at exactly the same moment in time. Notice how they are both mentioned as being created in the same verse as God is telling them to thrive and multiply. However, we know for a fact that God did not create Adam and Eve at exactly the same time. In Genesis 2:8-9 (KJV) we read:

> [8]And the Lord God planted a garden eastward in Eden; and there He put the man whom he had formed. [9]And out of the ground made the Lord God to grow every tree that is pleasant to the sight and good for food; the tree of life also in the midst of the Garden, and the tree of knowledge of good and evil.

Notice how Adam is by himself and God has just planted a garden for him (planted seeds would have been used). Once these seeds were planted into the ground they would have germinated, causing God's trees to grow for Adam. You will notice how the trees had to grow out of the ground. God did not just snap His fingers and the trees suddenly appeared fully grown. As a consequence, we have to realize that trees growing out of the ground in a natural fashion would have taken many years.

In verse 17, we read of God telling him, "But the Tree of Knowledge of Good and Evil, you shall not eat of it for in the day that you eat thereof you shall surely die." God instructs Adam not to eat of this one tree as it would lead to death. Many things are going on in this verse while Adam is by himself. Then in verse 18, we read, "And the Lord God said, 'It is not good that the man should be alone; I will make him an help meet for him.'" *Help meet* translates to, help mate. The woman, Eve, was to be Adam's companion and partner. But before this, we can see that Adam was living by himself in the Garden of Eden. So, let's look at what happened after Adam was created that occurred before Eve was created:

1. God planted a unique garden for Adam, put Adam into that area, then the trees and vegetation grew into a garden.

2. God instructed Adam that he could eat of all the trees except the Tree of Knowledge of Good and Evil. Then God tells Adam what will happen if he does eat of this tree.

3. In Genesis 2:19-20, God had Adam choose a name for every living species on the earth. There were millions of species that had to be named by Adam.

4. Then God put Adam into a deep sleep, removed one of his ribs, and created Eve.

After Adam was created, a lot of significant activity occurred before Eve was created. As a result, even though the creation of Adam and Eve is mentioned in the same verse in Genesis Chapter One, Eve was not created at that same time. This is contrary to what we initially assume when we read that they were both created in the same verse. When two events are mentioned in the same verse, we assume they occurred together.

Becoming convinced of incorrect assumptions like this will be the reason why we don't understand exactly what occurred. As we can see, many things took place before Eve was created. The only reason we know that our *timing* impression of Genesis 1:27 is incorrect, is because of the additional information in Chapter Two where God discusses the significance of the bond between a husband and a wife. Do you see how we assumed Adam and Eve were created at the same time just because they were introduced together in the same verse?

Couldn't this also be the case with the heavens and the earth which are mentioned as being created in the same verse in Genesis 1:1? If Adam and Eve were not created at the same time, then the universe and the earth may not have been created at the same time either. When God mentions that He created the heavens (the universe) and the earth, just as with Adam and Eve, they were not necessarily created at the same moment in time. Assumptions about the timing of events can be wrong. Admitting this does not undermine the Bible in the least. I feel we need to keep an open mind that some of our initial timing assumptions may not be correct.

God blessed mankind with the gift of a daily clock, knowing we needed it to live and manage our lives. Because of the manner in which Genesis is worded, it presented mankind with the opportunity interpret Chapter One in such a way that the construct of the seven-day workweek became evident.

Along with these first two *time-gifts*, God also gives us a third, a calendar. God accomplished this by revealing the relatively stable constellations of stars in our sky, our yearly cycle around the Sun, and the monthly cycles of the Moon. His did this on the Fourth Day of *Creation Week*. In Genesis 1:14 (KJV), "And God said, 'Let there be lights in the firmament of the heaven to divide the day from the night; and let them be for signs, and for seasons, and for days, and years.'" Mankind was to use this astronomy gift to celebrate Passover, the holy Sabbath of the first day of Unleavened Bread, and other holy days. This astronomy calendar allowed mankind to plant and harvest crops at the best times of the year, as well as learn how to keep track of the passage of the years. Mankind also uses astronomy for navigation.

Here is a summary of God's three time-gifts that mankind received during *Creation Week*:

1) The night/day cycle (modern era refers to it as the day/night cycle)

2) The seven-day workweek

3) The astronomy calendars derived from observations of the stars, the Sun, and the Moon

Now, if God did not deliberately structure *Creation Week* as being composed of seven days, then mankind would not have received the time-gift of the seven-day workweek. We would only have the time-gifts of the daily cycle and the astronomy calendar which allows us to track months, seasons, and years. We would be missing the construct of the weekly schedule. Do you see how structuring *Creation Week* as lasting seven days effectively gave mankind the time-gift of the weekly schedule? It defies logic to give mankind the daily, the monthly, the seasonal, and the yearly schedule, but leave out the schedule construct of the seven-day workweek. This is why I am convinced that creation was described by God in Genesis as lasting seven *Days*.

Human beings are the only creations on the earth that can measure and calculate from these three time-gifts. God knew we would need these designed time constructs to live and manage our lives. He does not require nor use them Himself. They were specifically engineered only for our use.

I mention this because, even though the first clock was in existence by verse 5 in Genesis Chapter One, the ticking of that clock did not begin until humans existed. This means the recorded measure of mankind's time did not start until Adam breathed his first breathe. Adam marked the moment when the clock functionally started ticking because this is the first moment that the passage of time was being recorded in a human brain. God created the first clock in Genesis 1:5, but it was like a new wind-up clock that we used to buy at the stores. The clock obviously existed when we bought it, but it was not ticking until we opened the package and wound it up. Once Adam was created, it was only then that mankind's clock was wound up and began to tick.

And just to clarify, time began at the moment when the universe was created. As I discuss in the next chapter, time is woven together with *space* in order to form the fabric of our *space-time* universe. While on the other hand, the first unwound clock existed in Genesis 1:5. As discussed, it was not functionally ticking until the moment that Adam was created. Therefore, Genesis 1:27, is when the first measurement of time began.

Since the earth was also created before the existence of a clock, the earth could be any age. The current consensus of science is that the universe is 9.2 billion years older than the earth. Once again, this makes the earth 4.5 billion years old. And since the earth could have been created at a different and later time than the universe, I agree with science that the earth is 4.5 billion years old. And one may ask: Why would the earth need to be 4.5 billion years old? Perhaps it takes that long for the earth to become hospitable for the ultimate arrival of mankind. And because this topic is so crucial, I'm going to reiterate that I can make these statements because a *clock* did not exist until **after** the Universe and fully formed Earth already existed.

I would also like to point out that Genesis Chapter One does not compel us to automatically assume that *Creation Week* started right after the earth was created in Genesis 1:1. This is because in Genesis 1:2 (KJV), we read, "And the earth was without form and void…." After the collision with planet Theia, Earth would have been a fragmented molten mess without form. This is why Genesis 1:2, makes perfect sense. Then, in Genesis 1:9 (KJV), we read, "Let the waters under the Heaven be gathered unto one place, and let the dry land appear…." It is at this point I believe that the earth has settled down, cooled down, and has firmed up into its final form which needs to have the waters separated from the land. In other words, Earth is finally fully formed.

When the earth was created, it was not fully formed yet. At some point later, God fashioned Earth into its fully formed state where life could now be introduced to Earth. The natural process of Earth settling down and becoming fully formed after its collision with planet Theia, was going to be a long time.

With that being said, if some people insist that the creation of the universe and the formless Earth are the beginning of *Creation Week* (Genesis 1:1), then Phase 1 of Day One would have lasted 9.2 billion years, while Phase 2 of Day One would have lasted 4.5 billion years. Phase 2 ended with the appearance of Adam and Eve. Phase 1 of Day One (9.2 billion years) can be longer than Phase 1 for all of the other *Creation Days* (12 hours) because the night/day cycle did not exist until 9.2 billion years after the universe was created and the earth settled down as fully formed.

If the universe and the earth are the beginning of *Creation Week*, this means *Creation Week* started 13.77 billion years ago when the universe was created. If this is when *Creation Week* really began, it just means that Creation Day One was longer than the other Creation Days. Either way, none of the *Creation Days* were 24 hours in duration.

I do not believe that I have presented anything concerning the age of the universe or the age of the earth that contradicts the Book of Genesis. This is because they were both created before the completion of the first night/day cycle which ushered in *Creation Week*. In addition, the Bible does not state how old the earth which allows for an argument to be made that there is more than one way to interpret, "And the evening and the morning were the first day."

I believe there is support for my assertion that the creation of the universe is separate from Earth's *Creation Week*. This is evidenced by the fact that Earth's rotation rate on its axis, which creates its night and day cycle, has absolutely nothing to do with the rest of the entire universe! The rotation of planet Earth has no impact on how the rest of the universe operates and functions. In fact, the planet Venus rotates on its axis once every 243 Earth days.[40] Since Earth and Venus are illuminated by the same Sun, this means that a solar day on Venus lasts 5,832 Earth hours.

It's obvious that Earth's 24-hour cycle has nothing to do with Venus. Why then, would Earth's 24-hour cycle have anything to do with the vast, two-trillion-galaxy Universe? This is the reason why I separate the creation of the universe in Genesis One, verse one, from Earth's *Creation Week* which began in verse three.

As a consequence, I have divided creation into two stages:

Stage One: Only includes Genesis 1:1, which started 13.77 billion years ago and pertains to the creation of the space-time universe, raw and formless Earth, and all of the other planets and moons.

Stage Two: Includes Genesis 1:2-28, which started 4.5 billion years ago and relates to God focusing His special attention only on Earth, with the initiation of Earth's *Creation Week* in Genesis 1:3. This is where God handcrafted Earth by making it fully formed, giving it an oxygen atmosphere, and fully populating it with life. Hence, *Creation Week* only pertains to planet Earth. All that has to be done to demonstration this, is to point out that Earth's 24-hour cycle has nothing to do with Venus' 5,832-hour cycle. This is why *Creation Week*, is only Earth's *Creation Week*.

Let's look at the statement, "And the evening and the morning were the first day." Do you see how this cannot be applied to Venus? One cycle on Earth takes 24 hours, while one evening and morning cycle on Venus (1 solar day) takes 5,832 Earth hours. Therefore, the verse, "And the evening and the morning were the first day," has a completely different duration on Venus. What is true on Earth, is completely false on Venus.

As a result, this verse cannot be applied to Venus. In the same way this verse cannot be applied to Venus, this verse cannot be applied to any of the other planets with different cycles either.

Almost none of the planets have the same evening and morning cycle. This means the verse, "And the evening and the morning were the first day," was never meant to be applied to other planets or the universe. It should be clear that this verse is only referring to Earth's cycle and only pertains to Earth. Hence, *Creation Week* only pertains to the work that God did on planet Earth. This is why I refer to Genesis 1:3-28 (KJV) as Earth's *Creation Week*. This Week does not include Genesis 1:1 which saw the appearance of the universe and formless Earth. This is why I feel that the creation of the universe has nothing to do with *Creation Week*, it's Earth's *Creation Week*. More specifically, Genesis 1:3-28, relates to the *Creation Week* of Earth in its fully formed state.

Let's remember, just because the creation of the universe and raw Earth are both mentioned in the same verse together (Genesis 1:1), this does not necessarily mean they were both created simultaneously with no gap in-between them. Therefore, I don't believe this evening/morning verse regarding the fully formed Earth, has anything to do with how old the universe is, let alone, infer how old the universe is.

This establishes that we can most certainly be living in a universe that is quite old. And because the universe being old does not contradict what is written in the Bible. an old Universe is not unscriptural. Likewise, the same goes for early Earth in its raw state before it was fully formed. Just to clarify, Earth was formless and in its raw state in Genesis 1:1. Then, the Holy Spirit surveyed the raw and formless condition of Earth in Genesis 1:2. This was in preparation for the initiation of *Creation Week* which started with Genesis 1:3. Genesis 1:3, is where God began the handcrafted process of fully forming Earth into a place that is hospitable to life.

Now let's turn to the Fossil Record which tells us that all the species on the earth are much older than 6,000 to 10,000 years. The traditional interpretation of Genesis makes the claim that everything that has ever existed can be no older than 10,000 years. This is the *Young Earth* interpretation of the Bible. The first step in discussing the discrepancy between the *Young Earth* and *Old Earth* positions has already been touched upon by drawing attention to the verse, "And the evening and the morning were the sixth day." If this verse actually means, "And the first evening and the last morning were the sixth day," then it is an example of how we are definitely dealing with very long *Divine Days*.

With that being said, I feel more needs to be said regarding the issue with timelines. Please allow me to introduce some more Scripture that sheds additional light on this *time* situation. In Genesis 1:24-25 (KJV) we read:

> [24]And God said, Let the earth bring forth the living creature after his kind, cattle, and creeping thing, and the beast of the earth after his kind: and it was so. [25]And God made the beast of the earth after his kind, and cattle after their kind, and every thing that creeps upon the earth after his kind: and God saw that it was good.

These verses contain extremely revealing clues! Notice in verse 25, God states the earth brought forth living creatures after his kind and the cattle after their kind. In other words, these individually created species are reproducing offspring of the same type. The earth supported the initial male and female couple of those species such that offspring "of their kind" were produced. This fact raises a critical question: How can parental couples reproduce offspring "of their kind," on the very first day of the parent's existence?

Let's consider the situation of just one particular species where God introduced the first mother and father of that species. I believe it is clear that within the span of one solar day, there would not be enough time for that couple to reproduce offspring in that same 24-hour period. At the end of Genesis 1:24, God states, "and it was so." This means God witnessed the offspring come forth as the same kind as their parents. We also see this on the Third Day and the Fifth Day.

The point to be seen here is that these cannot possibly represent actual 24-hour days. It is simply not possible to introduce a newly created male and female, have them mate, wait for the female to get pregnant, wait for the female to gestate, and then witness the female's newly birthed offspring, all in one solar day. This series of events could not possibly occur in one human day. Only by seeing into the future would it be possible for this information to be gleaned in one literal day. It should be clear these events could not physically take place in only one literal day. However, all of this activity most certainly could occur within the construct of a *Divine Day*, over the course of God's Time.

I also wish to point out that these early verses in Genesis also close the door to a prevalent scientific theory—evolution. The phrases, "after his kind" and "after their kind," indicate that God created the individual species to only reproduce offspring the same as their parents. None of God's creations were designed to give birth to offspring of *another kind*. None of God's species would give birth to offspring that would *evolve* into something that was not "after their kind." These verses in Genesis confirm that God did not create Earth's species through an evolutionary process. There is much more to say about this subject in Chapter Five.

With this being said, Day Seven marked a transition from God's Time to mankind's time. Every act of creation that occurred before Adam and Eve did so in God's Time. And because Adam and Eve were the very last species created by God, any amount of our time could have passed for the creation of all the other species during God's *Creation Week*. Remember, a clock did not **functionally** start to tick until Adam appeared. Therefore, every single event and every single species that came before humans, appeared before a functional clock began to tick.

This means all the billions of species could have appeared on the earth at different times when the Fossil Record reports they did. Once Adam was created by God, however, for the first time a clock started ticking because a human brain started to keep track of time. This means that a clock was not ticking for the creation of the universe, the creation of the earth, or the creation of all the species that would ever live on the earth. Essentially, a clock was not ticking at any point while God was creating all things. This means the Bible cannot be used to date anything in human time before Adam and Eve.

As I have mentioned, the first instance that mankind's time clock started to tick, was when Adam became aware of his existence and his surroundings. This marked the transition point to mankind's time in Day Seven. We have been living in mankind's time ever since. *This* is the 6,000- to-10,000-year history we traditionally associate with the Bible.

Another example of how the *Days* in *Creation Week* cannot represent 24-hours, comes to us from Genesis 2:8-9 (KJV). I mentioned this earlier, but I wish to remind everyone of this example as I mention it again:

> ⁸And the Lord God planted a garden eastward in Eden; and there He put the man whom He had formed. ⁹And out of the ground made the Lord God to grow every tree that is pleasant to the sight and good for food; the tree of life also in the midst of the Garden, and the tree of knowledge of good and evil.

Notice how God plants trees in this garden and then they have to grow out of the ground. This is not going to happen in one 24-hour day. This would have taken many, many years. Now, someone may argue that God made this garden grow very quickly. If that were the case, then why have the garden grow out of the ground at all? Why not just snap your fingers and have the garden appear fully grown right away? No, the fact that the garden was allowed to grow out of the ground means that it did so, naturally.

I am convinced that God did not create all things very quickly. He certainly has the power to do so, however, I am convinced that God prefers to use His created science to do most of His work. This requires waiting long periods of time as God allows "nature to run its course." The reason why I believe this is based on the scientific evidence and the Fossil Record. Genesis 2:8-9, is a perfect example, where God planted the Garden of Eden for Adam and Eve, and then He waited for the trees to grow. This demonstrates that God is willing to wait for His created nature to run its natural course. If God was not willing to wait for nature to run its course, then He would have simply commanded the trees to suddenly appear, fully grown.

Another example of how the *Days* in *Creation Week* cannot represent 24-hours, comes to us from Genesis 2:19-20 (KJV), regarding Day Six:

> [19] And out of the ground the Lord God formed every beast of the field, and every fowl of the air; and brought them unto Adam to see what he would call them: and whatsoever Adam called every living creature, that was the name thereof.
>
> [20] And Adam gave names to all cattle, and to the fowl of the air, and to every beast of the field; but for Adam there was not found an help meet for him.

It is here that God instructs Adam to name all of the species on the earth. There were millions and millions of species. A human being is not going to be able to name millions of species in one solar day!

In reference to my *creation seeds* concept, I would like to point out that the beginning of verse 19 states, "Out of the ground God formed every beast..." Well, seeds germinate out of the ground. In Genesis 1:24 (KJV), we read, "And God said, 'Let the earth bring forth the living creature...'" Then in Genesis 2:7 (KJV), we read, "And God formed man from the dust of the ground...'" Notice how God formed Adam from the dust, but the animals came out of the ground as they were brought forth by the earth. This is why I believe all animal species (except mankind) germinated out of the ground from planted *creation seeds*.

And in Genesis 1:20 (KJV), we read, "And God said, 'Let the waters bring forth abundantly the moving creatures...'" In this instance, marine life is coming from the water. Perhaps these species germinated from creation seeds that sat on the ocean floor. When we take all of this into consideration, we're left with the reasonable possibility that we can have old dinosaurs and the Bible at the same time. Please remember, the Bible does not state how old the earth is. And this allows the scientific timeline of an *Old Earth* to fit very nicely with the Bible's Scripture.

Let's take a breath and see where we are. Science tells us that the universe and the earth are billions of years old. Science also tells us the oldest dinosaur fossils are hundreds of millions of years old. This, of course, contradicts the historic, fundamental Christian interpretation of Genesis, claiming that the earth and all life can be calculated to be only about 6,000 years old. It is clear to me, that until an *Old Earth* interpretation is allowed to be accepted, the book of science and the Book of God will continue to appear to disagree. It is this canyon of timeline separation that makes some *Old Earth* people feel they cannot relate to what is in the Bible (like Francis Crick). They have a gut feeling that the earth's geology is old and that dinosaurs are old.

My objective is to bridge this separation and allow people who believe the earth is old to know that the earth may, in fact, be old. People can embrace the Bible without giving up their belief that

the earth is old. In addition, people need to realize that they are not automatically forced to accept evolution theory just because it is claimed to take place over a very long period of time. Earlier, I introduced a *creation seeds* concept. This concept demonstrates that evolution theory is not the only *Old Earth* explanation that exists.

Now, I'm not here attempting to convince people to *be Old Earth*. Most people of the world are already convinced of that (80%). Instead, I'm attempting to show people who are *Old Earth* that there is no disagreement with the Bible on this issue. You don't have to become

Young Earth to embrace the Bible. Becoming *Young Earth* is not required for you to believe in God and His Word. There are *Young Earth* believers and *Old Earth* believers. Neither is any more Christian than the other. Their differing beliefs are like two different Christian denominations. Neither position is any more 'saved' than the other.

With this being said, if our goal is to bridge most, if not all, of the significant timeline disagreements between science and the Bible, then we need to concede that *Creation Week* may involve very long *Divine Days*. Once someone who is *Old Earth* is told the Bible suggests that dinosaurs and the earth are no older than 6,000 years, they will stop listening to anything else said about the Bible. How do I know this? Because this is what Francis Crick did, and this is what I used to do. This poses a serious problem because if billions of people can't get past this first hurdle, which is a timeline hurdle, then they will give up trying to believe.

But suppose the Bible can also be interpreted with an *Old Earth* timeline. In that case, more people would seriously read the Bible and fewer people would gravitate toward the flawed theory of evolution. Most of the people who are *Old Earth* will never be *Young Earth*. A six-thousand-year-old Earth will never make any sense to us. When we look at dinosaurs and the geologic features of the planet, it seems obvious they are much older than 6,000 years. Let's at least allow people who are *Old Earth* to hear an alternative theory about how dinosaurs can fit in with the Word of God.

This is a battle for the truth that will never be won for many souls until this *time* hurdle is conquered. I'm not proposing that everyone change how they interpret the timelines in Genesis. People who believe in God will continue to interpret the Bible in the ways that they have. They are not the ones who need any assistance here because they are already saved. However, for those people who are plagued by doubt and don't believe, I propose an *Old Earth* alternative which will make it more reasonable for them to consider the Word of God. Even believers who struggle in their faith may have their faith strengthened when they realize they can believe in the Bible and an *Old Earth* at the same time.

Again, I'm not trying to change what is written. My goal is to navigate around certain, possibly mistaken, manmade calculations and timeline assumptions that don't agree with the scientific data and what many people think.

With all of this being said, it is here that I need to again mention the newly introduced *creation seeds* concept as a solution that connects the Fossil Record with the Word of God. Now, this concept may appear odd at first, but the reason I am compelled to propose a *creation seeds* concept is because it is the only way I can see to reconcile the Fossil Record with the Book of Genesis. Except for Adam and Eve, I believe every species started from planted seeds.

To reinforce that God did plant seeds during His creation process on the earth, I once again reference Genesis 2:8-9 (KJV), where we read:

> [8]And the Lord God planted a garden eastward in Eden; and there He put the man whom he had formed. [9]And out of the ground made the Lord God to grow every tree that is pleasant to the sight and good for food; the tree of life also in the midst of the Garden, and the tree of knowledge of good and evil.

Please notice that as God is planting this garden, He would have been planting seeds to create this garden, *creation seeds*. This is a unique garden that God planted just for Adam. It differs completely from the vegetation in the rest of the world because it had the Tree of Life and the Tree of Knowledge of Good and Evil. This garden had to germinate out of the ground as sprouts first and then grow into mature trees. God did not just snap His fingers and this garden appeared. No, instead, God planted seeds that would have had the DNA codes for these specific plant species in them in order to grow the exact types of vegetation that God wanted in this garden. Once again, this suggests that God planted seeds first.

Creation seeds either had a timer to make them germinate at the right moment, or God spoke to each pair of seeds to cause them to open at the right time. I feel that it is quite possible that God implemented a system where He created the DNA profiles for each and every species (for that particular *Creation Day*) and then *planted* them as seeds, all at the same time. Then they individually opened and germinated over the course of long ages at their predetermined times. Of course, regarding species that were not vegetation, God would have had to nurture the first couple of those species to maturity.

I propose a *creation seeds* concept for *Creation Week* because it allows for the creation of all the species for each particular *Creation Day* to be created within a short span of hours. They would later come to life at their prescribed times. The germination schedule would have occurred over the course of long ages. Because of the way in which Genesis Chapter One and Chapter Two are worded, I feel this *creation seeds* proposal helps to bring the Fossil Record into agreement with the Book of Genesis.

We see more evidence for this seed concept in Genesis 2:5-7 (KJV), (Creation Day Three):

> And every plant of the field before it was in the earth, and
> every herb of the field before it grew: for the Lord God
> had not caused it to rain upon the earth, and there was

not a man to till the ground. But there went up a mist
from the earth and watered the whole face of the ground.

God states that before He created humankind, there were no plants, herb shrubs, or trees. We are told the reason. It was because God had not caused it to rain yet. This means that God did not start off by putting fully grown plants and trees on the earth. They were in the ground waiting to be watered; they would have been waiting as seeds. Then, we see that a mist welled up and watered the entire face of the earth. Only then did the plants, herbs, and trees germinate and come forth.

Notice that the ground had to be watered first! This all happened before man was created. This reinforces the idea that seeds were planted into the soil and waited for water and their time to germinate. We see here that these seeds were planted and needed to wait until the time was right. Only then did God water them which caused them to finally grow.

Not only does this demonstrate that seeds were utilized by God during *Creation Week*, but this also demonstrates there was a timeline God was following during His creation process. God's creations were only going to come to life when the time was right for them. I believe God did this because managing the timing of when various species appeared allowed earlier species to prepare the earth for the later species, and so on, and so forth. Therefore, this watering that we see in Scripture seems to be evidence seeds were used that needed to wait until their time had come. Why would God water the face of the earth even before plants and trees existed? This tells me they were waiting as seeds that needed to be watered.

Reflecting on Genesis 1:11 (KJV), "And God said, Let the earth bring forth grass, the herb yielding seed, and the fruit yielding tree . . . ." The famous John Calvin commented:

> For neither was it [earth] naturally fit to produce anything,
> nor had it a germinating principle from any other source
> until the mouth of the Lord was opened.[41]

Calvin states the life-creating breath of God created a germinating principle in the earth's soil. Only then could the earth support life. This germinating principle fits right in with a *creation seeds* concept.

In Matthew 13:1-8, we read of Jesus telling the *Parable of the Farmer Scattering Seed*. The seed is God's message while the different types of soil are represented by the different types of people. Good people produce fruit while those who are not good, are lost, and do not produce fruit.

Then in Matthew 13: 24-30, we read of the *Parable of the Wheat and Weeds*. Here Jesus is telling people about a farmer who planted good seeds in his field. Jesus warns that God will separate the people of the good seed from the rest on judgment day.

In Matthew 13: 31-32, we read of the *Parable of the Mustard Seed*, where the smallest seed of them all grows into one of the largest trees in the garden. This example represents how our faith can start small, just like the mustard seed, and then grow enormously. This parable is found in all three Synoptic Gospels (Mark 4:30-32; and Luke 13:18-19).

Then we read in 1 Corinthians 3:6 (NLT), "I planted the seed in your hearts, and Apollos watered it, but it was God who made it grow." As we can all see, the seed is an essential and recurring theme presented in the Bible where God causes our attention to be focused on its germination principle. Once again, I feel this is consistent with a *creation seed* concept.

I believe God individually created all the species in this same manner and they emerged from their seeds in the ground (or seabed) when their time had come. The Fossil Record shows us the time when each species was activated. The only species God did not use a *creation seed* for was mankind. God formed Adam from the dust, and He formed Eve from Adam's rib. And as God was breathing the breath of life into Adam and Eve, God was delivering a unique soul to mankind that had the ability to form a Covenant with God.

For example, on Day Six (animal Creation Day), the first evening was used to formulate all of the DNA codes for the embryonic seeds for land animals. That would have been 4.5 billion years ago. Once molten Earth cooled down around 3.7 billion years ago, this is when the *creation seeds* would have been planted. And if we are just looking at Day Six, those seeds sat dormant until about 500 million years ago (possibly 600 million years ago). It was then that they started to slowly germinate and emerge as living creatures over the course of hundreds of millions of years.

I know there are many skeptical, science-oriented people who will be able to embrace the Bible if it agrees with the scientific findings. And this is why I propose aligning the Fossil Record with the Bible. I know that God made science, so I know there is a bridge that connects science and God together. I feel the concept of *creation seeds* creates a bridge of agreement.

A solution to this impasse does not require that *Old Earth* believers adopt a traditional interpretation of Genesis. Likewise, a solution does not require traditional fundamentalists to change their interpretation. No, all that is needed is for an *Old Earth* interpretation to be acknowledged as a permitted option that is allowed to be added to the toolbox. Once this occurs, the book of science and the Book of God can finally be reconciled.

There are famous scholars who agree that believing in the Bible does not require belief in a *Young Earth.*

Carl F. H. Henry (1913-2003) was one of the most influential theologians in the second half of the twentieth century.[42] Henry was a champion of Scriptural clarity and integrity. It was Henry who stated that an inerrant Bible does not rest on the age of the earth. Henry also stated that Chapters One and Two of Genesis do not require the belief in six literal 24-hour creation days. Henry goes on to declare it is unjustified to insist that twenty-four-hour days were involved or intended by the author of Genesis.[43] I feel a strong case can be made that we are NOT required to believe in 24-hour *Creation Days* and the author of Genesis (Moses) did not intend for us to do so.

Another dedicated champion of Biblical inerrancy is Old Testament scholar and Hebrew linguist Gleason Archer (1916-2004). Archer stated:

> On the basis of internal evidence, it is this writer's conviction that *Yom* (Hebrew word) in Genesis could not have been intended by the Hebrew author to mean a literal twenty-four-hour day.[44]

Notice how Hebrew linguist Gleason Archer, a champion of Biblical inerrancy, declared that the author of Genesis **could not have intended** for the Hebrew word for *Day*, to mean a literal 24 hours. If this Hebrew word was not intended to mean a 24-hour period of time, then what was its intended purpose? In this instance, I believe the use of the Hebrew word for *Day* was intended to have another purpose. Clearly it had a purpose, so what was it?

I believe there is evidence of the purpose for describing *Creation Week* over the course of seven days. Notice how God worked for six days and then took the seventh day off! Mankind was supposed to adopt the same schedule where they would work six days in a row and then rest on the seventh day. God called the seventh day, the Sabbath day. Hence, the purpose of using the word *Day*, in this particular instance, was to give mankind the blueprint for the time-gift strategy of the seven-day workweek.

Therefore, I am convinced the *Days* in *Creation Week* are not literal, 24-hour solar days. The fossil Record and the earth's geology are clearly very old. I understand the argument defended by those who support the traditional interpretation, but the physical evidence tells a different story.

With all of this being said, a workable solution for all the *Old Earth* believers out there would be for them to consider that the phrase, "And the evening and the morning were the sixth day," really means, "And the first evening and the last morning were the sixth day." This is where each *Creation Day* is a *Divine Day* of extended duration, making the earth very old. This interpretation works perfectly! However, with this being said, God said what he meant to say in Genesis because He was delivering the construct of the seven-day workweek to mankind by stating, "And the evening and the morning are the … day." By doing this six times in a row, and then adding a seventh day of rest at the end, the blueprint for the weekly schedule was revealed to mankind to adopt.

If 80% of the world believes in evolution, then 80% of the world believes the earth is old. This means 80% of the world does not believe that each *Day* in *Creation Week* was literally 24 hours, where all life that has ever lived on the earth existed within the span of the last 6,000 years. And I am one of those people.

I have presented how modern-day scientists have demonstrated that most of mankind does not really understand the dimension of time. In the same way mankind lacks full understanding of the dimension of time, mankind has traditionally been missing something with reference to the duration of *Creation Week*. Let's not forget 2 Peter 3:8. Many of the things we think we clearly understand, we actually do not understand. I feel the timeline in *Creation Week* is one of those things.

As stated, 80% of the world believes in the theory of evolution and that the earth is old. In this majority, there are billions of people who believe in God. This means there are billions of people who believe in God, who also believe the earth is old. These billions of believers clearly realize that something is being missed with respects to the timeline of creation when it comes to the use of the Hebrew word for, *Day*. The majority of the world inherently knows that something is being missed here because they don't believe the earth is young.

I feel consideration should be allowed for an *Old Earth* interpretation that can be placed next to the traditional interpretation as an additional option. In this way, the many people who are desperately trying to believe what they are reading in the Holy Bible will have an *Old Earth* alternative. This is like having an extra tool in the toolbox, just like having a pair of left-handed scissors available for the people who need it.

I fully understand there are folks who are trying to declare that God said what He meant, and the Bible does not have any errors in it. As a result, these folks insist on a literal interpretation of the Hebrew word for, *Day*. However, there are many scholars who disagree with this interpretation. I believe scholar Gleason Archer puts it best, when he declared the author of Genesis **could not have intended** for the Hebrew word for, *Day*, to mean a literal 24 hours.

As a consequence, it is reasonable to consider that God might have had another intended use for this word when it came to God's introduction of *Creation Week* to mankind. In other words, admitting that the Hebrew word for, *Day*, does not mean 24 hours, is not an admission that an error exists in Genesis. There is no error because God had a different intended use for that word in this highly illuminating and action-packed event. This is no different than keeping an open mind when we read a parable.

God delivers many types of messages; they have to do with love, belief, repentance, mercy, forgiveness, salvation, humanity, and obedience. With all of that being said, I strongly believe that one of God's messages contained in *Creation Week* was God revealing the seven-day workweek model to mankind.

The book of science states how old the earth is; the Book of God does not. By acknowledging these facts, we are able to move one step closer to reconciling the book of science with the Book of God. By demonstrating the way in which *Creation Week* could have actually occurred, that also finds agreement with the Fossil Record, people can have an old Earth, dinosaurs, and the Holy Bible, all at the same time!

CHAPTER THREE

The Big Bang

Before the universe existed, there was nothing in the physical realm, no space, not even time. Then, in one miraculous moment, a seed appeared. Scientists call this seed, the *Singularity*, a point of infinite density and infinite gravity.[45] Then this Singularity exploded and expanded via a process known as inflation at an unimaginable rate: ". . . in a trillionth of a trillionth of a trillionth of a second, the universe is thought to have expanded by a factor of 10^{78} in volume."[46] Here's the progression:

Nothing —> Singularity —> Quantum Inflation
and Big Bang —> Universe.

Once the Singularity exploded, its rapid expansion caused the Big Bang. Quantum inflation is essentially an expansion process that throws the escaping force from the Singularity outward as high-powered expanding plasma energy. After this plasma energy cooled it eventually formed into mostly hydrogen atoms. This was the birth of our universe and the Big Bang. By definition, *nothing* in the physical realm existed before the universe began. In my view, this is a demonstration of how God created the heavens and the earth. Apparently, God started it all with a seed that we refer to as the Singularity.

CERN, the European Organization for Nuclear Research, operates the world's largest particle physics laboratory on the border between France and Switzerland near Geneva. CERN describes what happened after creation:

> In the first moments after the Big Bang, the universe was extremely hot and dense. As the universe cooled, conditions. . . .would give rise to the building blocks of matter – the quarks and electrons of which we are all made. A few millionths of a second later, quarks aggregated to produce protons and neutrons. Within minutes, these protons and neutrons combined into nuclei. . . It took 380,000 years for electrons to be trapped in orbits around nuclei, forming the first atoms. . . . . the first stars formed from clouds of gas . . . 150–200 million years after the Big Bang. Heavier atoms such as carbon, oxygen and iron, have since been continuously produced in the hearts of stars and catapulted throughout the universe in spectacular stellar explosions called supernovae.[47]

When the universe plasma cooled, most of what formed were clouds of hydrogen atoms that coalesced into the first stars. After those stars exhausted their fuel they died and exploded. These explosions ejected heavier elements into space, serving as building blocks for the planets and moons. After about 9 billion years of this explosive ejection process, the building blocks for the earth were finally ready to coalesce, forming our planet. This occurred in our neighborhood which we refer to as the Milky Way galaxy about 4.5 billion years ago. The planets of our galaxy formed just after the formation of our Sun.

While this is the latest scientific explanation of what happened, mankind has grappled with questions about the origin of all things for thousands of years. The famous Greek philosopher Aristotle (384-322 BC), who has long been considered the ancient father of the Scientific Method, saw the heavens as constantly moving, requiring the presence of an *Unmoved Mover*. Aristotle believed the *Unmoved Mover* is God and that He always stays consistent. Aristotle stated:

> That God is the only being that is found to be distinct from the natural world. He is self-existing, and therefore necessarily exists apart from everything.[48]

Judging by this statement, Aristotle, who lived about 1,100 years after Moses wrote Genesis, clearly believed in a God who never had a beginning, never had an end, and was not bound by the laws of physics and the universe's dimensions. Aristotle knew God was separate and distinct from our physical universe. Aristotle knew that the universe is dependent upon God, but God is not dependent upon the universe. Undoubtedly, Aristotle would say God is not affected by constraints such as the absence of time. God existed before time because He is always consistent within Himself. Therefore, when nothing else could have existed without time, God did.

You will recall that Stephen Hawking claimed there was no possibility that God existed. Hawking stated since time did not exist before the universe began, there was no time for God to have existed in.[49] No time, means no God. But Hawking hadn't taken to heart Aristotle's great insight that God is separate and distinct from the natural world. God is not bound by or subject to time as the universe is.

If asked in his day, Aristotle would have undoubtedly declared that God existed before time and the universe began because He is self-sustaining. Physics can't exist without time, but God can. If Aristotle could have spoken with Hawking, I envision the old philosopher would have told the famous physicist that God does not need time to do anything. Aristotle would have told Hawking that God exists apart from, and is distinct from, the natural universe and time, which He created.

Anyone listening to Hawking on this point will be misled because of Hawking's complete lack of understanding. We have a famous modern-day scientist who could not comprehend something entirely understood by a more renowned scientist 2,300 years ago. To put it bluntly, the great Aristotle was correct, and Stephen Hawking was wrong.

With that being said, once our universe was born and the Big Bang cooled down it produced an enormous supply of hydrogen atoms that now existed in a platform of space-time. You may ask, "What is a platform of space-time?" To answer this question, we can start by realizing the universe is often times compared to a trampoline that you can walk around on. However, outside of the confines and borders of the trampoline, nothing can be supported. If you step off the edge of a trampoline, you will fall. Similarly, nothing can exist outside of the universe's confines except God, His Kingdom, and other beings He created in the spiritual realm. God and Heaven do not need the support of this universe trampoline, but everything else does.

In the context of a universe being described like a trampoline, just as a trampoline is composed of a woven fabric, the universe is likewise composed of a woven fabric. This fabric is referred to as, space-time. The fabric of a typical trampoline is a weave of fibers. In a similar fashion, the universe is a weave of two distinct fibers. Imagine space fibers and time fibers woven together to form the fabric of the universe.[50] I envision space-time as a woven flexible platform. You can't have a universe without *space*, and you can't have a universe without *time*.

Before our universe began, nothing physical existed, even time did not exist. However, once the universe was brought into existence with its space-time fabric, this is when gravity was made possible. Gravity is defined as the distortion of the space-time fabric caused by an object composed of mass existing in the space-time fabric. This is often times described to be like the downwards distortion of the fabric of a trampoline when you place a bowling ball in the middle of it. In the same way, when a planet exists in the space-time universe, it distorts the space-time fabric because of its mass.

This is a basic and common description of the interaction between mass and the space-time fabric. However, this is a severely simplified version of reality. The more accurate depiction would show a planet's mass residing inside a three-dimensional invisible lattice structure of space-time that puckers inwards from all directions equally toward the planet.[51] This reality is quite different from the common depiction of a planet sitting on top of a two-dimensional fabric, like a bowling ball sitting in the middle of a trampoline. The more mass a planet has, the more it distorts the space-time fabric. As a consequence, a larger mass causes a higher degree of gravity compared to a lesser mass which causes less gravity because it distorts the fabric of space-time less than the larger mass. Therefore, gravity equals the amount of space-time fabric distortion.[52]

That being said, gravity is actually very interesting because I believe it to be one of God's many designs that He has engineered into the universe. As mentioned, I actually refer to gravity as a phenomenon, *The Matter Converging Phenomenon*. This phenomenon occurs when we witness matter converge and merge together. Science describes this behavior as, gravity.[53] In the context of General Relatively, what is very interesting is that gravity is not actually a force and it is not a field. In astrophysics, the typical use of the word, *field*, is assumed to be referring to a gravitational field. Despite that, it may come as a surprise to realize that gravitational fields do not actually exist. There are no gravitational fields.[54]

In addition to gravity not being a gravitational field, it is my understanding that because gravity is not a field, it is likewise not the product of magnetic or electric fields either. As a consequence, because gravity is not a force or a field, this is why I refer to gravity as a phenomenon, *The Matter Converging Phenomenon*. The best example that I found online is in the same YouTube video I reference which tells us gravity is not a force or a field. This video explains how gravity works by using an example involving two people. I'm going to slightly modify the example presented in this video in order to accentuate the explanation.

Here is the example: Let's say we start with two people, where one person is in New York City while the other person is in San Francisco. Now, if they both start walking due North they will eventually converge on the same spot at the North Pole. Neither one of these people turned toward the other because they both walked North in a straight line. The reason why they converged is because the surface of the earth is curved.[55] In this same way, because mass creates 'distortion curves' in the space-time fabric, these 'curves' in the space-time fabric result in matter converging together. John Wheeler states:

> Matter (mass) tells space-time how to curve, while space-time tells matter (mass) how to move.[56]

As a consequence, because gravity is not a force and it is not a field, this is why I feel gravity can be referred to as, *The Matter Converging Phenomenon*, or *The Mass Converging Phenomenon*.

Once the universe was born and the Big Bang cooled down, essentially two realities existed in the physical realm. The first reality was the universe's platform of the space-time fabric. The second reality that existed was an enormous supply of hydrogen atoms (as well as some helium and a bit of lithium). These were the components that God used to craft the maturation of His expanding universe.

Our universe is very interesting because of its continued expansion. Like Spiderman shooting webbing from his wrists, the invisible space-time lattice of our universe just keeps stretching outward in all directions. Scientists don't know what caused the universe to occur or why it is expanding All of the expanding universe originated from a single point in space smaller than the size of an atom. This has been proven mathematically according to astrophysicist Hugh Ross who appeared on the televised religious program, The John Ankerberg Show. Ross proclaimed that the Big Bang has been proven.[57] He stated that whatever caused the universe, was not of the universe, because there was no universe.

It is now an established scientific fact that our universe did indeed have a beginning. The Big Bang was proven to be a fact when the cosmic microwave background radiation temperature (CMBR) maps of the universe were finally compiled in 1992. This confirmed that our universe had a 'hot' Big Bang beginning.[58] These background radiation temperature maps of the universe matched the predicted background radiation pattern. Physicists knew that if the universe had a beginning and a Big Bang, then a certain background of radiation temperature would exist.

Before the Big Bang was proven, some physicists figured that if our universe had always existed, then maybe it didn't need anything (God) to start it. Perhaps it was just always here. But if it was ever proven that our universe did indeed have a beginning, then physicists knew that *someone* outside of the construct of our universe had to have started our universe. Our universe could not have caused itself to come into existence before it even existed. This is why countless physicists worldwide became believers in a Creator in 1992 when the Big Bang was proven. The Big Bang is no longer a theory, it is now an accepted scientific fact.[59]

Because this is a critical revelation, I'm going to repeat it one more time. According to physicist Hugh Ross, many physicists became believers in God in 1992 because of the realization that our universe did have a beginning. This is the scientific evidence that convinced countless physicists that a Creator must exist.[60]

With that being said, in mankind's desire to investigate how our universe got here, some scientists have worked on calculating mathematical probabilities regarding our unique universe. One such scientist is Sir Roger Penrose who holds a Ph.D. in Physics and won the Nobel Prize in Physics in 2020. He is also a professor of Mathematics at Oxford University. It's also important to mention that Roger Penrose had collaborated in the past with Stephen Hawking while working on black holes.[61]

That said, regarding mankind's quest to unlock the mysteries of our unique universe, Roger Penrose has formulated a calculation of the mathematical probability of our highly precise and life-supporting universe. It's eye-opening to say the very least and is referred to as the *Penrose Number*.[62] The best technical description of the Penrose Number is that it represents "the probability of the initial entropy conditions of the Big Bang."[63]

It is important to point out that the Penrose Number is not the mathematical probability our universe created itself. This is because a universe cannot create itself, especially without any time to do so. Instead, I understand this calculation to represent the mathematical probability that our high precision and life-supporting universe even exists in the first place. This is compared to all of the other lesser types of universes that could have possibly existed instead.

Here's the bottom line, I believe this calculation demonstrates that the lower the calculated probability is, the higher the likelihood that an intelligence designed our universe. This is because the lower the probability for our precise and life supporting universe to exist, the lower the probability that our supremely ordered universe could somehow be the product of random chance.

This means that if a universe is very sloppy and functions imperfectly, it's extremely likely to be the result of random chance (for a few minutes we will pretend that a universe can create itself). In other words, it's much easier to make something that functions poorly.

Of course, in the real world, random chance will never produce anything functional, even something that functions poorly. On the other hand, it's very, very difficult to make a universe that is highly ordered and functions perfectly. As a result, random chance can lead to sloppy outcomes, but random chance will **never** lead to a perfect design. This is why Professor Penrose is quoted as stating:

> Bare probability or chance can never cause or create anything, let alone cause the creation of a Universe.[64]

I completely agree with this brilliant statement! With that being said, I must say this calculation was first brought to my attention while reading the comments of a science-oriented online blogger (whose name I can't remember). He stated that he had struggled in his faith, but once he came to realize the Penrose Number, it was only then that he became convinced that God must exist. Therefore, if this calculation can strengthen the faith of one person, then other people may also find this kind of inspiration from the Penrose Number. Of course, that's in addition to all the other ways that someone can be enlightened by this impressive and significant calculation.

It is at this point that we need to prepare ourselves with the ability to grasp the significance of this illuminating calculation. In order to do this, we need to first understand the components (variables) that are involved. This will more fully aid in our understanding of what has been calculated. To do this, I will start with the very basics and then build up from there. So, please be patient. I admit this part of my book may seem tedious, boring, and challenge the patience of some people, nevertheless, I need to present a description and explanation of this calculation's components. However, before I do that, I can tell you ahead of time that logic dictates this calculation is a demonstration of how our universe could not be the result of self-creation.

Now let's get started. There are three components or variables involved in the calculation of the Penrose Number that I need to explain. The first component has to do with the fact that the equation itself has numbers listed in **scientific notation,** (also referred to as the **power of a number**). The second component is defined as **entropy** (**thermodynamic entropy**). While the third component is the term, **phase-space.**

With that introduction complete, let's dive into the Penrose Number. The first component to understand that is involved in this calculation is referred to as, the *power of a number*. This describes how many zeros come after the first number listed. Let's say we have the number 10, which is a 1 with one zero after it. That translates into 10 to the 1st power. This is because there is one zero after the number one. If we look at the number 100, this translates into 10 to the 2nd power, because there are two zeros after the number 1. This can also be written as 10^2 which is 100, while 1,000 is 10 to the 3rd power ($10^{3)}$, and so on. This method is used in mathematics because it makes working with extremely large or extremely small numbers, more convenient. This method is referred to as, *scientific notation*.

Now, a probability of one in 10 to the 3rd power means the number is a fraction where the numerator is a 1, that is divided by the denominator, which is a 1, followed by 3 zeros (1,000). So, we have a probability of one chance in 1,000. This is not to be confused with 10 to the third power (10^3) which is not a fraction and equals 1,000. Likewise, a probability of 1 in 10 to the 600th power means a fraction exists where the number 1 is divided by a 1, with 600 zeros after it—a very tiny fraction of a probability! This can also be recorded as 10^{-600} or 1×10^{-600} (notice the minus sign in front of the 600). Both of these numbers are extremely small. This is not to be confused with 10^{600} which is a 1 with 600 zeros after it. 10^{600} is not a fraction and represents an extremely large number.

Many scientists wish to know what the chance is that any particular event will occur. This is also known as the *probability*. Most scientific authorities have established that 1 (one) chance in 10 to the 50th power (a fraction that is a small number, notice the minus sign: 10^{-50}) is the cut-off for an event to be mathematically possible. In other words, if an event is less likely than 1 in 10 to the 50th power then that event is not mathematically possible, no matter how much time is allowed.

A person may wonder what the size of this number is and how small is this probability? Well, there are 10 to the 50th atoms on the earth (not a fraction and therefore a large number, notice there is no minus sign: 10^{50}). That's a lot of atoms!

To explain the threshold where something is no longer considered mathematically possible, let's make up a hypothetical example in which a lottery is being played. In this lottery, instead of 9 billion people playing (population of the earth), imagine that you are playing against all the atoms on the earth where every single atom gets a lottery ticket. As a result, you and all of the atoms are playing and competing against each other. This means there is only one winning ticket out of 10^{50} lottery tickets. This is an extremely small chance to win and represents the cut-off for what is considered mathematically possible. *That* would be the chance of winning. Even so, winning this lottery is still considered to be mathematically possible.

Now imagine a second lottery where all the atoms on the earth are given 10 tickets instead just one ticket. This would mean there are now 10 to the 51st power number of lottery tickets in circulation.

It's at this point, that it would be considered mathematically impossible to win. To put this into perspective, if any chance event requires 10 times more lottery tickets than there are atoms on the earth, then that event cannot occur by chance, no matter how much time you allow. In effect, it is considered mathematically impossible (in practical terms).

Before I present Penrose's calculation, we also need to understand what is referred to as thermodynamic entropy. Entropy is a measure of disorder and randomness.[65] If something is very organized and orderly, it will have a low entropy value. If something is very chaotic, random, and disorganized, it will have a high entropy value. For example, when burning a log, the heat released would be considered to have a high entropy value because the dissipating heat is randomly escaping in all directions.[66] Because the dissipating heat is not orderly, it has a high disorder value.

That being said, a more accurate way to view entropy is to realize the dissipating heat can't be used for anything else. As a result, it is now considered "unusable," which means it can no longer be used to perform *Work*. The higher the value of unusable energy, the higher the entropy value.[67]

Now, according to Roger Penrose, a particle at the time of the Big Bang had an entropy (disorder/unusable energy) value of 10 to the 43rd power.[68] This seems like a very big number (10^{43}), but it is an extremely small number compared to the entropy observed in a particle in today's universe.[69] Therefore, the Singularity seed that started the universe possessed a comparatively low disorder value before it exploded (expanded). There is much more disorder now. The Singularity seed was supremely ordered compared to the expanding universe which is now much less orderly as it spreads out and loses heat. You will notice that Roger Penrose refers to *particle*s in his calculation. This is because numerous, small, subatomic particles are what form an atom. In this calculation, Singularity particle and universe atom number are the same.

This brings us to the last component of this probability calculation that needs explanation. It is referred to as, *phase-space*. A phase-space refers to one specific combination of variable values of a particular system.[70] Here's an example, let's consider a room light, it can either be on or off. The light cannot be in any other state; therefore, it has two phase-spaces. Let's say phase-space #1 has the light on while phase-space #2 has the light off. Now, if I told you that the situation was a #1, you would know the light was on. If we included the condition of a second light in the room, then there would be four phase-spaces because there are only four ways the lights (variables) can occur in combination:

Phase-space #1: The first light is on, the second light is on.

Phase-space #2: The first light is on, the second light is off.

Phase-space #3: The first light is off, the second light is on.

Phase-space #4: The first light is off, the second light is off.

If I tell you the phase-space situation is a #4, you know that both lights are off. As you can see, the use of phase-spaces is a logical way to catalog every single combination of all the interacting variables. Sometimes variables are referred to as *dimensions*. Think of phase-space as a snapshot photo and listed under the photo are the numerical values for each and every variable at that moment. Each phase-space is a different snapshot. Another example would be that of a ceiling fan with four different settings, however, in this case, the fan would have five phase-spaces because one phase-space is the "off" position. For every possible way that each of the variables in a system can be adjusted, there needs to be an individual phase-space to describe that exact snapshot. This is a highly logical way to thoroughly catalog every single way that a system can exhibit itself.

With all of that being presented, we are almost ready for what is referred to as the Penrose Number. As I have stated, it is clear to me that a universe cannot create itself. Therefore, the Penrose Number is not a calculation of the odds of our universe creating itself through a chance event, rather, it represents the odds that our universe exists in the first place. Other types of universes that would have lacked our precision and been plagued by countless imperfections, could have been here instead. This calculation represents the supreme precision involved in the engineering of our flawless universe. Therefore, the Penrose Number is a calculation of all of the different kinds of universes that could have existed (as the consequence of an intelligent Creator).

In my opinion, the Penrose Number is not telling us how perfectly designed our universe is and how well it functions. We are the ones who have evaluated how perfectly we think that our universe is designed and functions. Instead, the significance of the Penrose Number is that it allows us to compare our perfect universe with the total number of other possible universes that could have been here instead. Because we have determined that our universe is perfect, then most, if not all, of the other possible universe designs are going to be assumed to be less than perfect. This is especially true if there is a high number of other possible universe designs.

For example, if the Penrose Number was 10, then we would know there was a total of 10 possible universe designs. Since we are aware of how perfect our universe is, we would figure that our universe is the best one possible out of the 10 designs (this places our universe in the upper 10% of all possible designs). Hence, there would be a 10% chance that our perfect universe would be here. Let me explain further with a hypothetical example. Imagine a hypothetical scenario where we go to a far-away land where mankind never had any interactions with a Creator, had no history with a Creator, and doesn't even know what a Creator is? In this scenario, as far as this population is concerned, the Penrose Number would represent the total number of possible universe designs that would be assumed to be able to create themselves.

Now, if these people knew nothing about a Creator and our universe was imperfect, sloppy, and ugly, and the Penrose Number was calculated to be 10 (10 possible universe designs), then it would be assumed that our sloppy universe had between an 80-100% chance of creating itself as imperfect and sloppy. This is because these people would have figured out all the ways that our universe could have been designed better. They would certainly be assuming that our universe created itself by random chance and it didn't do a very good job. Since imperfection is easier to accomplish, the probability for a sloppy universe is high.

Let's add a change to this hypothetical example where our universe was perfect and functioned effectively, consistently, and logically. If our universe was so perfect that no one could imagine how it could have been designed any better, these people would be thinking that they got lucky. In this scenario, if the Penrose Number was calculated to be 10, then mankind would figure our perfect universe had a 10% chance of randomly creating itself as perfectly as it did. The probability would be 10% because our universe is assumed to be the best one out of 10 possible designs. Few questions would be asked by anyone because mankind would figure that we just got lucky and it would be reasonable to assume that having a 10% chance for perfection, could be the result of a random, self-creation event.

Now let's imagine these same people are faced with a Penrose Number that was 100. There is only about a 1% chance that our universe is the result of a random event. It's at this point that a few people are going to question the likelihood that our perfect universe created itself with just a 1% chance of doing so. Let's next imagine if the Penrose Number was 1000 (10^3). This means there is 0.1% probability that our universe just created itself randomly by chance. At this point, a lot of people are going to start asking questions. To some people, it no longer seems reasonable to assume the universe is here by a random chance event.

What if the Penrose Number is 1,000,000 (10^6), that's a #1, with six zeros after it. There would be a million possible universe designs. This would mean that our universe had a chance of one in a million of creating itself as perfectly as it did. There would definitely be a large group of people who would have serious doubts regarding self-creation. A random event of self-creation would no longer be seen as a reasonable explanation by many people who would now question if there is something in the cosmos that has the power and intelligence to create a perfect universe like ours? In this hypothetical example, this is where the concept of an intelligent Creator would first be considered by this population.

Let's now imagine if the Penrose Number was even higher. What if the calculation was 10^{1230}? That is a #1, with one thousand, two hundred, and thirty zeros after it! Would anyone still be thinking their universe was the result of a random event of self-creation? Would it be reasonable for anyone to assume the appearance of our fine-tuned, elegant, and perfect universe was simply the product of a random chance event of self-creation? No, no one who really understands the Penrose Number and its magnitude should continue to reasonably assume that our universe is still the result of chance.

In my opinion, the Penrose Number is significant because the larger that it is, the more likely it is that an intelligent Creator is responsible for our perfect universe. Please note that a very large Penrose Number equates to a very small probability of winning this universal lottery by chance. Hence, the Penrose Number is inversely related to the probability.

The Penrose Number should be telling mankind that the chances of an efficient and perfect universe just creating itself are impossible to imagine. This is because of the extreme number of inferior universes that could have possibly become a reality instead (by the hand of a Creator). The fact that the Penrose Number is so extremely large, means that most of the other types of universes in this calculation would be assumed inferior, lack our precision, and be plagued by countless imperfections. In my opinion, The Penrose Number is telling us how many other universe designs that we are superior to, and this tells us how many other inferior ways that a universe can be designed. As a consequence, the Penrose Number allows us to realize the level of work, precision, engineering, intelligence, and perfection of the being who created our universe.

Now that I have presented my opinion of how important this calculation is, I will finally explain how Roger Penrose came up with it. The manner in which Professor Penrose formulated this calculation is a technical point where he equated the Singularity with the characteristics of a black hole. Penrose used the Bekenstein-Hawking formula for the entropy of a particle in a black hole as if the universe were a giant black hole. As I have mentioned, 10 to the 43rd power is the comparatively low initial entropy (disorder) value that a particle had inside the Singularity in its highly ordered state. If the Singularity seems like a mystery, just think of it as a seed. I consider the Singularity to be the ultimate seed.

That being said, Penrose's calculation takes the total number of particles in the universe (estimated to be 10^{80}) and multiplies this by the entropy value for each Singularity particle (10^{43}). This yields an answer of 10 to the 123rd power (in scientific notation we multiply the exponents by adding them together—80 + 43 = 123).

Since entropy is on a logarithmic scale, like the well-known Richter Scale in which each interval is increased by a factor of the base of the logarithm, this calculation converts into 10 to the power of 10 to the power of 123. Notice the extra 10 in this calculation. Once again, this is because entropy is on a logarithmic scale.[71] Therefore, Roger Penrose calculated the probability of the initial entropy conditions of the Big Bang and the odds against such an occurrence. He came up with an answer of 10 to the power of 10 to the power of 123, to 1.[72]

I understand this number represents the total number of different kinds of universes that could have possibly occurred when our universe was born. It is a very, very large number. As far as I know, this is one of the largest numbers ever calculated by mankind. There were 10 to the power of 10 to the power of 123 (which simplifies to 10 to the power of 1230: 10^{1230}), different ways (phase spaces) to design a universe. Each possibility represents a different universe design with a different beginning. Out of all of those possibilities, our universe is in the rare category of being 'perfect.'

I am convinced that our universe is the most perfect design possible because God is only going to choose to create our universe in the most perfect way possible.

The probability chance of our perfect universe starting the way that it did is 1 out of 10^{1230}. This is way past the cut-off for being mathematically possible (10^{50}). I'm sure you can appreciate that our perfect universe was very precisely created and could not have occurred randomly.[73] This calculation supports the argument that our universe is the product of deliberate and intelligent design, not an example of a *"free lunch."* The Penrose Number allows us to realize that it defies logic to believe that our ultra-precise and life supporting universe is the result of a haphazard event. I imagine this is why the Penrose Number strengthened the faith of that science-oriented online blogger that I mentioned earlier.

Quoting Roger Penrose is John Lennox, the famous Oxford Mathematics professor who describes the significance of this calculation. He asks us to imagine the phase space of the entire universe, with each point representing a different possible way that the universe may have begun. The Creator holding a pin to be placed at some point in phase space, will determine how precise that our universe will be:

> Try to imagine phase space . . . of the entire universe.
> Each point in this phase space represents a different possible way that the universe might have started off. We are to picture the Creator, armed with a 'pin'—which is to be placed at some point in phase space. . . . Each

different positioning of the pin provides a different universe. Now the accuracy that is needed for the Creator's aim depends on the entropy of the universe that is thereby created. It would be relatively 'easy' to produce a high entropy universe, since then there would be a large volume of phase space available for the pin to hit. But in order to start off the universe in a state of low entropy–so that there will indeed be a second law of thermodynamics—the Creator must aim for a much tinier volume of phase space. . . . The Creator's aim must have been accurate to 1 part in 10 to the power of 10 to the power of 123, that is 1 followed by 10 to the 123rd power zeros. . . .[74]

Incorporating this explanation from John Lennox as he quotes Roger Penrose, I believe this calculation represents all the possible kinds of universes and the different ways that they could have started off. As a consequence, this calculation demonstrates the extreme precision necessary to create our universe with its initial, comparatively low entropy state.

According to Robin Collins, a distinguished professor of Philosophy at the Messiah College:

It is this extremely low entropy (disorder) value, that allows us to know that our universe had a beginning and did not always exist.[75]

The reality of our universe having a beginning, means that *someone* from outside the platform of the universe must have brought it into existence.[76] Nothing of our physical universe existed before the Singularity and its Big Bang, this includes the construct of *time*. Time did not exist before the universe began which means the universe could not have brought itself into existence. The universe simply did not have any time to create itself from nothing.[77]

What else does this tell us? Well, any event with odds of less than 1 in 10 to the 50th power will never realistically happen. This equals a zero probability in practical terms. Penrose's calculated probability of our particular universe existing and starting off the way that it did, is trillions upon trillions of times less than 1 in 10 to the 50th power.[78] The idea that our universe is simply here by chance is at least trillions of times more impossible, than impossible.

Notice that Penrose refers to phase-space in his quote. Penrose has calculated there are 10 to the 10 to the 123 phase-spaces or different universes that could have existed. Many of these universes would have had high entropy and been less ordered resulting in them being sloppy. Some of these universes would have exhibited moderate entropy, while a few would have possessed lower entropy and been more ordered. It is my understanding that our universe is the most perfect one possible. This makes sense because when God creates the universe, it's going to be perfect.

Now, let's stack all these types of universes on top of each other with the least ordered ones at the bottom while the more ordered ones are higher up. This universe stack would form the shape of an enormous pyramid of galactic proportions. This pyramid arrangement allows us to visualize how every single universe design that is under the most perfect one at the tip-top, is an inferior design as compared to the top one. It turns out that our universe phase-space is so supremely precise and orderly, it is magnificently perched at the tip-top of this pyramid.

The mathematical chance of our ultra-precise universe even existing in the first place and starting off the way that it did (which it can't do on its own in the absence of time) is the chance of one lottery ticket winning against a total of 10 to the power of 1230 competing tickets. Words cannot even describe how far away this is from the cut-off for what is considered mathematically possible. Most of these lottery tickets match with sloppy choices near the bottom of this universe pyramid. What are the odds that humanity is going to be lucky enough to receive the very best lottery ticket available that wins us the perfect universe positioned at the tip-top of this pyramid of possible universes? This kind of precision could not have occurred by chance. This is why Sir Roger Penrose states that:

> Bare probability or chance can never cause or create anything, let alone cause the creation of a Universe.[79]

For anyone still drawn to the idea that our universe just spontaneously created itself by chance, how do we explain that the cosmos came equipped with dozens of meticulous and consistent physical constants that describe precisely how our universe is perfectly designed to support life? This situation is characterized by the term "fine-tuning." A few of the physical constants on this "fine-tuning" list includes laws such as:

- **gravity**, a phenomenon where objects with mass converge together.
- **first law of thermodynamics**, which states that energy is neither created nor destroyed but only changed in form.
- **second law of thermodynamics**, which states the universe progresses toward entropy or disorder.

The list of highly structured, fine-tuning attributes goes on and on. All of them would have to have randomly popped up out of nowhere if the universe was somehow able to randomly form itself. This simply makes no sense.

At the very beginning of our brand-new universe, as we can see from the Penrose Number, the Singularity possessed the lowest amount of randomness of anything that has ever existed. This translates into the most order that has ever existed. This raises the question: *How could anything with the lowest amount of randomness in cosmic history be the result of a random event?* In the science of logic, there is what is referred to as the Law of Non-Contradiction which dictates that something cannot be both true and false at the same time, and in the same respect. So then, from a logic standpoint, how could the highly ordered Singularity, which is the least random entity known to mankind, have been formed randomly? This makes no logical sense at all. Therefore, our universe could not be both random, and not random, at the same time.

With that said, let's to return to Professor Hawking who is famous for his work on black holes. Recall that Hawking claimed that:

> You can't get to a time before the big bang because there was no 'before' the big bang. We have finally found something that doesn't have a cause because there was no time for a cause to exist in. For me, this means there is no possibility of a creator because there is no time for a creator to have existed in.[80]

Hawking is stating that because God could not have existed before time existed, and nothing else existed before time existed, this means that nothing caused the universe to come into existence. Despite this, because of the Penrose Number, we can see that it defies logic to believe that our precise and perfect universe somehow randomly popped into existence, from nothing. The Penrose Number confirms to me that our universe cannot be the product of a chance event. Therefore, in my opinion, the Penrose Number contradicts Hawking's claim that the universe did not have a cause (no God needed).

As we can see, our universe somehow randomly existing in the first place is **mathematically impossible**. With that said, what about the **physical probability**? Is such an occurrence physically possible? It turns out that we do have an answer to this question. Because of the Stephen Hawking quote just mentioned, the physical probability of our universe somehow being the product of random chance is ZERO. As Hawking points out, this is because there was no time.

Hawking stated that God could not possibly exist because there was no time for God to have existed in.[81] Basic logic dictates that if there was no time for God to have existed in, then there was no time for the physics of gravity to have existed in. There was simply no time for anything physics-related to have existed 'before' the Big Bang. This is why Hawking tells us that nothing existed 'before' the Big Bang.[82] The absence of time means it was physically impossible for any gravity magic to have existed. In fact, in order for there to be the claim that a universe could bring itself into existence, *Work* would have to be done. The creation of a universe requires *Work*. The equations related to *Work* are as follows:

Work = *Force* multiplied by *Displacement*.

Force = *Mass* multiplied by *Acceleration*.

Acceleration = the change in *Velocity* divided by the change in *Time*, without *Time*, there is no possibility of *Acceleration*. When *Time* equals 0, then *Acceleration* = 0.

As a consequence, when *Acceleration* = 0, then Force = 0, and *Work* = 0.

There is no possibility *Force* existed before *Time* existed. Without *Force*, *Work* = 0. As a result, no *Work* can be done. This means the *Work* necessary for a universe to create itself was not possible.

In addition, the *Power* necessary to drive the creation of a self-creating universe was not present either.

Power = *Work* divided by *Time.*

Time did not exist before the 'Big Bang,' this means there was no *Power* present. As a result, when *Time* = 0, then *Power* = 0.

In the absence of *Time*; *Work* = 0, *Force* = 0, *Acceleration* = 0, and *Power* = 0. In addition, *Space-Time* fabric = 0 because the *Space-Time* construct does not exist without *Time.*

I'm sure we are all familiar with the famous equation: $E = mc^2$. This is where (E) denotes the energy, (m) denotes the mass, and (c) denotes the speed of light. Here is the equation for the speed of light: $c = d/t$. The speed of light is equal to the distance divided by the amount of time. Therefore, when time equals zero, the speed of light equals zero. When the speed of light equals zero then $mc^2 = 0$, and this causes $E = 0$. Energy does not exist in the absence of time.

Therefore, when *Time* equals zero because it is not present, all entities in the realm of physics equal zero and can't exist. Nothing in the realm of physics exists outside of the construct of *Time.*

Despite this fact, there are present-day speculations that revolve around the idea that the universe somehow created itself from *quantum fluctuations*. It is beyond the scope of this book to discuss quantum fluctuations in detail but suffice it to say that any physical behavior like this would require the presence of *forces, energy*, and *time*. Since time was not present before the universe existed, this eliminates the possibility of the existence of the forces and the energy necessary for quantum fluctuations to exist. Therefore, any speculations that the universe created itself from random quantum fluctuations, gravity fluctuations, or any other phenomenon in physics are flawed and unsound because of the fact that *Time* = 0 before the universe existed.

In addition to this, when *Space-Time* = 0, this means *Gravity* = 0. As a consequence, gravity and gravity fluctuations could not exist before the construct of the universe existed. This is why anyone claiming that the law of gravity could bring a universe into existence (before it even existed) is not making any scientific sense. In the absence of *Time*, the absence of *Work*, the absence of *Force,* the absence of *Acceleration*, the absence of *Power*, the absence of *Energy*, the absence of *Space-Time*, the absence of *Gravity*, the absence of *Quantum Gravity,* and the absence of *Quantum Fluctuations*, it is a fairy tale fantasy to think that a universe could ever create itself from nothing. Nothing from nothing leaves nothing, it's that simple.

Nothing in the physical realm can exist in the absence of time. We can see in the last Stephen Hawking quote where he admits this. Despite this fact, some people argue that 'nothingness' was present before the universe existed. 'Nothingness' is more than 'nothing.' As a result, 'nothingness' is actually something. Their argument is that the universe created itself out of something called 'nothingness.' This idea is completely flawed because there was ABSOLUTELY NOTHING physical in existence before time came into existence with the Big Bang. This is why Stephen Hawking stated that there was NO 'before' the Big Bang.[83]

The point I am driving home here is, in the absence of time, it is scientifically impossible for a universe to create itself from absolutely nothing. **This leads us to the scientific conclusion: when nothing physics-related exists, self-creating physics is impossible.**

What Hawking has done is backward because time is not the consequence of gravity. The phenomenon known as gravity is dependent on time. Specifically, gravity is the consequence of space-time distortions. As a result, the physics (behaviors) of gravity are subject to the constraints of the construct of its space-time universe. This means gravity and quantum fluctuations are subject to the construct of time because they require the existence of time. As I have pointed out, when there is no *Time* to *Work*, no self-creating *Work* gets done. It's that simple.

By contrast, God is not subject to the constraints of a universe and the existence of time. This is why the only entity that could have presided before the universe and time existed, was the all-powerful intelligence who created the construct of the space-time universe in the first place. Our space-time universe was designed to depend and adhere to the constraint of time.

You will recall that Stephen Hawking made other statements indicating that science was at odds with God and religion. Remember the interview with Diane Sawyer where Hawking stated his opposition to belief in God by stating:

> There is a fundamental difference between religion, which is based on authority, and science, which is based on observation and reason. Science will win because it works.[84]

Hawking is declaring science is predicated on facts while religion is merely founded on obedience to an authority. Hawking is essentially stating this is a battle between the facts of hard science vs. the miracles of a fairy tale, where science will win.

In an interview in 2014, Hawking went further, stating, "But there is no God. I am an atheist."[85] Then he stated, "Religion believes in miracles, but they are not supported by science."[86] These interviews were about Hawking's book, *The Grand Design*, which many were calling the "No God Needed Book." Contrary to this, Sir Roger Penrose filmed an interview in which he commented on Hawking's book. Penrose stated that Hawking's M-theory was, "hardly science," and, "not even a theory," because testable data cannot be collected on it. He described Hawking's book as, "a collection of ideas, hopes, and aspirations." He said the book is misleading because it gives the impression that Hawking will explain how the universe started, instead, "it does nothing of the sort."[87]

Hawking tried to use string theory to claim the universe could allegedly create itself from nothing. However, Penrose pointed out that string theory has absolutely no support from observation. We should call it a *string hypothesis* to be more exact. Penrose called Hawking's ideas, "very far from testability," adding, "they are hardly science."[88] Remember, Penrose worked closely with Steven Hawking on black holes and singularity theorems.

And as a consequence, it is safe to say Hawking's *Grand Design* M-Theory only qualifies as a hypothesis that does not pass the Scientific Method. Professor Penrose stated M-Theory was only a collection of ideas. He stressed several times that M-Theory does not even qualify as a theory.[89] As a result, M-Theory fails to prove the universe can create itself in the same way that it fails to prove that it qualifies to be a theory. And if that wasn't enough, the "M" designation in M-Theory stands for the word, "Mother." This is because Hawking calls this the "*Mother*" of all theories. This means the "M" designation doesn't even represent a scientific term which we now realize has been exposed to not even qualify as a legitimate scientific theory.

Hawking, stating that religion is based upon authority while science is based upon observation and reason is implying that religion fails the Scientific Method while Hawking's science comes through with flying colors. As mentioned, Hawking's book, *The Grand Design*, has been called by some people, the "No God Needed Book." Nevertheless, what has become evident is that its foundation is "hardly science," and only constitutes a weak hypothesis.[90] This means that Hawking's "*science without a God*" does not have a stronger scientific argument than "*science with a God.*" In fact, I would argue that Hawking's "*science without a God*" doesn't even have a legitimate scientific argument.

It's ironic that the title of Hawking's book, *The Grand Design*, confirms that our universe was grandly designed! Random, haphazard accidents don't grandly design anything. Remember that Professor Roger Penrose stated:

> Bare probability or chance can never cause the creation
> of a Universe.[91]

Aristotle, the ancient father of the Scientific Method, and Sir Francis Bacon, the modern father of the Scientific Method, both believed in God. This means that "science with a God" is endorsed by elite champions when it comes to the topic of the Scientific Method. I say this because both of the fathers of the Scientific Method are not going to subscribe to a belief as crucial as God unless they are absolutely convinced through their own scientific observation and reasoning.

That being said, it appears that Sir Roger Penrose is not the only expert criticizing Hawking. The famous Oxford mathematics professor John Lennox states:

> As a scientist I'm certain Stephen Hawking is wrong.
> You can't explain the universe without God.[92]

Repeating Hawking's main argument:

> Because there is the law of gravity the universe can and
> will create itself from nothing—Lennox calls this claim,
> "triply ridiculous."[93]

Lennox states this declaration is a contradiction because a law of physics can't *cause* anything. Laws describe what things do; laws do not make things happen. Laws do not mechanically or physically **do** anything. This means Hawking told us something else that was not true.

Physical laws are descriptors, and as such, the law of gravity can only describe how objects are already behaving. Professor Lennox gives an example: when you add one dollar to another dollar, the law of mathematics dictates that you now have two dollars. The law of mathematics did not turn your one dollar into two dollars, you did that. This law merely describes what you did or what has already occurred. Therefore, the law is not the cause.[94]

You will notice that Hawking did not state the universe DID create itself. It should be clear Hawking does this because he can't prove what he is saying. As a result, he can't claim the universe **did** create itself because he has no proof which is supported by the statements of Professor Lennox and Professor Penrose. As mentioned, in the absence of *time,* before the universe existed, the platform of a universe with a space-time fabric was impossible. This is because the absence of *time* means one of the components of the universe's space-time fabric was missing. As a consequence, laws of physics like gravity did not even exist before the construct of the space-time universe.

The Singularity marks the beginning of the universe when *time* started. Before that, nothing—no mass, no energy, no space, no time, and no physical laws such as gravity—existed. When Hawking declared there was no *time* for God to create the universe, in effect, he was stating there was no *time* for anything to cause the Singularity—this includes the law of gravity. According to Hawking, the universe just popped up out of nothing and caused itself because there was no *time* for anything else to have caused the birth of the universe. This doesn't make sense.

This is circular reasoning on a galactic scale. If there was "no *time*," then there was absolutely nothing of the physical realm in existence. That includes the magical fairy dust of pre-universe gravity. There are about two trillion galaxies in the observable universe.[95] You can't get two trillion galaxies when nothing from nothing leaves absolutely nothing. Hawking's stance is ridiculous because he manages to give the law of gravity time to create the universe while somehow refusing to give God any time to do the same. That is unfair and defies logic. Therefore, I agree with Professor Lennox—Hawking is being triply ridiculous.

Of course, those who believe in God know that He was present at the beginning. Aristotle would have known this too. Since God, the "Unmoved Mover," exists outside of the dimensions of space and time, Hawking's limitations do not limit God. Only a Creator could have existed outside of the dimensions of a universe to cause the Big Bang. You can't physically get something from nothing unless God is present. Once the Big Bang had been demonstrated to be a reality, this meant that only God could have caused the universe to come into existence because there was no universe right before the Big Bang.[96]

It's a fact that our universe did have a beginning and did not always exist. Here are a few reasons why we know that our universe had a beginning:

1. The cosmic microwave background radiation maps of the universe match the predicted Big Bang maps.
2. The extremely low entropy (disorder) value of the Singularity particles.

Even Hawking acknowledged the Big Bang to be a fact. When the universe has a beginning, it means that something outside of the universe must be its Creator. Yet, Hawking's comments seemingly pit science against God. However, one could argue his remarks are pitted against each other as Professor John Lennox points out. More evidence of Hawking's ambivalence can be seen when he states there is no possibility of a creator because God had no time to exist, but then he contradicts himself with this statement:

One can't prove that God doesn't exist, but science makes God unnecessary.[97]

On the one hand he says you can prove that God doesn't exist, while on the other hand he says you can't. Furthermore, he says that, in a contest between God and science, science will win because it works—and presumably God doesn't. I feel this is another case of a scientist who takes what they know and contaminates and ruins it with what they want the truth to be. We witnessed George Wald do this. This is why Hawking's comments contradict each other and are flawed.

If science is properly understood, there is no conflict between God and science. Modern science, as a matter of historical fact, was born out of a Christian worldview. Many of the earliest scientists were professing Christians who sought to think God's thoughts after Him and uncover the mysteries waiting to be revealed in His Creation. Because they believed God is orderly, so too, His Universe would be orderly.

Speaking of scientific mysteries, I need to return to the topic of quantum fluctuations. Now, it's a fact that "nothing" was in existence before the Big Bang, as Stephen Hawking confirms to be the case. Nevertheless, there are now some scientists who speculate that "fields" exist, and they can even exist in empty space.[98] Within these "fields," there usually exists a particle which jitters or bounces around.

However, even if the particles are absent, as in empty space, the fields are still claimed to be there, and they can jitter all by themselves. Thus, both fields in empty space and particles can jitter. It is claimed that when a particle or a field jitters, it creates energy. This jittering energy producing phenomenon is referred to as quantum fluctuations.

Some scientists are claiming that quantum field theory makes room for quantum fluctuations as the temporary appearance of energetic "virtual particles" that jitter, even in empty space.[99] I would like to clarify that "empty space" is NOT nothing. This means that empty space would constitute, "nothingness," which is something. Therefore, regarding quantum fluctuations, a space-time universe must exist in the first place.

Some present-day scientists believe that jittering quantum fluctuations can give rise to transient energetic particles that pop into existence and then disappear.[100] That said, this magical fairy dust energy is being theorized to be capable of causing the universe to come into existence with a Big Bang. This means that instead of nothing existing before the Big Bang, something is being speculated to have existed before the Big Bang.[101]

The first problem with this idea is that it completely contradicts the assertion of Stephen Hawking that **nothing** existed before the Big Bang. Once again, here is Hawking's declaration:

> You can't get to a time before the big bang because there was no 'before' the big bang. We have finally found something that doesn't have a cause because there was no time for a cause to exist in. . . .[102]

This statement makes the topic of magical fluctuations crystal clear. Hawking's declaration is supported by the fact that empty space only exists inside the construct of the space-time platform that forms the structural foundation of our universe. Therefore, in the absence of time, the space-time fabric universe would also be absent. This eliminates any possibility of mystical creative fields of quantum fluctuations.

Despite this fact, some physicists try to work around this absolute limitation by speculating that "something" always existed. This is referred to as "nothingness". This directly contradicts another Stephen Hawking declaration that nothing existed before the Big Bang, there was no 'before' the Big Bang. It's impossible for the energy fields of quantum fluctuations to have existed in the absence of time because Energy = 0 in the absence of time. End of story.

Despite this, some scientists are promoting speculation that self-creation is theoretically possible because of quantum fluctuations. This speculation is being associated with the Uncertainty Principle which is being alleged to make room for this idea. The Uncertainty Principle states that the position and velocity of an object (like a particle) cannot both be measured precisely, at the same time.[103] It is beyond the scope of this book to discuss this principle in detail. However, I will state that it was developed by Werner Heisenberg who holds a Ph.D. in Theoretical Physics from the Ludwig Maximilian University of Munich. He is considered to be the father of Quantum Mechanics and was awarded the Nobel Prize in Physics for his work in Quantum Mechanics. That being said, he saw no conflict between God and science. On the contrary, Heisenberg declared:

> The first gulp from the glass of natural sciences will turn
> you into an atheist, but at the bottom of the glass, God
> is waiting for you.[104]

This is the reason why this book was written. The reason why many people are skeptics is because they are only half-way down the glass of scientific knowledge. This is the result of only being in possession of **some of the scientific facts**, which I refer to as pseudoscience. By contrast, if these people were in possession of **all the scientific facts** (sound science), they would graduate to the "bottom of the glass" where they find God waiting for them. Werner Heisenberg was a highly intelligent physicist who did not believe in fairy tales. Furthermore, he never intended for his Uncertainty Principle to be used by anyone as part of a speculation scheme alleging the universe could have created itself.

Henry Margenau, professor of Physics and Natural Philosophy at Yale University, had this to say about Heisenberg:

> There were, however, a few experiences I cannot forget. One was my first meeting with Heisenberg, who came to America soon after the end of the Second World War. Our conversation was intimate, and he impressed me by his deep religious conviction. He was a true Christian in every sense of that word.[105]

Professor Heisenberg clearly believed in God, and you will notice that his Uncertainty Principle did not cause him to believe the universe created itself. This should tell us something.

That said, if a few people still wish to throw their hopes behind speculation that proposes that magical quantum fluctuations existed before the universe existed, then we are able to ask them, where did such quantum fluctuations come from in the first place? If skeptics can ask where God came from, why can't we ask them to explain where their magical quantum fluctuations came from?

Science cannot provide any such underpinning source for whatever quantum physics is claimed to have created our universe. Science will never be able to establish an underpinning foundation that is the cause of it all.[106] This is especially true regarding the hypothesis that universes run through cycles where the end of the previous universe is claimed to have seeded this one. Regarding such an idea, we would need an explanation for how the very first cycle started? In other words, how did the very first universe create itself? If a validated scientific explanation is found to answer that question, then it would explain the genesis of our universe.

Therefore, the hypothesis that a cycling of universes is occurring does not solve the problem of explaining how this cycling started in the first place? Cycling universes puts us in the same position that we are in if we believe that our universe is the first and only one.

That being said, I used to hang on the words of scientists like Hawking, who promoted science as king and master of the universe. They presented a science that was self-driven and self-sufficient. No God was needed. It was full steam ahead with their, *"science without a God."* And when some of them, like Hawking, Francis Crick, and George Wald, talked about God and metaphysical matters, I figured they knew something that I didn't. I don't think that anymore, as a result, I don't care what Hawking thinks about religion and God because he clearly does not understand God.

In my opinion, it is unprofessional of Hawking to make false claims about God when there is no science to back him up. Science can't even prove how the universe came into existence. From Hawking's many statements, I find him to be filled with contradictions. Therefore, whenever we hear theological pronouncements from an expert who does not understand theology, we need to take such claims with a very large grain of salt. With that said, let's review five scientific realities that we come to realize when evaluating the comments of Stephen Hawking:

1) The Big Bang is a fact; our universe did have a beginning. This means that nothing in the physical realm existed before

the Big Bang. As a consequence, laws of physics and quantum fluctuations did not exist before the Big Bang.

2) There was no *Time* before the Big Bang occurred.

3) Hawking was 'mistaken' when he stated that laws of physics can cause things to happen.

4) Hawking was unable to establish how the universe began.

5) Hawking's book, *The Grand Design*, is based on a weak hypothesis, not a legitimate theory.

6) Hawking never proved that God does not exist. This is because God is not subject to the constraints of the construct of *Time*.

In light of these observations, I suggest we embrace the realities that Stephen Hawking has drawn our attention to, while at the same time, we should discard the ideas Hawking was unable to prove. The Scientific Method does not care what a scientist thinks. The Scientific Method is only concerned with what a scientist is able to establish and prove. And in my opinion, the proper use of the Scientific Method is not based upon hard science alone because it is meant to also include the incorporation of the science of philosophy.

Let's remember what Roger Penrose had to say: "The universe has a purpose. It's not there just somehow by chance."[107] This statement demonstrates that philosophy and science, when rightly understood, can coexist quite happily. With that, I would like to clarify that philosophy is the mother of science. Philosophy has been defined as the *Science of the Sciences*. Many people are not aware that hard science is a branch of philosophy. This means that philosophy has a higher rank than hard science does.[108] I mention this because many people think that hard science has more influence and is more serious than philosophy. Despite this impression, the exact opposite is true because hard science is a branch of philosophy, not the other way around.

One of the most famous scientists (and philosophers) in history was Sir Francis Bacon (1561-1626), who is described as the modern "father" of the Scientific Method and Empiricism. The Scientific Method is a logical process that starts with a hypothesis, then collects, measures, and observes experimental data in order to refine and formulate the hypothesis into a theory and then finally establish whether it is a scientific fact.[109]

On the other hand, Empiricism is defined as: "A former school of medical practice founded on experience without the aid of science or theory."[110] In Empiricism, the only component used is, *experience.* As we still say today, "There is no substitute for experience." Francis Bacon, being the modern father of these concepts, first proved something as a scientific fact (Scientific Method) and then combined that knowledge with his personal experience (Empiricism). On top of this, he infused the science of philosophy into his reasoning. This was Bacon's version of 'observation and reason.' And it can be demonstrated with an equation:

Observation and reason = Scientific Method + Empiricism + deep Philosophy

Bacon believed that depth in philosophy provides a deeper understanding than merely using strict, hard science. He explains why:

A little philosophy inclineth man's mind to atheism, but depth in philosophy bringeth men's minds about to religion.[111]

How similar this is to what Heisenberg stated about finding God waiting for us at the bottom of the glass of scientific knowledge. We don't find God until we get to the bottom. Most skeptics became nonbelievers because of their limited scientific journey. But when we dig deeper with philosophy, we complete the journey, and our minds are brought to God. This is what happened to me; Francis Bacon is 100 percent correct.

Bacon also stated, "I had rather believe all the fables in the legends and the Talmud and the Alcoran [Qur'an], than that this universal frame is without a mind."[112] The modern father of the Scientific Method knows that this universe must have an intelligent mind behind it.

Sir Francis Bacon included the following prayer in his will:

> When I thought most of peace and honor, thy hand [was] heavy on me, and hath humbled me, according to thy former loving kindness. . . . Just are thy judgments upon my sins. . . . Be merciful unto me for my Savior's sake, and receive me into thy bosom.[113]

As we can clearly see, famous scientists like Francis Bacon and Verner Heisenberg clearly believed in God.

Until hard science adds more philosophy to its practice, it will continue to incline minds to atheism and come up short when it peers back to the time of the Big Bang. Only those who dive deep and are equipped with the power of philosophy will see the entire picture. And when they do, they may find themselves at the same level of enlightenment as famous scientists like Aristotle, Verner Heisenberg, and Sir Francis Bacon.

At this time, I would like to introduce the highly esteemed astrophysicist Dr. Robert Jastrow, who holds a Ph.D. degree in Theoretical Physics. Dr. Jastrow was the first chairman of NASA's Lunar Exploration Committee, which established the scientific goals for exploring the Moon during the Apollo lunar landings in the 1960s. Dr. Jastrow hosted more than 100 CBS-TV network programs on space science. He was the special guest of NBC-TV with Wernher von Braun for the Apollo-Soyuz flights. Dr. Jastrow received the *NASA Medal* for

Exceptional Scientific Achievement and the *Arthur S. Fleming Award* for Outstanding Service in the U.S. Government.[114]

This is one of the scientists who was instrumental in getting us to the Moon! Who could be considered more 'space science' than Robert Jastrow and von Braun? We can all clearly see that Dr. Jastrow is an esteemed and accomplished space scientist. Now, with this introduction completed, let's see what Dr. Jastrow had to say about science proving that the Big Bang is a scientific fact:

> For the scientist who has lived by his faith in the powers of reason, the story ends like a bad dream. He has scaled the mountains of ignorance; he is about to conquer the highest peak; as he pulls himself over the final rock, he is greeted by a band of theologians who have been sitting there for centuries…. Astronomer now find they have painted themselves into a corner because they have proven, by their own methods, that the world began abruptly in an act of creation…. That there are what I or anyone would call supernatural forces at work is now, I think, a scientifically proven fact.[115]

Notice how this highly esteemed astrophysicist states that because science has proven the universe did indeed have a Big Bang beginning, this scientifically proves to him that a supernatural force (God) is responsible. This is because Jastrow understands that only a supernatural creating force could have existed before the universe began. Remember that Hawking stated there was no 'before' the Big Bang, because there was 'no time.'[116] In addition, notice how Jastrow points out that theologians have been correct, all along. Because Jastrow mentions theologians, this means his mention of a supernatural force is referring to God.

It is scientifically impossible that the universe created itself 'before' the Big Bang. Nothing can create itself before it even exists. This is a violation of the Law of Non-Contradiction because it is impossible for something to exist, and not exist, at the same time. Therefore, the universe creating itself before it existed defies logic. Whatever caused the universe to come into existence had to do so 'before' the universe existed. As a consequence, I fully agree with Dr. Jastrow, Dr. Ross, and John Ankerberg, when they proclaim it is a scientific fact that our universe could not, and did not, bring itself into existence. Therefore, it is a fact that a supernatural Creator is the cause of our universe.

There are many very famous scientists that most certainly do believe in God. As mentioned earlier, there is Aristotle, the ancient father of the Scientific Method. There is Sir Francis Bacon, the modern father of the Scientific Method. We have Verner Heisenberg, the father of Quantum Physics. We also have Robert Jastrow, NASA's *Dr. Space Science*. We can add to this list, Nicola Tesla and Sir Isaac Newton. In fact, evidence regarding Newton comes from Dr. William Stukely who was a medical doctor and prominent archaeology scholar in Isaac Newton's day. This is what William Stukely personally wrote of Sir Isaac Newton:

> No Man in England read the Bible more carefully than
> he did.[117]

This is a direct quote from Sir Isaac Newton:

> I have a fundamental belief in the Bible as the Word of
> God, written by those who were inspired. I study the
> Bible daily.[118]

I also wish to mention the world-famous astrophysicist Michio Kaku and what he revealed in an interview when he was asked about God? Professor Kaku revealed that:

Most top physicists do believe in God because of how the universe is designed. Ours is a universe of order, beauty, elegance, and simplicity.[119]

Dr. Kaku also revealed that the universe did not have to be ordered and beautiful, but rather, it could have been chaotic and ugly. I surmise that he means if the universe were here somehow randomly, that it would be chaotic and ugly, not perfect like it is. This reminds us of the Penrose Number which tells us how many other universes there could have been that would have been inferior to ours. Professor Kaku concludes with this assertion and declaration:

We are in a world made by rules created by an intelligence.[120]

Before I end this chapter, I wish to discuss what is referred to as *Causal Set Theory*. This new idea is hopeful speculation that the universe had no beginning and is explained in an article titled, "What If the Universe Had No Beginning?" by astrophysicist Paul Sutter.[121] I mention this article because I wish to address any speculation existing in a few people's minds that this article can be used to 'debunk' the Big Bang as being the very beginning. As a consequence, I intend to demonstrate that articles like this one, which support the idea the universe had no beginning, should not be viewed as having the scientific answers with which to base one's belief structure upon.

This article mentions current "contenders" for a microscopic description of strong gravity and states that one of these "contenders" is *string theory*. Well, string theory is what Stephen Hawking hangs his hat on in his book, *The Grand Design*. Hawking's M-Theory is the "Mother" of all string theories (that is what the "M" stands for). However, in Sir Roger Penrose's criticism of this book, he openly rejects string theory.[122] According to Sir Roger Penrose, one reason to reject

Hawking's idea is because testable data cannot even be collected on string theory. This is why Hawking does not even have a workable theory.[123] As a result, Hawking's book only contains a weak hypothesis.

This is important because it means that one of the alleged "contenders" in this article by Sutter has already been dismissed by a famous Nobel Prize winning astrophysicist. As a result, this weak *string* hypothesis isn't a contender at all.

Despite this fact, Sutter continues on as he explains how *Causal Set Theory* places strict limits on how close events can be in space and time. I would like to point out that this is an imposed condition. Who is to say these strict limits are valid for what actually occurred as the Singularity? How can anyone place strict limits on an event where current laws of physics crumbled? Sutter goes on by stating, "In our work instead, there would be no Big Bang as a beginning, as the causal set would be infinite to the past, and so there's always something before."[124] I need to point out that this is not what Stephen Hawking said where he is quoted as stating:

> You can't get to a time before the Big Bang because there was no 'before' the Big Bang. We have finally found something that doesn't have a cause because there was no time for a cause to exist in.[125]

Hawking clearly states there was no 'before' the Big Bang. As you can see, Sutter is severely contradicting Stephen Hawking and established scientific facts. If the universe has always existed as Sutter is implying, then time would have always existed which is not what Stephen Hawking has clearly stated. This article blatantly contradicts what Stephan Hawking has already clearly determined to be the case.

Remember that the entropy value in the Penrose Number prompted Robin Collins to state:

It is this extremely low entropy (disorder) value, that allows us to know that our universe had a beginning and did not always exist.[126]

If you add the fact cosmic microwave background radiation recordings "indelibly prove the occurrence of the Big Bang,"[127] it becomes clear Sutter's proposal that the universe has always existed is contradicting the scientific data. I believe all of these contradictions are evident once we look at them closely. For example, near the end of this article, Sutter admits:

> It's not clear yet if this no-beginning causal approach can allow for physical theories that we can work to describe the complex evolution of the universe during the Big Bang.[128]

What is being stated here is that it is unclear if this causal set idea will translate into a workable scientific theory. This means the causal set idea does not even qualify as a theory and is just a hypothesis. Remember how Roger Penrose described Hawking's book, *The Grand Design*, "It's a collection of ideas, hopes, and aspirations."[129] This is what Sutter's article appears to be as well.

And if someone wants to pose the argument that our universe bounced to life from the death of a previous universe in a *Big Bounce*, this idea violates General Relativity.[130] Such an idea proposes that a previous universe collapsed upon itself in what is termed a *Big Crunch*. This idea of a *Big Crunch* followed by a *Big Bounce* proposes that the universe goes through cycles of cosmic contractions and expansions which is referred to as "bouncing cosmology."[131] This idea seems to depend on a "regular" black hole at the center of the universe as opposed to an initial singularity being at the center. However, physicist Gonzalo Olmo states:

To mathematically implement this black hole trick in a cosmological model implies going from a homogeneous universe where all the spatial points have identical properties, to **inhomogeneous** models.[132]

Professor Almo is saying that in order to embrace this concept we would need to shift from the idea of a homogeneous early universe, and instead, believe that the early universe was not homogeneous. Almo goes on to state:

> Observations of the cosmic microwave background indicate a high degree of homogeneity in the early universe and it is unclear how this inhomogeneous model could yield a homogeneous universe like the one we scientifically observe.[133]

What physicist Gonzalo Almo is stating here is that the scientific observations of the cosmic microwave background radiation map of the universe demonstrates a high degree of homogeneity of our early universe. This contradicts the idea that an initial **inhomogeneous** universe model would then wind up as a **homogeneous** universe.

Another problem with this universe contracting idea is that it contradicts the scientific fact that our universe is **increasing** in its rate of expansion. If *Big Crunches* were a scientific reality, then our universe would have to decrease in its rate of expansion and then reverse direction to begin to contract. This is just the opposite of the scientific observation that our universe is accelerating in its expansion.[134] To give you an idea of the rate at which our universe is accelerating in its expansion, its distance is expanding at about 73.5 Kilometers per second per megaparsec (a parsec is a unit of length in astronomy).[135] Now, a 26.2-mile marathon race is 42 kilometers. This means that our universe is accelerating in its expansion a little less than 2 marathon distances with the passing of every second.

I present an example to help explain this. For demonstration purposes, let's say the size of our universe is 73.5 Km right now. One second from now, it would be 147 Km in size. Then it would grow to 220.5 Km in size two seconds from now. If we go backward in time, the universe expansion rate was less than 73.5 km/sec/Mpc. In some distant past, there was a time when our universe was expanding at a rate of one (1.00) marathon distance per second. And now it has accelerated to 1.75 marathon distances per second. To put this another way with a crude example, if our universe was a car moving at 42 mph at some point in the past, it is now speeding along at 73.5 mph. What I'm saying here is that our universe is not slowing down in its expansion, and it certainly is not contracting and going in reverse towards a *Big Crunch*. Therefore, the scientific reality of our universe contradicts the idea of a *Big Crunch* followed by a *Big Bounce*.

It's my personal belief that the universe was designed by God to continue to accelerate in its expansion until it burns itself out. I believe God designed His Universe to have a life span, and then die out. God is giving mankind the opportunity to live for Him while on Earth, and then join His eternal family when our physical bodies perish. This only needs to take place for a certain period of time. At some point, God will have a big enough family to fulfill His objective of having mankind join Him in His Kingdom. The universe will eventually fizzle out, leaving behind God's Kingdom filled with His Angels and His Family of loyal humans. This would explain why God created our universe in the first place and designed it to continually accelerate in its expansion.

Another idea also worth mentioning, is where some scientists think the universe has always existed and then suddenly started expanding. However, many physicists who reject this idea state that such a universe is not stable quantum mechanically.[136] These physicists state that a closed and static universe like this has a "non-zero" probability of collapsing quantum mechanically which means it could not have existed forever.

You will recall in the last chapter that I presented several examples of God using seeds. In comparison to the mustard seed, I believe that the ultimate seed planted by God was what we call the Singularity. God's seed for our universe was smaller than the size of an atom making it the smallest physical object that ever existed. And yet, it has blossomed into the expansive two-trillion-galaxy universe that we observe today! This is exactly like the smallest of all seeds, the mustard seed, growing into the largest tree in the garden (Matthew 13:31-32).

In conclusion, I'm pointing all of this out in the hope that it can be seen that our universe did have a Big Bang beginning. And because our universe had a beginning, this means there must be a Creator because a universe cannot create itself from absolutely nothing in the absence of time before it even existed! Self-creation from nothing, in the absence of time, is not how hard science works. All we have to do is follow the science which leads to the truth.

I would also like to point out that the scientific findings of the universe coming into existence first, reconciles and finds agreement with the Biblical account of God creating the universe first.

CHAPTER FOUR

The Hypothesis of Abiogenesis

Before I can begin discussing the theory of evolution, I need to start with abiogenesis. Abiogenesis is the hypothesis that the first living organism made itself from atoms in the ocean. Once that first life appeared, then evolution would have used that first life to produce every species on the earth, or so the postulation goes. Some people think both the hypothesis of abiogenesis and the theory of evolution are responsible for all life on the earth.

It is important to realize that abiogenesis is only a hypothesis, and evolution is only a theory. Neither one has been proven to be a fact. With that short introduction complete on the speculation of what some people think, let's dive into the scientific facts.

In order to get started, the first important fact for us to realize is that for an evolutionary process to exist, two conditions MUST be met:

- **Change** from an organism's normal genetic makeup must occur (mutation).

- **Natural Selection** (positive natural selection) which promotes advantageous mutations in an actively competing population member by increasing its ability to survive and prosper compared to the other members of its population. In addition, the population member who is now able to survive better, must also accomplish the **production of offspring** in order for their advantageous mutations to be passed on, thus causing the perpetuation of the increase in survival of its descendants and therefore its species. This is seen in nature and is defined as, **microevolution**. This is in contrast to the theory of **macroevolution**, where the advantageous mutations in the alleged splintered-off family line are so dramatic that they allegedly form a brand-new species (no observed evidence of this exists in nature to prove macroevolution ever occurred). Conversely, negative natural selection eliminates any negative mutations in an actively competing population member by decreasing its survival and eventually eliminating its presence in the population's gene pool.

In a nutshell, an evolutionary process has to spawn mutants who survive better and thrive better than their neighbors while producing offspring. Just to be clear, abiogenesis is a claimed evolutionary process just as evolution is claimed to be an evolutionary process.

Now, to really comprehend any evolutionary process, natural selection has to be thoroughly understood. Therefore, it is here that I wish to review the phenomenon of natural selection. Natural selection is said to occur when a population member is born with an advantageous mutation that allows it to adapt and survive better than its neighbors. It's worth noting that some mutated offspring are conceived as normal fertilized eggs. However, they become mutated because of errors during the rapid cell division that is necessary to transform the fertilized egg into an embryo and then a fetus. Regardless, if the mutant survives better, the reason it survives better is because its mutation qualifies as a biological improvement. When this occurs, that member has been 'naturally selected' to survive better, thrive better, and prosper.

It is this phenomenon that is speculated by the hypothesis of abiogenesis to be the mechanism that capitalizes on biological improvements that allegedly produced the very first species, a bacterium. In a nutshell, natural selection can be described as an increase in success and survival resulting from genetic code errors that produced biological improvements. In other words, an organism has been selected by nature (naturally selected) to be superior, and therefore the fittest, if it thrives and survives better because of its happenstance biological improvements. Natural selection can also be described as the advantage enjoyed by the fittest population member because of its acquired biological improvements that made the mutant thrive, survive, and reproduce better than its neighbors.

An evolutionary process can be described with the following equality relation:

Mutations (random genetic changes) resulting in biological improvements that increase survival, success, and reproduction = Evolutionary Process

This simplifies into a fundamental and core scientific equation:

Mutations + Natural Selection = Evolutionary Process

The term, *mutation*, refers to a random change in the information of the original DNA code. I use this term throughout this book and when I do so, I am referring to a typical genetic change (genetic variability) that is most often the result of errors during DNA replication. That being said, we need to keep in mind that random DNA code changes can also result from genetic recombination, translocation, and similar mishaps involving DNA strands.

Regarding the equation for an evolutionary process, notice how we need to combine mutations with natural selection in order to qualify as an evolutionary process. In other words, if an offspring is produced but there were no mutations present and they just happen to be fortunate enough to survive and thrive better than their neighbors, this does not qualify as an evolutionary process. Instead, the offspring that survives better must be a mutant with a change in its genetic code in order for an evolutionary process to be at work. Only in this way is a mutation able to be passed onto offspring which perpetuates the advantageous mutated trait. Luck does not qualify as a guidance system because it cannot be passed onto offspring.

It becomes evident the biological improvements that increase survival and success are what constitute the guidance system for the alleged advancement in the hypothesis of abiogenesis as well as in the theory of evolution. I say "alleged advancement" in the hypothesis of abiogenesis and the theory of evolution because such advancements have only been observed in nature regarding microevolution. Microevolution constitutes refinements of an already existing species. Microevolution cannot form a brand-new species (which is the theory of macroevolution) nor can it produce the first living species from lifeless objects (abiogenesis hypothesis). I will explain this more, later in the chapter.

Regarding natural selection, think of natural selection as the Olympics where members of a population compete for the gold medal. The member who wins and comes in first place gets the gold medal and is therefore deemed to be 'naturally selected.' This can be represented as an equation:

The Gold Medal Winner = The 'Naturally Selected' member

Therefore, in this Olympic analogy:

The Gold Medal = Natural Selection

To win the gold medal, the member has to come in first place by doing better than everyone else.

Only the winner gets naturally selected. And as such, natural selection is an active process because it requires active competition against other members in the population in order to establish the advantaged winner. I would like to point out that it is equally important to realize natural selection also requires the production of offspring. Therefore, only living organisms can be naturally selected because of the requirements of active competition and reproduction. It should be obvious that **only living organisms can actively compete and produce offspring.**

Natural selection requires active competition for an organism to survive, thrive, and reproduce, otherwise, success cannot be measured. Without competition, there would be no way to establish who the gold medal winner is. Without competition, there would be no way to tell if a mutation was truly advantageous or not. If a mutation does not demonstrate it is advantageous, then increased survival and prosperity would not occur, as a consequence, natural selection would not occur. Therefore, an organism must be naturally selected to survive, thrive, and reproduce better than its neighbors through mutations in order for an evolutionary process to be taking place.

There must be active competition for resources to prove that a mutation is advantageous. Only positive mutations would be able to move an evolutionary concept forward. Therefore, the proving ground occurs in the population when the members actively compete against each other in the same way athletes compete in the Olympics for the gold medal. This active competition must be present for natural selection to move the creatures with advantageous mutations forward. And of course, the successful mutants need to produce offspring to pass the advantageous mutations on. If the positive mutation does not get passed on to offspring, then the mutation is worthless because it dies off.

Let me present two standard definitions for natural selection. The first is from Merriam-Webster:

> A natural process that results in the survival and reproduction success of individuals or groups best adjusted to their environment and that leads to the perpetuation of genetic qualities best suited to that particular environment.[137]

The second is found on Dictionary.com:

> The process by which forms of life having traits that better enable them to adapt to specific environmental pressure, as predators, changes in climate, or competition for food or mates, will tend to survive and reproduce in greater numbers than others of their kind, thus ensuring the perpetuation of those favorable traits in succeeding generations.[138]

Notice how these definitions refer to living organisms in populations that are actively competing for survival and reproducing offspring. In addition, there is one crucial fact about natural selection: it requires that a mutation has to be significant enough to alter one's ability to survive. If a small change has occurred but does not increase survivability or success, natural selection did not occur. In this instance, the organism has not been *naturally selected* to survive better. Only if survivability and success have been changed does natural selection exist.

Therefore, not only does a mutation have to occur, but the mutation must be so significant that the organism gains an advantage in surviving better than its neighbors. In addition, the mutation also has to be passed on to offspring so that the genetic advantage to survive better does not die out. This is why natural selection can never exist with things that are not alive.

Here are the required conditions of an evolutionary process:

- The condition of *change* or mutation of genetic code must occur.
- The condition of *positive natural selection* must occur in a living and actively competing organism in a population where that organism survives and thrives better than its neighbors and produces offspring who perpetuate the advantageous mutations.

An evolutionary process has occurred if both of these requirements are met. However, if they are not both met, an evolutionary process has not occurred. Here is a slight variation of the evolutionary process equation that was presented earlier:

(A) mutations + (B) increased survival and reproduction

= (C) Evolutionary Process.

Of course, an increase in survival and reproduction = natural selection. It is critically important to realize that if (A) is absent or (B) is absent, then an evolutionary process is not present. As stated, **mutations** and **natural selection** must both be present for an evolutionary process to exist. And the natural selection that needs to be present is not referring to the relatively weak natural selection that causes the microevolutionary refinements we observe in nature. No, the natural selection that must be present is the alleged stronger version of natural selection that can allegedly cause the production of a brand-new species (macroevolution). This stronger version of natural selection has NEVER been observed in nature and has NOT been found in the Fossil Record either!

It is here that I need to clarify the difference between **micro-evolution** and **macroevolution. Microevolution** is defined in the Oxford Dictionaries as,

> An evolutionary change within a species or small group
> of organisms, especially over a short period of time.[139]

This means that small adaptations occur, but a brand-new species is not produced. We observe this phenomenon in nature with the production of COVID variants. These variants are the consequence of biological improvements from lucky accidental mutations. However, you will notice that a brand-new species is NOT produced with COVID mutations. In the case of microorganisms, only improved viral variants or improved bacterial strains are produced in micro-evolution. With that said, microevolution can occur in any species.

On the other hand, **macroevolution** is defined in the Oxford Dictionaries as,

> A major evolutionary change. The term applies mainly
> to the evolution of whole taxonomic groups over long
> periods of time.[140]

In other words, macroevolution refers to the idea that a brand-new species can be produced from the effects of natural selection. Nevertheless, the production of a brand-new species from accidental mutations has NEVER been observed in nature. I will discuss this more in the next chapter where I thoroughly analyze the theory of evolution.

I wish to stress that we really need to understand the huge difference between microevolution and macroevolution! Microevolution is true because it is found to occur in nature. Macroevolution is false because it has never been found to occur in nature.

Getting back to natural selection, not only do we need mutants to be formed, but the mutants that are lucky enough to possess a positive biological improvement need to demonstrate increased survival, and then reproduce. As mentioned, it is this increased survival that deems the lucky mutant to be 'naturally selected.' When it comes to the theory of macroevolution, natural selection is supposed to function as a guidance system by occurring as small, incremental, biological improvements which smoothly progress the mutations in a gradualistic manner until a brand-new species is created. However, with regard to the hypothesis of abiogenesis, the topic of natural selection becomes impossible as you will soon see.

Before we get to that point, we need to begin with a concise introduction clarifying the hypothesis of abiogenesis. The abiogenesis hypothesis claims that random *changes* occurred to clumps of atoms called molecules, which then came to life in the form of a complex living cellular machine called a bacterium. Once this allegedly occurred, the theory of evolution claims random errors in replicating the genetic-coded DNA of this bacterium eventually produced a brand-new species. Then somewhere along the line, that new species experienced random errors in the replication of its genetic-coded DNA, and this eventually produced yet another new species, and so on, and so forth. This lofty speculation is claimed to have occurred over five billion times, causing all the diverse life we see on the earth.

This fantastical idea claims that abiogenesis made the first living organism through an evolutionary process and then evolution turned that living organism into the ancestor of every species on the earth, also through an evolutionary process. Of course, positive natural selection must be present in both cases as the driving force.

When I went to school in the 1980s, I don't ever remember abiogenesis being separated from evolution. Nor do I remember the word 'theory' ever being placed after the word, evolution. As a result, not only was I given the impression abiogenesis and evolution were facts, but I was also left with the impression abiogenesis and evolution were interconnected. However, this interconnection is not what present-day proponents of evolution theory claim. Austin Cline is a former regional director for the Council for Secular Humanism. For those people unfamiliar with the word, *secular,* it is typically used to refer to someone who does not believe in God. In an article titled "Abiogenesis and Evolution," Cline states:

> The origin of life is certainly an interesting topic, but it is not a part of evolution theory. The study of the naturalistic origins of life is called abiogenesis. While scientists have not developed a clear explanation of how life might have developed from non-living material, that has no impact on evolution.[141]

This was news to me because I always thought that abiogenesis and evolution were linked together as the first and second steps of evolution. I mention this because I suspect many people believe abiogenesis is part of the theory of evolution. It is not. I'm sure that I am not the only one who is surprised by this clarification. I now realize the hypothesis of abiogenesis and evolution theory are separate. While still on this topic, Austin Cline continues:

> In evolutionary theory, life could have developed naturally through abiogenesis. It could have been started by divine power. It could have been started by aliens. Whatever the cause, evolutionary explanations begin to apply once life appears and begins to reproduce.[142]

Notice that Cline is not making any claims as to how the first life appeared. This is very important because Austin Cline is admitting a Divine power COULD have started the first living cell. Therefore, it is important for us to realize that evolutionary theory, as Austin Cline discusses here, does not claim the first living cell made itself.

Also take note that Austin Cline states that evolutionary explanations begin to apply **once life appears** and begins to reproduce. I'm sure he is referring to evolutionary explanations specifically related to the theory of evolution. By contrast, in the hypothesis of abiogenesis, evolutionary explanations specific to the hypothesis of abiogenesis are suggested by researchers in the field of abiogenesis, to begin to apply **before life appeared,** in order to make life appear. This is the difference between evolution theory (a 'life, from life' idea), as opposed to the hypothesis of abiogenesis (a 'life, from non-life' idea).

To further examine what the hypothesis of abiogenesis and the theory of evolution **do** claim, let's start with some basics. Let's start with a definition of abiogenesis by Oxford Dictionaries:

> The original evolution of life or living organisms from inorganic or inanimate substances.[143]

Abiogenesis states atoms floating around in the oceans of early Earth eventually clumped together. Atoms have a natural tendency to stick together like magnets. If we put ten magnets into a bag, shake them around and dump them out, they will be stuck to each other in a clump. In this same way, if we take carbon, hydrogen, nitrogen, oxygen, phosphate, and other atoms and mix them together, they will form clumps as they stick together through bonding. Some bond types require specific conditions to be met.

It is beyond the scope of this book to discuss the various types of bonds between atoms. Suffice it to say that these various types of bonds cause atoms to be clumped together in what we refer to as, molecules. Molecules are a clumped together configuration of atoms. Some of these clumps have been named with fancy terms such as nucleotides, amino acids, phosphate groups, nucleobases, and deoxyriboses. Essentially, they are all just building blocks (like bricks) that can be assembled together to build larger structures. The important fact to remember here, is that the random formation of a clump of atoms into a molecule is as lifeless as a bunch of magnets sticking together. The term 'molecule' sounds impressive, but it is just a clump of lifeless atoms, randomly and mindlessly stuck together.

Scientists have given each and every atom clump configuration its own name. There is no life in a molecule, just as there is no life in a clump of magnets. Water is a molecule, and water is certainly not alive. That said, please don't get too impressed with the names on these molecules. None of them are alive, and there certainly was never any life in the 'soup of life' of Earth's early oceans. There was as much life in the 'soup of life' as there is in a bag of magnets.

With that introduction complete, let's look at the claims of abiogenesis. Abiogenesis is claimed to have started through what is called, *chemical evolution*. Chemical evolution claims that atom clumps floating around in the ocean were supposed to have started doing things. The chemical evolution hypothesis states simple molecules randomly come together and randomly combine. And when molecule clumps get large enough, they are referred to as, polymers. The word, *poly*, means *many*. Therefore, the combination of many molecules forms a polymer.

An online researcher named Dr. Samanthi discusses Chemical Evolution and states:

> Furthermore, individual monomers transform into polymers which performed specific structural and functional roles. With evolution, these polymers interacted with each other thereby gaining the ability to reproduce and pass on genetic material to the next generation. This process leads to the origin of life. Hence, during evolution, chemical evolution took place prior to organic evolution.[144]

I feel it should be evident this comment is false. It is impossible that dead molecules randomly gained any reproduction abilities when they "interacted" and then passed on genetic material. How can dead objects actively "interact?" And where did the genetic material come from in a clump of lifeless atoms and dead molecules? What genetic material?? Who wrote the code for this alleged genetic material? There is no genetic material here. And there are no living interactions going on either. These are just lifeless inanimate objects that are simply floating around in the ocean.

Look at all of the *action* words being used here and applied to lifeless atoms in groupings that we call molecules. These are inanimate objects that have no internal agenda, no mission, and no life. Let's list the action words and phrases that have been attributed to lifeless molecules:

1) "Performed specific structural and functional roles"
2) "Interacted with each other"
3 "Gained the ability to reproduce"
4) "Passed on genetic material to the next generation"

Lifeless clumps of mindless atoms and dead molecules don't *do* anything on this list! The descriptors being used here are what living organisms *do*. What is being said here is, when enough lifeless atoms randomly clumped together to form dead molecules, they actively started doing things which will eventually bring them to life.

These dead molecules are not *doing* anything that living organisms do. They are barren atoms, barren molecules, and barren clumps of molecules. They are just as lifeless as a bag of magnets. Where did the written genetic code come from which was allegedly passed on to "offspring"? And I ask: what offspring can lifeless atom clumps and dead molecules have? None of these clumps of lifeless atoms and dead molecules were alive. None of these lifeless objects ever *did* anything that is even remotely associated with life. This sounds like science fiction to me and it certainly does not pass the Scientific Method.

Another article on chemical evolution is posted online by researcher and chemist Paul G. Higgs. In his article, we can see a bit more detail (compared to the last one) regarding what chemical evolution is all about. Higgs discusses *diversity* and *selection*. As we have seen earlier in this chapter, an evolutionary process must contain the two components of **mutations** and **natural selection** (which includes reproduction).

In the theory of evolution, when living organisms reproduce, sometimes errors occur in the replication of the genetic code of their DNA. This is where the mutations come from in evolution theory. However, in the area of abiogenesis, there is no DNA and there is no coded transmittable information. There is nothing but lifeless atoms and dead molecules floating around in the oceans of early Earth in what has been referred to as an organic soup. Evolutionary scientists discussing abiogenesis don't use the word, **mutation**. This is because there was no DNA before life began. Instead, they use the terms, ***diversity,*** or ***change***. These scientists claim the molecule components that magically became coded genetic material experienced *diversity* or *change*. This is in contrast to DNA which experiences mutations.

This raises the question: Why would lifeless molecules 'decide' to magically convert part of its molecule into information storing genetic material? Information storing genetic material (DNA) is the hallmark of highly intelligent engineering. I feel it should be obvious that mindless and lifeless molecules are not going to be able to handle that level of highly intelligent engineering. In fact, the only thing mindless and lifeless molecules would be able to handle, would be to float around and combine together just as mindlessly as magnets randomly sticking together.

Higgs states that diversity (*change*) is generated by random chemical synthesis.[145] Random chemical synthesis seems to boil down to the idea that if molecules bump into themselves enough times or are exposed to the right environmental conditions, then they can stick together forming new and larger molecules. I understand this random chemical bulking-up process is referred to as, *synthesis*.

Nevertheless, there are many insurmountable flaws regarding the hypothesis of chemical evolution and how it allegedly led to the spawning of the first living organism. The most critical flaws include the fact there was no instructional code storing device like DNA, and more importantly, there was no coded instructional information to be stored. When I say instructional code, I mean the operating system genetic code that instructs an organism's living systems to do what is necessary to live.

Notice how I make mention of "operating system genetic code." I find this to be the perfect time to discuss instructional code in order to explain what I mean here. Most people don't know this, but a Microsoft Windows operating system has 50 million lines of code on it. Your computer needs 50 million lines of very specific instructional code that was meticulously engineered to tell it what to do.[146] Everything from your sign-in window to your speakers need code. Once that code is written, it must then be loaded onto your new computer's empty hard drive. It just so happens that Microsoft genius Bill Gates made this statement about DNA:

> DNA is like a software program, only much more complex than anything we've ever devised.[147]

In the same way your computer needs millions of lines of intelligent instructional code, so does your DNA. Think of it like this, your

DNA is like a computer's hard drive and the intelligent instructional code on the DNA is like a Microsoft Windows operating system.

Regarding your personal computer, a Microsoft operating system is downloaded onto your computer's hard drive. In this same manner, your DNA's instructional code is downloaded onto your DNA molecules. Your DNA molecules function just like a computer hard drive that stores instructional code. As a result, DNA is actually composed of two components:

1) The molecule itself that functions as a biological hard drive data storage device

2) The downloaded instructional genetic code

As Microsoft genius Bill Gates explains, our DNA is more complex than your computer's operating system. I feel the conclusion to be drawn here is that your DNA has tens of millions of lines of very specific intelligent instructional code on it.

Abiogenesis is claimed to have produced the first DNA from the 'soup of life.' The very first living organism on the earth was a bacterium that appeared around 3.7 billion years ago.[148] We know this because we have a 3.7-billion-year-old fossil of this bacterium. That first life had the very first DNA molecule. It is here that I wish to describe exactly what DNA is. To more fully understand DNA, I will briefly describe the single-stranded DNA molecule found in the first living organism:

- DNA stands for deoxyribose nucleic acid.
- DNA is a polynucleotide.
- A polynucleotide has thousands of nucleotides in this instance.
- A nucleotide = nucleobase + deoxyribose + phosphate group.
- There are 5,000,000 nucleotides in the DNA of the very first living organism. This means there are 5,000,000 nucleobases, 5,000,000 deoxyriboses, and 5,000,000 phosphate groups.[149]

- This means that there are about 161,000,000 atoms in the first single-stranded bacterial DNA molecule if we consider that there are about 32 atoms, on average, per nucleotide.[150]
- However, most life on the earth has DNA that is double-stranded and is composed of 3 billion nucleotides compared to the 5 million nucleotides of the very first bacterium.

Therefore, DNA is a long strand of atoms strung together in just the right configuration and sequence. When you read of nucleobases, deoxyriboses, and phosphate groups, what this means is that atoms of carbon, hydrogen, oxygen, phosphorus, nitrogen etc. have been strung together as molecules that we have special names for. When these molecules are strung together, they form even larger molecules referred to as nucleotides—which are building blocks that get strung together like beads on a string to make up the very large molecule of DNA. In the case of most life on Earth, DNA it is composed of two long chains of nucleotides forming an impressive double-stranded molecule.

As I mentioned before, nucleotides are what the encoded instructional data is stored onto. And when chains of nucleotide building blocks are connected, they form polynucleotides. Polynucleotides are many nucleotides strung together. And if you add deoxyribose to the polynucleotides, you get deoxyribose nucleic acid, which is abbreviated as DNA. The first bacterial DNA had about 161 million atoms in it. And they all had to be very precisely sequenced. In comparison, I believe there are about 97 billion atoms in our double-stranded DNA molecule.

Part of the abiogenesis hypothesis claims that DNA formed itself in the ocean. Let's discuss the mathematical odds of that occurring with our DNA molecule. The chance of one typical DNA molecule randomly forming itself is less than 1 in 10 to the 600 th power.[151]

While the chance of the most simple replicating protein molecule forming itself randomly is less than 1 in 10 to the 450th power.[152] Both of these calculations are way past the definition of what is mathematically possible, which is 1 in 10 to the 50th power. Even though this DNA probability calculation seems to be for human DNA, bacterial DNA forming itself is also way past the threshold of what is considered mathematically possible.

I wish to stress that the churning ocean waves of early Earth did not write even one single letter of intelligent code. Random chance does not write intelligent code, let alone the millions of lines of intelligent instructional code that would constitute an operating system for the first living cellular machine. It is a fantasy to think the churning waves of the ocean with its atoms and molecules could randomly write even one single letter of intelligent instructional code.

To put this into perspective, imagine dropping a brand-new hard drive into the ocean. This new hard drive has no operating system on it. Then, 700 million years later, we come back and analyze this hard drive. Will it have tens of millions of lines of code downloaded onto it? Will the atoms and molecules floating around in the ocean write an operating system for this empty hard drive? The answer is, of course not. No one would ever believe this could happen. However, this is what you are being asked to believe regarding the hypothesis of abiogenesis. You are being asked to believe that millions of lines of precise instructional code were written as an operating system by mindless atoms and molecules floating around in the water.

As you may recall from biology class regarding the process of our DNA replication during reproduction, many precise processes must take place. The original DNA molecule has to unzip which sets the stage for replication to begin. This exposes the original DNA strand (the mother strand) in order for the new strand (daughter strand) to be assembled. I am referencing an educational online video that quickly demonstrates how this extremely precise and complicated process works.[153] As we can see from this basic video, replication was an extremely complicated and sophisticated process in the first living organism's single stranded DNA molecule.

In another referenced online video, we once again see details regarding the intricate mechanism of DNA replication involving various enzymes like Messenger RNA (mRNA) and Transfer RNA (tRNA) as they cause the correct assembly of absorbed nucleotides creating the new DNA strand (new daughter strand).[154] This video gets into more detail explaining the complicated coding and decoding process that is involved in the assembly of absorbed nucleotides which construct the newly replicated DNA strand (daughter strand). As we can see from this video, there is a high level of sophistication and precision involved in the coding and decoding involved in DNA replication. I believe it should be obvious this level of sophistication and precision is not going to be the invention of mindless molecules floating around in ocean waves.

It is here I wish to clarify a few terms you will come across. 'Encoding,' refers to the process of taking instructional operating system data and converting it into a usable genetic language of 'code.' It is the usable operating system genetic code that then gets downloaded onto a code storing device (DNA).

However, in the hypothesis of abiogenesis, since DNA is not going to just pop into existence, it is going to be claimed that DNA allegedly 'evolved' from a very simple molecule that got more complex as time went on. This means that in this hypothesis, at some point, part of a simple molecule (that was not DNA yet) had to decide to get into the business of data storage and magically become the very first information storing molecule segment in history. I ask: How was this quantum leap accomplished?? There is no logical reason why this magnificent biological technology invention would occur in nature. Because dead things can't be naturally selected, natural selection could not have been the guidance system for this 'life from non-life' idea.

In addition, in the case of the hypothesis of abiogenesis, an extreme amount of operating system data would have to magically come into existence. Then, all of this intelligent instructional data would have to be encoded as millions of lines of usable operating system genetic code. This encoded data would then need to be mysteriously downloaded (coded) onto the very first information storing segment of a dead molecule floating around in the ocean. Operating system code is not going to just jump onto the information storing segment of the first alleged DNA-like molecule floating around in the oceans of early Earth.

This would require the need for a download code that would command the transfer of the very first instructional code onto the very first DNA-like molecule segment. As mentioned, atoms floating around in the ocean do not have any kind of code on them. This raises the questions: Who wrote the intelligent instructional data for the first bacterium and who wrote the code needed to convert that data into the language of usable genetic code (encoding) in order for the very first operating system to be downloaded (coded) onto the very first biological information storing segments?

What I am saying here is this, if we were able to microscopically assemble atoms in a laboratory in order to synthesize a man-made DNA molecule, it would be empty. This artificially assembled DNA strand would have no code on it at all. This means millions of lines of operating system data would have to be written, encoded, and then downloaded onto this synthetic DNA molecule before it becomes viable to drive biological processes and reproduction. Therefore, without the millions of lines of intelligent instructional data, this synthetic DNA molecule is worthless. It's just like a brand-new hard drive that is empty when it is made at the factory.

Let's look at some of the requirements for the creation of the first living organism:

1) Millions of lines of instructional data
2) Code to convert that data into a usable language of operating system genetic code (encoding)
3) Code to command nucleotides with the ability to store the operating system genetic code
4) Code commanding the transfer of operating system code onto the information storing nucleotide molecules
5) Code to command the replication of both DNA and its code during reproduction

I'm sure that I'm probably leaving some steps out, but I feel that you should be getting the picture as to how complex this whole system actually is.

In the concept of abiogenesis, right before the first code was stored onto nucleotide segments,

let's not forget that at some point a randomly floating molecule would have had to delegate part of itself as the first information storing segment to receive encoded data. As stated, this raises the question: At what point was the decision made by this first random molecule to delegate part of its atom sequence with the power to store encoded data? How did such an astonishing achievement get accomplished by a lifeless molecule?? This sounds like a fairy tale.

An average nucleotide molecule is an assembly of a few dozen atoms. As mentioned, those nucleotides floating around in the water don't have any code on them at all. This raises the logical question: How did a lifeless nucleotide mindlessly floating around in the ocean suddenly gain the ability to store encoded data?

Let me give an example of this impossible situation. Let's say you are with a friend and the two of you sit on a short brick wall. You tell your friend that you need to back-up the data on your laptop. Your friend tells you that all you have to do is place your laptop on this brick wall and the data from your hard drive will magically jump onto the bricks in this short wall. Now, does that make any sense?

This is what you are being asked to believe in the hypothesis of abiogenesis. You are being asked to believe that intelligent instructional data wrote itself, translated itself into usable genetic code (encoding), and then magically jumped onto lifeless building blocks called nucleotides.

Nucleotides function as building blocks just as bricks function as building blocks. In the same way that bricks in a wall are lifeless building blocks with no data stored on them, nucleotides are also lifeless building blocks with no data naturally stored on them. Nucleotides don't naturally possess the ability to store encoded data. They are just the mindless combination of a few dozen atoms.

What I am stating here is two-fold:

1) The atoms composing molecules don't naturally possess the ability to store encoded data

2) The atoms composing molecules don't naturally exist loaded with stored code

In order for your friend's advice to be true, the lifeless bricks in this wall would need to magically gain the ability to store data. Then, more unexplained magic would have to occur that transfers all the data from your laptop onto the bricks in this wall. Does this sound reasonable? No, it does not sound reasonable.

Here are just four questions resulting from the many fatal flaws regarding the hypothesis of abiogenesis:

1) Who wrote the millions of lines of intelligent operating system data that became code?

2) How did lifeless atom sequences gain the ability to store encoded data?

3) How was the decision made to replicate these coded atom sequences?

4) How was the decision made to transfer data from established atom sequences (mother strand) to newly formed copies of the original atom sequences?

As we can see from this list of questions, not only do we need to discuss the existence of the first bacterium with the first coded DNA, but we also need to discuss this first bacterium initiating the first replication process of its DNA in order to engage in the activity of reproduction.

The process of reproduction involves the transfer of instructional code from this bacterium's mother DNA strand onto the newly formed nucleotide sequences as they were being assembled into the newly replicated daughter DNA strand. This requires a different set of codes that command the operating system code to be downloaded onto newly absorbed nucleotides which will, from now on, function as a data storage device, much like the hard drive in your computer.

Before this process began, these newly absorbed nucleotides were simply floating around in the oceans of early Earth without any code on them. But by the end of this process, these newly acquired nucleotides became fully loaded with instructional code transferred to them from the mother DNA strand.

Just talking about intelligent operating system instructional code should be enough to end all talk of abiogenesis. In addition, we are also talking about a system of different integrated codes with different functions that must work precisely together to attain the goal of transferring operating system code onto an information storing segment of a replicated molecule. In the case of DNA, the entire molecule is empowered with the ability to store encoded instructional data. As mentioned, there must also be command codes to duplicate/replicate the operating system code during reproduction, etc… Therefore, it is clear to me that layers of very specific integrated codes are necessary.

Suffice it to say this whole process is infinitely more complex than random churning waves containing the ocean's molecules would be able to handle, let alone think about. I don't believe most people fully realize everything that DNA is, everything that DNA does, and the various types of codes that DNA stores.

Nevertheless, in yet another article titled, "Origins of Life I," researchers very thoroughly go through the entire hypothesized process of how atoms became molecules which then, through environmental factors, ultimately became amino acids, small peptides, and even larger molecules.[155] This article discusses how membranes could form and then probably surrounded the enzymes, amino acids, and peptides floating around in the water. Then this article starts talking about some molecules copying themselves. These are referred to as *self-copying molecules.* You will notice the use of the words, **"could,"** and **"probably."** In the section of this article titled: "Moving to a DNA World," the author admits it is theoretical that larger and larger molecules would have formed on early Earth, and that this should have eventually led to molecules that could copy themselves.[156] The key words here are: "**theoretically,**" and "**should.**"

Then the author also states that, "it is likely that self-replicating molecules would emerge." The key words here are, "**likely**" and "**would.**" Then the author admits he does not know the precise pathway of abiogenesis but goes on to state that scientists have worked out the major steps and that those steps are "**possible,**" and they have **a good idea of how life probably started.**[157] The key words here are: "**possible,**" "**good idea,**" and "**probably.**" The use of words like these means **this is all speculation and does not pass the Scientific Method of proving.**

It is clear to me there is no proof establishing that self-replicating molecules actually occurred in the oceans of early Earth. Otherwise, we would not be reading an article that uses words like: "**theoretically,**" "**likely,**" "**could,**" "**would,**" "**should,**" "**possible,**" "**a good idea,**" **and "probably.**" We are all know how, 'could haves,' 'would haves,' and 'should haves,' pan out in the end. From reading this article, it is plain to me that talk about self-replicating molecules cannot be proven to be true, and as a consequence, certainly does not pass the Scientific Method.

In addition, to be relevant to the idea of dead molecules becoming alive, genetic code has to be involved. This is a severe problem for the hypothesis of abiogenesis because it means that not only would self-replicating molecules have to be proven to be a scientific fact, but it would also have to be proven that parts of these new and bulked-up molecules would have randomly gained the ability to store encoded data.

As I have mentioned, this is what DNA does. Not only would molecule segments have to randomly and magically gain the ability to store genetic code, but more importantly, someone would have to write the intelligent operating system code that would be self-copied/self-replicated. This operating system code would need to include commands for when the self-replication process begins, along with the specific commands for the download of code onto the newly duplicated molecule's information storing segments.

This means many types and layers of codes had to be written by someone. Why? Because, as I have mentioned, atoms don't float around loaded with operating system code. For example, the carbon atoms in your pencil do not contain bacterial genetic code. None of the atoms found in nature come loaded with bacterial genetic code (the first living machine was a bacterium). I'm afraid this is never going to randomly happen in the real world. Random luck is never going to write even one single letter of intelligent instructional code! In fact, random luck is never going to write one single letter of nonsense code either. For those of you who have ever meticulously written computer code, I believe you can readily understand that code is never going to just write itself.

And natural selection can't be the hero that saves the day here because dead molecules can't experience the phenomenon of natural selection. In addition to this, natural selection does not possess the ability, the power, nor the brains, to write intelligent instructional code. Once again, natural selection is not the magical fairy dust that makes this fantasy come to life in the real world.

Natural selection is simply the ability of an organism to survive better than its neighbors because of biological improvements caused by lucky errors in DNA replication.

We need to realize that natural selection does not write genetic code. The changes to genetic code (mutations) are what causes the organism to be naturally selected to survive better, not the other way around. Natural selection does not cause the genetic code mutations, the genetic code mutations cause the natural selection. It is very important for people to realize that natural selection can never be claimed to be how genetic code first appeared.

This raises the question: Why would the oceans of early Earth suddenly decide to get into the business of writing instructional code? Why would dead molecules suddenly become so determined and motivated that they learned how to start writing intelligent instructional code? It should be clear that dead molecules don't have the brains to write instructional genetic code. I'm afraid none of this makes any sense, especially once you get to the point where intelligent operating system code is needed.

This means that if you ever come across someone who is talking about self-copying molecules, or self-replicating molecules, they are talking about something they can't prove, something that would have to be manufactured through the manipulation of artificial selection in a lab, and something they are claiming possessed the presence of intelligent instructional codes.

Regarding the speculative topic of self-replicating molecules, we are not just talking about the magical appearance of an identical molecule. We are also talking about making a copy of the original molecule's code and then transferring that coded data to the duplicated molecule. This process is extremely complicated and requires the act of duplicating and transferring code. Therefore, self-copying molecules never existed because the multiple layers of necessary codes never existed.

This article also states that some of these self-copying molecules would be better at surviving than their neighbors.[158] The key words here are, "**would be.**" The author can't claim self-copying molecules

WERE better at surviving because he can't prove they even existed. As a consequence, the author has to say these theoretical molecules *would be better*, instead of stating that they *were better*. What can be seen in this statement, is that attempts are being made to apply the phenomenon of natural selection to dead molecules that are claimed to self-replicate. This article also claims that sometimes the replications would make errors.[159] This is an attempt to claim that the necessary diversity (change) was present for an evolutionary process to occur.

Let me pause here and ask a question. What if we observe many mounds of dirt in a field, but after a rainstorm only two mounds of dirt remain. At that point, can we say the two mounds of dirt 'survived' better than their neighbors? Can we claim the two mounds of dirt experienced the effects of natural selection because they 'survived'? And because the mounds of dirt 'changed' shape as a result of the rainstorm, can we also claim diversity and variability occurred? If so, these mounds of dirt could be claimed to be evolving because they experienced diversity coupled with natural selection. And if new mounds of dirt appeared, could we also claim reproduction occurred? As you can clearly see, if we stopped being sensible, it could be argued these mounds of dirt experienced the two requirements for an evolutionary process (change/diversity and natural selection).

Clearly this is ridiculous. With that being said, mounds of evolving dirt are no more ridiculous than clumps of evolving molecules. Once again, **dead things can't be naturally selected**. Therefore, if mounds of dirt can't experience natural selection and diversity because they are dead things and can't actively compete for survival, then a lifeless molecule can't evolve either. Lifeless objects can't participate in the active living processes of natural selection and the mutating of genetic code during reproduction.

If a molecule is fortunate enough to continue to exist compared to the fate other molecules, this is merely the product of chance. Dead things can only seem to get lucky because they can't actively compete for survival. Luck does not qualify as a guidance system. Only living organisms can be naturally selected. We need to be mindful that natural selection did not even exist until after life began.

In addition, the absence of genetic code prevents the claim that replications would make errors. Replication errors can only occur with genetic code. Therefore, the genetic diversity required for an evolutionary process is impossible in the absence of instructional code. As I have stated before, dead molecules and the ocean water are not ever going to write even one single letter of precise instructional code, let alone, millions of lines of intelligent instructional code! In addition, because there was no genetic material for self-copying and self-replication, this means "offspring" never existed. To be quite frank, none of this had any chance of randomly occurring in the real world.

Here is an updated list of fatal flaws contained in the hypothesis of abiogenesis:

1) Lifeless molecules can't compete for survival, so they can't be naturally selected. This means dead things can't survive better than their neighbors. **Dead things don't survive, they exist.**

2) Lifeless molecules can't convert part of themselves into an information storing segment like DNA.

3) Lifeless molecules can't write genetic instructional code for themselves.

4) Lifeless molecules can't self-copy/self-replicate because this includes duplicating genetic instructional code which did not exist. In addition, the genetic codes commanding replication and transfer of the operating system information did not exist either.

This is just a short list of the many reasons why the scheme of abiogenesis is impossible. There are many more reasons. For example, another reason that just came to mind is referred to as **Eigen's Paradox** which states:

> Accurate replication requires complex machinery. But to make complex replicators through evolution requires accurate replication-a chicken-and-egg problem (a catch-22). **There's no real evidence yet of experimental systems that solve Eigen's Paradox.**[160]

As you can see here, an accurate replicator requires complex machinery, but then the complex machinery first requires an accurate replicator. Eigen's Paradox confirms that the hypothesis of abiogenesis is stuck in a Catch-22. Abiogenesis is stuck between a rock and a hard place.

We can also see from this quote that this Catch-22 problem has never been observed to be solved in nature. Once again, all of this talk about replicators, self-replication, and self-copying is just Sci-Fi fantasy. Scientific observation and reason dictate that abiogenesis does not pass the Scientific Method. In addition, scientific observation and reason dictate that abiogenesis never occurred because it is not scientifically possible for dead objects to participate in living activities that then brought them to life.

I might also add there is yet another Eigen-like paradox that exists in my opinion. I refer to it as: **The Natural Selection Paradox:**

> In the hypothesis of abiogenesis, dead molecules allegedly came together to form the first living organism through the mechanism of natural selection, but the mechanism of natural selection first requires the competition of living organisms.

This is the same type of Catch-22 we see with Eigen's Paradox.

Besides Eigen's Paradox and my Natural Selection Paradox, the pivotal reason (there are many reasons) why this is all a fantasy revolves around the fact that nothing in the oceans of early Earth was going to write intelligent instructional code. Lifeless atoms and dead molecules floating around as an organic soup are incapable of writing instructional code! The writing of intelligent instructional code is NOT what mindless atoms and molecules do as they slosh around in the churning waves of the ocean. Quite frankly, an organic soup didn't have the brains for it.

In an article titled "The Tiny Code That's Toppling Evolution," Mario Seiglie reminds us that,

> It's hard to fathom, but the amount of information in human DNA is roughly equivalent to 12 sets of the Encyclopedia Britannica, an incredible 384 volumes worth of detailed information that would fill 48 feet of library shelves![161]

Contained inside each of your cells is the amount of information that is equivalent to 48 feet of library shelf space. The first bacterial cell's DNA had 5 million nucleotides (about 161 million atoms), compared to our 3 billion base pairs of nucleotides (about 196 billion atoms). I believe that you can see the titanic claims being put forth by the abiogenesis hypothesis.

This topic of genetic code is of the utmost importance because it is this absolute need for intelligent instructional code that became the precise reason why the world's most famous atheist in recent memory became a believer in God. Dr. Anthony Flew, as you will remember from the beginning of this book, is a noted scientist and author who was an outspoken, confident atheist. Because this is so very important, I'm going to repeat that Anthony Flew is described as the world's most famous and outspoken atheist of the second half of the twentieth century.[162] Recall that in an article titled, "How the World's Most Notorious Atheist Changed His Mind," Anthony Flew was asked if he had heard a voice that made him suddenly stop being an atheist and start believing in God. Professor Flew replied,

> "No, I did not hear a voice. It was the evidence itself that led me to this conclusion."[163]

The evidence that convinced Dr. Flew, the world's most notorious and outspoken atheist, can be seen in one of his other quotes:

> With every passing year, the more that was discovered about the richness and inherent intelligence of life, the less it seemed likely that a chemical soup could magically generate the genetic code.[164]

Notice how the complexity of the genetic code is what convinced the world's most notorious atheist in modern history to change his mind and believe in God! As a consequence, the absolute need for intelligent instructional code is the most important reason why the hypothesis of abiogenesis and self-creation would never work in the real world.

Instructional operating system code is never going to write itself.

There is one more fact about Professor Flew that I would like to point out. For most of his life, Anthony Flew lived with the conviction that atheism was presumed to be the true until God could be proven to be true. In other words, religion had to meet the 'burden of proof' in order to establish the existence of God before he would believe in God. This is very important because it means Professor Flew was only going to change his mind if he deemed there was sufficient proof of God's existence. As a consequence, when Anthony Flew changed his mind, this occurred because the burden of proof had been met.

As you can see, Professor Anthony Flew didn't just change his mind. No, there was a process of proving that had to be established first, and only then, did the world's most notorious and most outspoken atheist in modern history find himself in a position where the truth of the evidence convinced him to change his mind.

Now, getting back to the P.G. Higgs article, since mutations can't occur in the absence of information storing molecules like DNA, the hypothesis of abiogenesis instead uses the term, *diversity.* This is why articles regarding the hypothesis of abiogenesis replace the term, *mutations,* with the term, *diversity.* Diversity simply means that the molecule in question, somehow wound up with its configuration changed. Since an evolutionary process requires mutations, diversity is supposed to satisfy this requirement which it fails to do.

In addition, since an evolutionary process also requires the presence of natural selection, somehow, some of these dead clumps of molecules needed to compete for survival better than their dead neighbors and then reproduce. In other words, we need to see some evidence of natural selection, which is, of course, impossible to see with lifeless objects.

After discussing diversity, Higgs states that, "… 'selection' acts on physiochemical properties, such as hydrolysis, photolysis, solubility, or surface binding."[165] Notice that Higgs simply refers to **selection**, and it is being applied to mere physiochemical properties. Since Higgs is just using the word, '*selection,*' it leads us to conclude he is referring to *artificial selection.* This is why the word, *natural,* has been left out. Therefore, it appears that Higgs is referring to artificial selection. Any artificial manipulations by a scientist in a lab are not going to qualify as a natural process that could have occurred in the oceans of early Earth.

Artificial Selection is defined as:

> Selective breeding by humans involving the selection of breeding pairs in order to produce favorable offspring.[166]

Artificial selection involves human manipulations. Therefore, any talk about 'selection' regarding the topic of abiogenesis would be discussing scientists and their manipulations in a laboratory. Human manipulations are not going to occur naturally in nature and would therefore be disqualified from the discussion of life creating itself naturally. I wish to once again clarify that if you ever see the word, *selection*, used by itself, then whatever you are reading is not referring to **natural selection**. This is why the word, *natural*, has been left out.

At this point, I need to explain what physiochemical properties are because P.G. Higgs discusses them in his article. I can say that they are like the specifics or 'specs' of your car. Your car has specifics like what make, model, year, color, automatic transmission vs. manual transmission, etc. Therefore, in the same way your car has specific details, so do atoms and molecules. A molecule has specifics like its weight or mass, odor, color appearance, density, boiling point, solubility in water, acidity, hydrolysis, photolysis, and surface binding. It is beyond the scope of this brief overview to explain all of these physiochemical properties, but you can just think of them as the 'specs' on a molecule.

My first question in this discussion is: how can we interchange the actively competitive process of natural selection with 'selection'? First of all, artificial 'selection' can't be permitted in the discussion of 'life, from non-life' (abiogenesis) because it would never happen on its own. Secondly: how can we apply any form of 'selection' to mere properties of lifeless molecules? Not only are we prevented from naturally applying 'selection' to our discussion of the abiogenesis idea, but we are also prevented from applying 'selection' to mere physical properties of lifeless molecules! This is because properties don't compete for survival, they don't reproduce, and they don't pass on instructional code that has experienced, *change.* As mentioned, the hypothesis of abiogenesis poorly substitutes mutated *change*, with *diversity.*

A lifeless molecule clump can never experience being naturally selected because competition for resources and survival does not occur with dead things. In addition, this alleged process has to occur on its own in nature and not by the hands of scientists manipulating in a lab. Therefore, if this author is actually discussing artificial selection (which is implied by him not using the term, *natural selection*), then his conversation is meaningless because he is talking about something that would not occur naturally.

Here is a list of the problems with chemical evolution before life began:

1) Molecules are dead things
2) Genetic material and DNA did not exist
3) An operating system of genetic code did not exist
4) Physiochemical properties of dead things can't experience active competition to survive. They can't experience winning survival competitions which would prove they have been rewarded with increased survival. They can't mate, they can't have offspring, and they can't pass onto offspring successful genetic advantages. In other words, dead things and their lifeless physiochemical properties can't be naturally selected.

To be quite frank, the Darwinian, evolutionary process of abiogenesis cannot occur in the absence of genetic material, in the absence of genetic code, in the absence of offspring, and in the absence of natural selection. Essentially, a Darwinian evolutionary process cannot occur in the absence of life. Once again, this is why lifeless objects can't be naturally selected. chemical evolution would never work in the real world. Chemical evolution never happened.

The hypothesis of chemical evolution not only defies logic, but it also is a violation of the Law of Non-Contradiction. This is because these molecules cannot be both dead and alive at the same time. Not only can dead things not perform living activities, but as I have mentioned, dead things cannot compete for survival and reproduce offspring. In addition, there is no coded genetic material in existence that possesses *change* on it that can be passed on to offspring. The absence of coded genetic material would also prevent any molecule configuration *diversity* from being perpetuated.

And since dead things can't have offspring, any alleged molecule configuration *diversity* couldn't be perpetuated anyway.

To re-cap: the idea of abiogenesis would never work because of the absence of genetic information, the absence of a genetic information-storing device (like DNA), the absence of offspring, the absence of natural selection, and the absence of life. As a consequence, none of the evolutionary process requirements are satisfied which means that chemical evolution fails the Scientific Method.

In his article, Higgs also states,

> . . . I argue that chemical evolution, although Darwinian, does not quite constitute life, and that a good place to put the conceptual boundary between non-life and life is between chemical and biological evolution.[167]

Paul Higgs is admitting that nothing is alive yet.[168] This tells me that we cannot apply the living process of natural selection to the lifeless properties mentioned in the chemical evolution idea. This is supported by the fact that Higgs avoids using the term, **natural selection**. Instead, he is faced with the constraint of only being able to use the term, 'selection.'

We must be aware and focused when it comes to ideas like chemical evolution in order to avoid the claim that the non-random and actively competitive process of natural selection can increase the survivability of inanimate objects. In a nutshell, dead things cannot be naturally selected. Neither can they be 'selected' on their own in the absence of deliberate artificial manipulation.

Let me ask a few questions here. Has *diversity* been created when a bag of magnets is shaken and different magnet clumpings are produced? Can I claim the conditions of 'selection' exist, even if such conditions were the product of scientists manipulating in a lab? Can I claim this 'selection' then acted on the physiochemical properties of these magnets that make them stick together? And because I now have the components of *diversity* and '*selection,*' am I now able to claim that an evolutionary process is occurring in my magnet bag? Once again, this is ignoring the artificial manipulation that was necessary.

Remembering the Dr. Samanthi article, can I claim, with evolution, these magnets performed specific structural and functional roles, interacted with each other, gained the ability to reproduce, and passed on genetic material to the next generation? And because of all this, am I then able to claim, with evolution, my magnet-shaking process will lead to the origin of life? Molecules are lifeless and essentially stick together randomly like magnets do. The answer to all these questions—of course not.

Why am I spending so much time on this? The stakes are high because this flawed hypothesis is being used to convince people this is how life came about without the presence of a Creator. This is *"science without a God."* If all these abiogenesis claims sound like a sci-fi epic, just wait.

Scientists admit that the first bacterial cell was a living machine with proteins, cell membranes, a cell wall, a capsule, ribosomes that make proteins, mitochondria that make energy, and a flagellum that is used as a propeller for movement. The first bacterial cell was a complex and integrated living machine. Up to this point, I have only been discussing DNA and its code. All of these other components also had to be fabricated and assembled in working order!

All of this is what chemical evolution is ultimately trying to support with its claim that lifeless objects gained the ability to store instructional code and reproduce themselves. Chemical evolution is meant to be the spark that explains how dead objects started engaging in living behaviors and living activities. Chemical evolution is trying to infuse living behaviors into lifeless objects in order to claim this is how they eventually brought themselves to life. I also observe how the claims of chemical evolution do not pass the Scientific Method and run counter to how the real-world works. In my opinion, the lofty claims of chemical evolution are obviously false.

It should be clear chemical evolution is attempting to infuse living characteristics into lifeless molecules first, in order to then claim the molecules engaged in living behaviors and activities which eventually brought them to life. This is science fiction. This is not the practice of sound science.

But let's not just take my word for it; let's see what respected scientists think about the first living cell and its DNA, just creating themselves. For this, I turn to Marcel P. Schutzenberger who was a famous intellect, mathematician, and medical doctor in France. He conducted research at MIT as a great mind in the field of mathematics. Concerning the first bacterial cell, Schutzenberger stated:

> . . . there is no chance (< 10^{-1000}) to see this mechanism [mutation-selection] appear spontaneously and, if it did, even less for it to remain. . .Thus, to conclude, we believe there is a considerable gap in the neo-Darwinian theory of evolution, and we believe this gap to be of such a nature that it cannot be bridged within the current conception of biology.[169]

Notice that Schutzenberger states there is no real chance to see this mechanism spontaneously appear in nature, much less remain. It's obvious that 10^{-1000} is way beyond the point of being mathematically possible. I interpret this statement to mean that abiogenesis would have effectively been impossible, based on the reality of how biology functions on planet Earth.

Murray Eden was a prominent professor of Electrical Engineering at MIT who also worked at the Harvard Medical School. Eden was deeply involved in medical advancements such as PET scanners, computed tomography, and cognitive information processing. Eden said the following about life arising randomly from non-life using known physical laws:

> It is our contention that if "random" is given serious and crucial interpretation from a probabilistic point of view, the randomness postulate is highly implausible and that an adequate scientific theory of evolution must await the elucidation of new natural laws—physical, physio-chemical and biological.[170]

Here we see that Professor Eden rejected abiogenesis and evolution's random-based ideas. I'm interpreting Eden as saying that in order for any of this to occur randomly that you would need a new set of natural laws, physical laws, biological laws, physiological laws, and chemical laws. This tells me that abiogenesis and evolution have been deemed to be highly implausible on planet Earth with its current set of natural laws.

Dr. John Grebe was a chemist and former director of the Dow Chemical Company Physical Chemistry Research Laboratory in Michigan. Dr. Grebe was also the youngest recipient of the Chemical Industry Award. This quote is from Dr. John Grebe (n.d., as cited by McDougall 2012), who stated:

> That organic evolution could account for the complex forms of life in the past and the present has long since been abandoned by men (and women) who grasp the importance of the DNA genetic code.[171]

Notice how Dr. Grebe points out that people who really understand DNA, have abandoned the ideas of abiogenesis and evolution a long time ago. This is precisely what changed the mind of the former atheist, Professor Anthony Flew!

Two esteemed scientists who worked together as a famous team are N. Chandra Wickramasinghe, a famous mathematician and astrobiologist, and Dr. Fred Hoyle, considered the "father" of stellar nucleosynthesis (stars fusing atoms). Hoyle and Wickramasinghe (1981, as cited by McDougall, 2012) have been quoted as saying:

> ...life cannot have had a random beginning...The trouble is that there are about two thousand enzymes, and the chance of obtaining them all in a random trial is only one part in 10 to the 40,000 power… this simple calculation wipes the idea entirely out of court...The enormous information content of even the simplest living systems...

cannot in our view be generated by what are often called "natural" processes...For life to have originated on the Earth it would be necessary that quite explicit instruction should have been provided for its assembly...There is no way in which we can expect to avoid the need for information....[172]

I feel it should be clear this quote from these two highly esteemed scientists is stating that the components of the first living cell could not have randomly made themselves. In addition, the ultra-complex coded information that is required could not have written itself either. Notice the chance of all this randomly occurring was calculated to be $10^{-40,000}$. I could only present a truncated version of the original quote because of word count and copyright concerns. Therefore, I highly recommend that you access the website I reference and read the entire quote. It is even more convincing than what I am able to present here.

And natural selection is not the magic fairy dust that saves the day by neutralizing the random aspect of this idea that life could create itself from non-life. As I have stated, dead things can't experience the phenomenon of natural selection. In other words, natural selection cannot be used as an argument for why the hypothesis of abiogenesis is not a fatally flawed, random process idea. As a consequence, I agree with the conviction of all of these esteemed scientists that the hypothesis of abiogenesis is a fatally flawed idea.

I would like to repeat that ocean waves, atoms, and mindless molecules don't write instructional code! That is not what they do. Because of this obvious fact regarding the idea of abiogenesis, any speculation claiming the possibility of self-replication, the involvement of 'selection,' or any other kind of contrived *selection* in the oceans of early Earth, is worthless. The fact that genetic code is never going to write itself, makes chemical evolution and the idea of abiogenesis unworthy of serious attention. It is obvious that I completely agree with the assessments and quoted statements from these esteemed scientists that I have presented. And I greatly appreciate the Dr. Wickramasinghe and Dr. Hoyle comment where they discuss the absolute need for information (code).

Here's another fascinating quote from Hoyle (n.d., as cited by McDougall, 2012):

> Life originating by chance is like believing that a tornado sweeping through a junk yard might assemble a Boeing 747 from the materials therein.[173]

I believe this quote pretty much sums it up. The reason why this quote from Hoyle is so profound, is because a tornado whipping through a typical junk yard is never going to cause the creation a fully assembled 747 jet airliner. Why? Well, in order for a jet aircraft to be formed from the trash in a typical junk yard, the trash would have to be broken down into its atomic elements, recycled into the fabricated component parts of a jet aircraft, and then precisely assembled.

Are these activities the behaviors that tornadoes are known for? No, tornadoes violently and chaotically whip things around. That is what tornadoes do. As a consequence, a tornado could never create a fully assembled and fully functional 747 jet aircraft. The simple reason why this would never occur in nature is because tornadoes do not fabricate aircraft.

I say this because there are some people who believe abiogenesis had some remote random chance to occur, even if that chance was only once. These people argue abiogenesis might be calculated to be mathematically impossible, however, if it could happen even just once, then that is all it would take to make it a reality. This argument claims that an event can occur because the event had some remote mathematical chance to happen, even it has been calculated to be ***mathematically*** impossible. My response to this claim is simple: the mathematical impossibility of a DNA molecule forming itself should be argument enough, however, the strongest argument exists where focus is placed on the fact that atoms and molecules can't write intelligent instructional code!

What we are dealing with here is the fact that molecules writing intelligent instructional code is NEVER going to happen because that is ***scientifically*** impossible. There is a difference between an event being mathematically impossible and it being scientifically impossible. There are times when that difference is enormous, like it is here. As a consequence, if an event is deemed to be scientifically impossible, then it is meaningless to attempt to calculate if it's mathematically possible. If an event is scientifically impossible, this means there is NO POSSIBILITY IT WILL OCCUR.

As a result, the argument that 'it only needs to happen once,' does not work regarding abiogenesis because atoms and molecules writing intelligent instructional code for DNA is NEVER going to happen! Why? This is because the writing of intelligent instructional code is NOT what atoms and molecules do. Atoms vibrate and bind with themselves and other atoms forming molecules. Atoms and molecules are building blocks for substances and structures. Atoms and molecules did not, are not, and will not, ever write even one single letter of intelligent instructional code! Why? Because that's not what they do, in addition, they don't have the brains for it.

ONCE AGAIN, THIS IS NOT WHAT ATOMS AND MOLECULES DO. This is just like the analogy of how the fabrication of

functional aircraft from typical junkyard debris IS NOT WHAT TORNADOES DO.

In order for the 'only needs to happen once' argument to be considered for debate, the topic of discussion has to be scientifically possible. Therefore, in the same way that tornadoes do not create jet aircraft, atoms and molecules do not create intelligent instructional code for DNA.

With this in mind, anyone who believes for even one second that atoms and molecules wrote millions of lines of instructional code, even just one time, is clearly not grasping the reality of the universe that we live in. Anyone who clings to the argument that nothing is impossible, and therefore has a chance to happen once, is not talking about hard science. The people who cling to ideas like these are not practicing hard science, and they are not respecting the Scientific Method. This means they don't have a scientific argument at all. Instead, for those people, their argument is based on pure fantasy. What they claim would be the stuff that wild fairy tales are made of.

We saw an example of this type of thinking with Nobel Prize winner George Wald who stated that the existence of a Creator had been scientifically proven. However, because he did not philosophically like that fact, he chose to believe in the alternative which he admitted had been proven to be scientifically false. Thank goodness most top scientists don't abandon scientific observation and reason like this.

We don't live in a universe where atoms and molecules have the magical power to write intelligent instructional code. Therefore, for those who wish to cling to the argument that anything can happen once, I argue this has been proven false by the instructional code stored on DNA. Millions of lines of code will never write themselves. This is the precise reason why the world's most notorious and outspoken atheist changed his mind. Professor Anthony Flew refused to live in a fantasy world any longer. He finally decided to accept the truth of the scientific evidence regarding DNA.

This raises the question: How many millions of lines of code did that first living machine have to make it do everything that it did? It stands to reason that if DNA is much more complex than a Microsoft operating system, then there were tens of millions of lines of code needed for the first living machine. Here is a question to ask atheists: where did all of that code come from? Did the ocean write millions of lines of exact code just for DNA? We know that natural selection can't write code. Besides, natural selection did not even exist until *after* living organisms appeared.

I have one more point to mention. Abiogenesis claims the information storing molecule DNA was the product of an evolutionary process. If this were the case, then why didn't that powerful evolutionary process randomly produce other exotic forms of information storing molecules? Why didn't abiogenesis randomly invent ENA, FNA, and GNA? There is no possible explanation for why abiogenesis would have stopped randomly producing information storing molecules once it made DNA.

Random and mindless concepts don't know when to stop. Abiogenesis should have continued indefinitely producing a wide variety of exotic information storing molecules. But instead, DNA is the only one. Why didn't DNA itself, evolve into more advanced splintered-off versions? Why hasn't macroevolution spawned the production of new and advanced species of information storing molecules? DNA is the mother species of information storing molecules that should have spawned the evolutionary production of new evolved versions of information storing molecules.

All the species in the Fossil Record contain DNA. If evolution was a reality, then we would be seeing newly evolved versions of information storing molecules over time. And we don't see that at all. The species of the double stranded information storing molecule that we identify as DNA, has never evolved to become more advanced!

The fact that DNA is the only information storing molecule in existence, supports that a Creator is responsible. This is because a Creator would have known that only one type of information storing molecule was necessary. While if a mindless process was at work, we should have numerous and continuous, random versions of information storing molecules in existence. Intelligent design only needs one version. A mindless process would have randomly kept evolving and would still be evolving.

Now that we have debunked the hypothesis of abiogenesis, it's time to examine the theory of evolution in the next chapter. I think you will find its contents to be quite surprising.

CHAPTER FIVE

Evolution Theory

Let me start by saying that I concentrate on the theory of evolution as much as I do because I estimate 40-50% of the world refuses to believe in God because they believe the science of a self-driven evolution makes God unnecessary. Otherwise, I would not have any particular interest in the theory of evolution if it had no influence on whether people believed in God or not.

If believing in the theory of evolution had no impact on believing in God, then the only debate would be whether God set evolution into motion in order to produce all the species vs. God creating each and every species individually. If no one was being driven away from believing in God, then most of us would not think twice about the theory of evolution. However, this is not the case at all.

Many people are using the theory of evolution as their reason to reject God. As a result, this puts the topic of evolution front and center as a supremely important topic that needs to be thoroughly investigated. It is a sad reality that billions of people are using the theory of evolution to deny the existence of God. However, once this theory is revealed to be false, that demonstration of falsehood will inherently and ironically prove the existence of a Creator! As a consequence, the scientific facts listed in this chapter are going to be very surprising to countless people who believe that evolution is a fact.

The facts that happen to be repeated in this chapter are focused on delivering to you the scientific facts that contradict what you have been led to believe for your entire life. With that said, let's dive into the facts regarding evolution theory. In a nutshell, the theory of evolution claims that all species on the earth evolved from bacteria. Is this true, or is this a Sci-Fi fantasy?

To begin to answer this question, let's start with *molecular evolution* which basically refers to the genetic mutation errors that occur during reproduction. It is beyond the scope of this book to discuss all the steps in this process, but suffice it to say, that DNA must be duplicated in the reproductive process. It's a fact that errors occur in this complicated duplication process. The genetic errors that occur are called molecular evolution because the errors occur at the level of the molecules. Molecular evolution looks at changes at the level of the DNA and changes to proteins.[174] Therefore, accidental molecular errors during DNA replication are what constitute the mutations. I will be ignoring accidental DNA changes created by radiation.

Now, we need to remember from the last chapter that an evolutionary process has two requirements. Those two requirements are mutations and natural selection. If either one of these requirements is not present, then an evolutionary process is not possible. And according to the theory of evolution, positive mutations will be rewarded by *positive* natural selection which experiences increased survival success and reproduction. Conversely, negative mutations will be weeded out by *negative* natural selection which has a lower success for survival. And this raises the question: Did all of these mutations really occur billions upon billions of times (possibly trillions of times) in order to generate all of the billions of various species that have ever lived on the earth?

To investigate the answer to this question, we can start by looking at how many mutations occur in a human newborn. Geneticist Philip Awadalla and his team have determined that an average of 30 mutations are passed on to the newborn from each parent which amounts to about 60 mutations total.[175] So how many of these mutations are bad, and how many are good? Genetic Researcher J. Flegr states:

> … there are incomparably more negative mutations than positive mutations.[176]

Because there are "incomparably" more negative mutations, this means there are significantly more negative errors than positive errors. Most of the mutations are neutral, while the majority of the rest are negative. Only rarely does a positive mutation occur.

With that being said, let's look at two species that are supposed to be directly related through the theory of evolution, humans (Homo sapiens) and Homo erectus. Humans are claimed to have evolved directly from Homo erectus.[177] When we look at Homo erectus, it has a very ape-like head and its brain is significantly smaller. To turn a primitive Homo erectus brain into a super-computer human brain and completely change the skull is going to take an enormous amount of neurologic and engineering work.

So how many mutations would it have taken to significantly increase the brain size of a Homo erectus and produce a human super-computer brain? Also, how many bony mutations would it take to turn an ape-like head into a human skull? If this had really occurred, let's say it would have required 100 positive mutations all pointed in the same direction to finally wind up with a super-computer brain and a streamlined skull like ours. Those would just be the *positive* mutations. We know from Flegr there would be "incomparably more negative mutations."[178]

It's safe to say that if we add up all of the neutral, negative, and positive mutations, we are probably looking at an incredible number of mutations. All these mutations would be necessary to hypothetically produce the 100 (estimated) very specific, baby-step, positive mutations necessary to convert a Homo erectus into a Homo sapiens.

When someone is mining for gold, they have to process tons of rock and rubble before they get just one ounce of gold. In this case, countless mutations are needed to be sifted through to reach just one positive human-like mutation. And we would still need 99 more very specific mutations in exactly the right direction.

What else do we know about Homo erectus? Researcher Dennis O'Neil tells us that Homo ergaster allegedly evolved into Homo habilis, who evolved into Homo erectus. Then, Homo heidelbergensis, Neanderthals, and Homo sapiens (humans) all evolved from Homo erectus.[179] Homo heidelbergensis, Neanderthals, and Homo sapiens are all allegedly cousins that did not evolve from each other because they were all allegedly spawned from Homo erectus. Therefore, humans allegedly mutated from Homo erectus, not from the Neanderthals. O'Neil states:

> Homo erectus was a very successful human species, lasting
> at least 1.5 million years, though their numbers appar-
> ently remained relatively low. Some of them eventually
> evolved into our species, Homo sapiens.[180]

Here is my next question: If Homo erectus was present in such low numbers, then how do you get a high enough birth rate to cause the epic transformation from an ape-like skull with a small brain to a human skull with a significantly larger super-computer brain? There would have to be many miraculous genetic mutations (for the better!) to change an ape-like skull with a smaller brain into a modern human skull with a significantly larger brain. Some researchers estimate that a human brain is at least 30% larger than the brain of a Homo erectus.[181] I've even seen estimates that our brain is 50% larger.

Humans have had over 10 billion births during the last 100 years, and none of them are evolving mankind into another species. Out of 10 billion human births, none of them has hit the newspaper headlines as being the very first mutation exhibited by humans that is starting us on the long road to spawning a brand-new species. That being said, there are some rare examples of beneficial mutations scattered throughout the human gene pool. We see millions of examples of negative mutations causing birth defects and disabilities, but we only rarely see any examples of positive mutations occurring.

It is estimated that one in every 33 human infants is born with a birth defect.[182] That is more than 300 million infants who have born with birth defects over the last 100 years. Therefore, after 10 billion human births, I see no evidence at all, of a Darwinian evolutionary model that is fueled by a steady stream of positive mutations. Once again, the idea of evolution would never work in the real world, and as a matter of fact, it doesn't work in the real world.

With that said, how many hundreds of millions or billions of births would be needed to produce a chain of positive mutations that would produce a much larger refined super-computer brain along with all the other skull refinements to turn an ape-like Homo erectus hominid into a human? I ask: How many human births would it take to generate mutation No. 1 on the long list of specific positive mutations necessary to demonstrate that the evolution theory model is correct in seeding brand-new species? How many billions of human births would such a concept require?

At present, there is a negligible rate of positive mutations witnessed in 10 billion births. Would we be talking about needing hundreds of billions of births? Would we be talking trillions of births? And this is just to get the very first "new species" mutation. We would still need 99 more, very specific, positive mutations in exactly the right direction in order to theoretically create a brand-new species. Do you see the extreme reproduction capacity that would be required to make a concept like this work in the real world?

Now, getting back to Homo erectus, not only do we need the brain size and the skull's structural engineering to change, but we also need both of them to change *at the same time*. We are not talking about just one focused and directional mutation here. We need two components to simultaneously mutate in tandem. What are the odds of that? And one of those focused mutations fits *inside of* the other focused mutation. This is not the hallmark of random activity. If evolution took place, then both the brain and the skull would have needed to mutate in tandem to accomplish this very specific, highly engineered, and intelligent goal.

Referring back to Dennis O'Neil's quote, to get those kinds of quantum leaps in cerebral genetic upgrades, a *relatively low number* for Homo erectus is never going to work. And this miracle is not claimed to have happened just once; it is claimed to have happened three times! Homo erectus is supposed to have spawned humans (Homo sapiens), Homo neanderthalensis, and Homo heidelbergensis. Can you imagine the ultra-extreme number of births needed to fuel a random process like this three times? And we are only talking about the production of three species here. Can you imagine the reproductive requirements to produce billions of species through a concept like this?

The fact the upgrades to the hominids concentrated on their brains demonstrates that these changes were not haphazard, and they were not aimless. The concentrated brain improvements seen in the hominids demonstrate they were not the result of a random process. On the contrary, this concentration of advancements is a hallmark of intelligent design.

Now, let's analyze if a random process was really at work with Homo erectus. Let's say the first tiny mutation involved the brain. That mutant would have to splinter off forming a new family line. Why can't the next advancing mutation in this individual's new family line have been a small change in their descendant's backs starting the long process of sprouting wings (like the *Wizard of Oz* flying monkeys)? Then, the third mutation in this family line could have been a tiny mutation trying to sprout a third arm, while the fourth mutation could have been trying to sprout a third eye in the back of their head. How many body parts does a hominid have?

Yet, the differences seen between the hominids are localized to their brain and the skull that protects it. The fact that all of the alleged significant hominid mutations concentrate on the brain and its protecting skull, should eliminate the possibility that a random, error-based process occurred.

Mutations occurring on other parts of the body have every right to be naturally selected just like the first tiny mutation of the brain in our example mutant. Any change that increases survivability is going to be naturally selected, not just the ones concentrating on the brain and skull. This is why we should be seeing mutations all over the body of Homo erectus. But instead, the alleged mutations producing humans are concentrated on the brain and its protecting skull. That does not make any logical sense if a random process was at work.

The theory of evolution mandates that countless mutations were required for the production of the billions of species that have lived on the earth. In order to do this, each species that spawned a new species would have had a member of its population born a mutant. Then that mutant would have somehow formed a pocket of mutants that splintered off from the general population and experienced countless mutations that eventually produced a brand-new and distinct species. This hypothetical activity leaves the original species intact.

Let's pause here to clarify the theory of evolution. This idea of splintering off a new species is technically defined as *speciation*.[183] *Speciation* starts off with one species and ends up with two. In comparison, Darwin's original theory focused on the gradual transformation of one species into another, which is referred to as *phyletic transformation*. Darwin's main theory starts off with one species and ends up with one new species that is, of course, *changed*. Darwin's main mode of *change* did not turn one species into two. Therefore, what we presently refer to as evolution theory is actually a combination of speciation and phyletic transformation.[184]

In addition, there are a few more terms I would like to introduce. The term, *genotype*, refers to an organism's genetic code. While *phenotype*, refers an organism's physical appearance resulting from its genetics (genotype) being influenced by the effects of the environment.[185] It is my understanding that classic Darwinism concentrates more on genotype changes over time (purely genetic), while neo-Darwinism adds to this by also taking into consideration environmental influences that can affect survival, along with odd genetic mishaps that increase variability.

I will next discuss what is referred to as a *gene*. "A *gene* is a section of DNA that encodes for a trait."[186] That section of DNA is a series of nucleotides bonded together. One online research source states that for the typical human gene, at least 300 nucleotide pairs are needed to code for the most-simple type of gene. While the most complicated genes can require more than 1 million nucleotide pairs.[187] Clearly, one nucleotide pair is not enough to encode for a physical trait. We need many nucleotides connected together in a specific order to provide the space to store all the compiled information necessary to cause the physical manifestation of a trait.

If there is a subtle shifting of nucleotides that code for a gene, this is referred to as an, *allele*. An allele is technically an error (mutation) and can be viewed as a variant of the gene. An allele can be seen as a different variety of the same genetic trait. An allele is a mutation, but because it is not extreme and catastrophic, it constitutes a functional variant. Here is an example. Suppose someone has three pairs of shoes that are all the same style, but each is a different color. All three pairs of shoes function the same, but their differing colors makes them variants (different alleles). When the process of reproduction occurs, there is a combination of the mother's gene/allele and the father's gene/allele for that physical trait. It is this combination of genes/alleles for a particular gene in an organism that makes up their genotype (genetic code).

That said, let's get back to my discussion analyzing the concept of how Homo erectus was supposed to have spawned humans. This alleged process would need a Homo erectus female to give birth to a mutant. Well, how would this early mutant then mate and pass on its advantage? Only members of the same species can mate, by definition, right? In this situation, the very first mutation would not change the individual into a new species yet. That is allegedly going to take countless more mutations to do. As a result, this mutant who possesses mutation #1, is going to wind up mating with another member of the population who is normal. Remember, we still need countless more mutations in exactly the right direction to create a brand-new species.

However, one of the many fatal flaws with this concept of evolution involves randomness. When it comes to the idea of Darwinian evolution, when a mutant is born, that mutant becomes the matriarch (the Mother) or the patriarch (the Father) of an alleged new family line. The only way the alleged new family line can progress toward becoming a brand-new species is if all the later positive mutations occur, and are concentrated in, that new family. In addition, all those positive mutations must be concentrated in one area in order to add together. That means all the mutations have to have the same ultimate goal, like developing a larger brain. Humans have a significantly larger brain compared to Homo erectus.

Well, that is never going to happen in the real world because randomness would scatter later mutations out and around to the rest of the normal population members. In addition, later mutations could be any kind of mutation, not just brain size mutations.

Let me give an example relating to how the human species would have had to split off from the Homo erectus species. Now, to start this alleged process off, a Homo erectus female has to give birth to an infant that has a slightly larger brain than everyone else in the population. Since this is going to result in the infant being naturally selected to survive and thrive better than all the other members in the population, natural selection has occurred. This mutation is like winning the lottery. As a result, this infant is now the elder of a new family line.

Now, since this new family will still need at least 100 more positive mutations to produce a brand-new species, that's like this new family needing to win the lottery about 100 more times! Well, that is never going to happen in the real world. In the real world, 100 different families would win a lottery that is played 100 times. One family is not going to have a monopoly on winning the lottery every time. This is because winning the lottery is a random event, just like mutations are random events.

But the situation is even worse than this for the concept of evolution because not only does one family have to win the lottery 100 times in a row, but the lottery numbers have to always be only one digit greater than the last ticket's winning number. I say this because the same type of mutation must always occur which is just one tiny step improved from the last one. In this case, the mutations have to be focused on just the brain size. We can't have the next mutation trying to grow a third arm, webbed fingers, or wings on their backs.

I believe this lottery example is a great one because, as I have mentioned, looking at the last 10 billion human births, none of them has hit the headlines as being the first positive, natural selection mutation, that has produced and splintered off a new family line that will eventually become a super-human species. Clearly, the odds of winning a standard lottery are much, much better than attempting to win the evolution lottery, even just once. I personally estimate the odds of winning the evolution lottery just once, to be hundreds of millions to one. And this lottery would have to be won 100 times in a row, with each winning ticket just one digit different from the last winning ticket. Only in this way would the next mutation be the same type of mutation as the last one, allowing it to compliment and add to the last mutation.

As a consequence, splitting off a brand-new species is like one family winning the lottery 100 times in a row with the lottery numbers being different by only one digit, every single time. That is never going to happen! Why? Because winning the lottery is a random event in the same way that accidental mutations are random events.

Because mutations are random, when a second mutation occurs in a population it would have the likelihood of being in a normal member that has nothing to do with the original mutant member who experienced the first mutation. In addition, that second population mutation would be different from the first population mutation. Now we have two different mutations in the population being spread by two different families. As you can see, there is no way to predict or guide random accidental errors that occur in the duplication of DNA during reproduction.

Random mutations are not going to be concentrated in just one family. The first mutant and his/her offspring do not have a monopoly on any future random mutations. Random mutations can occur in any individual at any time throughout the entire population. Every population member has an equal opportunity to experience mutations from their parents. If we are to give any respect to the word, *random,* then one family is not going to concentrate all of the population's mutations just on themselves. In addition to this, all of the mutations are not going to concentrate on just one body part (the brain).

It's worth mentioning that some mutations occur after conception when the fertilized egg begins replicating its DNA during rapid cell division which is necessary to transform and grow the fertilized egg into a fetus. This could happen in anyone. In addition, random mutations can affect any part of a person's body. In order to create a brand-new species, focused biological improvements have to occur, not random ones. It's like one family winning the lottery 100 times. This will never happen. In addition, this super-miracle winning streak of 100 lotteries in a row was supposed to have happened not once, but more than five billion times in order to produce over five billion species from one original species.

This evolution idea seems riddled with holes that does not really make sense when you carefully analyze it. Therefore, I feel it should be evident that the evolutionary mutant concept of populating the entire planet with billions of different species from one species would never work in the real world. Remember, evolution is merely a theory, it is not an established scientific fact.

The only way to solve this problem of starting a new animal species is to have one male and one female with exactly the same genetic species code at the beginning. Posed with the need for this initial condition, I find it extremely interesting this problem is perfectly solved in the Book of Genesis where one male and one female of the same genetic make-up are paired to perpetuate that particular species.

Getting back to our discussion, let me present another example that is alleged to have occurred. All dogs are claimed to have evolved from wolves. Now, imagine a female wolf giving birth to an offspring that has a tiny change somewhere on its body. Let's say this initial mutant (somehow?) accomplishes a monopoly on mutations such that all subsequent mutations are concentrated on its new family line (contradicting the word, random). Anyway, this (non-random) activity would eventually lead to a chain of mutations in its offspring making them a few millimeters shorter than the other members of the population. The initial mutation is so subtle that it is not even perceptible.

The very first mutation in the initial mutant in this population, qualifies as **mutant intermediate #1**. Let's call this initial mutant offspring, 'Newbie.' Well, this 'Newbie' mutant is now going to be the first member that allegedly forms a pocket of mutants that splinters off from wolves. This new mutant family needs to somehow be 'lucky' enough to keep experiencing all the mutations necessary to convert a wolf into a dog. (Of course, in the real world, mutations would be randomly scattered all over the general population).

Anyway, the early mutations would be subtle. And over a long period of time, we would (allegedly) eventually see enough subtle changes accumulate that eventually increase the survival of the pocket of 'Newbie' mutants. Then, many more mutations would occur until the members of this pocket community eventually become the first dog species. That is the theory.

I see a problem with this claim regarding survival and success. How could a dog-like mutant survive better than a wolf? Wolves occupy a greater diversity of habitats than dogs can.[188] Since wolves are much more powerful than dogs are, it's no wonder that wolves are better at surviving in the wild. In the wild, a dog is not going to survive better than the more widely adapted and more powerful wolf. In the context of survival-based natural selection (survival of the fittest), wolves would have evolved from dogs, not the other way around. This means a dog-like mutant should have experienced **negative natural selection** where the 'Newbie' mutant family did not survive as well as their more powerful wolf neighbors. As a consequence, the 'Newbie' family line would have quickly died out and gone extinct.

The claim that dogs evolved from wolves through natural selection does not make any evolutionary sense because it would mandate the dog-like mutants were more successful and better at surviving than their more powerful wolf neighbors. This is clearly not the case. Therefore, in the context of the Darwinian model, this does not appear to make any sense and represents a contradiction. This is just one more problem regarding natural selection that gets added to the long list of reasons why macroevolution would never work in the real world. It's no wonder why so many experts have abandoned the neo-Darwinian model of evolution theory.

The next issue with evolution is something we can all observe. It is a fact that none of the earth's species are evolving into something else right now. Presently there are 8 million species on the earth. Evolution theory is a random and continual process, and it should be randomly chugging along right now. I should be able to see at least 1% of today's 8 million species (that's 80,000 species) with pockets of mutants in the middle of an evolutionary process. And that is only 1% of the current species number.

I should see a pocket of mutants where each member is 50% bear and 50% mutant. I should see a pocket of mutants where each member is 25% elephant and 75% mutant. I should see a pocket of mutants where each member is 75% horse and 25% mutant. A mindless and random process like evolution is not going to have a cut-off switch. It would never stop. Heck, it is claimed to have been evolving along for billions of years since the time of the first bacterium. There is no reason that can possibly exist to explain why there are no mutants roaming the earth right now!

The excuse that the conditions on the earth are different now compared to early Earth will not suffice as an explanation. That is because Homo erectus allegedly spawned three species, and the last one was just a few hundred thousand years ago (humans). The conditions on Earth are basically the same now as they were then. This begs the question: Why aren't there any living examples in the process of forming a brand-new species through evolution?

Anyone who believes in evolution will have to answer the question: Why don't we see any pockets of mutants of any species class in existence today? Where are the random pockets of mutants that are splintering off and *evolving* into new species? Where's the evolution? Evolution theory claims to be a random and continuous, mutant producing machine. There is no plausible reason why there are no mutants roaming the earth right now. The physical evidence to support the theory of evolution does not exist. It is the complete absence of obviously required evidence that scientifically proves evolution never occurred.

Some of us may remember that fast-food restaurant commercial from the 1980s where the woman shouts, **"Where's the beef?"** Well, I'm shouting, **"Where's the evolution?"**

Not only are there no living examples of evolution, but there are no dead examples either. It turns out that the fossil evidence for such a scheme is lacking. Dr. Michael Ebifegha holds a Ph.D. in Physics from the University of Toronto and a master's degree in Applied Geophysics from Ahmadu Bello University, Nigeria. In his book titled, *The Death of Evolution*, Dr. Ebifegha states:

> At a fundamental level of molecular structure, each member of a class seems equally representative of that class, and no species appear to be in any real sense "intermediate" between two classes. Nature, in sum, appears to be profoundly discontinuous.[189]

It turns out that there has never been any fossil evidence discovered of population members that were in-between two species. There are no mutant intermediates to speak of. There are no examples of mutants in the fossil record that link any two species. A T-Rex is 100 percent T-Rex, and a Raptor is 100 percent Raptor. All the species are of their *own kind* (like in the Book of Genesis). There is no fossil evidence of any evolutionary mutant intermediates. One species did not morph into another, otherwise, we would have fossil evidence of this littering the earth. And no such fossil evidence exists.

I'm sure we have all heard someone mention, "The Missing Link." Well, the truth of the matter is, ALL THE LINKS ARE MISSING! This paleontology research is severely important because it reveals a crucial fact that I was never aware of when I agreed to become a believer in evolution. Had my attention been drawn to the fact that no mutant fossils have ever been found that validate the theory of evolution, then I would have immediately deemed evolution to be an impossible theory.

This is devastating news for the theory of evolution. But let's not just take Dr. Ebifegha's word for it, Charles Darwin, the father of evolution theory, had this to say about the lack of mutant intermediate evidence (1859):

> The number of intermediate varieties, which have formerly existed on the earth, (must) be truly enormous. Why then is not every geological formation and every stratum full of such intermediate links? Geology assuredly does not reveal such finely graduated organic chain; and this, perhaps, is the most obvious and gravest objection which can be urged against my theory (Darwin, 1859, p. 292).[190]

And this is exactly right! Even Charles Darwin admitted that the earth should be littered all over with fossils of mutant intermediates if his theory were correct. You can see this confused him when he found that they don't exist. You will also notice that he admits the absence of these mutant skeleton fossils represents an obvious and grave objection to his evolution idea (macroevolution idea). The reason why the missing mutant fossils is a grave fact, is because you can't have a mutant process without any mutants!

It is clear to me that Charles Darwin knew this evolution idea was false as he is admitting the obvious and grave flaw. The word, 'grave,' essentially means to be dead. When Darwin used the word, *grave*, to describe his own theory, he was admitting that it was a dead concept. Hence, Dr. Ebifegha's book, *The Death of Evolution*, represents the reality of this failed idea. It is important to note that nothing has improved for Darwin's theory even after looking for mutant intermediates for the last 160 years.

You will also notice from his quote that he admits his evolution idea is only a theory. Evolution is not an established scientific fact! The theory of evolution will never become an established scientific fact because the evidence for it does not exist. And, of course, the evidence would most certainly exist if it occurred. This is what Darwin was stating in his quote.

Let's list the key points stated by the 'father of evolution' in his critical and revealing quote:

1) Notice that Darwin uses the word, *theory*, at the end of his quote. His evolution idea is only a theory. Evolution is not a scientific fact. Evolution was not established to be a scientific fact in 1859 when Darwin wrote his book about evolution, and to this day, it still is not an established scientific fact. Many people are unaware of this extremely important reality.

2) Darwin admits that in order for his theory to be true, there has to be a truly enormous number of mutated intermediates that must exist. He expected to find this evidence in every geologic formation and in every surface layer of the earth's crust. Did Darwin find this mountain of mutant evidence? No, just the opposite, he admits the absence of this mandatory evolution evidence.

3) He points out that this absence of evolution evidence is obvious.

4) This obvious scientific observation can be used to urge grave objections against his idea.

The fact that Charles Darwin made this quote should already tell people what they need to know when it comes to the reality of evolution theory. Charles Darwin tells you everything that you need to know about the concept of evolution, right here, in this single quote!

Over the course of the earth's lifespan between 5 and 50 billion species have lived here.[191] The theory of evolution claims they are all descendants of one original species. If this were the case, we would be tripping over mutant fossils because they would completely litter the earth. Charles Darwin essentially stated this when he proclaimed in frustration that he should be finding these mutant intermediates in every geologic formation, but instead, he found this was not the case.[192] Not only was Darwin frustrated because of not finding mutants in the Fossil Record, but Darwin was embarrassed by what he did find in the Fossil Record.[193]

In fact, as Darwin's investigations continued to fail to discover fossil evidence of mutants, he went on to say:

> If it could be demonstrated that any complex organ existed which could not possibly have been formed by numerous successive slight modifications, my theory would absolutely breakdown (Darwin, 1859, Battson, n.d.).[194]

And this "breakdown" is precisely what we observe from the scientific evidence. The evidence reveals that numerous, successive, slightly modified mutants, **do not exist** in the Fossil Record. As a consequence, the theory of evolution set forth by Charles Darwin absolutely breaks down as a failed idea.

We can all clearly see that Darwin could not find fossil evidence of mutants in the Fossil Record. This agrees with the fact that Dr. Ebifegha did not find any evidence of mutants either. But the cold hard facts stacked against evolution get even worse once we come to the realization that further evidence of not finding Darwinian evolution comes from Dr. David M. Raup and Dr. Henry Morris. Both of these esteemed scientists are world-renowned.

Dr. Henry Morris holds a Ph.D. in Engineering and Dr. David M. Raup holds a Ph.D. in Geology from Harvard and served as the Curator of Geology at the great Chicago Field Museum of Natural History. Dr. Raup has also taught at Johns Hopkins. Dr. Michael Foote, a highly respected professor in Geophysical Sciences at the University of Chicago, has this to say regarding Dr. Raup:

> Dr. Raup is a world-renowned expert in the fields of geology and paleontology and is considered by most, to be one of the most influential paleontologists of the second half of the 20th century.[195]

Dr. Foote, (n.d., as cited in Koppes, 2015) also had this to say about Dr. Raup:

> In the areas he chose to touch, nobody, in my view, surpassed him.[196]

Dr. Charles Marshall holds a Ph.D. in Evolutionary Biology from the University of Chicago and was director of the University of California's Museum of Paleontology. He was also professor of Integrative Biology at UC Berkeley. Dr. Marshall is quoted as stating:

> David Raup ushered in a renaissance in paleontology.[197]

I mention what these esteemed scientists had to say about Dr. Raup because I will be concentrating on an article Dr. Raup published regarding problems with Darwin's theory of evolution. That article is titled, "Conflicts between Darwin and Paleontology." Dr. Raup made his own observations regarding mutant intermediates, and Dr. Henry Morris made this statement regarding Dr. Raup's conclusions:

> He candidly acknowledges the complete absence of transitional forms in the fossil record and the complete absence of evidence for observable progressive evolution.[198]

What we can see here is that Charles Darwin, Dr. Ebifegha, Dr. Morris, and Dr. Raup, all failed to find evidence of mutant intermediates or any other evidence necessary to validate progressive Darwinian evolution.

This is crucial because there cannot be billions of species produced through billions and billions of mutations if there are no fossilized skeletons of any mutants to prove this! All of the countless fossilized mutant skeletons are not going to hide themselves while only leaving behind the evidence of the final species. Sure, most of the skeletons would not wind up being fossilized, but even a small percentage of billions upon billions of mutants still equals a tremendous number of fossilized mutants. Darwin confirms this when he states that we should be finding a truly enormous number of mutated intermediate fossils in the earth's crust. Instead, reality proves that we have no fossilized mutants to speak of demonstrating progressive evolution.

Charles Darwin predicted that he would find countless numbers of mutant intermediates in every layer of the earth's crust.[199] Dr. Raup stated that Darwin was embarrassed by the fact he didn't find any such evidence to support his (macroevolution) theory.[200] The Fossil Record consists of specimens and remnant specimens of about 250,000 distinct species that have been identified.[201] By contrast, there are no specimens or remnant specimens of any mutants that are evolutionarily in-between any two species in the Fossil Record. This obvious fact cannot be explained away by anyone who believes in the theory of evolution. Bottom line, you can't have a mutant process that is claimed to have populated the entire planet that is teaming with life, without any mutants! The absence of mutants means the absence of a mutant process, it's that simple.

Dr. Raup also stated the Fossil Record confronted Darwin's theory with several problems. Here is what Dr. Raup confirmed:

> There were several problems, but the principal one was that the geologic record (Fossil Record) did not then and still does not yield a finely graduated chain of slow and progressive evolution.[202]

All of these facts confirm that Darwinian evolution is a failed theory. Regardless, many scientists still claim the Fossil Record indicates evolution occurred simply because of the presence of *change*. This is based on the observation that the list of species alive today differs from the list of species that lived millions of years ago. This difference in species types is being claimed to be the product of evolution resulting from gradualistic and progressive mutations. Only in this way would it qualify as an evolutionary process. But as this chapter points out, it should become obvious that the Fossil Record indicates something entirely different has to be responsible for the appearance of all the species.

It is here that I wish to clarify what evolutionists mean when the say that *change* has occurred.

When evolutionists use the word, *change*, at first glance it appears they are pointing out that species are different now as compared to the past. Everyone would easily agree with this obvious observation. However, what evolutionists are actually saying is more than this. What they really mean is that species are different today compared to the past because of the effects of a mutant-based progressive evolutionary process. They are claiming it is this alleged process that *changed* the species types over time.

I warn people to not be so fast to get caught up in their assumption. We need to be mindful that evolutionists cannot prove that evolution occurred. As a result, they cannot claim that the comings and goings of species types is the definite result of evolutionary *change*. Evolutionists are ignoring the other possible cause (God) when they claim a self-driven process caused all the species to appear. All they can say for sure is that species are different today as compared to the past. This does not automatically force us to accept that species mutated, transformed, or *changed* into today's species.

Since science cannot prove that a Creator does not exist, science cannot automatically assume that evolution occurred simply because species are different today compared to the past. If a Creator replaced species over time, then this would explain how species are different today without there being a mutating or transforming evolution. Because this is a possibility, this explanation has to remain a consideration and a possibility.

Evolutionary scientists should be aware they cannot simply assume evolution occurred. Until it is proven precisely *how* species became different, evolutionists are basing their support of evolution only on assumptions. Therefore, just to be clear, without a demonstration of *how* species became different, scientists cannot legitimately claim that evolution occurred.

Billions of species cannot mutate through a series of successive skeletal mutations to produce the large variety of species that have ever lived on the earth and not leave behind some of their skeletal remains as fossilized evidence. All of these findings added together spell the death of evolution. Quite frankly, this is obvious once someone finally draws our attention to the fact there are no mutants to speak of in the Fossil Record. Charles Darwin was correct; this obvious flaw allows for grave objections to be made against his theory. None of us have to be scientists to figure out that no mutants, means no mutant process.

You will recall that for an evolutionary process to occur, mutations and natural selection must both be present. I am repeating these two requirements because, now that it has been demonstrated that mutants do not exist in the Fossil Record, everyone needs to realize that one of the requirements for an evolutionary process is obviously absent. As a consequence, it should be clear this fact eliminates Darwinian evolution as being responsible for the genesis of all the species that have ever populated planet Earth. This is a game-changing revelation!

At this point, I wish to turn our attention to the other requirement for an evolutionary process, natural selection. Now, if natural selection was involved in the appearance of species, its characteristics would appear in the Fossil Record. Dr. Morris reviewed Dr. Raup's detailed research and quotes Dr. Raup (January 1979, as cited in Morris, July 1979) as stating:

> Instead of finding the gradual unfolding of life, . . . geologists . . . find . . . a highly uneven or jerky record . . . species appear . . . very suddenly, show little or no change . . . then abruptly go out of the record. . . . it's rarely clear, that the descendants were actually better adapted than their predecessors. . . . biological improvement is hard to find.[203]

These findings are significant because they completely contradict the expected characteristics of a natural selection-driven Darwinian macroevolution. If natural selection had occurred, the Fossil Record would be smooth, gradualistic, progressive, and demonstrating biological improvements over time. In addition, species would be surviving longer over time instead of going abruptly extinct. Dr. Raup mentions this when he stated that he observed that species pop up and then go extinct without demonstrating the gradual changes that Darwin predicted.[204] I feel these observations of the Fossil Record demonstrate that it is scientifically impossible Darwin's theory of evolution occurred. Essentially, the predicted requirements to be satisfied by Darwin's theory, simply do not exist.

It is also important to note that Dr. Raup discusses the North American horse in his article. I mention this because many people believe that fossils of the North American horse demonstrate Darwinian evolution.[205] What I have noticed is that this is the one example that proponents of evolution have total faith in as a classic example of evolution.

Out of billions of species that have lived on the earth, this is the one that evolutionists point to as being a classic example of evolution. However, Dr. Raup states the idea that the horse can be depended upon to support Darwinian evolution is going to have to be discarded.[206] He says this because recent data shows that the course of the horse is far less gradualistic than initially thought. As a consequence, the Fossil Record for the North American horse is not gradualistic enough to demonstrate Darwinian progression.[207] Of course, this means the North American Horse can no longer be used as an example of evolution. This proves that Darwin's problematic argument for progressive evolution has grown weaker over time, not stronger, as Dr. Raup specifically points out.

None of these observations are consistent with the theory of evolution. Notice that Dr. Raup fully expected to find the Fossil Record gradualistic, but instead, he found the record to be jerky, highly uneven, sudden, and abrupt.[208] Also, note that biological improvement of organisms is effectively absent. But wait, if there are no biological improvements, then how can there be any natural selection going on? And Dr. Raup answers this question when he had this to say regarding the Fossil Record:

> Data appears to be much more complex and much less gradualistic. . . Darwin's problem has not been alleviated in the last 120 years and we still have a record which *does* show change but one that can hardly be looked upon as the most reasonable consequence of natural selection.[209]

It cannot be overstated that the Fossil Record is not gradualistic, and this clearly contradicts the theory of evolution. Notice that Dr. Raup admits that Darwin's theory still has the big problem of being unable to demonstrate gradualism and natural selection. As a consequence, Dr. Raup could not establish that natural selection is the mechanism responsible for today's species. In fact, in Dr. Raup's quote, he is clearly telling us that it is not reasonable to continue to believe natural selection was the reason for the appearance of the species that are found in the Fossil Record.

This is extremely important! This means that modern science has no idea what the mechanism was that brought all the species into existence. Without natural selection, there is no mechanism to guide mutations. But then again, there weren't any mutants found in the Fossil Record to begin with!

This means the Darwinian evolution idea is not only missing the guidance mechanism of natural selection, but it is also missing mutants to guide!

My summary of Dr. Raup's analysis of the Fossil Record concludes that if natural selection had occurred, we would expect to see a consistent Fossil Record that was smooth, progressive, gradualistic, and demonstrated biological improvements and adaptations in organisms over time. However, since we are observing just the opposite of what we expected, the theorized guidance system of natural selection regarding macroevolution has made no observable contribution to the Fossil Record. In other words, with respect to macroevolution, the fossil evidence for natural selection is effectively absent.

Now, I have referred to natural selection as the theorized guidance system (alleged guidance system for alleged macroevolution), but as I pointed out in the last chapter, it is more accurate to specify that the naturally selected mutant survives better because its mutation qualifies as a biological improvement. What should be evident is that the biological improvements that increase survival are what constitute the theorized guidance system for advancement in the theory of evolution. In other words, the mechanism of natural selection exists when biological improvements have increased survival. All things considered, instead of referring to biological improvements that increase survival, science simply uses the term, natural selection.

In the theory of Darwinian macroevolution, it is speculated that beneficial random mutations would be naturally selected with enough power to eventually create a brand-new species. However, there is no fossil evidence to suggest that natural selection is powerful enough to create a brand-new species. Observations of the Fossil Record's history reveal that whatever, or whoever, is responsible for the appearance of new species operates in a manner that contradicts what is expected from the effects of natural selection.

And we know what these expected effects are because we see them in environmental adaptation and microevolution. The effects of natural selection in environmental adaptation and microevolution include a smooth, progressive, and gradualistic journey as organisms acquire biological improvements and adaptations. When organisms enjoy an improvement that makes them survive better, they experience being naturally selected. This takes place over a smooth, progressive, and gradual course. Notice how none of this results in a brand-new species.

A classic example of microevolution is how bacteria become resistant to antibiotics. Bacteria form resistant strains and viruses form variants, but they don't *evolve* into brand-new species (macroevolution). I will discuss this more later in the chapter.

While on the other hand, what we see with respect to the appearance of new species is that they suddenly appeared, experienced a jerky and highly uneven existence without any notable biological improvements or adaptations, then abruptly went extinct.[210] Because these organisms did not enjoy any notable improvements, they did not experience being naturally selected. In fact, their jerky, highly uneven, sudden, and abrupt existence, further reinforces that they did not experience natural selection. The Fossil Record history of new species (claimed to be the result of macroevolution) is the exact opposite of the history of organisms experiencing microevolutionary improvements resulting from natural selection.

Let me give an interesting example. Let's say we have a situation where an elderly man falls into a river and is drowning. Then a woman jumps in and saves him. The woman then leaves once the man recovers and is safe. Now, the community want to thank her and praise her for her heroism. They describe her as being a woman in her 40s, about 5'3" and brunette. The community cannot find out who she is. Then a month later, a 60-year-old bald man comes forth to claim the praise for rescuing the elderly man. The townspeople ask him his name and he states, "I'm Mr. Natural Selection."

Well, it's a fact the town does not know exactly who the real hero is, but they do know that it cannot be this man. Why is that? Because the characteristics of Mr. Natural Selection are just the opposite of those possessed by the real hero, this means that without any doubt whatsoever, the town knows that Mr. Natural Selection is not responsible for this event.

I present this example because we have the same situation regarding the Fossil Record. The Fossil Record shows us that species suddenly appeared, fully formed, experienced a jerky and highly uneven existence with no biological improvements to speak of, then went abruptly extinct. These characteristics can be equated with those of the female hero in our example. But when Mr. Natural Selection presents himself as the hero, he has the characteristics of being gradualistic, smooth, progressive, and possessing biological improvements that have increased survival over time. Therefore, because Mr. Natural Selection's characteristics are completely different from the reality of the real hero who created the Fossil Record, we need to conclude that natural selection played no effective role in the creation of any of the species over time.

I believe that many people think microevolution and the theory of macroevolution are very similar. However, the Fossil Record shows us that the reality of the experiences of new species (some claim to be the result of macroevolution) is starkly different from the reality of microevolution. The appearance of new species compared to microevolution is like night and day. They cannot be seen in the same light. In reality, they are not even close to being the same. The limited modification of an existing species (microevolution) is completely different from the genesis of a brand-new species (macroevolution).

The reason why we witness the effects of natural selection in microevolution and not in the appearance of new species is because

natural selection is not powerful enough to create a brand-new species. This is why we observe none of the characteristics of natural selection in the Fossil Record.

God has designed His science to refine species (environmental adaptation and microevolution), but only God has the power to create species (macroevolution claims to have this power). If microevolution and the theory of macroevolution were linked parts of the same, autonomous, self-driven system, then their characteristics would not severely contradict each other. If they were linked or related, their tendencies would be the same. But instead, the Fossil Record shows us that they are not.

Natural selection has the ability to support advantageous errors resulting in refinements in an organism which increases its survival. As stated, this is defined as microevolution. However, natural selection does not possess the power to give birth to a brand-new species which is why natural selection is not observed in the realm of new species appearances.

But that's not the only bad news for natural selection. Dr. Raup points out that groups of species (much like a menu list) suddenly appeared, lasted on average 10 million years, showed little or no change, and then abruptly went extinct.[211] Dr. Raup states this pattern consistently repeated itself throughout history. This tells me that if natural selection occurred, then groups of species would be surviving longer and longer as time went on. Instead, the Fossil Record demonstrates that latter species groups did not survive any longer than earlier groups because they all lasted about 10 million years, on average. On a chart this would be a flat line instead of a line sloping upward over time as we would expect to see with natural selection.

For example, if natural selection was occurring, the first species group would have survived 10 million years, while the second species group would have survived perhaps 12 million years. And the third species group would have survived perhaps 15 million years, and so forth. Therefore, if biological improvements resulting in natural selection had occurred, then we would be seeing an upward sloping graph of survival times. But instead, we see a flat line on the survival graph because all species groups averaged about 10 million years. Regarding the concept of macroevolution, when there is no increase in survival over time, or otherwise, natural selection is not at play. This is additional observational data suggesting that natural selection is absent. Remember that Dr. Raup confirms this absence in his quote where he stated that the Fossil Record can hardly be looked upon as the most reasonable consequence of natural selection.[212]

You will recall that for an evolutionary process to occur, mutations and natural selection must both be present. I am repeating these two requirements again because, now that it has been demonstrated that evidence for natural selection does not exist in the Fossil Record, everyone needs to realize that the second requirement for an evolutionary process is also absent. As a consequence, it should be clear this fact also eliminates Darwinian evolution as being responsible for the genesis of all the species that have ever populated planet Earth. This is yet another game-changing revelation!

Once Dr. Raup eliminated natural selection as the Fossil Record's guidance system, he concluded that he needed to discard the Darwinian evolution model. After he did this, he reaffirmed that a guidance system was indeed still necessary to drive evolution, and that he needed to find out what it is. We see evidence of this when Dr. Raup states:

> A large number of evolutionary biologists these days are studying the question that I've just considered—it's called neutral or **non-Darwinian** evolution.[213]

This is the most important sentence in his entire article because it truly spells the death of evolution! Once Dr. Raup and a large number of evolutionary biologists began looking for a **non-Darwinian** evolution (another kind of evolution), this is clearly the point where the Darwinian model was abandoned. Please take note of this a game-changing event! It is scientifically impossible to continue to believe in Darwinian evolution after reading and understanding the earth-shaking conclusions of Dr. Raup and the large number of evolutionary biologists who he was working with.

In light of his findings, Dr. Raup started looking for a new scientific explanation for how species appeared over time. Dr. Raup did this because he continued to assume that evolution must have occurred simply because species are different now compared to the past.[214] However, Dr. Raup acknowledges that science still needs to find the scientific explanation for *how* species wound up different over time (phyletic transformation) and *how* new species appeared (speciation). And this is what makes Dr. Raup's article priceless to the people who believe in God.

Once Dr. Raup established the absolute need for scientists to find a non-Darwinian explanation for how species got here, this confirmed that science has no working model for the theory of evolution. This leaves only one explanation left, God. Without *science* having a viable explanation, *"science without a God"* only has an assumption that evolution occurred.

Why is this an assumption? This is an assumption because *science* cannot prove that God does not exist. This means that an intelligent Creator could be the reason for how the various species appeared over time. Because a Creator may exist, this means that Dr. Raup's assumption that evolution occurred is not the only possibility. This is why *science* needed to find that natural selection was *how* new species appeared. And because Dr. Raup found evidence that does not support but instead contradicts natural selection as being the reason for *how* species are different today, he began to look for another reason. We see this in his statement:

> The very obvious question at this point is: what alternative mechanisms do we have to explain the changes that we observe?[215]

As mentioned, once Dr. Raup was forced to abandon natural selection and Darwinian evolution, this caused him to begin looking for another explanation for how species are different today compared to the past. This other explanation needed to have another kind of guidance mechanism.

Once Dr. Raup realized he needed to abandon natural selection as the reason for the appearance of new species, he was likewise compelled to abandon Darwinian evolution. The abandonment of Darwinian evolution was the consequence of not finding any evidence for natural selection and not finding intermediate mutants in the Fossil Record regarding the theory of macroevolution. We can all see that Dr. Raup is not the only scientist who has come to this conclusion. He points out that many evolutionary biologists are now looking for another explanation which is being referred to as **non-Darwinian evolution**. Dr. Raup and other scientists are looking for 'another kind of evolution.'

This is earth shaking news because these statements are coming from the famous scientist described as one of the most influential paleontologists of the second half of the 20th century.[216] Because a large number of evolutionary biologists are now searching for another kind of evolution, with another kind of driving mechanism, this means that Darwinian evolution has officially been laid to rest. It's very important for us to take notice that nobody has any idea of how 'another kind of evolution' would have worked? Scientists don't have a model for it, and they have no ideas for a driving mechanism either. Thus, Dr. Ebifegha's book has the right title: *The Death of Evolution*.

This is where I would like to discuss neo-Darwinian evolution a bit more. The theory of neo-Darwinian evolution, also known as the *Modern Theory of Evolution*, requires genetic change (genetic variability) and natural selection in the same way that Darwinian evolution has these two requirements. In addition to mutations from DNA replication, neo-Darwinism adds to this by also taking into consideration genetic recombination, translocation, hybridization, and genetic drift.

That being said, neo-Darwinism suffers from the same problems that the classic Darwinian model suffers from. The first critical problem revolves around the fact that you can't have a mutant process without any mutants. The second critical problem for neo-Darwinism is the fact that it also requires natural selection, which we know from Dr. Raup's extensive and comprehensive research, can hardly be seen as the mechanism responsible for the Fossil Record. As a consequence, neo-Darwinsim (*Modern Theory of Evolution*) does **not** represent, 'another kind of evolution' which evolutionary biologists are still looking for in order to prove that evolution occurred.

Dr. Raup spent the rest of his illustrious career looking for another kind of evolution, but he never found it. However, what is important is what he ***did*** find. He found the fossil evidence led him to abandon Darwinian evolution. This is what caused Dr. Raup to search for another evolutionary model that actually works, which he never found. This is because the non-Darwinian evolution he searched for, does not exist. This truly spells the death of evolution.

I suspect that many of the evolutionary biologists that Dr. Raup is referring to, who were looking for another evolutionary explanation, wound up attending the Wistar Institute Symposium held in Philadelphia in 1966. This is where scores of mathematicians, biologists, physicists and engineers openly rejected the theory of Darwinian evolution.[217] This conference was titled, "Challenges to the Neo-Darwinian Theory of Evolution," and was hosted by the Nobel Prize winner Sir Peter Medawar where scores of scientists voiced their dissatisfaction about there being no scientific basis for testable evolutionary theory.[218] I might add that the situation for evolution is actually worse than it was in 1966 because the North American horse can no longer be argued to be a classic example of gradualistic Darwinian evolution.[219]

Now, because this topic harbors such a powerful revelation which can deliver a life-changing impact, I wish to review what we have learned here one more time:

1) The evidence for mutant intermediate fossils DOES NOT EXIST. The fossils of mutated organisms that would be necessary to validate Darwin's theory of evolution, DO NOT EXIST. And to be clear, if Darwinian evolution had occurred, countless fossils of mutated intermediates would certainly exist.

2) Evidence for production of new species from genetically induced biological improvements that increased survivability, DOES NOT EXIST. As a consequence, the evidence in the Fossil Record that would be necessary to validate that natural selection is responsible for *how* new species appeared, DOES NOT EXIST. And to be clear, the characteristics of the Fossil Record prove that natural selection is not what caused the appearance of species over time that compose the Fossil Record. This means

natural selection did not cause the appearance of any species that has lived on the earth.

3) A legitimate working model for evolution DOES NOT EXIST. Present-day scientists have no idea what mechanism was responsible for causing the appearance of new species over time. Present-day evolutionary biologists are still searching for another kind of evolution!

Now, I don't want to give the impression that Dr. Raup did not believe in natural selection; he did. He stated, ". . . natural selection, as a process, does work."[220] He acknowledged the existence of natural selection. After all, we see the effects of natural selection in microevolution. However, even though microevolution does exist in nature and does manifest the effects of natural selection, our discussion is concerned with macroevolution because microevolution cannot produce a brand-new species. Therefore, Dr. Raup is correct that natural selection as a process does work. It works regarding microevolution. However, it clearly does not work regarding the idea that macroevolution caused the production of brand-new species.

With that being said, because Dr. Raup was a steadfast evolutionist, he found one small niche in the Fossil Record that he felt compelled to assume was the result of natural selection. Dr. Raup believes natural selection was somehow involved in rare examples of optimal design structures like Pterosaur wings[221] and Trilobite eyes.[222] Optimal design structures are biological solutions that could not be any more perfect for an organism's needs.[223] Dr. Raup assumes these rare optimal designs resulted from natural selection because he could not imagine another mechanism or process that could accomplish this.[224]

Regardless, regarding the world's vast variety of species that compose the rest of the Fossil Record, Dr. Raup abandoned the belief that those species are the consequence of a natural selection mechanism.[225] In other words, natural selection could not be how all of the other species got here, but natural selection is the only mechanism Dr. Raup could think of, that could possibly be responsible for these optimal designs. It's important to point out that Dr. Raup admits he cannot prove his presumption,[226] which I consider to be merely an assumption. Why is this merely an assumption? It's an assumption because Dr. Raup is overlooking the possibility that a Creator is responsible for the Fossil Record. Evolution is not the only possibility.

I wish to stress that Dr. Raup assumed natural selection as the only possible way he could imagine for Pterosaur wings and Trilobite eyes to exist, but at the same time, he found the rest of the Fossil Record could not reasonably be seen to be the consequence of natural selection. At first glance this appears to be inconsistent. However, I think that Dr. Raup was reasoning, for the most part (over 99%), the Fossil Record is not the result of natural selection. But in the case of rare optimal design examples (less than a fraction of 1%), this is the only time that natural selection was assumed to be the mechanism at work. This is because Dr. Raup simply could not imagine any other way that these optimal designs could be accomplished.

Dr. Raup experienced an inconsistent dilemma here, and I believe this is the result of his assumption that there is only one possibility for why species are different today compared to the past. At the top of page 26 of his article, Dr. Raup admits he has no proof these structures are the product of natural selection. However, he still feels that he has a strong circumstantial argument that they are. His argument only exists if evolution is the only possibility and there is no other possibility to consider. However, this is not the case! He is failing to consider the other possibility of God existing and personally designing these perfect structures.

It should be clear that evidence of natural selection is nowhere to be found in the Fossil Record. Therefore, a strong circumstantial argument has not been established to exist that claims natural selection was responsible for optimal design structures found in the Fossil Record. I feel that Dr. Raup's dilemma supports that the Fossil Record is the product of intelligent genetic engineering. Genetic engineering does not present any of the inconsistencies, roadblocks, and contradictions that Dr. Raup experienced.

Another very important point to realize, is that when Dr. Raup assumed natural selection was the only way he could imagine for the existence of the perfect Pterosaur wings and Trilobite eyes, he was admitting that he has no idea whatsoever for any other mechanisms to explain these rare structures in the Fossil Record. Otherwise, Dr. Raup would have used that new mechanism to explain Pterosaur wings and Trilobite eyes. This means Dr. Raup has no ideas for what mechanism was responsible for the appearance of species on Earth. I also find it very interesting that Dr. Raup is so impressed with the optimal optical design of the Trilobite eye that he states:

> Thus, the Trilobites 450 million years ago used an optimal design which would require a well-trained and imaginative optical engineer to develop today…[227]

My response to Dr. Raup is that these brilliant optimal designs were indeed developed by a genetic engineering genius, and His name is God. These examples of perfect and optimal designs are obvious proof of God's handiwork!

In fact, I am convinced that Divine genetic engineering caused new species to appear from slight alterations in the existing code of earlier created species that were used as starting templates. In this scenario, a brand-new species is produced in one shot. Hence, there won't be any mutant intermediates, let alone dozens and dozens of mutant intermediates (possibly hundreds or even thousands) which evolution requires. Since the Fossil Record demonstrates that no mutant intermediates have ever been found to exist, this correlates perfectly with the Divine genetic engineering scenario.

In thoroughly examining the Fossil Record for his entire illustrious career, Dr. Raup abandoned his belief that natural selection was the cause for the evolution that he assumes to have occurred.[228]

The foundation of Darwinian evolution mandates that natural selection had to have been the guidance system and guiding force. However, this was not found to be the case. As I have mentioned before, an evolutionary process requires both mutations and natural selection to be present. Therefore, the absence of natural selection eliminates the possibility that an evolutionary process ever occurred. This confirms the death of evolution theory.

As I have mentioned, even though Dr. Raup cannot prove *how* new species appeared, he declares that because species are different today compared to the past, this demonstrates evolution must have occurred.[229] This is an assumption. This *change* in species types refers to earlier species allegedly metamorphosizing into new species over time along with the addition of the new species which allegedly splintered off. However, because Dr. Raup abandoned natural selection regarding macroevolution, he has no scientific evidence that species transformed themselves into new species over time.[230] Without a proven model for the theory of evolution, there is no proof the evolution of phyletic transformation (metamorphosizing *change*), or speciation (splintered off species) ever took place.

Furthermore, without the mechanism of natural selection being demonstrated to transform a single original species into a single new species or being demonstrated to splinter off new species, there is no known mechanism for the evolution of phyletic transformation or speciation to take place. Therefore, Dr. Raup's assumption that ancient species evolved into, and/or spawned today's species is unfounded. Dr. Raup's claim is unfounded because of the other possibility that exists. If a Creator exists who cycled species groups in and out every 10 million years, then species did not metamorphosize over time, they were replaced over time. This represents a huge difference.

If species evolved over time, then the Fossil Record would be progressively smooth, gradual, and we would see mutants with biological improvements. The fact that the Fossil Record experienced a jerky, highly uneven, and abrupt history demonstrates that species were suddenly replaced. The logic behind cycling species in and out revolves around a system of using earlier species to prepare the earth for more sophisticated species scheduled to appear later.

Until *science* proves that God does not exist, God will remain a viable explanation. Therefore, evolution cannot be automatically assumed to be the genesis of species just because species are different today compared to the past. This is especially true in the absence of a working model for the theory of evolution. Dr. Raup assumes evolution occurred, but for all Dr. Raup knows, a Creator could have been the reason. And if this is the case, we would be looking at a situation where species did not evolve over time but were replaced over time. When I say replaced, I mean that a *creation seed* opened and suddenly introduced the next species. That said, it is also possible that God created the species at the time they were due to appear.

Regardless, Dr. Raup still assumes that species being different today is somehow a natural transformation because he makes no mention of a Creator. Despite this, Dr. Raup does not need to mention the possibility of the existence of a Creator in order to be useful to me here. This is because he established the need to abandon the explanation of natural selection regarding the theory of macroevolution.[231] As a consequence, this mandated that he discard Darwinian evolution and begin searching for a *non-Darwinian* evolution.[232] Therefore, what Dr. Raup **did** find is crucial because it confirms the death of evolution. Quite frankly, this earth shaking-news is a complete game changer!

Once again, what Dr. Raup has established is extremely important. Even though Dr. Raup's search for another kind of evolution was never successful, this is of no consequence. The Scientific Method does not care about what a scientist is searching for; it only cares about what a scientist can demonstrate and prove. And what Dr. Raup successfully demonstrated is that Darwin's natural selection-based macroevolution has no support from the Fossil Record and should be abandoned.[233] I feel it is evident that not only is there no support from the Fossil Record for Darwinian evolution, but the Fossil Record actually contradicts and eliminates Darwinian macroevolution from having ever taken place.

Dr. Raup also mentions artificial selection in his article. Now, for the most part, I ignore discussions involving artificial selection because mankind's artificial 'selection' manipulations are not going to occur 'naturally' on their own in nature. This is why natural selection is *natural* while *selection* (artificial selection) is not. Even so, Dr. Raup mentions the artificial selection employed by plant and animal breeders.[234] This work is referred to as hybridization because it creates hybrids. This is completely different from Darwinian macroevolution.

The impression I come away with as Dr. Raup discusses plant and animal breeders is that artificial selection is seen to work with hybrids while natural selection is seen to work with **Darwinian micro-evolution**. I agree that better adapted types result in both of these examples. However, using microevolution as an example, we can see that a "better adapted type" does not mean a brand-new species. We need to be very careful to scrutinize the way in which certain sections of Dr. Raup's article are worded in order to not come away with any misinterpretations.

I say this because these examples of artificial selection and micro-evolutionary natural selection have no connection with the alleged creation of brand-new species through **Darwinian macroevolution.** As a consequence, the artificial selection seen with regard to hybridization, and the natural selection seen with regard to microevolution, are NOT seen with regard to macroevolution.

This is one of the sections of Dr. Raup's article where we really need to clarify precisely what he is actually saying in order to avoid any possible misimpressions. My impression is that Dr. Raup is just trying to state that natural selection is seen to work sometimes. I agree that it works regarding microevolution, environmental adaptation, and artificial selection manipulations. However, it does not work regarding the theory of macroevolution, and it is not responsible for why species are different today as compared to the past.

Instead, I see a pattern of Creation where previous species were introduced to the earth in order to prepare it in some way for the benefit of the species scheduled to follow. This *creation seeds* theory introduces species groups suddenly, who then experience an erratic existence without any observable biological improvements. And when their time is up, they quickly and unpredictably go extinct and are replaced by the next species group as their *creation seeds* open. And this is precisely what we observe in the Fossil Record which scientifically supports that species are replaced over time instead of evolving over time through mutations.

As a result of this clear possibility, **mutations cannot be assumed to be the only possible reason for today's species.** I will go one step further and state that because there are no mutant intermediates to speak of in the Fossil Record, this scientifically proves that mutations are **not** the reason for today's species. This means what we witness in the Fossil Record does not demonstrate that mutating *changes* occurred.

When Dr. Raup states that we are witnessing *change*, he means that species mutated into something else over time. However, since he cannot prove this, he can't even establish that mutating *changes* have occurred. As a consequence, this is the reason why Dr. Raup can't assume evolution occurred. Dr. Raup has no basis at all for evolution. All he can state with certainty is that species groups are different today as compared to the past.

It's clear that the theory of evolution is missing both mutants and natural selection which is more than enough to end any argument for an evolutionary process. In carefully analyzing this situation, Dr. Raup's argument is missing the evidence that species experienced *change*. As a result, **Dr. Raup's statement is unfounded when he claims the Fossil Record demonstrates *change*** (mutation-based change)**.** Dr. Raup has no proof that species *changed* (mutated) over time. And since there is the possibility that a Creator replaced species over time, Dr. Raup can't just assume that transforming *changes* took place.

As you will recall, an evolutionary process requires the presence of both mutations and natural selection. And because of the absence of evidence for natural selection, the presence of an evolutionary process is not possible. Once evolution theory lost natural selection as its guidance system, the concept of an evolutionary process was also automatically lost. This compounds the fact that the absence of mutants in the Fossil Record also makes it impossible that an evolutionary process occurred.

When spontaneous generation was proven false, it involved experiments using flasks of broth. It was proven that life could not just pop into existence spontaneously.[235] When science examines the earth's Fossil Record, geologists and paleontologists don't find any evolution mutants, and they don't find any evidence that natural selection is the reason why species are different today compared to the past. This means that evolution theory has been proven false in the same way spontaneous generation was proven false.

We actually have a present-day example to prove that macroevolution does not occur. That example is bacteria. Bacteria experience genetic mutations which allows some of them to luckily also experience positive natural selection. Their positive mutations allow them to survive antibiotics and then those lucky survivors reproduce. In this way, present-day bacteria exhibit the two conditions necessary for an evolutionary process to occur, mutations and natural selection (survival). And what does that produce? It merely produces a new strain or variant of the same species. Bacteria experience an incredible reproduction rate which produces lots and lots of mutations. It is crucial to note, when advantageous mutations occur that cause these offspring to be positively naturally selected, it **does not produce a brand-new species.**

Because of their ultra-high reproductive rate, bacteria will produce far more genetic mutations than any animal species ever could. And let's not forget to factor in the benefit that they reproduce on their own without requiring a mate to pair up with. This eliminates any limitations caused by combining a mutated recessive gene with a normal dominant gene. Asexually reproducing organisms like bacteria don't experience issues like this because they don't need a mate.

Microorganisms are the species group that experiences the most ideal conditions to support an evolutionary process. They have the highest chance to realize an evolutionary process. And with all that being present, they **do not evolve** into a new species (phyletic transformation) and they also don't splinter off a second, brand-new species (speciation).

This proves that when all of the ideal conditions for an evolutionary process are met, it does not result in the creation of a brand-new species! Neither speciation nor phyletic transformation occurs. I feel this clearly demonstrates that natural selection is able to cause microevolution, but natural selection is not powerful enough to ever cause macroevolution. As mentioned, this mutant strain phenomenon observed in nature has been defined as Darwin's microevolution. And for simplicity, I will also group environmental adaptation into this category. Microevolution is entirely different from Darwin's macroevolution idea, where a brand-new species is allegedly produced.

As discussed in Chapter Four, microevolution is defined in the Oxford Dictionaries as:

> An evolutionary change within a species or small group
> of organisms, especially over a short period of time.[236]

This means that small adaptations occur, but a brand-new species is not produced. On the other hand, macroevolution is defined in the Oxford Dictionaries as:

> A major evolutionary change. The term applies mainly
> to the evolution of whole taxonomic groups over long
> periods of time.[237]

In other words, macroevolution refers to the idea that a brand-new species can be produced.

Natural selection has the ability to manifest microevolution. I feel it's clear that natural selection does not possess the power to create a brand-new species. This can be observed in nature when we look to bacteria and viruses as the perfect examples. And this is why the effects of natural selection are not found in the Fossil Record. The Fossil Record has been found to not be the consequence of natural selection. This demonstrates to me that natural selection is a weak event that merely rewards a mutated organism with a positive change, that gives it the ability to survive better and adapt better to its environment. And that's it.

Personally, I feel the inclusion of, *evolution,* in the word, *microevolution,* may cause some people to think that if microevolution occurs in nature, then macroevolution must also be true. This is completely false because microevolution is not creating a new species while macroevolution claims to create brand-new species. These two terms are vastly different despite the fact they sound very similar. I feel this can cause someone to associate microevolution with macroevolution. Because of the reality of the Fossil Record, we now know that microevolution (along with its natural selection) had no perceptible influence on the appearance of today's species. Therefore, we need to avoid the potential confusion of microevolution and macroevolution sounding so similar.

Along these same lines, it is false to claim that many changes to a species from microevolution will add up to eventually produce a new species (macroevolution). Here are the reasons why this is false:

1) As mentioned, positive natural selection is able to reward mutant bacteria with survival against antibiotics. This is clearly

microevolution. If microevolution added together to produce macroevolution, then a series of bacterial microevolutionary mutant strains would have added together to produce a brand-new (macroevolutionary) bacterial species. Because this does not occur, it proves that microevolution does **not** add together to produce macroevolution.

2) Microevolution demonstrates the progressive and gradualistic effects of natural selection, which includes the presence of biological improvements. As we can see, this is in stark contrast to the Fossil Record regarding the theory of macroevolution which does not demonstrate progressive biological improvements and gradualistic effects of natural selection. Therefore, if macroevolution was the product of adding up microevolutionary events, the natural selection that produced the microevolutionary events would be added into, and consequently observed, in the Fossil Record history. This is clearly not the case.[238]

3) We also know this claim is false because the Fossil Record does not produce mutant intermediates that would be necessary to demonstrate progressive evolution.[239] In other words, because there is no working scientific model for evolution that proves macroevolution occurred, this means microevolution cannot be claimed to have added up to something (macroevolution) that did not occur. Present-day scientists have no evidence, or clear idea, for how species wound up different over time.

It is here that I wish to state that some of the ideas that Darwin had were correct. It is true that if two physically fit parents reproduce, they will have fit offspring. As a consequence, those fit offspring have a better chance to survive and thrive than those who are less fit. Thus, survival of the fittest does work in nature. Darwin's microevolution also works where mild genetic changes that are advantageous in a particular set of circumstances benefit the population members that possess those changes.

Darwin was also correct about natural selection with respect to environmental adaptation and microevolution. It is true that if a genetic code error occurs in a population member, and that error causes an increased ability to survive and adapt, then that member has been positively naturally selected. Therefore, Darwin had several successful ideas, however, macroevolution was not one of them. He acknowledged this when he admitted that he should be finding mutant remnants littering every layer of geology, but they were not there.[240] This demonstrates to people the need to be mindful of how microevolution is very different from macroevolution.

The last comment I wish to make regarding natural selection is that I believe the realistic power of natural selection has been grossly overestimated. To help demonstrate this, I wish to present an example of how I personally view natural selection. The situation of natural selection is like placing a lawnmower engine in a Daytona 500 race car where it gives the car enough power to facilitate eventually crossing the finish line, but that engine does not possess the power to ever win a race.

Natural selection possesses enough power to cause environmental adaptation and microevolution, but it does not possess the power to cause the genesis of a brand-new species. As mentioned, bacteria are the prime example that proves this. With all of the ingredients present for evolution to occur, natural selection was responsible for the production of a new strain (microevolution), but it was not powerful enough to produce a brand-new species (macroevolution). Therefore, Darwin was correct about natural selection being able to handle microevolution, but he grossly over-estimated its power when he suggested that it had the ability to cause macroevolution.

I would also like to state that Darwinian evolution is not automatically rejected just because someone believes in God. When I was younger and thought there might be a God, I reasoned that God could have created all the species on Earth through the process of evolution. Evolution could have been a Divinely created process for the purpose of creating billions of species. However, because there are no mutants to speak of in the Fossil Record and no signs of natural selection guiding the genesis of new species, this tells me that God did not create all of the life on Earth through the process of Darwinian macroevolution. These are the reasons why I reject evolution and refer to it as pseudoscience. Following sound science has caused me to reject the pseudoscience. We need to *follow the science.*

The great detective Sherlock Holmes was said to not only look for clues at the scene of a crime, but he also looked for what was not present at the scene of the crime. In this case, what is not present are mutant intermediate skeletal fossils proving that evolution really occurred. No physical evidence of mutants in the Fossil Record means there never were any linking chains of progressive mutations. There are no such links and no such chains in the Fossil Record that connect any two species together in an evolutionary chain. This is definitive proof that evolution theory never occurred.

In order to produce the billions of species that have lived on the earth, it would mandate that billions and billions of mutants had to have been born. And for us to find no proof of this in the Fossil Record tells us that Darwinian evolution could never have been a reality. Simply put, the absence of mutants means the absence of an evolutionary mutant process. It is that simple.

But the great Sherlock Holmes would not stop there because in this evolution mystery case there is actually one more piece of missing evidence which spotlights, *The Case of the Missing Natural Selection.* This is why I find the solution to this mystery case to be, well, elementary my dear Watson and Watsonettes. All we have to do is apply the same type of logic to this investigation that Sherlock Holmes would. And when we do, the answer becomes quite clear.

The Scientific Method does not care what a scientist hopes and assumes. The Scientific Method is only concerned with what a scientist can actually prove that they found. And when we very carefully examine Dr. Raup's findings, what Dr. Raup actually found from the Fossil Record can be summarized as four facts.

First, he admits that he does not find gradual and progressive chains of intermediate mutants slowly transitioning from one species to another (Raup, Conflicts, 1979, p. 23). Both Dr. Raup and Darwin fully expected to find mutant intermediates and they are simply nowhere to be found. And please be aware that in the Dr. Raup article that I reference, he uses phrases like, "there are not enough" and "there are very few cases." This raises the rhetorical question: Is this just a nice way of Dr. Raup saying there aren't any? I think so.

Dr. Raup is a steadfast evolutionist and he is going out of his way to be kind to the theory of evolution. But if we snap back to reality, we see that Dr. Raup admits that not finding mutants is the biggest problem with Darwin's macroevolution theory (Raup, Conflicts, 1979, p. 23). And I agree. The absence of mutants means the absence of a mutant process.

We don't need to be Sherlock Holmes to figure this out; all we need is common sense. But we can't easily figure this out for ourselves if we are not told about the fact that mutant intermediates are not present in the Fossil Record! If people are not made aware of the absence of mutants, then people will be led to believe and accept an idea that has already been scientifically proven false.

The second fact he found, is that it cannot be established the vast fossil record is the result of natural selection (Raup, Conflicts, 1979, p. 25). In fact, Dr. Raup could not even prove that natural selection was responsible for as little as 0.9% of the Fossil Record (Raup, Conflicts, 1979, p. 26). This means that Dr. Raup found no proving evidence that natural selection played any part at all in why species are different today as compared to the past.

If natural selection had occurred, the Fossil Record would have been smooth, gradualistic, progressive, and slowly demonstrating biological improvements. But instead, Dr. Raup found that species suddenly appeared, experienced a surprisingly jerky and highly uneven existence showing no biological improvements, who then went abruptly extinct (Raup, Conflicts, 1979, p. 23). Therefore, the characteristics of the Fossil Record prove that natural selection was not the guidance mechanism responsible for the creation of the species on the earth.

The third fact involves rare examples of optimal design structures. Even though Dr. Raup mentions these rare examples, he admits that he found **no proof** they are the product of natural selection (Raup, Conflicts, 1979, p. 26). Instead, he admits he only has a circumstantial argument. However, this circumstantial argument is flawed because it contradicts his finding that it is unreasonable to believe the Fossil Record is the consequence of natural selection. If you ask me, optimal design structures were created by God exactly the way they were found in the Fossil Record and represent clear evidence of deliberate intelligent engineering. In addition, his circumstantial argument is also flawed because it is entirely based on the assumption that no other possibility exists. Dr. Raup completely ignores the fact that a Creator may have caused the creation of all the species on the earth.

It is clear to me that a Divine microevolutionary natural selection process does exist. However, a Divine macroevolutionary natural selection process DOES NOT EXIST. Apparently, God created an auto-piloted microevolutionary process that refines species over time. But when it comes to creating new species, God reserves the right of doing that Himself. I feel this is why God has limited the power of natural selection to only being able to cause microevolutionary refinements. Only God has the power to create.

Finally, the fourth fact regarding Dr. Raup, is that he found the need for scientists to start looking for a non-Darwinian evolution to explain why species are different today as compared to the past (Raup, Conflicts, 1979, p. 26). Why do scientists need to do this? Because until they find a viable explanation, science has no working model for the theory of evolution.

These findings constitute the realities Dr. Raup established as scientific evidence as it pertains to mutant intermediates and natural selection with regard to the theory of Darwinian macroevolution.

With that being said, all of Dr. Raup's other talk in his article where he steps back and "very generally" mixes in artificial selection (selection), hybridization, microevolution, and optimal designs, is just his way of telling us what he hoped and wished was the case concerning natural selection with regard to Darwinian macroevolution.

It is clear to me that Dr. Raup was hopeful he would find proof that mutant intermediates existed, and that natural selection actually had something, anything, to do with Darwinian macroevolution. But much to Dr. Raup's disappointment, he was never able to prove any of this and his hopes were never realized. This is why he started looking for a non-Darwinian evolution. (Raup, Conflicts, 26). Dr. Raup never found a working model for the theory of evolution. Therefore, in conclusion, we need to embrace what Dr. Raup actually found and discard what Dr. Raup hoped for.

The last expert that I wish to present is Stephen Jay Gould who is considered to be an expert in the fields of paleontology and evolutionary biology. He served as professor of Geology and Paleontology at Harvard University, and is quoted as stating (1977, as cited by Battson, n.d.):

> The history of most fossil species includes two features particularly inconsistent with gradualism (evolution):
>
> 1) Stasis – most species exhibit no directional change during their tenure on Earth. They appear in the fossil record looking much the same as when they disappear; morphological change is usually limited and directionless;
>
> 2) Sudden appearance – in any local area, a species does not arise gradually by the steady transformation of its ancestors; it appears all at once and 'fully formed' (Gould, 1977).[241]

As researcher and scholar Art Battson points out, Professor Gould honestly admits that neo-Darwinian evolution is not supported by the Fossil Record evidence, as he concludes that neo-Darwinian evolution:

> "…is effectively dead, despite its persistence as textbook orthodoxy" (Gould, 1980).[242]

Just to make this crystal clear, this means the theory of evolution, which is being universally presented as an accepted explanation for how species appeared on the earth, has already been **disproved** a long time ago. This Harvard professor's statements are so important that

I ask you to please read his quotes one more time. Please remember, this is coming from an evolutionary expert who didn't necessarily believe in God. Professor Gould defined himself as Agnostic.

Notice that Dr. Gould confirms that species did not transform from ancestors through a gradual progression. Instead, they suddenly appeared in their fully formed state.[243] When species appear fully formed, and all at once, this means they did not 'evolve' slowly over time from another species. This completely contradicts the theory of Darwinian evolution. And this most certainly causes the theory of evolution to "breakdown." Whatever caused all of the species to appear on the earth, it should be clear that Darwinian evolution was not that cause. This is why I suggest that species were introduced over time through a *creation seeds* strategy that was genetically engineered. This would explain why species appeared suddenly, fully formed, and displayed no evidence of species transformations.

And there you have it. Notice how Dr. Gould's findings completely agree with what Dr. Raup came to realize in his investigations of the Fossil Record. I fully agree that evolution is dead. The theory of evolution has been dead for a long time. Dr. Ebifegha's book, *The Death of Evolution*, has the perfect title. This spotlights the fact that the scientists who really know their evolutionary biology are well aware that Darwinian evolution is a failed theory. By contrast, everyone else on planet Earth who is not well versed in evolutionary biology is under the impression that Darwinian evolution is a sound scientific explanation for how all of the species appeared on Earth.

With that said, I need to stress that Stephen Jay Gould was a steadfast evolutionist just like Dr. Raup. Dr. Gould continued to look for 'another kind of evolution' throughout his career just as Dr. Raup did. However, to date, no one has found another kind of evolution to replace the neo-Darwinian model. What this means is that **science presently has no working model for the theory of evolution**.

I might also add that both Dr. Raup and Dr. Gould made no mention of the possibility of a Creator.

I mention this because it demonstrates that Dr. Raup and Dr. Gould did not determine neo-Darwinian evolution to be false because they were influenced by a religious affiliation. No, just the opposite; I don't believe either one of them had a religious affiliation. This is important because it demonstrates they both eliminated neo-Darwinian evolution purely based on the scientific evidence.

Now, there is another topic that I wish to mention here. Some people believe that the process of stars converting simpler atoms into more complex atoms is an example of evolution. But let me be clear, the creation of the higher atoms at the cores of stars is not some automatic, evolutionary process that just happens randomly by itself. It is a creation process invented by God. As we see in Psalm 147:4, "He tells the number of the stars; He calls them all by their names." I feel that God calls His stars by their individual names as He commands them to perform their work for Him. All of this science exists and functions the way it does by Divine design.

Stars are God's designed science and not an example of automated atom evolution. Evolution can't exist in the core of a star because natural selection cannot occur, in the center of the furnace of a blazing star. As stated, natural selection requires the active process of an organism competing in a population for survival, and then reproducing.

Clearly, there are no living organisms competing for survival in a star. This means there are no newly gained survival advantages that are then passed on to living offspring. Natural selection is simply not possible in a star. This is not a random evolutionary process where simpler atoms *evolve* into more complex ones because they survived better. This is a designed fusion process. Atoms are being fused together by brute force, and that's all there is to it.

Now, I do not wish for people to think that I naturally oppose the concept of evolution. When I was younger and trying to believe in God, I reasoned that if God existed, then He could have created the life on Earth through the process of evolution. However, once I came to the recent realization that scientific evidence actually eliminates evolution from being a scientific fact, I had to reformulate my belief structure. In order for anyone to properly formulate their belief structure, they need the truth. And the truth has been found in the Fossil Record demonstrating it has been scientifically proven Darwinian evolution never occurred.

You may hear sophisticated, detailed, and convoluted arguments put forth by some evolutionary biologists and some geneticists who promote the idea of evolution as a self-driven progressive process. And because these arguments and explanations are presented in a confident manner, you may be prompted to become convinced by them if you are unaware of the evidence presented in this chapter. Therefore, there are two critical points that you need to remember when you hear lofty technical arguments from scientists who are nonbelievers:

1) If the claims you hear actually occurred, then the Fossil Record would contain fossilized mutated skeletons demonstrating a methodical and progressive evolutionary process. What these researchers are claiming would mandate the existence of countless mutant intermediate organisms that lived and died during their life cycles in the alleged progressive process of Darwinian evolution. Because such fossilized mutated skeletal remains are

not found to exist in the Fossil Record, this proves the claims of Darwinian evolution are unfounded and false. The fossils of mutated skeletal remains would indeed be found if Darwinian evolution actually occurred, even Charles Darwin admitted this. We have found hundreds of thousands of fossils of normal specimens which means we should have found countless more fossilized specimens of the mutants that allegedly produced billions of brand-new species. All you have to do is ask these researchers why there aren't any fossils of mutated intermediate skeletons in the Fossil Record? Here is the bottom line: You can't have a mutant process without any mutants, now can you??? Therefore, Darwinian/neo-Darwinian evolution has been proven false by the Fossil Record itself.

2) The researchers who present their complex and convoluted arguments cannot prove that God does not exist. Because they cannot prove that God does not exist, this means their explanation is not the only argument that exists. A Creator could have utilized a methodical process to create the genetic profiles of every single species. This would be referred to as, genetic engineering. Then, species groups could have been cycled in and out over time. If this was the case, it would certainly give us the impression that a methodical and progressive process occurred. Researchers cannot prove this did not occur. Therefore, there are two arguments for how all the species got here over time.

As stated, there are two arguments that exist. However, what is interesting here is that point #1 demonstrates that one of the arguments in point #2 has already been proven to be invalid. The absence of fossilized mutated skeletons in the Fossil Record proves Darwinian/neo-Darwinian evolution never happened. As a consequence, this eliminates evolution as a possibility and only leaves one possibility left. This proves the existence of a Creator and explains how all the species got here.

Once again, evolution is not the only long ages proposition for how all of the species got here. This is so, because God could have methodically, genetically engineered all the species and then slowly introduced them over a long period of time. If God used the code of earlier species as the working templates for subsequent species and then introduced the replacement species who were spread out over a long period of time, it would give the impression that later species evolved from the earlier species.

For example, the genetic code for the species scheduled to be the 109th species to appear on Earth would be used as the starting template for the genetic code for the species scheduled to be the 110th species to appear. Then, the genetic code for species 110, would be used as the working template for the genetic code for the 111th species scheduled to appear, and so on.

A method like this would result in the creation and appearance of new species over the course of a long period of time. It would give the impression of a progressive process. The code difference between species 110 and 111 would be dramatic enough to produce a brand-new species. While at the same time, the genetic codes of species 110 and 111 would be similar enough for a resemblance to be noticed. It is the similar appearance of species 111 when compared to species 110 that causes us to assume 111 evolved from 110. Despite this, species 110 is a distinct, full-fledged species. Species 111 is also a distinct, full-fledged species. There are no transitional intermediates in this genetic engineering method. And this is precisely what we see in the Fossil Record.

This is in contrast to the theory of evolution that proposes the production of a series of mutant intermediates that exhibit small, incremental, baby-step mutations, that slowly transition into new species. This is the definition of an evolutionary process and this is how the theory of evolution is defined.

At first glance, this genetic engineering method seems similar to evolution theory because they are both progressive. However, the difference is that the theory of evolution requires the existence of countless transitional mutants in-between the two distinct species that are claimed to be related by way of evolution. Because there are no fossils of transitional mutants in-between any two species on the earth, this eliminates the possibility that Darwinian evolution ever took place. The scientific evidence actually supports the proposal of a Creator because the absence of transitional mutants in the Fossil Record closes the door on the theory of neo-Darwinian evolution.

From bacteria to galaxies, evolution theory has been shown to be an elaborate fairy tale and a science-fiction fantasy. All things considered, some people may ask the question: If evolution has been proven to have never occurred then why is it still being taught and supported? If evolution is a failed theory, then why does 80% of the world still believe in it? The reason evolution has not been put to rest is because no working model of another theory exists to take evolution's place. That's why!

For those people who will only accept a self-driven scientific explanation for where all of the species came from, they have no choice but to hang their hats on a science fiction fantasy that we know never occurred. Until 'another kind of evolution' is found as a viable explanation, Darwinian/neo-Darwinian evolution will continue to be the status quo as it continues to sit on its throne. Hence, there is a dead king on the throne.

As I close out this extremely important chapter, I wish to repeat that Charles Darwin admitted the absence of mutant intermediates was an obvious and grave problem with his macroevolutionary theory.[244] Dr. David Raup agrees, even though there has been over a 100 years of researching, this significant problem with Darwin's theory still exists and has not been alleviated.[245] And let's not forget that Professor Stephen Jay Gould agrees that Darwinian evolution "is effectively dead, despite its persistence as textbook orthodoxy" (Gould, 1980).[246] I wish to remind you that these two scientists are not making these statements because they are trying to promote the existence of God. No, these scientists made these statements because they are declaring the scientific truth of the matter.

Finally, I feel it is important for everyone to realize that proponents of a self-driven Darwinian evolution have been proven false with the death of evolution. Because these researchers have not proven the other possibility (God) is false, the only explanation still left standing, is God. The existence of God is established with the demonstration of how self-creating Darwinian evolution never happened.

This is exactly like flipping a coin. There are only two possibilities, either 'Heads' or 'Tails.' If another person flips this coin, covers it with their hand, peeks under their hand, and then tells us that 'Tails' (evolution) did not come up, this tells us the result must be 'Heads' (God). We don't need to see the coin to know that 'Heads' came up. Once we discover that 'Tails' is not the truth, it is unreasonable to refuse to believe that 'Heads' came up until we are finally able to see the coin with our own eyes. We don't need to do this to know the truth.

Regardless, there are people who are "on the fence" regarding the existence of God because they are not willing to commit to the existence of God until they observe concrete proof. These people require a level of proof that is extreme. Considering the coin flipping example in the last paragraph, a person "on the fence" would not be satisfied with being told that the coin did not come up 'Tails.' Many of these people require the concrete proof of being able see that the coin came up 'Heads.' This may seem like a reasonable position to take, however, I feel their requirement of absolute proof is too much to ask. I say this because on Judgement Day, it is logical to conclude that unbelievers wind up in the same category as nonbelievers.

Let me give an example of how the need for absolute proof is not necessary. Let's say that the great Sherlock Holmes was investigating a "whodunit" mystery where there were only two suspects left. As the investigation progresses, detective Holmes finds that it is impossible for one of the suspects to have been responsible for the evidence that was left behind (in this case the evidence would be the Fossil Record). By eliminating one of the two suspects, only one remains. You will recall in the introduction of this book that I mentioned the great Sherlock Holmes is quoted as stating:

> When you have excluded the impossible, whatever remains, however improbable, must be the truth.[247]

It is clear how intelligent and true this statement really is. And it's no wonder this is being declared by a fictional detective who was designed to be brilliant. In this Sherlock Holmes example, we can see that simply knowing 'Tails' has been eliminated is enough for Sherlock Holmes to determine that the answer must be 'Heads.' I feel it is important for people to recognize that Sherlock Holmes did not demand seeing the absolute proof of 'Heads' in order to come to the logical conclusion.

Darwinian evolution has been scientifically proven to be false. This is not my opinion. This is a fact. This means that Darwinian evolution should be excluded because it is impossible. Even so, many people may still wonder: if evolution has been proven to be false, then why do most people still believe in it?

I actually feel there are three reasons for this situation. The first reason that I have mentioned has to do with the fact there is no replacement for the theory of evolution. The second reason has been pointed out by Stephen Jay Gould who states that evolution is still taught as textbook doctrine even though it is effectively dead.[248] I feel that people believe what they are taught in school, and this is why they believe in evolution. The third reason people will continue to believe in evolution, even after it has been demonstrated to be a failed theory, is because humans are resistant to change. We are creatures of habit. This imperfection in the human condition can best be realized in a quote from the great Benjamin Franklin who was a famous intellectual statesman, inventor, and scientist. He has been quoted as stating:

> You will observe with concern how long a useful truth
> may be unknown, and exist, before it is generally received
> and practiced on.[249]

As we can see, the great Benjamin Franklin has observed that it is common practice for society to ignore useful truths for an extended period of time. This is precisely why the theory of neo-Darwinian evolution is still taught as textbook orthodoxy, even though it has been disproved by the Fossil Record. In addition to this very wise observation, the great Benjamin Franklin also made a powerful statement regarding his belief in God:

> Here is my Creed, I believe in one God, Creator of the Universe. That He governs it by His Providence. That He ought to be worshipped. That the most acceptable Service we render to Him, is doing good to His other Children. That the Soul of Man (Mankind) is immortal, and will be treated with Justice in another Life respecting its Conduct in this…[250]

It is clear from this quote that the great Benjamin Franklin believed in God. He believed that we should serve God by serving humanity. He believed that we all have an eternal soul. He believed that we will be held accountable for our deeds. And he believed in Heaven and Hell.

I reference Benjamin Franklin and what he had to say because he was an influential source whose level of wisdom was impressive. In an effort to demonstrate his influence and credibility I will list some of his significant achievements. Benjamin Franklin engineered the U.S. Postal system and started the first lending public library.[251] As a scientist, Benjamin Franklin invented the bifocal, the odometer, and the urinary catheter. He also invented the lightning rod because he understood electricity and the danger it posed to mankind. He knew that the power of electricity could be harnessed. Benjamin Franklin was also the first person to coin the electrical terms: "battery," "charge," "positive," and "negative." He never sought to patent any of his inventions because he wanted mankind to enjoy them freely![252]

As a statesman, Benjamin Franklin helped the Patriots win the Revolutionary War against Great Britain through his diplomatic genius as he appealed to the Nation of France to aid the colonists during their epic struggle for independence.[253] To put this into perspective, if the Patriots had never received support from France to break free from Great Britain, this would have prevented the United States of America from existing and becoming an industrial superpower that would go on to vastly exceed Great Britain's industrial capacity to manufacture war-goods during WWII. We witnessed America's dominant industrial might during WWII. I can't remember the source, but I read an online blog that was asking people who the best Generals of WWII were? One online blogger put it best, he stated:

Three Generals won WWII, General Motors, General Electric, and General Mills.

Now, I fully recognize the entire world is to be praised for uniting together to rise up and courageously fight against the tyranny of the Axis Powers during WWII. With that being said, if Benjamin Franklin and the colonists had failed to win their independence, the United States of America would have never existed. As a consequence, the Axis Powers most probably would have won WWII and the world would be a very different place right now. This is how important the Nation of France is to America's history, and this is how important Benjamin Franklin was as a statesman.

Some of Benjamin Franklin's history presented here may seem unrelated to the topic of this book, however, I argue this additional information helps to establish the genius and significant influence of Benjamin Franklin and how his thoughts and quotes should be taken very seriously to heart.

These are just a few of Benjamin Franklin's greatest achievements as a statesman and as a scientist. However, with all of this being said, I feel Benjamin Franklin's greatest overall achievement was his strong belief in God. Benjamin Franklin did not believe in fairy tales.

God is not a fairy tale. The same cannot be said for Darwinian evolution.

CHAPTER SIX

Earth Is Special

On the televised program, *The 700 Club*, host Pat Robertson read a letter from a viewer whose biggest fear of the future was not seeing her children and husband in God's Kingdom because they believed that the Bible could not explain the existence of dinosaurs. In his answer, Robertson said that Christians should not cover up scientific evidence that shows the earth to be much, much older than traditional interpretations. He told her that the Bible doesn't say that the world and everything in it is just 6,000 years old. Robertson also told this woman, "If you fight science, you're going to lose your children and I believe in telling it the way it was."[254]

I completely agree! The moment has come for us to solve this *time* dispute. On the one hand, we have what science declares, while on the other hand, we have mankind's traditional interpretation of the Book of Genesis. The purpose of this book is to reconcile the book of science and the Holy Writ of God. I seek to explain that God made science and that these two books are in agreement.

This particular chapter seeks to harmonize science with its Creator by revisiting the topic of *Creation Week*. In Chapter Two, *Creation*

Week was discussed as it relates to the topic of time. In this chapter, I revisit *Creation Week* as it relates to the earth becoming fully formed and fully populated with a diverse variety of species. This includes a discussion of the scientific engineering that went into creating planet Earth which serves to demonstrate how our finely tuned planet is not the product of lucky chances.

As discussed in Chapter Three, God created the cosmos with the Big Bang 13.7 billion years ago. By God's hand the dust and gases of creation began to coalesce into untold billions of glowing galaxies, each composed of untold billions of stars bursting into the cosmic void.[255] When the universe plasma cooled, most of what formed were clouds of hydrogen atoms that coalesced into the first stars.

After those stars exhausted their fuel, they died and exploded. These explosions ejected heavier elements into space, serving as building blocks for the planets and moons. After about 9 billion years of this explosive ejection process, the building blocks for the earth were finally ready to coalesce into our planet. This occurred in our neighborhood which we refer to as the Milky Way galaxy about 4.5 billion years ago. The planets of our galaxy formed just after the formation of our Sun. Our Sun is one of the newer generations of stars that began from coalescing hydrogen molecules and helium atoms along with clouds of debris dispersed from explosions of nearby nebulae.

God is a Master Engineer and Designer. We can see from the universe's development that the stars He made produced the materials that would compose our Earth and Moon—materials out of which you and I are made! Once the Big Bang cooled down, it produced an enormous supply of hydrogen atoms, some helium atoms, and a bit of lithium. You will recall from Chapter Three, I mentioned that one of God's many inventions which He has designed into the universe includes what I refer to as, *The Matter Converging Phenomenon*. This intriguing behavior is what we describe as gravity.

Now, once the Big Bang produced all these hydrogen atoms, they combined into molecules. Then God's *Matter Converging Phenomenon* (described as gravity) caused these hydrogen molecules to merge into large spheres. Once a sphere of hydrogen gas gets large enough and dense enough, it starts to crush the molecules at its core. This initially causes them to split back into hydrogen atoms. Then, *The Matter Converging Phenomenon* (described as gravity), coupled with pressure, friction, and heat causes the atoms in the core to get squashed together. This crushing process is the initial phase of what ultimately results in nuclear fusion.[256] The crushing and fusing of hydrogen atoms together, forms a new element called helium.

You will recall from high school chemistry class that hydrogen has one proton and helium has two protons. The actual process is rather complicated, however, to simplify a complex process, suffice it to say that 1 + 1 = 2. Essentially, two hydrogen atoms crushed together make one helium atom. The intricate details of this process are beyond the scope of this book.

That being said, when the star runs out of hydrogen atoms to crush together, it has run out of hydrogen fuel. And to simplify this complex process, I will simply state that at this point the star begins to crush the helium atoms together forming an even more complex atom. The star is now using its helium as fuel. Nuclear fusion is like combining building blocks together to produce more complex atoms. This process is referred to as stellar nucleosynthesis and is acknowledged to be a scientific fact.[257]

Let me give a simplified example. Do you remember the Lego building blocks we used to play with when we were younger? They were the size of those pink handheld erasers. Well, imagine that a single red Lego building block is a hydrogen atom. If we snap another red Lego block on top of the first block, then we have two blocks stuck together. In the case of this example, they are now fused together. These two blocks fused together now represent a helium atom. And if we stick another single Lego block on top of those two, we have three blocks fused together. This now represents a lithium atom. If we stick three more blocks on, we have six blocks fused together which now forms a carbon atom. If we fuse another hydrogen block onto carbon, we have seven blocks. This now represents a nitrogen atom, and so on, and so forth.

There is one point that I should clarify regarding my simplified example. When atoms and molecules commonly stick together, this represents molecular bonding (it is beyond the scope of this book to discuss the various types of bonds). When atoms are merged together to form another element, this represents nuclear fusion (stellar nucleosynthesis). There is a huge difference between molecular bonding and nuclear fusion. The relatively sedate process of chemical and molecular bonding does not require the immense amounts of pressure and energy that are necessary to accomplish nuclear fusion.

This process continues until the star finally runs out of the fuel necessary to remain functional. This usually results in the star exploding, releasing the heavier elements—carbon, oxygen, nitrogen, iron, aluminum, and quartz–into space. Then, God's *Matter Converging Phenomenon* (described as gravity) causes these released star-fused elements to merge together and form rock-solid spheres known as planets and moons. This is how science explains the origin of all the atoms more complex than hydrogen. This also explains how the planets and moons were formed.

You will recall a chart on the wall in high school chemistry class that had a lot of boxes on it. That is the Periodic Table which lists all the elements in the known universe. Essentially, all atoms are made in the center of a star except for the initial atoms resulting from the Big Bang. This phenomenon also includes pulsars (pulsating stars). In addition, collisions of neutron stars are believed to produce some of the very heavy metals.[258] God created the universe first and then had His *Star Science* produce the materials for the earth. Science dates the universe to be 13.7 billion years old, while the earth is 4.5 billion years old. Apparently, about 9 billion years after this stellar nucleosynthesis process first began, the elements composing our Earth were finally merged together solidifying into what we call home.

I would like to point out how logical, elegant, and productive this stellar nucleosynthesis process is. Stellar nucleosynthesis is a brilliantly designed fusion process that creates light, heat, radiation, and complex atoms. The complex atoms that are produced become the construction materials that make up the planets and the moons. Stars also serve mankind with all of the benefits we experience from the science of astronomy which includes calendars, knowing when to plant and harvest crops, and how to navigate from one place to another.

What I also find fascinating about stars is that they demonstrate how God prefers to use His created *Star Science* to produce the raw materials for His Universe instead of just snapping His fingers causing the materials to suddenly appear. However, God's choice to create in this fashion can give some people the false impression that science is a self-driven phenomenon. This is clearly not the case.

As I have stated in Chapter Two, because the first clock was not created until after the universe was already in existence, this means the universe could be any age, even billions of years old. Scripture does not contradict this scientific finding. It is my opinion, that the age of the universe and the age of the earth cannot be proven to contradict Scripture. Why is this? This is the case because the Bible does not state how old the earth is and the Bible was not meant to be used as a calculator. As a result, I feel a case can be made that the Book of Genesis is not in conflict with science regarding the age of the universe and the age of the earth. Therefore, I agree with the scientific consensus that the universe is billions of years old.

Also discussed in Chapter Two is Earth's collision with the planet Theia which brings into alignment the timeframe of when the earth started spinning and the date that *Creation Week* started. This serves to date the start of *Creation Week* to 4.5 billion years ago.

With that being established, it is time to focus our attention on the life that populated the earth. It is one thing to find harmony between the age of the universe and the earth, and the Book of Genesis, however, it is another thing to find harmony between the Fossil Record and the Book of Genesis.

The traditional fundamental interpretation of the Book of Genesis seems to have come to the conclusion that the universe, the earth, and all the life that has ever lived on the earth were created over an actual seven-day week, just 6,000 years ago. Some Biblical scholars have dated Adam and Eve to have lived anywhere from 6,000 years to as far back as about 10,000 years ago. As discussed in Chapter Two, because Adam and Eve were created at the end of the same '*Week,*' in which all other living creatures were created, this makes it appear to some scholars and others who traditionally interpret Genesis, that all the life that has ever existed on the earth must be no older than 6,000-10,000 years.

How do we solve this multi-billion-year disagreement with the Fossil Record? As mentioned in Chapter Two, during the seven-day

Creation Week, I propose that God created *creation seeds* of all the different species. They would go on to germinate at different, precise, and staggered times throughout the earth's history. You will recall that a *creation seed* contains the DNA profile for a particular species along with a possible timer which is pre-set to open the seed when its scheduled germination date has arrived.

This interpretation would perfectly reconcile the Fossil Record with the Scriptural Record. Even if all of these *creation seeds* were created during an actual seven-day '*Week*,' the germination of these seeds took place in God's Time over the course of billions of years. This would agree with what the evidence from the Fossil Record tells us. According to this proposal, all *creation seeds* would have to have been created over four billion years ago, right after Theia collided with Earth.

In science, we see the first species appeared 3.7 billion years ago.[259] Then, more species slowly appeared over millions of years. This conflicts with the traditional religious timeline of 6,000 years for the appearance of every species on the earth. Some people may wonder: If the earth was formed 4.5 billion years ago, then why did it take until 3.7 billion years ago for the first life to appear? Why did it take 800 million years for the first life to appear on the earth? The answer is pretty straightforward. After Theia collided with Earth, this severe trauma caused Earth to become a very hot, molten lava planet.[260] The earth eventually cooled down. After 800 million years the earth was settled down to the extent that it became hospitable for the first living organisms 3.7 billion years ago. The earth was finally ready to support its first life that germinated from the *creation seeds* for Day Two of *Creation Week*. As a consequence, all *creation seeds* made 4.5 billion years ago had to wait until the earth cooled down before they could be planted 3.7 billion years ago.

Events that occurred during *Creation Week* explain how the earth became populated with life. Therefore, it is at this point that I'm going to revisit *Creation Week* and repeat some of what was presented in Chapter Two. Then I'm going into a bit more depth so that the complete picture of *Creation Week* becomes evident.

Science tells us that plants, birds, marine life, and land animals appeared on the earth before mankind. And this is what the Book of Genesis tells us as well. So far, so good. However, disagreements exist because of the timelines.

Do you remember the clock that was made for mankind on Day One? It was created for mankind who appeared at the end of Day Six. During God's creation of all the other species on the earth, mankind was not yet around to determine the amount of time that had passed. As a result, God created all the other species on *His Time*. As we saw in Chapter Two, that was not mankind's time, but God's—the difference between the two is something that humans will never be able to comprehend. God manages and controls *time* in ways that we cannot even imagine and is beyond the grasp of our limited intelligence.

With that in mind, a *creation seeds* proposal is a problem-solving solution that functions to explain how God's creations started their existence as seeds during *Creation Week* which started 4.5 billion years ago. Then, over the course of long ages, all of these *creation seeds* opened and introduced species at their prescribed times. The last of God's creations occurred about 10,000 years ago with His creation of Adam and Eve.

At the very beginning of the *Creation Days* involving living organisms, I admit the creating of the *creation seeds* could have occurred over the course of a very short period of time. However, the actual germinations of these seeds would have taken billions and millions of years to unfold, opening at their prescribed times as God determined. All the species came forth in a staggered fashion when God wanted them to in order for simpler species to prepare the way for the more complex species that would appear later. This means that each *Creation Day* lasted for a very long period of time.

This *creation seeds* proposal serves to reconcile the Word of God with the Fossil Record. Because Adam and Eve effectively started the first functional clock when they came into existence, the 6,000- to 10,000-year timeline for Adam and Eve that some scholars attempt to calculate from the Bible's genealogies, can be true regarding how far back mankind's history goes.

Here's where we are, there are two categories of creation, each with its own category of time:

>**Category 1: God's Time** applies to the creation of the universe, the earth, and all the life that came before Adam and Eve.
>
>**Category 2: Mankind's time** applies to Adam and Eve and all of the earth's history from that point forward. This includes the last 10,000 years.

The first six *Creation Days* are in Category 1 while Day Seven is in Category 2. The first six *Days* all came to an end at the same time which ushered in the beginning of Day Seven. The end of Creation Day Six is what brings Genesis Chapter One to a close.

At this point, in an effort to clarify *Creation Week* and this *creation seeds* concept, I will present a condensed summary of what could have happened. Before I begin, I wish to repeat that the reason I am proposing a *creation seeds* concept is because it is the only way I can see to reconcile the Fossil Record with the Book of Genesis. For the people who may find this *creation seeds* concept to be unusual, please keep in mind that it succeeds in its function to bridge the gap that separates the Fossil Record evidence from the Holy Writ of God.

As stated, I believe God used His Light to simulate 24-hour, day/night cycles to mimic what our Sun would do once mankind appeared. I also believe the very first evening of each *Creation Day* that involved *creation seeds*, was when the *creation seeds* were genetically engineered. In this way, each *Creation Day's* creation phase (Phase 1) can be said to have occurred within the span of what we now consider to be, one day. As mentioned in an earlier chapter, if we take the first creative period (the first evening) of each *Creation Day* (which is Phase 1 of each *Creation Day*) and add these seven periods together, this could very well equate to a literal seven-day week. However, this seven-day week only represents the creation phase for each *Creation Day* (Phase 1). The germination phase (Phase 2) for each *Creation Day* lasted for billions of years.

I will now quickly run through a synopsis of *Creation Week* to refresh what we went over in Chapter Two.

Creation Days had their starts staggered by what we now consider to be a 24-hour day. I say this because there was no functional clock until Biblical Adam was created. Day Seven is the only exception which started only after the first six *Creation Days* ended.

Day One kicked off *Creation Week*. This very first evening period would represent Phase 1 of Day One where God turned His Light on. All subsequent *Day Periods* would constitute Phase 2 of Day One.

Day Two obviously started before Day Three began.

Day Three started before Day Two ended, and before Day Four began.

Day Four started before Day Three ended and before Day Five began.

For example: Day Four allowed the Sun to become visible. And even though Moses is told that God saw the light was good before Day

Five is discussed, Day Five started before Day Four was completed. This is because it took a very long time for the effects of God's *Matter Converging Phenomenon* (described as gravity) to clear the atmosphere of orbiting debris.

We must be mindful that Genesis was given to Moses by God through angels. They told Moses about things that had taken place long before. This means that when God states that each *Creation Day* had unfolded as He planned, this was ancient history by the time Moses wrote about it. This allowed God to mention His Commands for each *Creation Day*, along with the outcomes for each *Day*. By the time that Moses wrote Genesis, any gaps in time that existed when *Creation Week* took place, were not deemed to be important enough to include. The fact that God created, and the general order in which he created, were the only details deemed to be significant. It is very probable the fundamental timeline interpretations that have been traditionally assumed when examining this text, do not represent what actually occurred.

Some people may ask, "If this was not important to know when Moses wrote the Book of Genesis, then why would we need to know this now?" My answer is that we did not have scientific literature that claimed that the earth, the universe, and the fossils are incredibly ancient. There was no scientific literature that contradicted how we have traditionally interpreted *Creation Week*. Please take note that I am only seeking a solution concerning a few parts of Genesis 1—all having to do with *time*. Because of the way in which *Creation Week* is worded, and because of the way the *Days* are numbered, we get the impression that previous *Creation Days* had to be completed and come to an end before the next *Creation Day* was started. We naturally assume that each *Creation Day* only lasted for 24 hours. I don't believe this is what actually occurred because the Fossil Record tells us this is not what happened.

For example, Day Five did not have to come to an end before Day Six started. It is true that Day Five started before Day Six started, but Day Five did not have to end in order for Day Six to begin. Most of Day Five and Day Six ran concurrently. As stated, I now believe that Moses is actually describing *Divine Days* in *Creation Week* that lasted much longer than a 24-hour day.

Continuing on, we see that Day Five started before Day Four ended and before Day Six began.

Day One, Day Two, Day Three, Day Five, and Day Six, were all running at the same time while God's *Matter Converging Phenomenon* (described as gravity) was slowly clearing the debris from Earth's orbit in Day Four. This means Creation Days One through Six all wound up running simultaneously for billions of years.

As mentioned, God had Moses record, "And the evening and the morning were the …. day," for the first six *Creation Days*. However, God did not have Moses record, "And the evening and the morning were the seventh day." Notice how God did not close out Day Seven. I feel the absence of this verse indicates that we are still in Day Seven which has not ended yet, it only started 10,000 years ago! As a consequence, the fact that God does not state, "And the evening and the morning were the seventh day," proves to me that *Creation Week* is actually composed of seven, very long, *Divine Days*.

This supports the possibility that Genesis 1:13, is really stating, "And the first evening and the last morning were the third day." This makes perfect sense and would mean that the first six *Creation Days* were billions of years long and have ended. This would be a demonstration of how God's Time during *Creation Week*, was vastly different from mankind's time. What we are witnessing here are *Divine Days*, not solar days. We know these *Creation Days* are not solar days because the Sun is not even mentioned until Day Four.

As previously mentioned, Phase 1 of Day Seven included God resting from the work of implementing the infrastructure for *Creation Week*. Phase 1 also includes the establishment of the weekly Sabbath and God's Covenant with mankind, while Phase 2 of Day Seven includes all of mankind's history until the *End of Times* occurs. As a consequence, I believe Phase 2 of Day Seven will end with the *End of Days*. I suspect this term, *End of Days*, actually means, the *End of Creation Days*, where Phase 2 of Day Seven finally ends.

At this point I am going to more thoroughly explain what I believe occurred during *Creation Week* as it completed the earth's development, refinement, and populating.

The very beginning of Day One of *Creation Week* occurred after God had already created the universe (the heavens) and the earth. I consider *Creation Week* to be what occurred on the earth once a clock was established. I think of *Creation Week* as, *Earth's Creation Week*.

Genesis 1:2 tells us the earth's history started in a state of darkness. Then in Genesis 1:3, God shined His Light onto the earth, probably as He was casting the planet Theia into Earth to complete Earth's formation which put Earth into its spin. This is why the darkness of evening comes before the morning light. The earth initially sat in darkness when it was void and without form (Genesis 1:2), after this, God shined His Light. This dark/light sequence is a reflection of the beginning of Earth's history. Then in Genesis 1:4, we read that the light was good and then God was able to divide the light from the darkness. This was accomplished by God causing the earth to spin. In Genesis 1:5, we read that God called the light, as day, and He called the darkness, as night. Then God states, "And the evening and the morning were the first day."

This is how the night/day cycle began. In ancient Jerusalem, the night phase occurred first, followed by the daylight phase. This Hebrew tradition most likely has its roots in the earth's beginning and the verse, "And the evening and the morning were the first day." I feel we can all agree that Day One of *Creation Week* started off by giving mankind the time-gift of the night/day cycle. This established the construct of a standard day. This is why God had Moses record, "And the evening and the morning were the first day." It is true that *Creation Days* were composed of 24-hour days, but they were composed of billions of years of 24-hour days. This is the case because *Creation Days* were *Divine Days*. It would have only caused confusion if Moses had written,

> And the evening and the morning were the first day, of
> Day One. Hence, the first evening and the last morning
> were the entirety of Divine Day One.

Apparently, God left out the long ages between the first evening and the last morning because simple mankind would not have been able to wrap their heads around anything more complicated than what God had Moses record. The confusion that this detailed statement would have caused would have prevented mankind from easily recognizing the seven-day workweek model. Therefore, we can reconcile the Fossil Record evidence with how Genesis Chapter One is worded if we take all of this into consideration. I can't find another way to bring the scientific findings into agreement with the Holy Writ of God. If you can find a better way, use it.

In addition to Earth's spin, the collision with Theia created other benefits. This tremendous collision sheared off lots of the earth's crust and added the iron core from Theia to the earth's iron core. As a result, Earth is an extraordinary planet because it has a much larger iron core and a much thinner crust than most planets in the universe. The large core protects us from solar radiation because of the produced electromagnetic field that functions like an umbrella shielding the earth from much of the Sun's radiation.[261] This is referred to as the magnetosphere.

In addition, the collision with Theia sheared off much of the earth's crust. This resulted in Earth's thin crust which established the conditions that created the moving plate tectonics that keeps the earth *alive*.[262] And as scientists have discovered, the earth's crust debris from Theia's collision makes up our Moon which significantly supports life on the earth.[263]

Our Moon supports life on the earth by keeping Earth's axis of rotation constant at 23.4 degrees off vertical. If our Moon was not present, Earth's axis could be swinging wildly causing the polar ice caps to dramatically shift position on a regular basis causing severe climate shifts that would be enough to trigger ice ages.[264] This would make living on the earth very different, and very difficult. All of this makes our earth special and fully engineered to support mankind's existence.

Therefore, in addition to the earth's spin, I believe that God cast Theia into the earth as part of Earth's forming and refinement process. And just to clarify, *forming* and *refinement*, are different from *creating*. The earth was formed and refined after it had already been created.

On Day Two of *Creation Week*, we read in Genesis 1:6 (KJV), "And God said, Let there be a firmament in the midst of the waters." The firmament is the oxygen atmosphere. It sits above the oceans and below the rain clouds. I propose that Phase 1 of Day Two started 4.5 billion years ago when its *creation seeds* were produced. This was followed by Phase

2 of Day Two when the first *creation seed* germinated which brought forth the first life, a bacterium. This bacterium appeared around 3.7 billion years ago.[265] The appearance of this first bacterium started the long process of reducing Earth's atmospheric methane levels.[266]

After this, large amounts of existing carbon dioxide fed later bacteria called Cyanobacteria which produced oxygen as a waste product which accumulated as Earth's oxygen atmosphere.[267] Cyanobacteria are famous for producing the earth's oxygen. We refer to this process as, *terraforming*. It took billions of years for various bacteria to terraform the earth. This combined activity of different types of microorganisms served to terraform the earth into a place with an oxygen-rich atmosphere that is hospitable to supporting complex life.

Made by God, that first bacterium had very complex DNA. These primitive bacteria have a single-stranded chromosomal DNA. DNA is the most complex coding mechanism ever discovered. Many scientists admit the instructional code on DNA is so ultra-complex, that it would not have been able to just invent itself as the theory of abiogenesis claims. What I have just presented answers the question: Why would God start with bacteria as the first life on planet Earth? Why didn't this get mentioned during Creation Week? God knew that mankind would not understand unseen microscopic life. As a result, God only revealed what was necessary. God started with bacteria because the earth's atmosphere needed to be bioengineered. This is all the product of a Master Engineer at work.

As mentioned, the first bacteria reduced methane levels. Then the *creation seeds* for cyanobacteria and other particular bacteria germinated. Cyanobacteria proceeded to use the existing atmospheric CO2 as food.[268] God even equipped cyanobacteria with the miracle pigment, chlorophyll, which converts light into food! Chlorophyll can work with God's Light or sunlight and represents the first solar panel. I don't believe the miraculous chlorophyll pigment is a coincidence. This magnificent photosynthetic innovation did not just magically invent itself. I don't believe the appearance of these special bacteria that produce oxygen as a waste product is a coincidence.

Cyanobacteria form the oldest fossils on the earth and are found in Australia, the Bahamas, and Utah's Great Salt Lake.[269] These cyanobacteria fossils are called stromatolites and prove that life was here over 3.5 billion years ago. Stromatolite fossils are sedimentary structures produced by the activity of blue-green algae, which are really Cyanobacteria (not really algae). The oxygen-hating bacteria (anaerobes) were seeded here first (when there was no oxygen) over 3.7 billion years ago. Next, oxygen producing cyanobacteria were seeded around 3.5 billion years ago. [270] Notice how the oxygen-hating bacteria (anaerobes) were followed by the oxygen producing bacteria which prepared the way for animal life.

Scientists who wish to see Mars able to support human life, propose introducing microorganisms like our Cyanobacteria, and others, to make the atmosphere of Mars breathable.[271] Therefore, this concept of terraforming makes perfect logical sense. It seems this is how God made the earth's oxygen atmosphere which we read about during *Creation Week* on Day Two in Genesis. Cyanobacteria also pulled nitrogen from the air and deposited it into the soil to promote plant life.[272] I don't believe it is a coincidence that these bacteria also possessed the ability to deposit nitrogen into the soil.

Let's review the three benefits we witness from cyanobacteria:

1) This species of bacteria converts light into food (photosynthesis).

2) This species of bacteria produces oxygen as a waste product which complex life will need.

3) This species of bacteria takes nitrogen from the air and deposits it into the soil which vegetation will need.

All of these activities were crucial in helping to terraform the earth into a place that is now hospitable for complex life. Prior life supports subsequent life. Indeed, God is logical and methodical.

Next comes Phase 1 of Day Three where God makes the seeds for vegetation. Phase 1 of Day Three would have also started 4.5 billion years ago. It is important to note that Earth was a hot molten planet for a while after its collision with Theia. This means that *creation seeds* would have probably needed to have waited to be planted until the earth cooled down. As a result, the *creation seeds* could have still been created 4.5 billion years ago (Phase 1), but they would not have been physically planted until the earth cooled down 3.7 billion years ago. This would be the case for all the *Creation Day's* seeds.

The first vegetation to appear were the fungi which date back to over a billion years ago. Most of the other vegetation seeds sat in the soil for billions of years before finally emerging 500 million years ago when most of the vegetation seeds started to germinate during Phase 2 of Day Three.[273] With that in mind, Phase 2 of Day Three would have stalled until it was able to accelerate once the point was reached where Day Two had produced enough oxygen to support vegetation. Vegetation needs carbon dioxide to make sugars, but vegetation also needs oxygen to break the sugars down into usable energy.[274]

We can clearly see how the success of Day Three depended on the success of Day Two. While Day Two and Day Three were still running their course, Day Four, Day Five, and Day Six, were started (Phase 2). A week after *Creation Week* started, *Creation Days* One through Six were all running simultaneously.

In Genesis 1:9-13, we read that the grasses, the plants, and the trees were created in Day Three. Because molten Earth had to cool down first, I believe the first hours of Day Three involved God creating the *creation seeds* (Phase 1). Once the earth had cooled down hundreds of millions of years later, then God separated the land from the water, thus creating the seas, the lakes, and the rivers during Phase 2. It would have been at this point that God could have planted the vegetation *creation seeds* into the soil (Phase 2).

Day Three of *Creation Week* is where God ordered the earth to support His *creation seeds* for vegetation and to bring them forth once those seeds germinated at their prescribed times in the future. The only thing that **physically** happened in Phase 1 of Day Three (first 12 hours) was the creation of the seeds. Non-physical activity in Phase 1 would have included statements made by God as He gave the earth the command to support His creations in the future. Then God looked into the future to see that His creations would be good. Finally, God commented on those visions. All of these things could have transpired within the span of 12-24 hours. The only physical activity in Phase 2 would have been the planting of the *creation seeds*.

In Genesis 1:12 (KJV), we read, "And the earth brought forth grass and the herb yielding seed…" Once the timer went off for the vegetation *creation seeds*, the earth did indeed support these germinations and brought them forth, one at a time. I believe God is making this comment to Moses around 1440 BC about the grasses and vegetation that came forth just as He had commanded. Therefore, what Moses records for Day Three includes God's plans, creation of the seeds, God's commands, and God's visions of the future outcomes. Because God delivered this message to Moses after the fact, this message can include the initiation of this process as well as the outcome of this process, from start to finish. Therefore, if we only considering everything that physically happened (Phase 1 and Phase 2), I favor the phrase, "And the first evening and the last morning were the third day." Notice how this phrase also includes everything from start to finish for Divine Day Three.

Let's now look at *Creation Week* regarding Day Four. Genesis 1:14-18 (KJV), states:

> And God said, 'Let there be lights in the firmament of the heaven to divide the day from the night; and let them for signs, and for seasons, and for days, and years. And let them be for light in the firmament of the Heaven to give light upon the earth: and it was so. And God made the two great lights; the greater light to rule the day, and the lesser light to rule the night: He made the stars also. And God set them in the firmament of the Heaven to give light upon the earth, And to rule over the day and over the night, and to divide the light from the darkness:' and God saw that it was good.

Day Four does not involve any *creation seeds* but may have included God giving His *Matter Converging Phenomenon* (described as the law of gravity) the command to begin the process of clearing Earth's orbit of debris. By the end of Day Four, all of the orbiting debris was cleared from the atmosphere, thus creating a path for the star's light, the Sun's light, and the Moon's light to finally reach the earth's surface. This would have *made* the stars, Sun, and Moon finally visible.

It is my understanding that '*creating*' and '*making*' have two different meanings in the Bible. *Create* means something that is newly produced, while, *made*, or *making*, means to fashion a new use for something already in existence. If we look at the original Hebrew of Genesis 1:14-19 (KJV), in particular verse 16, we read, "Elohim (God) is making the two illuminaries (lights), the great illuminary (light) to rule the day and the small (lesser) illuminary (light) to rule the night..." Because the word, "*making,*" is used, this could very well mean that our Sun and our Moon already existed. However, they were obscured by orbiting debris, then God **made** them visible, and therefore, useful by the end of Day Four. I say this because we know that our Sun existed millions of years before the earth and our Moon did. Our Sun is definitely a bit older than the earth.

Notice how there is no mention of the Sun or the Moon until Day Four of *Creation Week*. With Day Four discussing the Sun, also take notice that we now have TWO major light sources during *Creation Week* (God's Light and the Sun). Science tells us the Sun is a bit older and existed a bit earlier in our galaxy than the earth. As a consequence, we are posed with the question: How can we reconcile the Sun being older than the earth, but the Book of Genesis does not mention the Sun until Day Four of *Creation Week*? How is this possible?

As I have briefly mentioned earlier, the only way this can be reconciled is if the Sun was not visible to Earth before Day Four, even though it was still there. How is this possible? Well, if there was enough rocky debris orbiting the earth from its numerous meteor collisions, this would have blocked out the Sun. This means that on Day Four, God 'created' the conditions (God created the path) that allowed the Sun's light to finally reach Earth. The clearing of this debris from the skies would have been the consequence of God's *Matter Converging Phenomenon*, which we describe as gravity.

What seems to be happening is that God cleared the cloudy atmosphere around the earth so that the Sun, the Moon, and the stars would become visible to the earth. Once mankind is created, this will give them the ability to develop calendars, navigate, and keep track of the seasons. This is why it seems that the light given on Day One was God's own Light.

I believe that these details help to substantiate that we are not dealing with a contrived tale. Why would a fable writer conjure up a myth of creation in which there was one light source for the first three days of creation and then introduced another light source that took over at some point later? Does that make any sense? What would be the logical purpose of structuring a fable in this way? No reader 3,500 years ago would understand its implications; it would just confuse the reader.

This is why I find it extremely interesting there were two different light sources during *Creation Week*. This was probably because lots of crust debris and soot were orbiting the earth from its collision with Theia in the past. This would have blocked out the light from the Sun and would explain why God supplied His Light for the first *three days* (at least) of creation. And once God's *Matter Converging Phenomenon* (described as the law of gravity) finally cleared the atmosphere of the soot and debris on Day Four, the Sun's rays were now able to penetrate the skies and reach the earth. This also made the Moon and the stars visible as well.

This explains why there were two different light sources during *Creation Week*. Since science tells us that the Sun is a bit older than the earth, this means that what God did on Day Four in reference to the Sun, the Moon, and the stars, was to 'make' them visible. God had already created the Sun, the Moon, and stars in the past, but on Day Four God *created* the clear path to make them visible.

The fact that we see two different light sources mentioned during creation tells us that the details of this account came from a Divine source and not from a fable writer.

As I have stated, a human would never conjure up a creation story with two different light sources. Because God allowed His Science to take its time and run its course, this caused *Creation Week* to begin with God's Light on Day One and then later switch over to the Sun's light when it was available. God has no problem waiting for His designed science to run its course.

I believe the Sun took over at the very end of Day Six and has been doing its job well in Day Seven as it supports mankind and all the species on Earth. I believe we are in Day Seven right now. As I have stated, I believe we are currently in Day Seven because in Genesis 2:3-4, where God Blesses Day Seven as a Sabbath and a day of rest, He does NOT state: "And the evening and the morning were the seventh day." I believe this is because the Seventh Day isn't over yet.

Since the Sun was not mentioned until Day Four, this means that God used His Light (for sure) on Day One, Day Two, and Day Three. And remember, it's on Day Three that we see the appearance of vegetation which includes plants, flowers, and trees. This means that the world's vegetation was grown with God's Light, not with the Sun's light. God definitely did not use the Sun to create on the first three days of Creation Week. By the end of Day Four, the Sun's light was finally able to reach the earth's surface. However, I believe this happened at the end of Day Five and Day Six. God could have continued to have His Light on for Day Five and Day Six. Hence, I believe the first six *Creation Days* all ended at the same time and were all illuminated by God's Light.

I believe this is the case because this scenario allowed God's Time to continue to dictate the duration of a Divine evening and morning cycle during *Creation Week*. In other words, Day Four, Day Five, and 99.9% of Day Six, were still on God's Time, just like Day One, Day Two, and Day Three. Day Seven is the only exception. Even though it is a *Divine Day*, it's illuminated by the Sun's light. Even though Day Seven is now on mankind's solar time, mankind's time still exists within the construct of Divine Day Seven.

Next, we have Day Five, which is seen in Genesis 1:20-23. Phase 1 of Day Five includes God creating the seeds for marine life and birds. These seeds would have been created 4.5 billion years ago but not deposited in the water and soil for germination until the molten Earth cooled down. The same *creation seeds* explanation I used for Day Three would be applied to Day Five. In Genesis 1:20 (KJV), we read, "And God said, Let the waters bring forth abundantly the moving creature that has life and fowl that may fly above the earth. In the open firmament of heaven." All these creatures came forth on their predetermined birth dates, not all at the same time.

At this point I wish to clarify research has found that land animals appeared before birds appeared. This is not the order we read in Genesis. However, because the creation seeds were created billions of years ago, they sat dormant until it was time for them to open. This allowed some land animal seeds to open before the birds appeared. *Creation seeds* could open at any time because Day Five and Day Six overlapped and ran concurrently. Therefore, the order of creations listed in Genesis Chapter One, reflect the order the *creation seeds* were created during the first, seven evening periods (Phase 1) of *Creation Week*. This is not necessarily the order that the seeds germinated in Phase 2. The order of the germinations was dictated by God's design which was sometimes, slightly different from their *creation seed* production order.

Let's look at the *creation seeds* for sharks which were created 4.5 billion years ago at the beginning of Day Five of *Creation Week*. They were probably deposited on the ocean floor about 3.7 billion years ago once molten Earth cooled down. They sat on the ocean floor for billions of years and then began emerging around 500 million years ago.[275] These *creation seeds* began to open and slowly introduced sharks over the course of 500 million years during Phase 2. Because God delivered this message to Moses after the fact, this message can include the initiation of this *Creation Day* as well as the outcome of this *Creation Day* which came later. This is why I believe in the phrase, "And the first evening and the last morning were the fifth day." This phrase includes everything from start to finish for Divine Day Five.

Then we have Day Six, which is described in Genesis 1:24-31. In Genesis 1:24 (KJV), we read, "And God said, Let the earth bring forth the living creature after his kind, cattle, creeping thing, and beast of the earth after his kind: and it was so." Phase 1 of Day Six includes God creating the seeds for all animals, including the prehistoric reptiles, dinosaurs, and the hominids.

The *creation seeds* that were planted for dinosaurs on Day Six of *Creation Week* sat in the soil for billions of years and began emerging about 240 million years ago.[276] After the dinosaur seeds had opened, they roamed the earth for millions of years. Then a significant event occurred about 65 million years ago, which is a few million years after T-Rex started to roam the earth. Scientists tell us that an asteroid the size of Mount Everest struck the earth and killed all the dinosaurs.[277] This asteroid is referred to as the K-T Meteorite (the Cretaceous–Tertiary extinction) and the devastation it caused wiped out all the dinosaurs and large animals of that era, clearing the way for the mammals.[278] That asteroid prevented dinosaurs from being involved in the history of Adam, Eve, and mankind.

Some may wonder why God made the dinosaurs in the first place? As mentioned, God created earlier species to support later species that in turn support mankind. During their era, dinosaurs, and especially the pre-historic vegetation of that period, would go on to decay and form our fossil fuels which currently provide for much of mankind's energy needs.[279] If it wasn't for all those dinosaurs and all of that pre-historic vegetation, we would not have our coal, natural gas, and oil reserves. Pre-history supports our history. God designed the universe and the earth to support His prime creation of mankind. God's creativity is unlimited, and all of these spectacular dinosaurs are a display of His infinite power, imagination, and brilliance. A *creation seeds* concept demonstrates how people can have dinosaurs and the Holy Bible at the same time.

As a side note, this creation seeds proposal also helps to explain the Noah's Ark story to some degree. If species came and went extinct over long ages, many of the species that roamed the earth before Adam and Eve would not have wound up on Noah's Ark. They were already extinct by the time Noah was alive. Therefore, this *creation seeds* concept also explains how there would have been a much lower number of species to load onto Noah's Ark than originally thought. A much lower number of species to load makes the Noah's Ark story much easier to visualize.

Phase 2 of Day Six really kicked into gear about 500 million years ago when those *creation seeds* began to open, slowly introducing them as living organisms over the course of 500 million years. Phase 2 of Day Six ended with Adam and Eve roughly 10,000 years ago. I believe

God turned His light off the moment He created Adam. This began mankind's time of the 24-hour 'solar' day. However, since Eve was not created right away, this means that a very short segment at the end of Day Six was now on mankind's time. Only with the appearance of Eve can Creation Day Six truly end and Day Seven begin.

By the time God turned off His glorious Light at the end of Day Six, the stars, the Sun, and the Moon would have been visible and able to be experienced by all life on Earth (especially mankind). Once each *creation seed's* first male and female couple were birthed, God nurtured these first couples to maturity.

Right before the appearance of Adam and Eve, the last *creation seeds* to germinate on Day Six occurred between 125,000-150,000 years ago when *Scientific Adam* and *Mitochondrial Eve* appeared (who I discuss shortly). I say this because Biblical Adam and Eve were not created with seeds. I believe mankind is the only species that was not created by using a *creation seed*. At 10,000 years ago, when the earth was fully prepared, God finally created Biblical Adam and Eve. It was at this transition from God's Time to mankind's time, and in the presence of Adam and Eve, that God ushered in the Seventh Day. It was at this time that God created the holy Sabbath as a perpetual celebration and a day of worship. In addition, this is when God established a covenant relationship with Adam and Eve.

Here is a list of some of God's creatures and when their *creation seeds* opened. One of the first animals known to exist was aquatic and belongs to Day Five (Dickinsonia). The rest are land animals belonging to Day Six. The Fossil Record provides the following data:

- Dickinsonia (the first animal fat) - appeared 560 million years ago.[280]
- Dinosaurs – started appearing 243 million years ago.[281]

- Horses - started appearing 55 million years ago.[282]
- First Primates - started appearing 55 million years ago.[283]
- Apes and Old-World Monkeys - started appearing 30 million years ago.[284]
- Chimpanzees - started appearing 6 million years ago.[285]
- Tigers - started appearing 2.5 million years ago.[286]
- Homo erectus – appeared around 1.4 million years ago.[287]
- Homo heidelbergensis - appeared around 800,000 years ago.[288]
- Homo neanderthalensis - appeared around 400,000 years ago.[289]
- Homo sapiens/primitive human-like hominids - appeared around 200,000 years ago.[290] (This group also includes *Scientific Adam/Y-Chromosomal Adam* and *Mitochondrial Eve* who appeared about 130,000 years ago).[291]

Biblical Adam and Eve had no *creation seed*; they were created as "*mankind*," on a monumental and celebrated day about 10,000 years ago.

At this time, I would like to direct your focus on the primate hominid list. We can see how researcher Colin Schultz has listed many of them:[292]

- Homo rudolfensis
- Homo habilis
- Homo georgics
- Homo erectus
- Homo floresiensis
- Homo ergaster
- Homo cepranensis
- Homo antecessor
- Homo heidelbergensis
- Homo neanderthalensis (Neanderthals)
- Homo sapiens

In addition, there were more hominids such as Cro-Magnon and Homo denisovan. As we can see, God enjoyed creating hominids because he made a lot of them. It is important to note this is not a list of *evolving* hominids. That is because each and every one of these hominids has their own species name. They are not mutant intermediates linking two distinct species together, because if they were, they would not possess their own species name. The hominids listed above are all separate and distinct species. Therefore, this long list does not represent evolutionary progression.

God made billions of species and about 20 of these species were hominids that are more advanced than apes and monkeys but less advanced than humans. The Neanderthals are a good example. The Neanderthals are not monkeys, and they are not human.

When you line up theses 20 species of hominids, at first glance it appears they represent an evolutionary line of progression. But they don't! As mentioned, each one of these hominids represents their own species and there are NO mutant intermediates in-between any of them that connect any of them together in an evolutionary chain. It is critical for us to realize that when hominids are lined up on alleged 'evolution charts,' what you are looking at does not represent evidence of evolution! What has been done is the simple lining up all of the hominids that God made, and that's it. If they were the product of evolution, then there would also be countless mutated hominids in-between each of these individually distinct hominid species. The Fossil Record clearly demonstrates that NO mutated hominid intermediates have ever been found. This means they never existed.

Therefore, the hominids lined up on alleged 'evolution charts' are not a demonstration of how mankind evolved from ape-like species!

I believe that many people look at this list and think it represents a procession of evolution, and it does not. If a procession of evolution existed, the most crucial aspect would be the countless mutants in-between linking the distinct species together. However, reality demonstrates that no such chain of linking mutants has ever been found in the Fossil Record.[293] Science does not have any fossil evidence linking any of these species together with a chain of mutated fossils.

Dr. Henry Morris has pointed out that the prominent scientist, Professor David M Raup,

> … has candidly acknowledged the complete absence of transitional forms in the fossil record and the complete absence of evidence for observable progressive evolution.[294]

Once again, none of the species on Earth have been found to be linked together by fossil mutations demonstrating a connection. As Morris has pointed out, there are no fossils of mutants at all.[295] Therefore, this is not a simple case of, "the missing link." There are actually billions upon billions of missing links. In fact, **all of the links are missing!**

Let me give another example. Let's say that a shelf of books in a library can be used to explain Darwinian evolution. Imagine that a library exists, and it is named, "Evolution Library." And in this library, there are five billion shelves. Each shelf represents the five billion species that have ever existed on planet Earth. Each shelf is very long because each one has room for about 1,000 books to be placed on it.

Why so many, you ask? Well, in the theory of Darwinian evolution it would take at least 100 baby-step mutations (that are all positive), to theoretically splinter off a brand-new daughter species from the original mother species (speciation). And because there would be at least 10 times more negative mutations than positive mutations, this calculates to 1000 negative mutations. By adding all of the negative mutations to the lucky positive mutations we come out with 1,100 total mutants that would need to be born in order to theoretically produce a brand-new daughter species. Let's round this number down to 1,000.

On each shelf, the first book is the mother species, while the very last book on the shelf is the brand-new daughter species. There should be about 1,000 books in-between, representing the incremental and progressive evolution that would be necessary to finally produce the brand-new daughter species book at the very end. This means the books numbered 2-999 would all be the 'intermediate' mutant books. Is this what we find in the Fossil Record? No, this is not what we find. Instead, we find the first book (mother species) and the very last book (alleged daughter species), but there are NO mutated books in-between! The Fossil Record very clearly demonstrates this.

Therefore, in this "Evolution Library," every single shelf is very long but only has two books on it. There is the first book on the far left and there is the last book all the way down on the far right side of each shelf. There are NO other books in-between that have ever been found. This is a very strange library indeed where every shelf only has two books on it when there should be at least several hundred books on each shelf.

Now, I admit that every mutant is not going to wind up fossilized, nevertheless, for each alleged daughter species that did get fossilized, there should have been at least a few dozen mutant fossils found. And NONE have been found. This means that in the entire "Evolution Library," there should only be one book on each of the five billion shelves. The missing books on each shelf mean that a connection cannot be established between the first book and the last book on each shelf. And because a connection will never be established between the first (mother) book on the far left and the last (daughter) book on the far right, this means the last book should not be on that shelf at all.

That last book should be on its own shelf because it is unrelated to the book on the far left. Hence, there is only one book on each shelf. The Fossil Record demonstrates that each shelf in "Evolution Library," should only have one book on it because there are no connections between any of the species books. "Evolution Library" is essentially empty and barren.

This clearly makes "Evolution Library" a failure. Once you realize that no mutant intermediates have ever been found in the Fossil Record, it becomes clear that Darwinian evolution is a failed idea that has been proven false by the Fossil Record. As a consequence, since there are no mutant fossils to speak of on Earth that connect any two species together, this means *someone* had to have created the species, one by one. The complete absence of fossils demonstrating progressive evolution means that a Creator must exist. This means the Creator had to create each and every one of the billions of unique DNA codes.

At this point, I wish to draw your attention to the last animal species that God created on Day Six which scientists refer to as *Y-Chromosomal Adam* and *Mitochondrial Eve. Y-Chromosomal Adam* is also referred to as *Scientific Adam*, and he lived between 125,000 and 156,000 years ago.[296] The *Scientific Adam* term is now being used by genetic scientists who declare that all men on Earth have the same genetic marker on their Y-chromosome. Geneticists declare that this means every single man on Earth is the descendant of one single male.[297] **Most people in the world do not know this!** And by examining the mitochondria of women, science has also found that every single female on Earth is the descendant of one single female, referred to as *Mitochondrial Eve.*

Most people in the world do not know this! She is thought to have lived between 99,000 and 148,000 years ago.[298]

This means that modern-day science finds that all men on Earth are descended from one single male and all women are descended from one single female. I was surprised to learn of this and I'm sure that most people are unaware of this fascinating genetic research. And since modern-day science cannot accurately pinpoint Eve's first appearance, this means that Scientific Adam and Mitochondrial Eve could have been a couple who lived together somewhere between 125,000-148,000 years ago. Either way, this supports the Book of Genesis which documents it only took one man and one woman to populate the entire planet. Therefore, it is not a fairy tale that billions of humans can result from just two parents.

It appears to me that Scientific Adam and Mitochondrial *Eve* were the last, in the long line of hominids, that God created. They would have been the species created right before Biblical Adam and Eve. I'm not counting Biblical Adam and Eve as hominids. Therefore, Scientific Adam and Mitochondrial Eve were animal hominids, while Biblical Adam and Eve were human and referred to as *"mankind"* in the Old Testament.

This brings up the question of whether animals have souls? There has been some debate in the past as to whether animals have a soul. What is interesting to know is that the first Pope to declare animals had souls was Pope John Paul II in 1990.[299] And recently, Pope Francis has reaffirmed that all animals have souls and will go to Heaven.[300]

There is actually support for animals going to Heaven that comes from near death experiences (NDEs). Reports exist where animals have been commonly seen in Heaven that were unknown to the person experiencing the NDE. First of all, a person in a NDE is not expecting to see an animal they have never seen before and don't know. Secondly, there is no emotional connection with an unknown animal. This supports the fact these animals were really seen and wasn't just a wishful dream of the observer who longed to see their deceased pet again.[301] In addition, there was a very credible instance where a woman was declared dead after she had been in a coma for several days. She suddenly woke up and later reported seeing her mother greeting her cat who had just arrived in Heaven. Her cat was alive when she fell into her coma, however, while she was still in her coma, her cat suddenly died. This allowed her cat to be seen when it newly arrived in Heaven and was being greeted by her mother.[302]

This report is exceptional because it tells researchers that when this woman arrived in Heaven, there would have been no reason for hoping to see her cat who she thought was still alive and well on Earth. This is amazing evidence that animals do go to Heaven when they die. This is remarkable evidence for several reasons:

1) This demonstrates there really is a Heaven.
2) This demonstrates that all animals go to Heaven, and some people do.
3) This demonstrates that we go to Heaven right away. We don't rest in limbo until the world ends at some point after the return of Jesus. This correlates with what the thief was told who was crucified next to Jesus. In Luke 23:43 (KJV), Jesus states, "Verily I say unto thee, today shalt thou be with me in paradise." Notice how Jesus tells the repentant thief that he will be in paradise with Jesus, "today."

We have been given vital information through the careful observations and documentation of NDE research scholars. Let's make full use of this critical information while we still can.

All things considered, I believe the souls of Biblical Adam and Eve and mankind are in a different category than animals because it is my understanding that God separates *mankind* from the animal kingdom. In other words, God's most prized creation of mankind is not considered to be an animal. Support for this conclusion comes from the fact that only Biblical Adam and Eve had the mental capacity to form a Covenant (which is an agreement) with God. In addition, only Adam and Eve were created in God's image, not the animals.

Now, when most of us view the earth, which is teaming with life, we become convinced that a progressive process produced all of these species that we observe. There is something inside of us that just knows that some sort of a methodical process created all of this life which somehow seems connected. Therefore, in order to show people that the concept of evolution is not the only progressive concept that exists, I am going to present a technique that could have been used by God during the creation process.

But before I do that, let's first review that DNA is composed of two parts. The first part is the string of the billions of atoms forming the information storage device that we refer to as DNA (the hardware). The second part of DNA is the operating system code downloaded onto these atoms (the software). Therefore, God had to generate billions of DNA molecules to create all of the species, but more importantly, God had to write the tens of millions of lines of unique, intelligent, instructional code for each and every species.

Now, for God, this is not as all-encompassing as it sounds. Although an omnipotent and all-knowing God would have no problem doing this, it is possible God utilized some logical process to efficiently produce the billions of different DNA codes in the short span of a single day, at the very beginning of each *Creation Day*. All the *creation seeds* for each particular *Creation Day* could have been quickly and efficiently formulated in a 24-hour period by using the DNA profile of the last created species seed as the working template for the next species seed to be created. This would amount to what we refer to as genetic engineering.

Evolution is not the only long ages proposition for how all of the species got here. This is so, because God could have methodically, genetically engineered all the species and then slowly introduced them over a long period of time. If God used existing code of earlier species as the templates for the next species, and then spread this out over a long period of time, it would give the impression that a later species evolved from the species that existed just before.

For example, the genetic code for the species scheduled to be the first to appear on Earth would be used as the working template for the genetic code for the species scheduled to be the second species to appear. Then, the genetic code for the second species would be used as the template for the genetic code for the third species scheduled to appear, and so on. A method like this would result in the creation of new species that could be set to appear over the course of a long period of time. In addition, a method like this would give the false impression that the second species evolved from the first species and the third species evolved from the second species.

The code difference between the first species and the second species was dramatic enough to produce a brand-new species in one shot. The first species is a distinct, full-fledged species, and the second species is also a distinct, full-fledged species. There are no transitional intermediates in this Divine genetic engineering scenario. In other words, the genetic engineering differences that exist between the first and second species occur in one step, and all at once. You will recall that this agrees with what Stephen Jay Gould found who reported that species appeared, "…all at once and fully formed."[303]

This is in stark contrast to the theory of evolution that proposes the production of a series of mutant intermediates that exhibit small, incremental, baby-step mutations, that slowly splinter-off a brand-new species. This is the definition of an evolutionary process; this is how the theory of evolution is defined.

A process like this would necessitate dozens, hundreds, or even thousands of genetic mutations that are theorized to slowly splinter off a brand-new species. In fact, if we carefully scrutinize this theory, we must also include all of the negative mutants that would have also been produced. Most of the mutants would be negative ones. The negative mutants would also have had the opportunity to become fossilized because they would have been born and tried to survive. Once their failure to thrive and survive occurred, they would die. However, their physical remains would still be left behind with the same chance to be fossilized as any of the other creature's physical remains.

If we add all of the positive and negative mutants together that would be necessary to theoretically splinter-off distinct animal species #2002 from distinct animal species #2001, this could be over a thousand mutants. By contrast, a Divine genetic engineering method would create each new species in one step without any mutant intermediates. And this is precisely what we witness in the Fossil Record. This is just the opposite of the theory of evolution which requires the production of countless mutants (positive and negative ones) in order to attempt to theoretically accomplish the production of just one new and distinct, hypothetical species.

At first glance, this Divine genetic engineering scenario seems similar to evolution theory because they are both claimed to produce billions of species over an extended period of time giving the impression of a progressive process. However, the difference is that the theory of evolution requires the existence of countless transitional mutants in-between the two distinct species that are claimed to be related by way of evolution. However, because there are no fossils of transitional mutants in-between any two species on Earth, this eliminates the possibility that evolution ever took place. The scientific evidence actually supports the proposal of a Creator because the absence of transitional mutants in the Fossil Record closes the door on the theory of neo-Darwinian evolution.

I will now present an example in order to fully demonstrate the genetic engineering technique that could have been used by God which gives the *feel* of a progressive process. One way that God could have created the billions of DNA coded sequences in a progressive fashion, could have included a process like the drag-and-drop technique that we used to make music playlists.

For anyone who has ever created a music playlist, you will quickly recognize what I am saying here. We start by loading 20 songs into our first CD playlist that we label as, *Playlist #1*. If we hear a new song the next week that we really like, instead of making a new list from scratch, we could simply delete the one song that we like the least from our first CD playlist and then add the new favorite song. We substituted the least favorite song with the new favorite song. We still have 20 songs, but the new playlist is better than the first playlist. Since this new playlist is not exactly the same as the first playlist, we need to give it a new name, *Playlist #2*. *Playlist #2* is 5% different from *Playlist #1*. We keep doing this where the last playlist created will be used as the template for the new playlist.

If we do this every week for a whole year, we wind up with 52 playlists that got better and better as the year progressed. Your friends may even say that your collection seems to be 'evolving' over time. And notice how easy it was. Each week, you only had to delete one song and then replace it with your new favorite song. This would prevent you from having to start from ground zero every single week. This technique also allows you to perpetually keep your most favorite songs in your list that you will never want to delete. Every single new playlist would always be better than the last one. In this way, your playlists are progressing, giving the impression that they are evolving. If we did this for ten years, we wind up with 520 playlist CDs. *Playlist #520* would look nothing like *playlist #1*.

Now, imagine that the first life on Earth (the first bacterium species) is *Playlist #1*. Next, imagine that humans are *Playlist #5 billion*. It appears to many people that *Playlist #5 billion, evolved* from *Playlist #1*. Regarding the music playlists, everyone knows they did not evolve on their own.

They were clearly the result of a deliberate process of creating better and better playlists even though your friends instinctively use the word, *evolving*, to describe your playlists over time. Likewise, when it comes to the species that have lived on Earth, people easily and instinctively use the word, *evolving*, when describing the appearance of species over time. However, in this case, they don't understand that this is a deliberate creative process of an intelligent Creator.

When it comes to the topic of evolution, people are easily able to accept the concept of an evolutionary process. And in this case, billions of people think that it happened all by itself. This is not the case because there are no mutated skeletons in the Fossil Record to demonstrate evolution. The only reason why we get the impression that a progressive evolution occurred is because of the progressive genetic engineering that was used by their Creator (like the playlists).

Now, if God utilized a system to create billions of species by taking the DNA profile of the last species made and removed a fragment from the end of its code and replaced it with a new end fragment, this would have resulted in a new species. This concept is very similar to genetic engineering or genetic modification.[304] This type of work involves taking fragments from one species and inserting them into the DNA of another species. Mankind already utilizes this technology. However, in the case of Divine genetic engineering, a fragment of new code is written and transferred to a prepared area on the existing code of the template species. A prepared area on the template DNA would be the area on the DNA molecule where code was deleted to make room for the insertion of the newly written code. This is much like the drag-and-drop process I used to make my music playlists. Such intervention would create a brand-new species.

Therefore, I'm suggesting something similar where God could have utilized a drag-and-drop genetic engineering system to create billions of species over a short period of time. Instead of starting from scratch by rebuilding 100 percent of the genetic code for each new species, God could have simply removed and replaced a few percent of the code from the last species created (the template species) and this would have quickly produced a brand-new species.

For example, the genetic code of the Great Apes is only about 5 percent different from that of the Neanderthals. If we start with the code for the Great Apes, take out the 5 percent fragment that is only found in the Great Apes, and then replace it with a 5 percent unique Neanderthal fragment, we now have a brand-new species, the

Neanderthals. This is just like creating a music playlist and constitutes a basic drag-and-drop template process. If this is what actually occurred, it is not presently on mankind's radar screen of possible mechanisms for species genesis. As a result, mankind naturally assumes that species who appeared later, must have automatically evolved from earlier species. However, in reality, earlier species were used as the templates for the genetic engineering of the later species.

Remember that Homo heidelbergensis, Neanderthals, and Homo sapiens, are all allegedly cousins that did not evolve from each other because they were all allegedly spawned from Homo erectus.

Based on what I have described, this would mean that the genetic profile for Homo erectus was used as the template for Homo heidelbergensis, Neanderthals, and Homo sapiens. Then, after some Homo erectus code was deleted, unique code would have been added to this template code in order to create the DNA profiles for Homo heidelbergensis, Homo neanderthalensis (Neanderthals), and Homo sapiens, respectively.

Now, I'm not saying that God was compelled to use this exact process while creating the billions of DNA profiles for each and every species. With that being said, whatever process God did use to create the billions of species on Earth, we can be sure that it was logical and methodical. I am using this drag-and-drop example because many of us are familiar with moving data around by dragging and dropping it. With a drag-and-drop template engineering technique, notice how the simpler species would be created first, and as time progressed, the species would increase in their complexity, just as our music playlist improved and advanced over time. And this is precisely what we observe in the Fossil Record. If a similar technique was utilized by God, then it would explain why creation seems to have an evolutionary *feel* to it.

I think many of us get the ***feeling*** that a progressive process occurred because species seem to be somehow connected as they became more complex over time.

This is why, if we place similar species in a line-up (like on those ape-to-man 'evolution charts'), they appear to be related and represent links in a progressive process. However, THIS IS NOT THE CASE AT ALL. Those alleged 'evolution charts' actually demonstrate how the previous species (the species on the left) was used as the genetic engineering template to design the next species (the next species to the right of it). This would explain why a more recent species seems to be similar, related, and descended from the slightly less-complex species that existed right before them. The prior species was used as the genetic template for the very next species. The newest species seems descended from the species that came just before it. This is because there was just a tiny modification of the genetic code of the prior (template) species.

This is much like the engineering of our music playlists where we only changed a small fraction of the total list (5%). In fact, with genetic engineering, we could change as little as 1% or less if we wished.

This brings me to the claim that humans are the evolutionary down-stream product of Chimpanzees. Chimpanzees have 24 pairs of chromosomes (48 total chromosomes) while humans have 23 pairs (46 total chromosomes). Allegedly, two Chimpanzee chromosomes fused end-to-end (2A and 2B) which is claimed to have evolved into a new single chromosome. Thus, because Chimps have 24 chromosome pairs and humans have 23, this is used by some people to support the claim that we are related by way of an evolutionary process. Apparently, this is not supported by the reality of the world that we live in. Not only are there safeguards in nature against this occurring with chromosomes, but read what expert Geneticist Fazale Rana states:

These articles actually undermine the Chimpanzee-to-human hypothesis. Because the synthetic biologists had to undertake such extensive and precise genetic editing, that there is no way such fusions would have occurred through undirected random processes.[305]

Notice how this fusion would never occur in nature on its own. This reminds me of the artificial manipulations mentioned in Chapters Four and Five regarding *selection* (artificial selection). Many types of schemed artificial manipulations performed in the laboratory are never going to occur on their own in nature. This is the very reason why artificial manipulations are employed in some research projects. When this is done, it equates to stepping outside of the realm of how the real-world works. It's not reality.

Regarding the claim that Chimpanzees contributed to the spawning of humans, researcher Hugh Henry goes on to state that other hindrances to this hypothesis include genetic instability and possible carcinogenesis.[306] Now, for just one moment, let's ignore that Fazale Rana is telling us how impossible this alleged chromosome fusion would be on its own. If we push that fact aside for a moment, Hugh Henry points out that offspring would have no one in the population with the same exact mutation to mate with. Thus, the mutant with 23 chromosome pairs would have had to mate with a normal member with 24 chromosome pairs.

This represents a really big problem for this hypothesis because this is not how viable fertilization works in the real world. Chromosomes from each parent have to pair up evenly. As a consequence, such a mating would almost certainly **not** result in fertilization. And when no offspring are produced by the mutant, the mutation dies off in one generation when that mutant dies.

This conclusion is reinforced by experiments conducted in Russia in the 1920s when three Chimpanzees were inseminated with human sperm. None of these attempts resulted in fertilization. Hugh Henry concludes that it is unlikely that an ancient Chimpanzee union could have resulted in fertilization, let alone, go on to produce fertile mutant offspring.[307] This means there is no proof that Chimpanzee chromosomes fused together on their own to produce the 23 pairs of chromosomes found in advanced hominids. The only way this fusion and fertilization fantasy can be assumed to be true is if it can be proven that God does not exist.

And because there are many experts who would agree that this chromosome fusion hypothesis never had a realistic chance to occur, let alone get passed onto any offspring, this means there is only one logical conclusion; a Creator must be responsible for this genetic engineering work. Just look at the statement by Fazale Rana where he states there is no way such a fusion occurred on its own. The first hominids to exist with 23 pairs of chromosomes could have easily been accomplished through the genetic engineering of a Creator. An intelligent Creator would have used Chimpanzee code as the template and then implemented high precision manipulation and editing to successfully fuse chromosomes 2A and 2B in order to create the first human-like hominids. By contrast, such extensive and precise genetic editing was never going to happen randomly on its own in nature, as many genetic experts point out.

Therefore, if a drag-and-drop genetic engineering technique was used by a Creator, this would explain why it *feels* as if species *evolved* over time, just like our music playlist seemed to *evolve* over time. The possibility that methodical and intelligent genetic engineering could have been utilized by a Creator, demonstrates that evolution theory is not the only progressive concept to be considered. Regarding the Chimpanzee hypothesis, random fusion was never going to occur. By contrast, this could have easily been formulated by an intelligent Creator. A drag-and-drop genetic process could have been the systematic method utilized by God. And because it is so methodical and progressive, it projects the illusion of a progressive evolutionary process!

Just as our music playlists seemed to *evolve* over time, it only seems that way because of the manner in which they were created. This is similar to the example of the 7 years of car model designs that I mentioned earlier in this book. That example also gave the impression of an evolutionary process that never occurred, it just seemed that way. Simpler species followed by slightly more complex species, creates the illusion of a self-driven, progressive process.

So yes, I believe that a progressive process occurred, but it was not Darwinian evolution. God clearly progressed from the simplest life at the beginning and then finished *Creation Week* with the most complex life. If you line up the species that were created, they progressively became more and more complex, they did not evolve (just like those monkey-to-human charts). This is the case because mankind was created last.

This would also explain why Scientific Adam and Mitochondrial Eve appear to be our ancestors when in fact they are not. They were merely the last hominid species created right before mankind.

In other words, Scientific Adam and Mitochondrial Eve were the last animal species created by God. We can think of them as *pre-mankind hominids*. As a result, their genetic code would have served as the template for our unique code. God only needed to tweak Scientific Adam and Mitochondrial Eve's code just a little bit in order to formulate our code. This is the reason why they appear to be our ancestors and the same species that we are.

Scientific Adam and Mitochondrial Eve are not the same species as Biblical Adam and Eve. And I believe we can see evidence that we are dealing with two different species when we read Genesis Chapter One regarding creation on Day Six. In Genesis 1:24 (KJV), we read:

> And God said, Let the earth bring forth the living creature after his kind, cattle, and creeping thing, and beast of the earth after his kind, and it was so.

We can see how the words, "creature," and, "beast," are used. Then in Genesis 1:26 (KJV), we read, "And God said, 'Let us make man in our image and after our likeness….'" Notice the distinction that has been drawn where mankind has been separated out from the categories of the beasts and the creatures.

God did not make Homo erectus or Neanderthals in His image. And this puts them into the category of an animal. By contrast, God made Biblical Adam and Eve in His image and likeness. As a result, they were not in the category of an animal. Even though Scientific Adam and Mitochondrial Eve may appear very similar to Biblical Adam and Eve (genetically very similar), they were not created as, mankind. And because they were not, mankind, they were an animal species just like the Neanderthals. The three fundamental differences between mankind and Scientific Adam and Mitochondrial Eve are:

1) God breathed His breath into Biblical Adam and Eve delivering them each a mankind soul.

2) God specifically created Biblical Adam and Eve by hand as mankind, His most prized creations. This is in contrast to the marine life that came out of the waters, and the land animals that came out of the ground.

3) God created a covenant relationship with Biblical Adam and Eve.

Therefore, even though science may not consider Scientific Adam and Mitochondrial Eve to be different from Biblical Adam and Eve, God considers them to be very different. As a result, God considers mankind a different creation (species) compared to all the other creatures, beasts, animals, and hominids. Scientific Adam and Mitochondrial Eve's descendants existed for well over 100,000 years, and they are not suspected to have had a relationship with God. By comparison, as soon as Biblical Adam and Eve were created, they lived in God's presence in the Garden of Eden and talked to God on a daily basis. Therefore, it should be clear that Scientific Adam and Mitochondrial Eve were not in the same category as Biblical Adam and Eve.

As mentioned, because they were the last animals created before mankind, it would make sense that Scientific Adam and Mitochondrial Eve's genetic code would be the most similar to our code. If a system similar to a genetic drag-and-drop was utilized, then very few changes to their hominid code, if any, would be needed to create our code. I strongly believe Scientific Adam and Mitochondrial Eve's genetic code was used as the templates for our code. This would explain why our DNA code is so very similar to that of Scientific Adam and Mitochondrial Eve.

This explains why all the men alive today, have the same genetic marker on their Y-chromosome which matches the genetic marker found on Scientific Adam's Y-chromosome. This is also why the mitochondrial DNA of all the women alive today can be traced back to one single female, Mitochondrial Eve.[308] I was very surprised when I learned of this scientific fact.

Therefore, if God used pretty much the same DNA profile to create us that He used to make Scientific Adam and Mitochondrial Eve, this would allow the Fossil Record timeline for Scientific Adam and Mitochondrial Eve to be correct (about 130,000 years ago). This also allows Biblical Adam and Eve's timeline to be correct (about 10,000 years ago). In other words, the archaeological evidence for Scientific Adam and Mitochondrial Eve does not contradict the history of Biblical Adam and Eve because they are two different species that lived in two different eras. This represents another problem-solving realization that allows the book of science to be reconciled with the Book of God.

What is important here is that a significant genetic difference is not what made Biblical Adam and Eve a different species from Scientific Adam and Mitochondrial Eve. As far as a new species is concerned, significant genetic *changes* did not make the difference here. Instead, non-scientific changes constitute the majority of what makes mankind a different species. These changes include, being created in the exact image of God, and being given a human soul that was able to form a Covenant, allowing us to experience a personal relationship with God.

All things considered, I also believe Scientific Adam and Mitochondrial Eve had souls. However, just like their animal counterparts, their souls were not designed to form a covenant relationship with God. God loves His animals, however, only one species was created in His Image and designed to form a covenant relationship with Him. God's definition of a new species creation is different from our definition. This will create a stumbling block for science because it does not include measuring and analyzing these kinds of *changes*. Even though science lists modern humans as a hominid species, I would argue that mankind was created in the image of God and is uniquely distinct from the animal hominids.

And once we realize all of this, it allows us to reconcile the Fossil Record with the Book of Genesis in reference to Adam and Eve.

Upon carefully evaluating this situation, we are presented with the conclusion that Scientific Adam and Mitochondrial Eve cannot be the same species as Biblical Adam and Eve (mankind). This is important because it solves the problem of science reporting that Homo sapiens existed over 100,000 years ago. By comparison, religious believers commonly accept that mankind is no older than 10,000 years. Therefore, by establishing that we are technically dealing with two different species, the book of science and the Book of God can both be correct.

We are no more descended from Scientific Adam and Mitochondrial Eve than we are descended from the Neanderthals. This means that all the human-like skeletons found around the world that are 200,000 years old in Africa, 100,000 years old in Israel, and over 12,000 years old in the Americas, are not, mankind. Any skeletons older than 11,000 years, belong to descendants of the last hominid species that God created, Scientific Adam and Mitochondrial Eve.

I would also like to point out that all of the hominids were extinct by 11,000 years ago. All hominid species went extinct except for one, Homo sapiens sapiens. This coincides with the well-known extinction disaster referred to as *The Younger Dryas Event.*[309] This mass extinction catastrophe occurred all over the world where 120 mammal species suddenly died out. As a result, whatever hominid species were still in existence 11,000 years ago, were finished off with this brief catastrophe. Don't you think it's a bizarre coincidence that all of the hominids were eliminated from existence except for just one? Allegedly Homo sapiens were the only survivor. What a coincidence! And this occurred right before Biblical Adam and Eve appeared. What are the odds that **all** hominids, except for one, would no longer be in existence right before mankind was created by God?

It is my opinion that ALL hominids went extinct 11,000 years ago including those related to Scientific Adam and Mitochondrial Eve. I believe this was no coincidence and was designed to remove any human-like hominids that could potentially interbreed with mankind. The fact that the last of the hominids went extinct right before Adam and Eve appeared gives me the strong impression this was not a coincidence. I suspect the Homo sapiens species that allegedly survived *The Younger Dryas Event*, did not survive at all. This would serve to wipe the slate clean of hominids to make way for Biblical Adam and Eve.

If that was the case, then there were no human-like species for about 1,000 years. Science would not be able to detect this small gap. Then around 8,000 BCE (10,000 years ago), God created Biblical Adam and Eve. This is why scientists believe that Homo sapiens were the only hominid species to survive that catastrophe. Why would just one hominid species survive when **none** of the others did? I believe that once the dust of that catastrophe settled, no hominids survived. This served to make way for God's final and most prized creation, mankind. And if this is what actually happened, then the Fossil Record's history of hominids, and the Bible's history of Adam and Eve, can reconcile and both be correct.

Now, I understand there is talk about humans having some Neanderthal genes in them from interbreeding. Apparently, a few percent of our DNA have been found in the Neanderthals. The situation of inter-species mating is also known as *hybridization.* Scientists at the University of Cambridge make this statement:

> Our work shows clearly the patterns currently seen in the Neanderthal genome are not exceptional, and are in line with our expectations of what we would see without hybridization.[310]

As this research has discovered, if interbreeding did occur between Neanderthals and Homo sapiens, it was minimal and did not have any notable genetic impact. In other words, the evidence clearly does not suggest that Neanderthals must have interbred with Homo sapiens. Therefore, our genetic profile is not suspected to be from interbreeding with Neanderthals. That being said, these scientists do presume the code that is similar between humans and Neanderthals is from the two species being related by way of a common ancestor.[311]

I wish to point out that if any interbreeding did occur, it would have been between Neanderthals and the Homo sapiens descendants of Scientific Adam and Mitochondrial Eve. I also wish to point out that "humans" (actually Scientific Adam and Mitochondrial Eve) and Neanderthals are suspected to be related by way of a common ancestor because that earlier hominid's DNA was used as an upstream template for Neanderthals, Scientific Adam, and Mitochondrial Eve.

From what I can see, from a purely scientific standpoint, the descendants of Scientific Adam, Mitochondrial Eve, Biblical Adam, and Biblical Eve, can all be placed into the same general category of 'Homo sapiens sapiens.'

From what I understand, if we carefully analyze the genetic code, the descendants of Biblical Adam and Eve are a distinct species who are not exactly the same genetically as the descendants of Scientific Adam and Mitochondrial Eve. The slight differences in genetic code are assumed by scientists to be from genetic drift and other reasons. However, because our DNA is slightly different from that of Scientific Adam and Mitochondrial Eve, I argue this is because we are actually two different species. By the time of the end of *The Younger Dryas* catastrophe, all of those hominids who were descendants of Scientific Adam and Mitochondrial Eve would have gone extinct. As a consequence, I believe *The Younger Dryas* event marks the point in time during Creation Day Six, right before Genesis 1:26-31 (where God creates mankind).

Humans are all descendants of Biblical Adam and Eve. Any similarities of our genetic profile with any ancient species are explained by the genetic engineering of God retaining fragments of Homo ergastor, Homo erectus, or Neanderthal code, making sure they wound up in our genetic profile. This would explain why it appears that we are related to hominids. This is just a simple case of retaining DNA fragments found in earlier species making sure they survived into our DNA profile (genetic engineering). In this way, the misconception of evolution is completely explained by the genetic engineering that God could have easily used to create every species.

There are many geneticists who do believe in God. However, regarding the geneticists who do not believe in God, whatever explanations they suggest as to how evolution occurred because of similar or identical gene fragments that are found in different species, I have a simple defense.

That defense is as follows: If DNA profiles of different species are lined up to show similarity, this does not prove evolution because, as mentioned, it could also be the product of the deliberate genetic engineering of a Creator. Since geneticists who don't believe in God can't prove deliberate genetic engineering did not occur (they also can't prove that God does not exist), this means evolution is not the only possible explanation. Furthermore, because of the evidence presented in Chapter Five on the theory of evolution, we can actually eliminate the arguments of geneticists who don't believe in God because the theory of Darwinian evolution has already been proven false by evidence found in the Fossil Record. In other words, evolutionary genetic arguments are all null and void because of, *The Death of Evolution.*

The only way I can imagine that evolutionary geneticists who don't believe in God can win this argument, is by them first finding "another kind of evolution." Because Darwinian evolution has been scientifically proven false, people who don't believe in God need to find "another kind of evolution" that they can prove produced all the species on the earth. Until they do this, all of their arguments fall severely short because they are scientifically impossible. And this is just to get on even footing with the scientists who do believe in God. However, in order for this argument to be won by scientists and others who don't believe in God, they will also have to prove that God does not exist. As a result, it is clear to me that scientists and others who don't believe in God hold the indefensible low ground in this battle over the truth.

Now, I don't wish to come across as being harsh on geneticist who don't believe in God. I'm merely attempting to demonstrate to them, and anyone who follows them, that a better answer exists compared to the impossible evolutionary idea they endorse. God wants all of his children to return to Him. And this includes scientists and anyone else who presently refuses to believe in Him. People who believe that the false theory of evolution makes God unnecessary are using a falsehood to reject the truth. I find this to be tragic.

Now, getting back to the Neanderthal genetic code, some people may ask why God would give us some of the Neanderthal's code? Well, if the Neanderthal's code happened to have a great immune system sequence in it, then the God would want to duplicate that superior gene sequence in the design of subsequent species. This would especially be true in God's most prized species, Biblical Adam and Eve.

This is just like retaining a favorite song so that it survives and makes it into your next playlist.

Therefore, God seems to have retained fragments of Neanderthal code, ensuring they stayed in the template that was used for our genetic profile. If this superior immune system code was in the genetic profile for Homo erectus, then God simply kept that code sequence in the Homo erectus template code that was used for Neanderthals, Scientific Adam, Mitochondrial Eve, and later Biblical Adam and Eve. It really doesn't matter whether this special immune system code was originally present in the Homo erectus profile or not.

Either way, God could have easily dragged the Neanderthal immune system code out of their profile and dropped it into the genetic profile for our code. This also holds true for how this immune system code got into the genetic profiles for Scientific Adam and Mitochondrial Eve. This represents the supreme flexibility that a Creator has with genetic engineering.

As a consequence, I believe God used most of Scientific Adam and Mitochondrial Eve's code as the templates for Biblical Adam and Eve's code (mankind's code), while leaving in the Neanderthal's immune system code. Clearly, God did not significantly modify the code for Scientific Adam and Mitochondrial Eve because our code is **almost** identical to their code. The impressive situation that exists with a genetic template system that also utilizes a drag-and-drop technique, is that it nicely explains how two different species can possess a few DNA fragments that are the same, without those two species being related to each other or interbreeding with each other.

Because this is so very important, I am going to say it one more time, if God created all the species on Earth through a methodical process of drag-and-drop, template genetic engineering, this explains why it seems that a progressive process of evolution occurred. For some people, it will be hard to let go of evolution even after it has been demonstrated to them that it never occurred. This is because people are convinced that a progressive process unfolded where more and more complex species emerged over a very long period of time. As a result, until an alternative explanation is presented, some people will continue to believe in evolution theory even after they realize the Fossil Record completely contradicts and disproves the Darwinian model.

This is why I am presenting the alternative explanation that God sequentially created the DNA profiles for the simpler species first, then added or replaced DNA fragments to produce ever more complex species. As stated, a method of creation like this would give the false impression of a progressive evolutionary process.

God could have stored all of these DNA profiles in seeds where the simpler ones opened first, and the more complex seeds opened later. This would explain why species suddenly appeared, experienced a surprisingly jerky and highly uneven existence, did not enjoy biological improvements, and then abruptly went extinct. You will recall that Dr. Raup documented these Fossil Record observations.[312] Because these Fossil Record observations are the exact opposite of what we would be seeing if Darwin's theory was a reality, we know that Darwin's theory of macroevolution has been scientifically proven to be false.

By contrast, the Fossil Record's behavior is exactly what we expect to see if God cycled species in and out at regular intervals with an efficient species replacement system, possibly a *creation seed* system. We actually have an estimation of the time interval for such cycles from Dr. Raup who states he observed that the average duration of a species living on Earth is less than 10 million years.[313] Therefore, it appears that God may have cycled species groups in and out about every 10 million years.

As stated in the last chapter, I do not naturally oppose the concept of evolution. I admit that when I was younger, as I was trying to believe in God, I imagined God could have created the life on Earth through the process of evolution. However, once I realized that scientific evidence actually eliminates Darwinian evolution from being a scientific fact, I had to reformulate my belief structure. In order for anyone to properly formulate their belief structure, they need the truth. We need all of the truth (sound science), not some of the truth (pseudoscience).

It is severely important to realize that it has been scientifically proven that Darwinian evolution is a failed theory. This goes for neo- Darwinian evolution as well. And because at least 40% of the world rejects God because they think the science of evolution makes God unnecessary, I feel the need to set the record straight. It makes no logical sense for me to say nothing about evolution once I found out that it was a failed theory that billions of people are using as the reason for rejecting God. Why is this so important? This topic is critical because those billions of people are in dire straits as their souls hang in the balance.

As the title of this chapter indicates, Earth is special . . . and so are we. We are all special to God.

CHAPTER SEVEN

The Bible Is Not a Book of Fables

In this chapter I will revisit and finally explain the extremely interesting story presented at the very beginning of this book.

As previously mentioned, Anthony Flew is a noted scientist and author who was an outspoken, confident atheist. He is described as the world's most famous atheist of the second half of the twentieth century.[314] In an article titled, "How the World's Most Notorious Atheist Changed His Mind," Professor Flew was asked if he had heard a voice that made him suddenly stop being an atheist and start believing in God? As you will recall, Anthony Flew replied:

> No, I did not hear a voice. It was the evidence itself that led me to this conclusion.[315]

Professor Flew reveals the nature of this evidence in his next quote:

> With every passing year, the more that was discovered about the richness and inherent intelligence of life, the less it seemed likely that a chemical soup could magically generate the genetic code.[316]

Notice how Professor Flew's belief in God revolves around what he has learned about the genetic code. While he stands head and shoulders above most of us regarding scientific credentials, many of us can also experience following the scientific evidence to the truth, just as he did.

As we continue on our quest to find the truth, in this chapter we will take a close look at Scripture in order to find evidence of the truth. I feel there is proof in Scripture that demonstrates the Bible is not composed of fables, but instead, documents actual history. You will be surprised to discover that some of this evidence comes directly from Scripture as it discusses the earth.

To begin, let's discuss the earth by using the fascinating Book of Job, which will shed more light on the authenticity of the Bible. In Job, we encounter several references describing the engineering of the earth. In Job 38:16, God says to Job (KJV):

> Hast thou entered into the springs of the sea? or hast
> thou walked in the search of the depth?

Here God is referring to the vents on the ocean floor when he speaks of "springs of the sea," along with mentioning the deepest part of the oceans. God knows there is the deepest part of the oceans which He refers to as the *depth*. If we were able to walk on the ocean floor, we would have to search for this deepest part. Apparently, it is a sight to behold. He is asking Job if he has ever walked on the ocean floor searching for the deepest part or entered into the ocean's venting springs? Obviously, no man knew that there was a deepest part of the ocean floor, and no man knew there were springs in the ocean either. Only God did. It is well known that before scientists invented sonar, many people, believed the bottom of the ocean was completely flat and even.[317] I would say this belief was especially true of ancient people. As it turns out, the deepest part of all the oceans is the Mariana Trench,[318] which does indeed have venting springs nearby.[319] Only God knew they were there over 3,000 years ago.

This mention of the springs (vents) and the depth (meaning the deepest trench) makes me ask why a scribe would make this up as a fable? No one could see the ocean floor. You would think that a myth writer would mention great plains, vast valleys, and high mountains as parts of the earth that people could see and relate to. Only God Himself would have known the ocean floor had a deepest part that just happened to have venting springs nearby. Considering all the topics that a myth writer would choose to write about, what human could relate to a story about the bottom of the ocean?

Steve A. Austin, a scholar who holds a Ph.D. in Geology, explains that the word for "springs" is *nebek* (transliterated from Hebrew), meaning a place where water bursts out of the earth.[320] But Austin states that in this case, it was water bursting out of the earth, underwater. Austin states:

> No man knew about water bursting forth from the earth under the water, and no man would have seen anything like this or known what this verse meant. Only in the 1960s did we finally discover vents springing up water on the ocean floor. Before that, we had no idea that they even existed.[321]

Austin adds that the Mid-Oceanic Ridge wells up lots of water that circulates through springs as a major geologic process. He states, "The discovery of ocean springs ranks as one of the foremost scientific accomplishments of the last ten years."[322] Dr. John M. Edmond of the Massachusetts Institute of Technology states that 40 cubic miles of water flow out of ocean floor springs every year.[323] Therefore, since the Book of Job mentions special underwater features that no human would have ever seen nor understood, this demonstrates an example of Scripture that cannot logically be the product of a myth writer. A myth writer is never going to invent confusing details that no one can relate to.

For further support of the authenticity regarding the Bible, let's take a look at Noah's Great Flood story. In Genesis 7:11, we read (KJV):

> In the six hundredth year of Noah's life, in the second month, the seventeenth day of the month, the same day were all the fountains of the great deep broken up, and the windows of heaven were opened.

Notice how the flood begins with the ocean floor of the *great deep* breaking up first. The very first event mentioned in this flooding process is not the rain falling from the sky but the great deep breaking up. The great deep breaking up would be the breaking up of the portion of the earth's crust that forms the ocean floor.

Most people don't know this, but there is actually three times more water inside the earth than in all its rivers, lakes, and oceans, combined.[324] If this flood story were merely a fabricated tale, the writer would not be thinking about the deep ocean floor breaking up while writing a raining flood story. However, God would have been thinking about the immense water reservoir under the earth's crust because it was going to be used to assist in the flooding of the surface. There are two crucial points to be seen here. First, if this story is merely a myth, there is no logical reason why a myth writer would start this raining flood story off with the ocean floor breaking up. If this were a fable, the writer would have drawn attention up to the sky in order to cause his readers to imagine the deluge pouring down from above. If this flood story is a myth, an ancient audience would be confused and not understand why the ocean floor is being mentioned.

Therefore, to add an ocean floor detail like this into a raining flood fable, severely defies logic because it makes no sense to the reader and would only serve to confuse people. In no way, does the ocean floor qualify as a necessary component for the telling of a raining flood story. This single detail is only significant if someone is aware of the earth's massive freshwater reservoir underneath the ocean floor and that the surface of the earth can be flooded by forcing this massive water supply upward. As water crashes up through the ocean floor, this would cause it to be, "broken up." The earth's water reservoir was pushed upward by God with such tremendous force that this explosion of water up through the ocean floor would have produced geysers shooting upward with tremendous gushing force.

The fact this account starts off with this very specific detail convinces me that this story could not have been conjured up by a human. This story was indeed written by a human, but that person was merely writing what a Divine source instructed him to write. There is no other explanation for the existence of this very specific detail in this account. I find this to be fascinating evidence that tells us these are indeed the Words of the Creator and the Great Flood really happened.

The second point to be noticed here is that because God decided to well water up from below to initiate this flooding process, the amount of water that needed to rain down from the atmosphere was much lower than if all the water needed to rain down from above. There are experts who point out that the atmosphere does not hold enough water to flood the entire surface of the earth and cover the mountains. Therefore, because most of the water came from below, this solves the problem caused by having only a limited amount of atmospheric water. Because the ocean floor broke up first, the first step in this flooding process was water welling up from below. Then the rest of the water that was needed rained down from above. This greatly reduces the amount of water necessary to fall from the atmosphere in order to flood the earth. Once we realize this, it is easier to envision this monumental flooding event.

Let's not just take my word for it. We see evidence of a massive global flood from an investigative research project led by Allegra LeGrande, a graduate student in the department of Earth and Environmental Sciences at Columbia University. This article states that:

> Scientists from NASA and Columbia University, New York, used computer modeling to successfully reproduce an abrupt climate change that took place 8,200 years ago. The article states that the current warm period was caused by a massive flood of freshwater into the North Atlantic Ocean. This work is the first to consistently recreate the event by computer modeling, and the first time that the model results have been confirmed by comparison to the climate record, which includes such things as ice core and tree ring data.[325]

This event occurred in 6200 BC which means the Great Flood occurred 8,200 years ago. Because Genesis 7:11, records that The Great Flood event started with the fountains of the great deep breaking up, this NASA and Columbia University research confirms to me that God caused a massive amount of fresh water under the earth's crust to come crashing upward causing it to well up and initiate the flooding process. And there you have it. We have scientific proof that a massive global flood really did happen within the timeframe of mankind's existence during the last 10,000 years.

Scholar Owen Omid Borville makes this statement regarding The Great Flood:

> Ancient Flood stories have been recorded all over the world and from every continent. As many as 500 or more have been recorded, giving strong evidence of the Book of Genesis account of the flood.[326]

If cultures all over the world have generated as many as 500 versions of this event, it means this flood actually happened.

Now, let's get back to the Book of Job. So, who wrote the Book of Job, anyway? This question has a bearing on our quest to check the reliability and truthfulness of the Bible. Ancient Jewish belief credits the authorship of the Book of Job to Moses, who wrote the first five books of the Bible after leading the Israelites out of Egypt. The first five Books of the Old Testament (the Torah) are referred to as the Pentateuch. This belief is reinforced in the Babylonian Talmud which claims:

> Moses wrote his own book, and the passages about Balaam and Job (Baba Bathra, 14b, 15a).[327]

Biblical Scholars state:

> Certain words used in the book of Job appear also in the Pentateuch, but nowhere else in the Old Testament; many other words common to both Job and the Pentateuch are seldom used by other Bible writers. An example of this is the title 'El-Shaddai,' "The Almighty" which is used 31 times in the book of Job and 6 times in the book of Genesis but doesn't occur in this particular form anywhere else in the Bible.[328]

Therefore, it is logical to conclude, as many scholars have, that a particular descriptor that only appears in two books in the whole Bible must have been written by the same person. I agree and believe the author of Job is also the author of Genesis. Did Moses hear about the account of Job from the oral Hebrew tradition passed down while he was still in Egypt? Moses probably wrote Job from the oral Hebrew version, the language of which is referred to as *Oral Abrahamic-Hebrew*. Scholars have long held that Job was probably the first book that Moses wrote.

There are others, however, who insist that Job is a fable—certainly not actual history! However, let's look at why this assumption appears to be flawed. There are a lot of historical details in the Book of Job as to where he was from and the exact names of his friends. This allows us to investigate Job's story. For example:

> Now when Job's three friends heard of all this evil that had come upon him, they came each from his own place; Eliphaz the Temanite, Bildad the Shuhite, and Zophar the Naamathite. (Job 2: 11, KJV)

Later these three are joined by Elihu the Son of Barachel the Buzite (Job 32:2, KJV). Finally, scholar Dr. John Osgood goes through how each of Job's friends can be traced:

> ***Eliphaz the Temanite***: He is introduced in Job 4:1 (KJV): Temanites were descended from Teman, who was the first son of Eliphaz, who was the son of Esau, as mentioned in Genesis 36:9-19. The names of both father and son help us to identify the geography where the descendants of Esau lived, i.e. Edom. . . .

> ***Bildad the Shuhite***: He is introduced in Job 8:1 (KJV): The Shuhites were a tribe descended from Shuah, son of Abraham via his concubine Keturah-Gen.25:2. They . . . lived just east of the Syrians on the south bank of the Euphrates river (mid-Euphrates region)...

Elihu the Son of Barachel the Buzite . . . He was of the kindred of Ram. Buzites were descended from Buz, who is listed as a son of Abraham's brother Nahor and would have been an inhabitant of the city of Nahor. . . [329]

I could only present a truncated version of the original quote because of word-count/copyright concerns. That said, I highly recommend that you access the website I reference and read the entire quote. It is even more convincing that what I am able to present here.

Osgood has clearly indicated how these real names were of real people who were from real places. Therefore, Job cannot be an allegory because he has a physical history here. Allegories are falsehoods made up to get a moral of a story across. Allegories have also been referred to as "symbolic narratives," which are used to teach a lesson. But in this instance, we can see that Job is not a falsehood or a symbolic narrative. The Book of Job, which skeptics have attacked as an ahistorical fable, has solid support from ancient geographic history showing that it is a trustworthy account of a real person. What's more, is the fact none of these skeptics can prove that Job was not a real person. Therefore, Job lived in a real place with real friends and he went through a real trial.

As far as the time frame of when Job lived, we find clues in Job 42:12-16 (KJV). Researcher Eric Lyons states, "Unlike Israelite Law, where the family inheritance was passed on to daughters only in the absence of sons, Job gives his daughters 'an inheritance among their brothers.'"[330] This indicates old patriarchal times. Also, Job measures his wealth, not in money, but in livestock that he owned. This is also indicative of patriarchal times. Finally, Job lived long before Moses because of the fact his life span was so long. Job lived a life span comparable to patriarchs who lived around 2200 BC.[331]

* * *

Reference Alert! Please be advised that at least one of the authors that I have criticized in this book has re-written two of his online articles after the release of this book. This book was originally released in September of 2022.

The re-rewriting of articles can cause the deletion of important quotes, the addition of new material, the changing of section names, and the shifting around of paragraphs of text. When this occurs, the endnote references may no longer correlate with the altered website article. This will cause confusion when someone tries to refer back to the original online article. You will know when this occurs because the online article publication date will be after September of 2022. And in the case where no publication date is posted for an online article (n.d.), if it does not correlate with the referenced endnote, it can be concluded that the online article was also changed after the initial release of this book in September 2022.

* * *

With that being said, we now come to the crucial topic of provenance, which is the earliest known history of something. And in this case, we are investigating the truth behind the earliest known history of the stories in the Bible. As I stated earlier, when I was younger, I heard that the stories in the Bible had been written first by the Mesopotamians as myths. This devastating news caused me to view the Bible as a collection of myths from other cultures. However, as a result of extensive research, I have come to realize that Oral Abrahamic-Hebrew stories about God existed way before the first written language was invented. The Sumerians were the ones who invented the first written language around 3,000 BC.[332]

For example, the story of Creation and the Great Flood story recorded in the Bible and the Torah tell of Hebrew history that predates the cultures that first put them into print. I did not know this because I had never heard anyone mention this fact. Because of this knowledge that the Oral Abrahamic-Hebrew traditions predate all of the written Mesopotamian myths, it completely changes the perceived credibility regarding the authenticity of the Bible.

To begin to discuss this extremely important topic of provenance, we need to go back to the beginning. This brings us to an archaeologist named George Smith who was the first person to decipher fragments from the ruins of Nineveh that were written in cuneiform.[333] Smith assembled these fragments back together and translated them in the 1800s. What he found is entitled, *The Epic of Gilgamesh*, which is an ancient Mesopotamian flood story.[334] Smith found that *The Epic of Gilgamesh* had been written before the Bible was written. And because of this, some people have taken what Smith found and falsely claim this to be proof that the Books of the Bible were copied by the Hebrews from the Sumerians and the Babylonians.

To demonstrate this flawed claim, I will present actual quotes from a freelance writer and professor. I must point out that he is not the only person saying things like this. I am more concerned with *what* critics like this are claiming while I am less concerned with *who* is making these claims. I believe it is important for people to see exactly what is being claimed by critics in order to know what to expect and be prepared when they see and hear such claims regarding this topic.

The freelance writer I present is Joshua Mark, who discusses this provenance topic by mentioning the work of George Smith.[335] He states that because Smith deciphered ancient Cuneiform, this has caused mankind to alter what they perceive to be historically correct.

What mankind thought they knew about ancient history has been demonstrated to not be the case because of what George Smith has uncovered. This can be seen in a direct quote from Mark where he states (March, 2018):

> Many Biblical texts were thought to be original until cuneiform was deciphered. The Fall of Man and the Great Flood were understood as literal events in human history dictated by God to the author (or authors) of Genesis but were now recognized as Mesopotamian myths which Hebrew scribes had embellished on in *The Myth of Etana* and the *Atrahasis*. . . .[336]

Notice how he claims that once George Smith translated cuneiform, it allowed us to see that Hebrew scribes modified existing Mesopotamian myths in order to write their own stories. This of course means he is saying the Bible is not literal history dictated by God. Why does he think this? Before we can answer that question, we need to evaluate one more of his quotes (March, 2018):

> These advances in understanding were all made by the 19th century CE archaeologists and scholars sent to Mesopotamia to substantiate biblical stories through physical evidence.[337]

This writer is referring to the archaeological and deciphering work of people like Smith. But notice his mention of *physical evidence* and recall that the Sumerians invented the first written language. The physical evidence that is being referred to, are the written manuscripts of Mesopotamian myths which have been deciphered, cataloged, and dated. What is happening here, is that only written works can be considered as *physical evidence*. Before the Sumerians invented the first written language of cuneiform, only oral traditions were utilized to transmit historical accounts from person to person and from generation to generation.

So here is the catch, since oral history was not *physically* written down, there is no *physical evidence* of oral history. What this freelance writer appears to be doing is leaving out the oral Hebrew history because it is not considered physical evidence, like the physically tangible manuscripts of the Mesopotamian myths. In another article by this same writer, he goes on to state (March, 2011):

> There is no question that a number of Biblical narratives of the Old Testament have their origins in Sumerian Works.[338]

Notice how Mark claims there is no question about this. This is a serious and definitive statement, and it is completely false. By making a statement like this, he is essentially declaring it is uncontroversial that many stories of the Old Testament were copied from Sumerian Works. I find this to be shocking because in order to claim this, the original Oral Abrahamic-Hebrew Bible traditions have to be completely ignored. This seems to be equivalent to only presenting *some* of the histories instead of *all* of the histories. What kind of history is that? Therefore, what this writer is claiming is most certainly controversial and raises serious questions. It's obvious that orally passed down histories in the ancient world are what constitute the evidence that establishes the origins, not the publication dates.

This writer also discusses the Book of Job where he states that many scholars think that Job was written in the 7th, 6th or 4th centuries BC.[339] This of course conflicts with Moses writing Job and the Pentateuch in the wilderness in the 15th century BC.[340] In addition, this writer states that the Book of Job is not about a real person's trials and sufferings. He also states that the Book of Job should be viewed as having its roots in the earlier Mesopotamian myth, *Ludlul-Bel-Nimeqi.*[341] This claim that the Bible is not the original source for the Book of Job and its story not being about a real person contradicts the detailed research of John Osgood, who established that Job was a real person, who had real friends, and was from a real place.[342]

In another article, Mark states that he believes the story of Job was taken from an earlier Sumerian work titled, *Man and His God*, which he claims dates back to 2000 BCE.[343] Even if this date is correct, the details listed in Job's story, such as laws of inheritance and Job's extended lifespan, date back to the Patriarchal Times. This places Job living as far back as 2200 BCE.[344] Therefore, the oral Hebrew account of Job predates this Sumerian work by about 200 years. This is another example of Hebrew history taking place first, then the Mesopotamians adopted it, adapted it, and printed it as another one of their myths.

It seems clear from the details that Job lived several hundred years before Moses. Job's story finally got to Moses while he was growing up in Egypt. Perhaps as his fellow Israelites were voicing their woes and sufferings to Moses, one of them told him about the woes and sufferings of Job. It is possible the Israelites felt as if they were suffering just like Job had suffered. Maybe this is how the historical account of Job was passed on to Moses, who would eventually write it down. Therefore, the Book of Job, which skeptics have attacked as an ahistorical fable, has solid support from ancient geographic history showing that it is a trustworthy account of a real person.

What this freelance writer seems to be doing is overlooking all of the oral Hebrew histories that occurred before the invention of the first written language. From a logical perspective, it is impossible to just ignore mankind's oral history and focus only on written physical evidence.

This freelance writer also believes that the Garden of Eden story and the Book of Genesis are derived from the Mesopotamian myth *Enuma Elish*.[345] He states that Hebrew scribes used *Enuma Elish* to fashion the Book of Genesis. To present opinions from respected scholars regarding such claims, I present scholar Stefan Stenudd, who makes a comment in his article titled, "Enuma Elish3,-The Babylonian Creation Myth." Stefan Stenudd states:

> Of course, it is still possible that the Enuma Elish text is based on an oral tradition - this is implied by the repetition of long parts of it, and its ritualistic ingredients.[346]

Stenudd specifies why it is possible that the Mesopotamian myth *Enuma Elish* appears to have been based upon established oral accounts. He states this conclusion is implied by this myth's long repetitive parts and ritualistic components. This lends support that written Mesopotamian myths were based upon prior oral traditions and oral history.

And to further support my argument here, I reference a brilliant article by scholar James Rochford. The article is titled, "(Gen. 1:1) Did The Jews Steal Their Creation Story From the Babylonian Enuma Elish?" This article lists many scholars who contribute to the analysis of the Babylonian tale of *Enuma Elish* and very thoroughly addresses this question. The archaeologist and Egyptologist, James Hoffmeier, is mentioned as describing how different the creation story of *Enuma Elish* is from the Genesis account.[347]

Kenneth A. Kitchen, a leading Egyptologist, is quoted (1966, as cited in Rochford, n.d.) as stating:

> The common view that the Hebrew account is simply a purged and simplified version of the Babylonian legend (applied also to the flood stories) is fallacious on methodological grounds. In the Ancient Near East, (the)

rule is that simple accounts or traditions may give rise
(by accretion and embellishment) to elaborate legends,
but not vice versa. (1966, as cited in Rochford, n.d.)[348]

We can see that because the Biblical Garden of Eden story is the more simplified account, this implies that it is, by rule, the original account. While the more drawn-out and elaborate *Enuma Elish* story, would most likely be the embellishment. Rochford also goes on to state that the Babylonians could have taken Hebrew stories they had heard and used them as the material for their copied versions.[349] Yes, this is exactly right! By now we should be able to recognize that the Mesopotamians could have been the ones who were embellishing from long-standing oral Hebrew histories.

Rochford's statements are very important because they confirm that the Babylonians could have been the ones embellishing from the Hebrews. In my opinion, anyone failing to keep this very real possibility into consideration is not logically approaching this history. I also agree with Kenneth Kitchen that the idea of the Hebrew account being a copy of the Babylonian legend is fallacious and mistaken.[350] And when Kitchen states that it does not happen vice versa (the other way around), he is saying that a more elaborate *Enuma Elish* is not going to spawn a more simplified Garden of Eden version. Therefore, based upon this rule, the Garden of Eden account should logically be the original story while a more elaborate rendition would be a copied version. This all makes perfect sense. I also fully agree with all the experts presented in Rochford's article that there are huge differences between *Enuma Elish* and the Garden of Eden story.[351]

There is one last comment that I wish to present from this freelance writer that I find to be quite revealing. He states:

. . .In this, the poem follows a paradigm of Babylonian writers borrowing from earlier Sumerian pieces as exemplified in *The Epic of Gilgamesh* where the Babylonian scribe Shin-Leqi-Unninni (c. 1300-1000 BCE) drew on the separate Sumerian tales of the King of Urek and formed them into the now famous epic.[352]

Notice how Mark is admitting that the Babylonians *borrowed* from the Sumerians. And when he states this was a followed paradigm, it tells us there was a pattern of borrowing that was practiced by Babylonian writers. Therefore, Mark is admitting there was a practice of Babylonian borrowing at that time. So why can't both the Babylonians and the Sumerians have *borrowed* from the original oral Hebrew accounts? Is it not possible that "The Borrowing Babylonians," as I call them, were also busy pirating oral Hebrew accounts as material for their *works*? Simple logic dictates that this was quite possible. Furthermore, I believe this was quite probable. What we have learned here is that *borrowing* was not only practiced, but it was a deliberately followed standard, a paradigm.[353] I feel that it is just plain common sense that the borrowing Babylonians would have been practicing the same *borrowing* from anything Hebrew that they had heard as well.

Let's not forget, that the Sumerians and the Babylonians lived close to the Hebrews and were all descendants of Noah. They were all one big extended family. This allowed them to put into writing what they had been hearing for a long time from their related Hebrew neighbors. The Sumerians would likely have been quite familiar with the oral Hebrew accounts that they had heard throughout their lives. Then they adopted and adapted them into their own oral traditions before using their invention of cuneiform to be the first culture to put these stories into print.

The Sumerians and the Babylonians could have most certainly embellished earlier Oral Abrahamic-Hebrew accounts by providing these stories as outlines to their scribes for the epics that they would put into print with cuneiform. Since the Sumerians and Babylonians would have been familiar with these wonderful oral Hebrew stories, they probably felt empowered to claim them for themselves because they held the advantage of inventing the first written language. Therefore, there exists a very real probability that the Sumerians and the Babylonians used already well-known Oral Abrahamic-Hebrew history to create their own written epics.

And for those who may not be convinced that the Mesopotamians were descendants of the Hebrews, this does not matter. Whether the Mesopotamians were descendants of the Hebrews or not, this does not change the fact that the close proximity of the Mesopotamians to the Hebrews, would have caused the Mesopotamians to hear all of the Hebrew histories in the form of circulated oral traditions and stories.

I would also like to add that the Greek myths of creation and their numerous fanciful gods, were all written thousands of years after the first Hebrew stories were initially spoken as oral traditions. And as far as the Bible's first written manuscripts are concerned (Job and the Pentateuch), the first Greek myths date back to around 700 BC which is over 700 years after Moses started putting the oral Hebrew stories into print.

It is clear to me that the Mesopotamians, the Sumerians, and the ancient Greeks, all used the original oral Hebrew stories as the magnificent inspiration for their myths. I believe the ancient Greeks adopted and adapted the original Hebrew stories, along with seeking inspiration from the Mesopotamian and Sumerian myths.

I do not see how anyone can assume that just because the culture that invented the first written language and consequently put stories into writing first must therefore necessarily be the original source of those stories. The earliest written publication does not prove provenance. In the ancient world, provenance was established by whoever *told* the story first, not who wrote of it first. Remember that I mentioned Scholar Owen Omid Borville who makes the same argument when he states that ancient flood stories have been recorded all over the world giving strong support for the Great Flood account in the Book of Genesis.[354] The Great Flood story was told worldwide while the *Epic of Gilgamesh* was not. The Great Flood is universally recognized and dwarfs the Sumerian culture and its epic myths. I feel it is clear that *The Epic of Gilgamesh* did not invent the Great Flood story.

Borville also makes this statement:

> Noah's descendants passed on the history by word of mouth throughout the generations as his descendants spread from the Ararat region in all directions throughout the world in 4,500 years until today.[355]

This statement is extremely important because it reminds people that history used to be transmitted by word-of-mouth. There were no written histories before the Sumerians invented writing. Borville makes the point that even though the *Epic of Gilgamesh* was written before the Book of Genesis, people need to be mindful that the oral Hebrew version existed way before Moses had the opportunity to finally write it down. Borville also makes the point that Noah's descendants spread out and populated the entire earth after the Great Flood. This is why the Great Flood story can be found all over the world. Noah's descendants passed this history down, generation-to-generation, through oral traditions. In conclusion, Borville states that just because other cultures put their flood story into print before Moses did, this does not mean the Book of Genesis is not the original source.[356]

I would also like to point out that the *Epic of Gilgamesh* makes absolutely no mention of the ocean floor breaking up. This epic is a raining flood story that starts off with black clouds filling the skies that rumbled (thunder) where all the light had turned to blackness. These raining storm clouds are the only source of flood water. And as it rained, the winds blew strongly as a storm with the rising water destroyed everything on land as it submerged the mountains.[357] But nothing at all is mentioned about the ocean floor or *fountains of the great deep* breaking up in this myth. I feel the reason for this is clear. That part of the Hebrew story made no sense to the Mesopotamian and Sumerian scribes.

When the Sumerians wrote this myth, they were quite familiar with the oral Hebrew history of the Great Flood. The Sumerian scribes adapted this oral Hebrew history by using it as the framework for their myth, *The Epic of Gilgamesh.* The Sumerians did not understand what the *fountains of the great deep* were. This reference made no sense to them. This is why it makes perfect sense for them to leave it out and make no mention of the *great deep.* They understood this to be a Hebrew raining flood story, and that is why their copied version leaves out anything referring to the ocean floor. All things considered, I suspect that the *fountains of the great deep* did not make any sense to Moses either. Still, he includes it because Moses wrote what he was instructed to write. By contrast, the Sumerians wrote what they wanted to write and what made sense to them.

Also found in *The Epic of Gilgamesh,* we read that the dimensions of the ship to save mankind made it as long as it was wide, "The boat which you are to build, its dimensions must measure equal to each other: its length must correspond to its width."[358] It is evident that the boat in this epic was shaped as a square. However, we read in Genesis 6:15 (KJV), that Noah was given the following dimensions:

> And this is the fashion which thou shalt make it of:
> The length of the ark shall be three hundred cubits, the
> breadth of it fifty cubits, and the height of it thirty cubits.

We can see that Noah's Ark was six times longer than it was wide. Over the course of history, marine engineers have determined the most stable and efficient designs for cargo vessels. This has resulted in modern cargo vessels being constructed about six times longer than they are wide.[359] Today's Chinamax vessels (popularly called Valemax) have a length to width ratio of 5.5 to 1.[360] Therefore, from an engineering standpoint, a six to one ratio is a sound design. By comparison, the square vessel in *The Epic of Gilgamesh* is not what present-day engineers would ever recommend. No one constructs square cargo vessels that have a length to width ratio of 1 to 1. This means the Mesopotamian design for the ark is flawed, while the Hebrew design is perfect.

Some people assume the Sumerian version of the Great Flood is the original because it was put into print first. By contrast, the Hebrew version can be claimed to be the original because the instructions on how to construct the ark were given to Moses by a Divine source. Since we find sound engineering in the design of the ark in the Hebrew version, this supports the Hebrew claim that their version came from God, the Master Engineer.

Finally, let's recall that Kenneth Kitchen stated that a simpler account tends to give rise to a more elaborate copied version.[361] Anyone who has read *The Epic of Gilgamesh* and the Book of Genesis can see that one flood story is a lot longer than the other.

The scribe who wrote, *The Epic of Gilgamesh*, heaped on embellishment after embellishment onto the original Hebrew account to produce a drawn-out and protracted myth. As mentioned, I feel the scribe who wrote Gilgamesh left out the ocean floor breaking up because that did not make sense to him. Regarding the vessel dimensions, the scribe apparently put in his own length to width ratio of 1 to 1, which makes no sense from a marine engineering standpoint. This overzealous scribe went on and on with his fanciful elaborations of the original oral Hebrew account.

The reason why this is so very important is because some people try to use these Sumerian and Mesopotamian myths to discredit the Torah and the Bible by claiming embellishment. With all of this being said, no one can deny the historical fact that oral traditions existed *before* cuneiform was invented. This first written language provided wildly eccentric and unhinged Sumerian scribes the opportunity to put their own distorted versions of these Hebrew histories into print first. This occurred before the Hebrews had a chance to start writing down their original oral histories. This provenance topic is as straightforward and elementary as that.

CHAPTER EIGHT

Ten Plagues, the Red Sea, and a Shepherd Named David

T he story is told of Napoleon Bonaparte asking the scientist Pierre-Simon Laplace why he had never mentioned God in his scholarly book about the universe. Laplace haughtily answered, "I had no need of that hypothesis." There are a number of scientifically minded people today that have the same view, seeing miracles as mythical, unwanted, and unneeded hypotheses to explain reality.

Yet, what if we took a different view of miracles—not as fantastic, unpredictable, magical intrusions on the natural order, but as the way God sometimes chooses to work in His Creation? I am convinced that for the most part, God does not micromanage the earth. However, when He does choose to intervene, He uses His designed science to carry out His Will. Take the Ten Plagues, where God exposed Pharaoh to the wrath of His created nature to free the Israelites under Moses from Egyptian slavery. You can read about them in Exodus 7-12. There were plagues of blood, frogs, lice, flies, pestilence, boils, hail, locusts, darkness, and the death of the firstborns. Let's examine the

10 Plagues from a scientific perspective, paying special attention to the order in which they were recorded to have occurred.

Most researchers agree that the Nile water turning red happened first because of a bacterium known as, '*Burgundy Blood*.' It has been observed in nature that green lakes can turn blood red in a very short period of time. This is from bacteria and toxic algae.[362] Such bacteria or toxic algae would have infected the area's water supply and quickly turned the Nile red (first plague), leading to more plagues. This would have brought disease to people forced to drink from it because they were desperate for water.

The second plague on the list includes the amphibious frogs that would have been the only life that could have escaped the infected foul water, although many would still die. The frogs that did manage to escape would have wound up all over the place. The gnats and lice (third plague) and the swarms of flies (fourth plague) would have multiplied because of the enormous number of dead frogs and decomposing fish floating in the Nile River. This allowed the insects to thrive.

As dehydration set in, the animals and the Egyptians desperate for water would have swallowed the foul and infected water. Because of this, the livestock died (fifth plague), and the Egyptians got boils (sixth plague). I'm sure other infections spread as well. The list goes on in the exact order that the Bible states in Exodus.[363]

From the Institute for Atmospheric Physics in Germany, Dr. Nadine von Blohm reports that a volcanic eruption may have ejected ash and debris into the atmosphere that mixed with thunderstorms. If this occurred, it could have caused a dramatic hailstorm of fiery hail (seventh plague).[364]

By this time, the locusts came to devour the dead and rotting livestock. All of these events created the ideal situation for locusts to multiply and swarm (eighth plague). And of course, this ash and debris from the eruption could have blocked out the Sun once dispersed, causing darkness to fall for several days (ninth plague).[365]

Years ago, I read that a fissure in the earth's crust from this eruption could have allowed carbon dioxide to be forced up from below the earth's crust and into the households of the Egyptians. Carbon dioxide is heavier than air and would therefore sink and collect close to the floor. And since the Egyptians placed their young newborns on the floor (or close to the floor) so they could not roll out of bed and fall, this caused the Egyptian babies near the floor to breath in the carbon dioxide which caused them to die. I apologize that I cannot remember the source of this information, someone else deserves credit for this theory. That being said, I did find a source that confirms carbon dioxide causes death by displacing oxygen which causes asphyxiation by hypoxia.[366] In addition, it is common knowledge that carbon dioxide is heavier than air.

With all of this being said, scientific researchers admit they can scientifically explain most of these events in the precise order that the Bible records them. In other words, from a scientific perspective, these miracles and their order of occurrence are quite possible. Therefore, instead of science stating that they have just proven this Biblical account to be impossible, science demonstrates that it was indeed possible and that the order of the plagues makes logical sense. It's amazing the sequence of events for these plagues is so precise. I feel this is an example of how God can utilize the science that He created to carry out His commands. Of course, what makes these Divine miracles, is their timing.

Let's look at another amazing miracle recorded in Scripture to see what we can learn. In Exodus 14 we read about the parting of the Red Sea. You'll recall that when Pharaoh and his armies chased the departing Israelites, their way of escape was blocked by the Red Sea, and a mass slaughter seemed imminent. But Exodus records that God parted the waters using a strong East wind, and the people walked through on dry land. When the Egyptian armies attempted to follow, they were swallowed up by the surge of the sea, returning to its natural state. The first detail of this account to take note of is found in Exodus 14:1 (KJV), where the Israelites were instructed by God to camp at a very specific site. This indicates that the parting of the Red Sea did not occur at a random location. Instead, God had selected the best spot for the crossing.

We now have scientific research that reveals water can indeed be parted in a phenomenon referred to as, *wind setdown.* This is where very strong winds blow in from one direction creating a storm surge in another part of the body of water which completely clears the water from the direction where the wind was blowing. This effect can last several hours. Research states that a 63-miles-per-hour wind can produce a dry channel in the Red Sea that could have been crossed.[367] It has been proven that if a strong directional wind can move enough water, an exposed land bridge can be created.[368] God is capable of directing a wind that is far more powerful than the wind in any model experiment. This means that God could have easily cleared a tremendous amount of water in the same way. I find it very convincing that in Exodus 14:21 (KJV), we read of a strong East wind which lasted all night long. The longer the wind pushes, the greater the amount of water it will move.

This event is very convincing to me because it starts off with a strong wind along with the location where the strong wind would be delivered. A strong wind is exactly what *wind setdown* requires. This proves two things to me:

1) This account must have really occurred because it starts off describing the exact required condition of a strong wind which was necessary for *wind setdown* to occur.

2) This account once again demonstrates that God did not just snap His fingers to cause this event to occur. Instead, He preferred to use His created science to carry out His Will.

What I also find extremely interesting is that the direction of the strong wind was listed as being form the East. The Israelites were crossing from the West side to the East side of that channel in the Red Sea. When the speed of an East wind starts to slow down, the water will start to fill back in on the West side first. This would have prevented Pharaoh's armies from retreating. This would have also given the Israelites the greatest amount of time to cross because they were running from the West to the East, just as the returning sea would have been moving from the West to the East.

As a consequence, because the direction the Israelites were running coincides perfectly with the direction of the strong East wind listed in the Book of Exodus, this strongly supports the authenticity of this documented event. Therefore, I am convinced the parting of the Red Sea really occurred and is not a fairy tale.

Now, there are historians who are quick to point out the Egyptians don't record this destructive event in their history. And I ask: why would they? If they told the entire ancient world they just lost all of their armies in the Red Sea, what do think would happen next? They would have been invaded by every single one of their hostile neighbors, of course. Not only was this a significant embarrassment to Pharaoh, but it created a **severe** national security emergency. The Egyptian Empire would have ceased to exist if their enemies found out they were completely vulnerable. I'm sure that Pharaoh immediately decreed that nothing be said about this situation or written about it. This makes perfect logical sense.

I would like to take a moment to pause here in order to comment on the occurrence of natural disasters like tornados, hurricanes, and earthquakes which cause destruction and death. I don't believe these events happen because God has necessarily willed them to occur. I think that some people feel when these disasters occur, God is sending them as judgement, just like the 10 Plagues. However, I believe disasters sent by God are rare. The 10 Plagues were necessary in order for God's people to be set free from the tyranny of their bondage in Egypt.

Earthquakes occur because of the molten lava at Earth's core while tornados and hurricanes tend to occur primarily because the earth is spinning 1,000 miles an hour on its axis. Therefore, when natural disasters occur, it is usually the consequence of living on planet Earth, not necessarily because of God's Will. In other words, I don't believe God is the reason for these disasters.

When God does choose to intervene and assist, this constitutes what we call a miracle. Otherwise, God typically allows nature to take its course. However, if it was God's Will for one of these events to occur, then it would constitute, judgement. As stated, I believe almost all of these disasters are the consequence of the reality of Earth's physics. Apparently, Adam and Eve were initially protected from these events but their fall from Grace removed those protections exposing them, and us, to the reality of living on planet Earth.

This brings up a similar topic. Some people may wonder why God allows bad things to happen to good people from the actions of others. In my humble opinion, the bad things that happen to people at the hands of others are a result of the abuse of free will. God grants all of us free will and He will not violate our free will when we choose to abuse it, otherwise, we would be robots. If God stepped in and stopped abusive behaviors every time they were just about to occur, then mankind would not have the freedom to make choices. This means that we cannot blame God for the abusive actions of others. I believe the reason why abuse occurs stems from the influence of our selfish sin natures. We are all born with a sin nature that was passed down to us through Adam and Eve. God did not make mankind this way. Mankind became this way because Satan tricked Adam and Eve into abusing their free will. This resulted in disobedience which was against God's Ways.

I believe that sin can be summed up by one word, selfishness. The root of all sinful and wicked behavior is the result of mankind being selfish (and greedy). Let me give a relevant example on how this is not God's fault. If parents teach their children the difference between right and wrong, but one of their children grows up and chooses to engage in criminal behavior, do we prosecute the parents? No, society does not seek to hold the parents responsible because everyone knows that the parents did not commit the crimes, their adult child did. Their offspring knew the difference between right and wrong and chose to be abusively and criminally selfish (in this case). In the same way that society does not prosecute parents for the actions of their adult children, mankind cannot blame God for the abusive actions of some of His children.

Now, getting back to the Egyptians. There are some people who cast doubt that the Egyptians held enslaved people who they forced to make mud bricks for them. These critics claim the Hebrews never lived as enslaved people in Egypt. However, proof exists that slaves were forced to make ancient Egyptian bricks from clay, mud, and straw. This evidence comes to us from archaeologists who are also experts in the field of brickmaking:

The evidence of this can be seen today at ruins of Harappa Buhen and Mohenjo-daro. Paintings on the tomb wall of Thebes portray Egyptian slaves mixing, tempering, and carrying clay for sun dried bricks.[369]

The images documented on this fresco in the Rekhmire Tomb are quite clear. Scholar Kim Phillips who is a research fellow at the Institute for Hebrew Bible Manuscript Research points out that we can see from the paintings that the slaves were being forced to mix mud and water to make bricks, mold the bricks, dry the bricks in the Sun, and then carry the bricks off for use. This was all done under the watchful eye of rod-wielding overseers.[370] The people tasked with making the bricks were described as being, servants. A servant is a slave. Only slaves would be subjected to rod-wielding overseers.

In addition to the frescos, Egyptian papyri have been discovered that document brick quotas and how straw was used in the brick-making.[371] Dr. Gary Baxter is a Biblical scholar who a holds a Ph.D. in Organic Chemistry and he makes this statement about one of these papyri:

> The Papyrus Anastasi VI from around 3200 years ago describes how the Egyptian authorities allowed a group of Semitic nomads from Edom who worshiped Yahweh, to pass the border-fortress in the region of Tjeku (Wadi Tumilat) and proceed with their livestock to the lakes of Pithom.[5] More evidence of the presence of Semitic[6] people in Egypt.[372]

This papyrus represents physical evidence confirming that ancient Egypt allowed Semitic Hebrews worshiping Yahweh to move into their empire. And why would ancient Egypt have allowed this? It appears logical to conclude the reason why they were allowed to move in, was because these Israelites were going to be forced into slave labor. Despite this, some skeptics still claim that physical evidence of Israelite habitation in Egypt does not exist. However, there are natural explanations for this which include decomposition, erosion, and the ravages of time.[373]

As stated, I feel we need to also be mindful that Israelite habitation in Egypt would have been deliberately erased. After the stunning defeat of his armies, it makes perfect sense that Pharaoh could have decreed that all signs of the Israelites be destroyed. Pharaoh would have done this in an attempt to erase this horrible experience from Egyptian history. Its logical to surmise that a proud and aggressive leader like Pharaoh would want nothing left behind to remind him of his devastating humiliation.

Next, there is the Biblical story of the destruction of Jericho and how the walls suddenly came crashing down. Archaeologists have confirmed the ruins of the fortified city of Jericho and that its walls really did abruptly come crashing down, just as the Bible describes.[374]

Another story that we are all familiar with is the Great Flood. As I mentioned in the last chapter, scientific research evidence exists proving that a massive global flood really did happen in 6,200 BC.[375] This indicates to me that the Great Flood mentioned in the Book of Genesis occurred 8,200 years ago.

I would like to point out that this Hebrew history pre-dates cuneiform and the Mesopotamian myths by thousands of years. As a consequence, the Hebrews would have been passing this particular story down by word-of-mouth, generation to generation, for thousands of years before the first Mesopotamian myth was ever written.

In fact, the Hebrews would have been passing this Great Flood history down by word-of-mouth, generation to generation, for about four thousand years before the first Mesopotamian myth was ever written. As a consequence, if you ever read a comment from a 'scholar' who claims the Bible stories are loosely based upon previously written Mesopotamian myths, you can be assured that 'scholar' is mistaken. Those 'scholars' are mistaken because they have left out the early Oral Abrahamic-Hebrew histories that existed thousands of years before the first written myth was ever contrived and put into print with the first written language (Cuneiform).

Next, we have research from scholars that around 6000 BC the historical city of Nineveh was built. One of these scholars is Julia O'Brien who holds a Ph.D. from Duke University, majoring in Hebrew Bible and Semitic Studies and minors in Judaism and Literary Criticism. We see from O'Brien that she places the founding of Nineveh to be perhaps as early as 6000 BC.[376] Nineveh was a post-flood city. Since Nineveh has been dated to around 6000 BC, this tells me that it took roughly 200 years for the descendants of Noah to establish Nineveh after the 6200 BC Great Flood subsided. This timeline makes perfect sense.

Therefore, it took Noah's children and their descendants around 200 years to multiply to the extent that there were enough people concentrated in this area to begin the construction of this post-flood city. This is possible because Nineveh could have initially started off as a small village with just a handful of buildings. Then, over time as the population grew, Nineveh would have slowly grown and spread out as the sprawling and grand metropolis that history reveals that it ultimately became.

If anyone has reservations about this event in history not seeming to sequence properly as far as timelines are concerned, then see if dating the Great Flood to 6200 BC solves those issues. This would mean that Adam and Eve were created over a thousand years before 6200 BC. This is why I personally date the appearance of Biblical Adam and Eve to about 10,000 years ago.

Some may ask, just who were the descendants of Noah that built the post-flood cities like Nineveh? We get this information from Dr. David P. Livingston, a Ph.D. in Archaeology from Andrews University. Dr. Livingston directed excavations of ancient cities in Israel for 24 years. Dr. Livingston tells us that a descendant of Noah named Nimrod was the one who initiated the building of many ancient post-flood cities. Two of these cities were Nineveh and Babel. Babel was also known as Babylon. In Genesis 10:1-12 (KJV), we see mention of Noah's offspring which mentions Nimrod who was the great grandson of Noah.[377]

In Genesis Chapter 11, we read that Noah's descendants repopulated the earth and proceeded to build the Tower of Babel. Apparently, this tower was planned and constructed out of mankind's arrogance and complete defiance to God. It is my understanding this tower was mankind's attempt to ascend to the Heavens in order to raise themselves to God's level.

Professor Mark Miller, who served as the State Archaeologist of Wyoming for 30 years, focuses our attention on a baked tablet found in ancient Babylon.[378] This tablet depicts a structure that looked like a pyramid of sorts and had a temple at the top. Dr. Miller presents Dr. Andrew George, professor of Babylonia at the University of London who examined this baked clay tablet that was discovered a century ago that depicts a tower. It had seven steps and shows a king with his conical hat and staff. This tower is thought to be the Tower of Babylon. Below is the text that describes the commissioning of the tower's construction. George said:

This is a very strong piece of evidence that the tower of
Babel story was inspired by this real building.[379]

The chiseled text reads, "Etemenanki, Ziggurat Babel." Professor
George states, "the Ziggurat or Temple Tower of the City of Babylon
(is depicted as a) building with its builder on the same relief." This
find seems to prove that the Tower of Babel was real.[380] In a Smithsonian video, Miller also includes this quote from Professor George,
"After Darwin cast doubt on the story of a six-day creation, people
began to ask what else in the Bible might not be true,"[381] Dr. George
made this statement to *Breaking Israel News*:

> In the 19th century there was a discovery that the Assyrian
> kings described in the Bible were real and corroborated
> by archaeological evidence, making us ask now, how
> much more in the Bible is true?[382]

As more archaeological evidence is discovered over time, more
stories in the Bible are being demonstrated to document actual history.

Then, in Genesis 19:24-29, we have the destruction of Sodom and
Gomorrah around 1700 BC. The Bible account states that the Lord
destroyed the cities with what is called fire from heaven. Researchers
have found convincing evidence that a meteor exploded above the two
cities and rained down platinum and molten lava.[383] Apparently, the
cities were exposed to temperatures between 4,000 and 12,000 degrees
Celsius, the latter of which is as hot as the surface of the Sun. Zircon
crystals were formed that confirm the extreme heat exposure was brief.
From this evidence, many scientists now believe that a meteorite explosion burned Sodom and Gomorrah to the ground.[384]

What matters is that scientists have discovered both Sodom and
Gomorrah abruptly burned to the ground, just as the Bible states.
This is not a coincidence or a fable. God used His created science

to carry out His Will as He cast a relatively small meteorite to Earth with the intent to destroy sinful Sodom and Gomorrah.

As I have mentioned, in the past, I did not believe the stories in the Bible because I was under the impression that they were all recycled myths from other ancient cultures. However, in heavily researching for the truth over the last few years, I have discovered that just the opposite is true. Other cultures were the ones who recycled already established oral Hebrew stories. This realization has allowed me to see the truth and embrace the stories in the Bible as being authentic. With that said, there was one Bible story that I still had questions about. That was the story of Jonah and the whale.

The story of Jonah and the whale is where God sends Jonah to the sinful city of Nineveh to get them to repent and turn from their sinful ways. Nineveh was considered a city of sin and a city of "embellishment."[385] In the Book of Jonah, 4:11 (KJV), we see that there are "six score thousand" people in Nineveh. This means that 2,000 years ago, Nineveh was a city with 120,000 people. It was an enormous mega-city in its day.

As I proceeded to investigate this story online, apparently other people had the same question I did and were arguing on an online forum about how Jonah could have survived in the belly of a whale for three days and three nights. Unfortunately, I cannot recall the name of this blog forum, but I do remember what one of its members had to say. Because people were arguing about how Jonah could have survived, this blogger told people to listen and realize that Jonah did not live in the belly of that whale for three days. Rather, Jonah died and was then resurrected three days and three nights later. Jesus used Jonah as an example in Matthew 12:40, because Jesus would also die and then resurrect after three days and three nights. As soon as I heard this, I was able to understand this part of Jonah's story.

This blogger also said something that was fascinating. He stated that being in the stomach of a whale for three days would have exposed Jonah to acids that would have bleached his skin white and burned off his hair, eyebrows, and eyelashes. It was at this point that I disconnected from the forum because I had found an explanation regarding Jonah's experience inside of that whale.

In Jonah 1:17 (KJV), we read that Jonah was swallowed into the belly of a large fish. However, most people associate the creature that swallowed Jonah to have been a whale. A whale breathes air while a fish does not. Therefore, a whale is not a fish. That said, it turns out that the largest fish in the ocean is a whale shark. A whale shark is not actually a whale, it's a fish that is the size of a whale.

All things considered, there is one way to bring these two interpretations into agreement. If we consider that Jonah may have been swallowed by a whale shark, we have a situation where, Jonah may have been inside the belly of a fish that was the size of a whale and is called a whale. I say this in case there are any people out there who argue over whether a large fish or a whale swallowed Jonah. If we can accept that he may have wound up in the belly of a whale shark, then perhaps we can all agree that he was inside of a whale fish. In this way, both interpretations can be correct and find agreement.

After considering all of this later that night, I started to have more questions. I questioned how an outsider such as Jonah could have possibly convinced a mega-city like Nineveh to repent of their sins? I had difficulty imagining how a foreigner like Jonah could go into Nineveh, a huge city of 120,000 people, and convince them of anything, let alone to repent of their sins? In addition, this was accomplished in just one day. I must admit that I struggled to imagine this part. Nineveh was a pagan city with pagan gods. Why would they listen to Jonah?

But then I remembered that the online blogger described how Jonah would have looked. Then I reasoned that if Jonah was bleached white with no hair, no eyebrows, and no eyelashes, people would have gathered around him asking what happened to him? Human curiosity would have collected a large crowd around him in this vast city. Then he would have told them that he died in the belly of a fish the size of a whale and his God brought him back to life. The people who gathered around him would have probably thought about this and then said, "That makes sense because you look like you have been dead for three days." And I'm guessing that he smelled like he had been dead for three days as well.

They could see with their own eyes that Jonah was acid bleached. And I can assure you that they had never seen anything like this before. Then he would have told them how his God saved him and brought him back to life. I would like to add that I believe once Jonah died in the whale fish, that God prevented Jonah from decomposing and preserved the general condition of his body. However, Jonah's outward appearance would have been shocking because of being immersed in stomach acid. This makes a lot more sense than God allowing Jonah to decompose over the course of three days and then God reversing all of that decomposition.

Since God is able to create an entire universe along with all of the species that have ever existed on the earth, He can certainly reverse decomposition. However, because I find God to be logical and method-ical, I believe that God probably took the more logical approach by preventing decomposition in the first place. Likewise, I believe the bodies of Lazarus and Jesus were preserved in this same way in order to keep them in a prepared state for their resurrections.

With that being said, as the citizens of Nineveh listened to Jonah's story, they would have believed all of this. Once they became convinced of the first part of his story because of how he looked (and smelled), they would have also believed the rest of his story. The physical evidence they could see with their own eyes, coupled with his testimony convinced the citizens of Nineveh that he was telling the truth.

Then they would have asked him why he came to their city? This is where Jonah would have told them that his powerful God had brought him there to warn them of the planned destruction of their city if they did not repent of their sins. I believe it is not too hard to imagine that once these people believed what happened to Jonah and could see with their own eyes that he should still be dead, that they immediately presented him to their king. Everyone would have believed everything that he had said and realized what a powerful God that he served.

I'm sure the king of Nineveh interviewed Jonah and also believed everything Jonah had said. Once the king saw what Jonah looked like, smelled like, and heard his testimony, I'm sure that he became convinced of Jonah's credibility and almighty God. Then the king would have ordered a decree for the entire city to obey his command for all of them to repent of their sins and change their behavior immediately. The king would have done this to protect his metropolis from destruction. That would have been his main duty as king.

In this way, I can see how a foreign visitor to an ancient megacity is going to possess the influence necessary to cause the entire city to repent and turn from their sins, in just one day. At first glance, to some people this may sound like an impossible fable. However, it does make perfect logical sense if we carefully analyze the situation.

Once Jonah is resurrected by God, what happens after that follows a very logical progression of human behavior.

Now, we have all heard the story of David and Goliath. And to some, this is another story that sounds too good to be true. How could a much smaller shepherd boy defeat a highly experienced, fierce, and imposing warrior? This seems like a fairy tale at first glance. But not so fast, let's look at this fascinating account in more detail.

A bit before 1000 BC, we have David whose birthplace was Bethlehem. He was a shepherd boy who could play instruments and sing very well. King Saul (the first King of Israel) and the Israelites found themselves challenged by the Philistines to a single combat contest. The Philistine's put Goliath on the battlefield as their representative for this contest. Goliath was giant, who was imposing and ferocious with a sword. Everyone feared Goliath. Many people around the world have heard about King David. David's first claim to fame was him being the Israelite who volunteered to meet Goliath in this single combat challenge. Thus, we have a battle between a shepherd boy, who chose not to wear armor, versus a much larger, fully armed, and battle-hardened soldier. This battle seemed lopsided and doomed for David and the Israelites.

This situation is well explained in a Youtube video titled "The Unheard Story of David and Goliath."[386] As Malcolm Gladwell's video explains, it turns out that what David had for a weapon was a sling. You will note that a sling is not a slingshot. A sling, as it is whizzed in a circular motion several times a second, once released, actually generates a projectile like a large, low-velocity bullet. Shepherds tending their flock used these slings to protect themselves and their livestock from predators. Some shepherds got so good with slings that they could hit a bird in the air.[387] Therefore, people who got good with slings were deadly accurate, just like a sniper. This is how David drove off or slew deadly animals with his sling to protect himself and his flock.

Goliath had no idea what would be thrown at him at close range. He was actually dead before that fight began. Goliath was probably standing 10-15 feet away from David. Goliath held an imposing sword that he was not using yet because he thought David would approach and get closer. David had what amounted to a low-velocity gun with bullets larger than the diameter of a silver dollar.

Gladwell states that these stones can be thrown at speeds of 35 meters per second.[388] This is about 80 miles per hour. This is about the average speed that a baseball pitcher throws a baseball. What we have here amounts to a heavy bullet the size of a silver dollar travelling the length of a football field in less than 3 seconds.

For 2,000 years ago, that was really fast. But in this case, the stone only has to go 15 feet and straight into the forehead of Goliath. Recent research has even discovered that these slings threw stones with the stopping power of a .44 Magnum handgun.[389] And unlike David's other victories with his sling, where the target was erratically moving in a threatening manner as a charging animal, Goliath waited and stood still. As a result, David had a stationary target which is much easier to strike.

Gladwell also states the rocks David used were made of barium sulphate and were denser and heavier than normal stones.[390] Granite has a density of around 2.7 g/cm^3. Basalt has a density of approximately 3.0 g/cm^3. While barium sulphate, has a density that is around 4.5 g/cm^3. Clearly, barium sulphate would make for a very heavy and dangerous projectile. Shepherds knew exactly what they were doing with their slings.

David was not getting close enough for a sword to reach him, this is why he rejected the offer to borrow King Saul's armor. In addition, wearing someone else's armor would have been cumbersome and thrown off his aim. Many people who have heard this story wondered why David would have turned down the opportunity to wear Saul's armor. But David knew what he was doing, and the armor would have been a hindrance. David began to whip his loaded sling around and around until he revved it up to top speed. Then he let it loose and dropped Goliath on the spot. Goliath was probably dead when he was struck in the forehead at close range. David made sure by taking Goliath's sword and cutting off his head.

This battle was not as lopsided as most people think. A highly experienced and accurate sniper gunned down Goliath. This giant Philistine was actually at a severe disadvantage. This history is important to me because it demonstrates that what some people have called another improbable fairy tale story found in the Bible, is actually not improbable at all. David was highly favored to win that contest because of his supreme skill and his choice of weapons. And let's not forget that David was favored by God as well. Therefore, it makes perfect sense that Goliath lost because he brought a knife to a gun fight.

When we examine the facts that Gladwell presents, the account of David and Goliath is actually not an improbable fairy tale at all. Science proves this account was very possible, and I would venture to say that this account was highly probable. Remember that shepherds were so accurate that they could hit a bird in the air with their stones. They were used to defending themselves and their livestock against deadly animals that were charging at them. Goliath stood still right in front of David and waited. And as you can see, science and history are supporting this account that we read of in the Bible.

Science is not disproving this account. The Bible is full of seemingly implausible stories like this one, that upon closer inspection, turn out to be fully compatible with science and reality.

Clare Fitzgerald holds a Ph.D. in Art History and is a Curator and Egyptologist. In an online article, she states that slings are today recognized to have revolutionized warfare in the ancient world.[391] They were used by Hebrew warriors and Roman soldiers alike. Slings used as weapons even appear in the ancient Greek writings of Homer. The oldest surviving examples of slings were found in the tomb of King Tutankhamen (King Tut).[392] Therefore, the sling was a real weapon that really worked.

I believe God prefers to use His created science to carry out His Will when He intervenes in human affairs. We are privileged in these instances to view His miracles—and be warned. The editing author of Bible History.com states:

> What is amazing is that modern archaeology has confirmed that the Bible has never made one error or given any clear contradictions in all of its text in matters of historical fact. Every archaeological discovery that describes people, places, or events mentioned in the Bible has pointed to the accuracy of the Biblical record. In fact, many archaeologists have become believers in the Bible because of its accuracy.[393]

During all of the research it took to compile this book, I found story after story where science, history, and archaeology never contradicted the accounts found in the Bible. In fact, they appear to support the accounts found in the Bible.

The Bible is not just a collection of allegories to get morals of stories across to the reader. The Bible is a history book that accurately documents ancient Hebrew history, as fantastic as that may sound. And because this is so important, I'm going to state it one more time, the Bible is not a collection of recycled Mesopotamian myths because the first oral Hebrew traditions and stories (histories) existed thousands of years before the first Mesopotamian myth was ever written.

CHAPTER NINE

You Gotta Have Soul

Despite the impressive list of famous scientists that I have presented earlier who strongly believe in God, there are some people, some of them scientists, who severely doubt the existence of a Creator. Years ago, one of these doubtful skeptics online posted the pointed question: Why would a Creator (if there was one) have suddenly decided to create the universe, the earth, and mankind in the first place? *I apologize for not remembering the online blog or the blogger's name.*

This person was vexed as to what reason could possibly exist for a Creator to suddenly decide to create everything? In this person's analytical mind, if there was a Creator, then there had to be a justifying explanation of epic proportions. Perhaps one of the reasons this person was a skeptic, was because he simply saw no logical motivation for why an intelligence would abruptly cause the creation of everything in our physical universe, which was initiated with the Big Bang. What rational purpose could possibly exist to explain the sudden decision to initiate the genesis of our perfectly designed universe along with mankind?

I have one simple answer to this great question. God is many, many things. God is magnificent, God is merciful, God is forgiveness, God is salvation, and God is logical. With that being said, what God is best known for is His Love. And like anyone filled with love, they want to share it with someone else, especially if you are God. This is why I believe God wanted an eternal family with which to fellowship and share His Love. This is the fundamental explanation for why God decided to create a universe that was engineered to support life and mankind. All of the other species that were here in the past, and are currently here, support the earth's ecosystem and mankind in one way or another. All of creation was designed to serve and support mankind. We are God's most prized creation. When God created us, it was with the intention that we would join His eternal family. Simply put, God wanted a family.

I am convinced this is the reason why we observe in *Creation Week* that God created mankind as His most precious creation. As you will recall, mankind was created in the image and likeness of God which culminated with God forming a covenant relationship with mankind. However, in order for mankind to join God's eternal family, a special part of mankind has to survive the physical process of death and live on. And this brings us to the topic of this chapter.

In this chapter, we will discuss the special part of mankind that was designed by God to exist forever, our soul. Jesus Christ assumed both the existence and the utter importance of the soul when He asked in Mark 8:36 (KJV):

> For what shall it profit a man, if he shall gain the whole world, and lose his own soul?

Our eternal destiny, He said, hangs on whether we keep our soul or lose it. His followers have taught that the salvation of the soul leads to the union with God in heaven. By contrast, the loss of the soul leads to eternal separation from God. It results in serving an eternal sentence in Hell. Ecclesiastes 12:7 (KJV) states:

> Then shall the dust return to the earth as it was: and the spirit shall return unto God who gave it.

The body has an expiration date, but the soul does not. After hearing this, a person may ask the question: If some people are going to Hell for eternity, then why would all souls return to God upon their deaths? I believe this may indicate that all souls are first brought to God the Father to be judged. Then after that official proceeding, our souls go to their final destination. Therefore, it seems there may be a process involved with death.

Of course, many people in the modern world do not believe in the existence of the soul. Like Karl Marx before them, they consider such a doctrine to be a means to keep the people in their place as they await heavenly rewards. Religion, they assert, is the "opium of the people."[394]

Suppose we can find evidence that we really do have souls. In that case, we are forced to confront the very real possibility that Heaven and Hell exist not in the dusty pages of ancient religious texts but as non-negotiable pillars of reality itself. This brief chapter will present evidence that human beings possess souls with eternal destinies

To establish this, we will consider three YouTube videos of medical doctors. The first is titled, "What Really Happens When You Die / End-of-life Phenomenon: At Home with Peter Fenwick."[395] This is the video that runs 59:28, where Peter Fenwick is wearing a tan-colored suit. Dr. Fenwick is both a neurologist and a psychiatrist who holds an M.D. degree and a Ph.D. In addition, Dr. Fenwick has served as a senior lecturer at King's College in London and is a highly respected neuropsychiatrist who presents his evidence for near-death experiences, known as NDEs.

Earlier in life, Dr. Fenwick didn't believe in these experiences and thought they were all nonsense. Nevertheless, his medical work exposed him to many patients who had NDEs. As a consequence, Dr. Fenwick is now considered by many to be an esteemed expert in the field of near-death experiences. As a medical doctor and a scientist, Dr. Fenwick collected and analyzed his scientific observations on these patients' experiences. Eventually, he came to the realization that there was an actual "process to death." He describes patients who, just before they died, would suddenly sit up in bed and say, goodbye, to the people around them and then lie back down and die.

What Dr. Fenwick finds even more fascinating are clinical observations of paralyzed patients sitting up to acknowledge people around them just before they died. Astonishingly, Dr. Fenwick states that for those few moments, their central nervous systems seemed to work again appropriately. This should have been impossible! Even more intriguing, Fenwick notes Alzheimer's patients, whose brains were entirely overtaken by dementia and have lost their memories many years ago, will sit up, fully recognize their friends and relatives, say goodbye, and then lie back down and die.[396] Dr. Fenwick emphasizes that it is physically impossible for paralyzed people to sit up and Alzheimer's patients to suddenly and completely remember. Something outside of the realm of physics, chemistry, and biology is occurring here. This renowned neuropsychiatrist has documented it many times with meticulously collected scientific data.

Dr. Fenwick discovered a fascinating fact involving people who did not believe anything existed after death. Many of his subjects thought that everything would "just go into blackness" when they died. They were convinced there would be nothing afterward, and that would be it. However, he states, "What is quite clear, as they come into the death process, they have *all* given up that idea."[397]

All of these doubting people gave up their belief that they would simply fade into blackness. Dr. Fenwick goes on to state, "They don't say that they don't believe in anything anymore. . . . They *all* start looking forward to what's happening to them, and they don't say that they don't believe in anything anymore."[398]

Dr. Fenwick mentions an example, "And one woman who was absolutely sure that there was nothing there, kept waking up from a coma saying, 'Come on, get on with it, because I want to move on.'" What Dr. Fenwick finds vital for us to note is that every one of his subjects who believed that nothing exists after death, completely changed their minds. They quickly realized something was happening to them, not explained by physics, chemistry, or biology. Dr. Fenwick documented that *all* of these nonbelievers realized they were wrong about this right before they died. They were all wrong in believing that they would just fade into blackness.

As a consequence, what was previously thought to be something no one could ever know until after they died, has been scientifically demonstrated through meticulous clinical observations, interviews, and documentation. This is all based on science and the Scientific Method. Dr. Fenwick is a detail oriented medical doctor and researcher. He does not have the time nor the patience for nonsense. He used his scientific mind and extensive medical training to establish whether near-death experiences were real or not. Dr. Fenwick now knows they are valid and that something does exist beyond our realm. Therefore, instead of realizing these facts while we are in the process of our own deaths, we are fortunate enough to get this information ahead of time because of the work of Dr. Fenwick. I feel this is critical information to be aware of.

This raises the question: Did these people's souls take possession of their damaged physical bodies in order to sit up these paralyzed patients and do the thinking for these Alzheimer's patients? Well, what other explanation is there? I'm thoroughly convinced with this scientific data that Dr. Fenwick has collected and presented here. It firmly establishes that something special occurs at death that defies biology, chemistry, and physics. And the only thing all of this can mean is that we move on after death and our soul is how we get there.

Now let's turn to the second video from Dr. Lloyd Rudy who is a renowned cardiovascular surgeon. Dr. Rudy "was the youngest member of the first heart transplant team at Stanford University. He has pioneered quantifying surgical procedures that have drastically increased the survival rate of heart patients."[399] Dr. Rudy is considered one of the most respected cardiac surgeons of all time.

In a video titled, "Famous Cardiac Surgeon's Stories of Near-Death Experiences in Surgery," Dr. Rudy recounted a few amazing experiences that occurred in his operating room.[400] For example, one patient on the operating room table who was pronounced dead for 20-25 minutes, came back to life. This patient was in a coma for one to two days before eventually waking up. Dr. Rudy visited this patient to see how he was doing and assess expected neurologic deficits. When the patient appeared to have no neurologic deficits after being pronounced dead for about 25 minutes, Dr. Rudy asked him what he remembered, if anything?

Dr. Rudy states the patient first told him of seeing a bright light, which many people who have out-of-body experiences report. The surgeon did not seem to be impressed. Then the patient said he was floating up and around the room, and again, Dr. Rudy was unmoved. The patient also reported that he didn't know where the anesthesiologist was? Then the patient tells him that he saw the surgeon and his assistant standing in the doorway with their arms folded. When he told Dr. Rudy this, it caught Dr. Rudy's attention. This patient later witnessed the surgeon, the anesthesiologist, and the nurses all running back into the room while he was dead.

Considering all of this, Dr. Rudy knew for sure that something phenomenal had occurred here when this patient mentioned seeing all of the post-it-note messages left for him during the surgery. These messages were placed on a monitor while the surgery was taking place. Dr. Rudy states this patient could not have known about or witnessed the presence of his post-it messages because this patient was put to sleep way before the messages were placed there.

In addition, I know that when a patient is on the operating table for open heart surgery, the anesthesiologist is positioned directly behind the patient's head. And when the patient is flat on their back, it is impossible to see the anesthesiologist behind them, unless the anesthesiologist is leaning over them. In this patient's testimony, it made sense to me that the only reason he did not know the whereabouts of the anesthesiologist, was because he could see behind his head to notice that the anesthesiologist was gone. This would support this patient's report of floating up and having an overhead view.

Also, heart surgery patients have their eyelids taped closed during the surgery, so their eyes don't dry out. The eyelid taping also prevents accidental abrasions of the patient's corneas. There is no way this patient was viewing anything with his physical eyes, and Dr. Rudy confirms that visual processes were not possible. Dr. Rudy stresses that this patient's physical eyes could not have seen what he later reported seeing. This man was dead with his eyes taped closed and he did not wake up for another day or two.

Dr. Rudy found this to be quite astounding because this man could describe what was going on in the operating room, not only after he was anesthetized, but also while he was dead. Because of all of this, especially the patient seeing the post-it messages, Dr. Rudy came to the conclusion this man had to have left his physical body. Dr. Rudy was talking about this man floating around as he was pointing up to the ceiling. This is when Dr. Rudy exclaimed, "He was up there!"[401] In utter amazement, Dr. Rudy stated:

> "He described the scene, things that there is no way that
> he knew."

I would like to point out that while this man was floating around, his soul was able to visually store all of this information such that he could recall it once he came out of his coma. I find this to be fascinating.

At this point, Dr. Rudy asks the only logical question that he can, which is, "Was that his soul, up there?"[402] As you can see, Dr. Rudy's only logical explanation is that this patient's observations appear to be the result of this man's soul being able to float above his body. What other explanation is there? And because this allowed an overhead view of the operating room, this man was able to report seeing things that his physical body could not see.

How could this happen? We have all heard accounts before of people who reported they could see their bodies on operating tables or hospital beds while another part of them was floating in the air. Many books have been written about NDEs, some more credible than others. Even though I doubted them for the most part, there were a few that did seem credible. However, overall, I was not convinced of out-of-body experiences. I figured that maybe some brain activity was still going on in these patients that made it seem like they were really experiencing what they remembered. I thought these experiences were akin to having a dream.

However, this case is different because of the incredible testimony of a very famous cardiovascular surgeon. Dr. Rudy was most impressed by the fact this patient had been able to see his post-it messages on a nearby monitor which were placed there while the surgery was going on, well after the patient's eyes had been taped closed and was anesthetized.[403] Also remember, that while this patient was dead on the operating room table, he was also able to see through the open door which allowed him to report seeing Dr. Rudy and the assistant surgeon standing outside the room with their arms crossed.

Dr. Rudy knows this man had to have left his physical body in order to visually store all this information. This means that our souls possess visual perception and the ability to store what they see, into our brain's memory. That is why this patient could comment on visual observations his physical body had never experienced. As Dr. Rudy states, there is no other way to interpret this evidence.

The last video that I wish to present here involves an orthopedic surgeon who was struck dead by lightning. His name is Dr. Tony Cicoria and he posted his testimony in a YouTube video titled: "Doctor Struck By Lightning; Learns The Secret Of Creation And Consciousness (NDE)."[404]

Dr. Cicoria was using a payphone during the beginning of a rainstorm which caused him to be struck dead by lightning through the phone line. Here, Dr. Cicoria shares with us the vivid description of what he experienced. I welcome you to check out his video for the details. In this brief video, Dr. Cicoria very definitively concludes:

Whoever I am, I always am. There is no break in consciousness. There is no such thing as dying. Yeah, we die, but we don't cease. We continue and the consciousness continues on.[405]

From what we have seen here, we do indeed appear to have souls that separate from our physical bodies as we are dying. Contrary to popular belief, we do not just fade into "blackness" at our deaths but instead separate from our bodies for what happens next. What happens next is not bound by the constructs of physics, chemistry, or biology. The Master Engineer has designed each one of us with an element that has no expiration date which separates from our physical bodies at death. We are engineered just as the Bible states in the Book of Ecclesiastes 12:7 (KJV): "And the dust returns to the earth as it was, and the spirit returns to God who gave it." From what has been presented in this chapter, Ecclesiastes 12:7, appears to be spot-on.

We have been given vital information about our soul's existence before our own deaths through the careful observations of first-class medical professionals and research scholars. Let's make full use of this critical information while we still can.

Unfortunately, most people only find this out upon their deaths. But by then, it's too late to change what they believed in, change how they lived, and change their soul's eternal destination. We need to remember one thing, forever, is a long time!

CHAPTER TEN

Jesus Christ

The first part of this book established that God exists. God is the only one who could have created the universe from nothing in the absence of time. And God is the only one who could have created every species that has ever lived on Earth, since they did not produce themselves. Many people will only see God if they first see that 'science' is actually God's Science. Some people feel that their understanding of science contradicts God or proves that God is not necessary, this causes them to reject God. However, reality demonstrates the claim that science created itself has been proven false. As a consequence, science cannot contradict its Master. Bringing the book of nature into agreement with the Book of God is necessary in order to fully demonstrate this.

But this is not the whole story. God the Father has a Son named Jesus Christ. I feel that my discussion of Jesus should start with who He is and His position with respect to the Holy Trinity. The Trinity was always difficult for me to wrap my head around. Therefore, to begin, I would like to present my impression of the Holy Trinity. To do this, I need to present a few examples.

The first example I will start with is the simple example of an alloy. One particular alloy we are all familiar with is stainless steel. It is a blend of distinct elements combined together to form a unique and valuable metal. If any of the distinct elements are not present, then this prized alloy does not exist. In this same way, God the Father, Jesus His Son, and the Holy Spirit blend together to form one perfect Divine essence. All three of them must be present and unify together as one.

Now, even though God the Father, Jesus His Son, and the Holy Spirit are blended together as one perfect unity, they are different from each other and they have different roles. To explain this, I will incorporate the example of the Roman Empire and its hierarchy of structured power.

The Caesar of ancient Rome was the one who possessed supreme power, while numerous Roman officers supported and assisted Caesar. Typically, these Roman officers were generals. And since Rome had governing authority over vast stretches of land, Caesar needed to delegate powers equal to his own to these Roman generals. Accordingly, they were tasked with governing the various provinces of the Roman Empire. These governing generals were given the title of Primary Imperial Legate.

In the provinces they governed, they were given the same power to rule that Caesar possessed in Rome. When a Roman subject was brought before a Primary Imperial Legate in, let's say, the province of Syria, it was just as if that subject had been brought before Caesar himself in Rome. Caesar needs to remain in Rome where he controls the helm of the entire Empire. In order to also control the various Roman provinces, Caesar needed to delegate to his supporting associate officers, powers equal to his own.

I present this Roman delegate example because I feel that it functioned much like the Holy Trinity does. I view God the Father as the ultimate authority. And one of His roles is to reside in Heaven to control the helm of His Kingdom in this same way that Caesar remained in Rome to control the helm of the Roman Empire. And just as Caesar sent his generals out as delegates, God the Father has delegates to send out on special missions. Jesus and the Holy Spirit are God the Father's Divine delegates. And as such, Jesus and the Holy Spirit possess the ability to separate from God the Father when they are sent on missions as Divine delegates.

And just as Caesar granted powers that were equal to his own to his governing generals, God the Father grants Jesus His Son and the Holy Spirit with powers equal to His own. While on their missions, they possess the same power as God the Father. Thus, the Holy Trinity is perfectly blended together with the ability to separate from each other when duty calls.

When Jesus and the Holy Spirit are sent to do the will of God the Father, they function like two very powerful and holy, Divine delegates. Jesus and the Holy Spirit depart from God the Father to carry out His Will, and once they complete their particular task, they return to reunite and merge with God the Father. Therefore, the Holy Trinity is a fusion of the three Divine beings who live and reign as one God, where Jesus and the Holy Spirit can be sent out as Divine delegates to do the work of God the Father.

As mentioned, God's two Divine delegates, Jesus and the Holy Spirit, have been given the same level of power that God the Father possesses. God shares His power equally with them. God the Father refers to Jesus as His Son. And because these two Divine beings have been given the same level of power as God the Father and are part of God the Father, they are God as well.

I used Rome's delegate governors as an example because they followed a similar pattern of structure. Their governors were granted the same degree of power as Caesar and then they were sent out as delegates to effectively serve him. I used Rome's logical structure of rule as an example by which to attempt to explain the Holy Trinity. I believe that God is logical and methodical, and I see the Holy Trinity as being logically structured. For those of us still perplexed by the Trinity, perhaps understanding Rome's adopted pattern of logical organization may help us wrap our heads around the perfection and genius of the Holy Trinity.

Imagine in God's Kingdom that Jesus sits in His throne chair at the right hand of God the Father. Jesus is sent out to do the will of His Father, and after this work is completed, Jesus returns to His throne, seated at the right hand of God the Father. Likewise, the Holy Spirit resides in His place of honor near God the Father. The Holy Spirit is sent out to do the will of God the Father, and after this work is completed, the Holy Spirit returns to His place of honor. Both Jesus and the Holy Spirit reunite with God the Father as one.

Some people may find an equation helpful in visualizing the Trinity:

God = God the Father + Jesus His Son + The Holy Spirit

There is one last example I wish to present for those still vexed by the Holy Trinity. Most of us are all familiar with the corporate structure of companies. Imagine that God the Father is the CEO (Chief Executive Officer), the Holy Spirit is the COO (Chief Operating Officer), and Jesus is the CFO (Chief Financial Officer). Jesus could be seen as the Financial Officer because He **paid** the **price** for our sins with His precious blood. I believe that each member of the

Holy Trinity serves a specific role. I admit this is a crude example to use, but some people may find it helpful as they strive to comprehend the Holy Trinity.

It seems to me that the members of the Holy Trinity each have their particular purpose and duties. God the Father remains at the helm of His Kingdom. Jesus was sent to the earth to teach and heal mankind before He died as the perfect sacrificial Lamb for mankind's sins. While the Holy Spirit, is sent to the earth to sweep down and deliver God the Father's Power. Of course, the purpose and duties of the Holy Trinity are much more than this. For this is only an introduction attempting to explain how I comprehend the Holy Trinity.

In Scripture, we see examples of Jesus following the directives of God the Father as a delegate would. In John 5:30 (KJV), Jesus states:

> I can of mine own self do nothing: as I hear, I judge: and
>
> my judgement is just; because I seek not mine own will,
>
> but the will of the Father which hath sent me.

This demonstrates the relationship that Jesus and the Holy Spirit have with God the Father. Both Jesus and the Holy Spirit answer to God the Father.

And just as Caesar must remain at the helm in Rome, God the Father remains at the helm in His Kingdom. This requires the existence of the two equally powerful Divine delegates that do God's work on Earth. And when God's work is completed, Jesus and the Holy Spirit return to rejoin God the Father.

One critical task that needed to be accomplished was the sacrifice of God's Son as the perfect sacrificial Lamb for the sins of all mankind. And it is no coincidence that Jesus died for mankind's sins as the perfect sacrificial Lamb on the day of Passover Proper, at exactly the same time the Passover lambs were being sacrificed that year (AD 30).

This was not a coincidence! This was by design, and it represents the main reason why Jesus was sent to the earth.

We see other examples of God's designs in Scripture. After Jesus rises from the dead. Mary Magdalene wishes to hug Jesus, but Jesus tells her not to hug Him yet. In John 20:17 (KJV), we read that Jesus said unto her:

> Touch me not; for I am not yet ascended to My Father: but go to my brethren, and say unto them, I ascend unto my Father, and your Father; and to My God, and your God.

Notice how Jesus needs to rejoin God the Father before Mary is allowed to even touch Him. What we see here is that God the Father sent Jesus to the earth to complete a monumental task, and now that this task is completed, Jesus needs to first return to His Father. And if anyone touches Jesus before He rejoins God the Father, this would appear to make Jesus unclean. This demonstrates to me that a strict protocol had to be followed by Jesus and it was part of His duty to remain clean until He returned to His Father in Heaven. I feel this represents a strict protocol that was designed by God the Father.

This designed protocol needed to be satisfied as the last part of the Crucifixion and Resurrection process. Only then was Jesus able to meet up with His Disciples in Galilee. This indicates there was a strict process involved with the Crucifixion and the Resurrection. Everything had to be done exactly right. This is why Jesus had to be sacrificed as the perfect sacrificial Lamb on Passover at the exact time when the Passover lambs were being sacrificed! And once that glorious mission was completed, Jesus returned to God the Father.

Likewise, when the Holy Spirit is finished completing God's work, He also returns to God the Father. And this is how I see that the Holy Trinity is blended together as one God. Some of you may have a different view of the Trinity, which is fine. I'm just explaining how I understand the Holy Trinity.

And for those people who question the existence of the Holy Trinity, I point to Genesis 1:26 (KJV), translated straight from the original Hebrew Torah:

> And God said, 'Let us make man (mankind) in our image
> and after our likeness: Let them (man and woman) have
> dominion over the fish. . . the fowl. . .the cattle…all the
> earth, and over every creeping thing. . .on the earth.'[406]

This verse is extremely important because we can see that God specifically uses the word, "us," when God is preparing to create mankind. God also uses the word, "our," to reflect whose traits mankind is being modeled after. Here is another Hebrew Torah translation of Genesis 1:26,

> And Elohim (God) is saying, 'We shall make human in
> the image of us and the likeness of us.'[407]

In this translation, God is using the word, "us," and the word, "we." If God was only a single being, then God would not have used the words, "us," "our," or "we." Instead, God would have stated, "Let me make man in my image and after my likeness." Thus, I believe it is clear that God's word choice here, proves that God is composed of more than one being! To further clarify the Holy Trinity let me state that God the Father is a He. Jesus is a He. And the Holy Spirit is a He. They are three different people who unite as one God.

This verse is also important because it demonstrates that a myth writer did not conjure up this story. If a myth writer invented this as a fable, then he would have had God state, "Let me create man in my image." Why would a myth writer conjure up a story where a God states, "Let us create man in our image"? It would make no sense for a scribe to insert this into a myth. As a consequence, I feel this verse establishes that the creation story is authentic. We need to remember this verse was written in the Jewish Torah over a thousand years before the New Testament was written. I say this because I am pointing out that this verse was not written by a Christian promoting the Holy Trinity. The first five books of the Jewish Torah were written by Moses who wrote what he was Divinely instructed to write.

This verse does not make any sense until it is applied to the reality of the Holy Trinity. In other words, God is three people composing the Holy Trinity. This is why God stated, "Let us make man in our image and after our likeness…" A myth writer is going to fabricate a story where everything makes sense and is easily understood by his readers. This is why Genesis 1:26, demonstrates that it is not part of a fabricated myth.

This brings us back to God the Father's most important task delegated to His Son, Jesus. I have already briefly mentioned this critical task. God the Father sent His only begotten Son to the earth in order to die for our sins as the perfect sacrificial Lamb so that we may be cleansed of our sins with His precious and perfect blood.

It is here that I wish to explain the difference between the Old Testament and the New Testament.

The Old Testament is God having a Covenant agreement with mankind that resulted in over 600 commandments or laws. These are referred to as the Laws of Moses. However, because mankind was constantly seeking loopholes with which to violate these laws, mankind violated their end of this Covenant agreement. As a result, God decided to form a New Covenant with His Son, Jesus.

This New Covenant includes Jesus agreeing to come to the earth in order to die for our sins. And because this New Covenant is not between God and mankind any longer, mankind cannot violate this agreement. That is the difference between the Old Testament (Old Covenant) and the New Testament (New Covenant).

Keeping that in consideration, let's get back to my acknowledgement that Jesus was the perfect sacrificial Lamb. In doing so, I need to discuss the need for blood sacrifices. It is here that I need to explain that one of God's Ways (how God does things) is that when a sin is committed, that sin must be paid for with the blood of a living sacrifice. In the Jewish Torah we see that a "sacrificial system" was implemented in Judaism where the blood of a sacrifice was needed to atone and cover the sins of mankind.[408] The need for a "chatat" (sin offering) removed the consequences of sin. In the Book of Leviticus 5:6 (KJV) we read:

> And he shall bring his trespass offering unto the LORD
> for his sin which he hath sinned, a female from the flock,
> a lamb or a kid of the goats, for a sin offering; and the
> priest shall make an atonement for him concerning his sin.

In other words, the priest must make a blood sacrifice for sins, and only then will sins be forgiven. The High Priest's blood sacrifices also atone for the sins of their congregations during Yom Kippur. In the King James Version of Leviticus 17:11, we read:

> For the life of the flesh is in the blood: and I have given
> it to you upon the altar to make an atonement for your
> souls: for it is the blood that maketh an atonement for
> the soul.

Therefore, blood sacrifices were understood to be necessary for the atonement of sin. The Jews would sacrifice lambs on special celebration days like Yom Kippur and Passover. Because the sacrificed animal had to be only one year old and free of imperfections, it meant that the sacrificed animal was very valuable. Hence, the sinner was paying a significant financial price for their sin. This was God's Way.

This relates to the story of Cain and Abel.[409] Abel presented his blood sacrifice of an animal to God for his sins. By contrast, Cain's sacrifice was that of fruits and vegetables from his crops. Well, God accepted Abel's sacrifice and God rejected Cain's sacrifice. It is my understanding that only a blood sacrifice was acceptable. This appears to be why Cain's sacrifice was rejected. It was 'God's Way' that blood sacrifices were from a living entity. God's Ways and God's Covenant with mankind are what constitute Judaism. However, because the sacrifice of Jesus put an end to blood sacrifices, Christians don't need to sacrifice animals for their blood any longer. The Jewish people who don't believe Jesus is the Messiah (non-Messianic), are in a different situation. This is where Christianity separates and becomes distinct from Judaism.

Since Jesus was Jewish, this meant He was going to be the blood sacrifice on Passover. Jesus states at the Last Supper that we need to eat of His Body (bread) and drink His Blood (wine) in order to live. This means that His precious blood had to be spilled as a sacrifice in order to atone and cover mankind's sins, once and for all. Only the blood of Jesus was powerful enough to accomplish this. The blood of goats and lambs was not powerful enough to cover mankind's sins. Only those who believe that the sacrifice of Jesus was the only way to make them presentable to God the Father will be able to enter God's Kingdom. This is what Jesus meant when He stated we would "live" because of His sacrifice. Jesus is **The One** who makes us 'right,' with God.

We can see another example of this in Matthew 7:13-14 (KJV), where we are told that the highway to Hell is broad with many people on it. While the gate to the Kingdom of God, is narrow that few will find. It is my understanding that the narrow gate is Jesus. Only belief in Jesus dying for our sins will open the narrow gate to God's Kingdom. In other words, Jesus is the gate. This critical mission that God the Father delegated to His Son, Jesus, can be seen in John 3:16-17 (KJV):

> [16]For God so loved the world, that He gave His only begotten Son, that whosoever believeth in Him should not perish, but have everlasting life. [17]For God sent not His Son into the world to condemn the world; but that the world through Him might be saved.

After we die, we return to God to be judged. Those who pass judgement are received into God's Home. However, we are not worthy to enter unless we have first been cleansed of our sins and have Jesus residing in our hearts. In the past, goats and lambs were sacrificed by mankind to atone for their sins, but this failed to truly cover mankind's sins. Jesus is the perfect sacrificial Lamb as he is perfect and has never sinned. It fulfilled a prophesy that He be sacrificed for the sins of mankind, then rise from the dead and sit at the Right Hand of the Father. His Kingdom will have no end.

There is a special process of requirements that must first be satisfied in order to transition us from our earthly bodies and into the Kingdom of God. Only the blood of the perfect sacrificial Lamb would be powerful enough to cover all of mankind's sins and transition all of us who believe into God's Kingdom.

What I intend to do in this chapter, is establish that what is documented in the New Testament about Jesus is actual history, not a fairy tale. In this way, we can see what is proclaimed of Jesus is true. I will discuss the Crucifixion, the Resurrection, and the ministry of

Jesus. Finally, I will establish that Christianity is not only something that we can believe in, but that Jesus Christ is someone to live for.

With that being said, there are critics of Christianity that I have noticed on the internet. I was always afraid to read what they may have to say, so I avoided anything that a critic posted. However, I now feel that confronting what critics claim, actually functions to clearly demonstrate they don't have a case against Christianity. Therefore, I will spend a large part of this chapter addressing what is being claimed by critics. Since many of them are saying the same things, I feel that it is important for me to present *what* is being claimed.

That being said, I will present many criticisms, some from different sources. It does not matter who they are from. These complaints are considered, *common*, because they are generated by numerous people who have similar complaints. My objective is to present and address these criticisms in a professional, structured, and logical fashion. This is not unlike defending a legal case against claims that serve to discredit Christianity as a false religion.

The first criticism that I would like to mention comes from critics who try to claim that Jesus was a prophet and not God, as the Son of God. Some critics claim this because, in Mark 13:32-33 (KJV), Jesus states, "But of that day and that hour knoweth no man, no, not the angels which are in Heaven, neither the Son, but the Father." This refers to the Tribulation and the return of Jesus. Because Jesus admits that He does not know when this date is, some critics claim this means that Jesus either lied about being Divine or He is not omniscient.

Referring back to my description of the Holy Trinity, people have to understand that Jesus is the Son of God. He is not God the Father. They are two different beings. Jesus and God the Father are supremely woven together, but they are not the same person. And as

I have stated, the relationship that Jesus shares with God the Father is such that Jesus is sent out by God the Father to do His Will. We see this where Jesus is sent by His Father to come to the earth to die as the perfect sacrificial Lamb for the sins of mankind.

And just as God the Father gives Jesus instructions, He also decides what He wants Jesus to know. God the Father does not want anyone to know when the *End of Times* will be. God the Father knew that mankind would ask Jesus when this time would be, and since Jesus is not going to lie, not telling Jesus makes perfect sense. God the Father tells Jesus what He wants Him to know and needs to know in order to serve His will.

Therefore, it is by the design of God the Father that only *He* has complete knowledge. Jesus accomplished His mission perfectly when He mentored and healed mankind; then He died as the perfect sacrifice for mankind's sins. This was what Jesus was sent to the earth to accomplish, and He succeeded at that task. Because of how the Holy Trinity functions, God the Father is at the helm. And the fact that Jesus is not told everything that the Father knows does not detract from the fact that Jesus performed His duties perfectly. Jesus is without sin and He is the Son of God. Those are the only qualifications that He needs in order to die as the perfect sacrifice for mankind's sins.

I have witnessed critics online who point to a list of things that Jesus did not know while He was on the earth. God the Father delegates duties and missions for the Holy Spirit and Jesus to accomplish. And it appears that Jesus does not need to be given all of the knowledge that God the Father possesses in order to accomplish these duties and missions. Therefore, knowing everything that the Father knows is not required for Jesus to be God, as the Son of God. In addition, it is possible that God the Father withheld some information from His Son so as to allow Jesus to more fully experience the human condition.

As mentioned, the Holy Trinity is composed of three distinct Divine beings. They are not the same, and they all serve different roles. Therefore, the only person who needs to be omniscient is God the Father, and He is. This is how God the Father, Yahweh, has designed the Holy Trinity to function. And the fact that this is how God has structured His Holy Trinity to work, means this the best way to achieve His supreme level of organization. The Holy Trinity is the first example of supreme organized leadership which mankind has subsequently adopted as their CEO, COO, and CFO upper management model.

Next, I will discuss the Crucifixion and Resurrection because they form the foundation of Christianity. And as a result, I will now discuss criticisms directed at the Crucifixion and the Resurrection and then work backward in time from there.

Before I get to the criticisms regarding the Crucifixion, I would like to point out that it involves some Roman history. I feel this is important because it draws our attention to the fact that the Roman history recorded in the Bible is historically correct. I saw a T.V. special documentary on Roman crucifixions years ago on the History Channel titled, "Crucifixion."[410] And the reason why I mention this is because it demonstrates how perfectly Roman history agrees with what we read in the New Testament.

This documentary discussed the two parts that made up the crosses used in crucifixions. The vertical beam of a cross is called the *stipe*. Now, this vertical beam would tend to fall over and lean one way or another if it was not well secured in its hole in the ground. This instability posed a difficult problem for the Roman guards responsible for conducting the crucifixions. In crucifixion after crucifixion, keeping the stipe vertical was a severe challenge if you keep taking the cross out of the ground and then repeatedly, keep putting it back into the same hole. As a solution to this stability problem the Romans used concrete cement, which they invented.

The Romans began to cement the vertical stipes into the ground, securing them permanently. In this way, they would never tip over to one side or the other. As a result, these vertical beams no longer came out.

Then there was the horizontal beam called the *patibulum*, which weighed about 100 pounds. This beam had a hole in the middle. When the beam was raised, this hole would slide over a peak in the vertical stipe forming the shape of a cross or a "T." Two Roman guards were needed to hoist the patibulum up with the victim nailed or tied to it. The victim was first secured to the horizontal beam, then hoisted onto the stipe. Once in place, the victim's feet were nailed to the stipe. There were a few variations of that basic design. However, many believe that the Crux Immissa type was probably used for Jesus. [411]

Now, to start to investigate the Crucifixion, we first need to see what year Jesus was crucified and on what day of the week he was crucified. Everyone pretty much agrees that Jesus was crucified on Passover Day. And the day after Passover is the high holy Sabbath of the first day of the Festival of Unleavened Bread. For those who are not Jewish, Passover Day is the day before the Sabbath day of the Festival of Unleavened Bread. Therefore, if Passover is on a Wednesday, then the first day of the Festival of Unleavened Bread is the next day, which is Thursday. We need to remember that Passover is not a Sabbath, but the next day is. I used to think that Passover was a Sabbath because I knew that it was an important Jewish celebration, but Passover is not a Sabbath day.

I'm discussing all of this because I feel that we need to understand some Jewish history in order to more fully comprehend what happened 2,000 years ago. With that being said, I am going to explain several things that you probably don't know, unless you are Jewish.

First, the ancient Jewish day started at 6 p.m. A Jewish day began with the night phase first. Then 12 hours later, the day phase began. I believe the reason for this can be found in Genesis 1:5 (KJV), "… And the evening and the morning were the first day." Notice how the evening came first and then the morning followed, concerning the cycle that God defined as a day. Jewish tradition preserved this order. This seems a bit confusing at first, but you will get used to it the more you go over it. And when I refer to the word "Nisan," this is the Jewish word for the first month of the year. Therefore, Nisan 14, would mean the 14th day of the year's first month. And please note that some sources use the word, "Abib," instead of, "Nisan." For example, Nisan 14 is the same as Abib 14.

Since Jesus was crucified on Passover, I need to explain Passover. The first Passover involved the 10 Plagues of Egypt where Moses told the Egyptian Pharaoh to let the Israelites go free. The 10th plague was God sending the Angel of Death to pass over Egypt and strike down the firstborn in every household that did not have the blood of a sacrificed animal painted on the doorway.

Now, I used to think that Passover was the day that the Angel of Death passed over Egypt, but that is not correct. To protect one's household from the Angel of Death, who would pass over Egypt at midnight on Nisan 15 in 1445 BC, the blood of a sacrificed animal had to be applied to the doorposts. To get the blood of that animal, it had to be sacrificed about 12 hours before which was around noon on Nisan 14. Therefore, Passover is the day the lambs were sacrificed for their blood which was applied to the doorway later that evening. And that is why it is called Passover.

The first Passover was on Nisan 14, over 3,400 years ago when the Israelites were still enslaved people in Egypt. This is when the lambs were sacrificed for their blood which was applied to the doorposts. At 6 p.m. of that evening, this started the next new day of Nisan 15. And six hours later, at midnight, the Angel of Death passed over Egypt in 1445 BC. Because of the death of the Egyptian firstborns that night, Pharaoh had been pushed to his limits as the Egyptian mothers were screaming throughout all of Egypt. I would imagine that the Egyptian mothers were screaming at Pharaoh for allowing this to happen and they wanted him to do something about it. And he did.

It was at this point that the relentless carnage that befell Egypt, finally resulted in the Israelites being ordered to leave Egypt immediately. The people that knew God and knew God's Ways were finally free! And thus, they began their trek to the Red Sea. This exodus probably started as soon as the Sun came up. Many scholars believe that the Exodus was in 1445 BC. Moses probably started writing the Pentateuch while in the wilderness shortly after this, perhaps between 1445-1440 BC.[412]

As they were on their trek, they ate their unleavened bread, which they had brought with them for food. However, because they left Egypt abruptly and there was no time to wait for the yeast to make the bread rise, they ate unleavened bread instead. Thus, we celebrate the freedom of the Israelites on Nisan 15, which is the day after the Passover lambs were sacrificed on Nisan 14. And that first day of freedom is referred to as the first day of the Festival of Unleavened Bread, a high holy Sabbath.

I feel this is an excellent place to present the major Jewish celebrations for those who are not familiar in order to learn about Jewish customs and festivals. What I have learned about Judaism has helped me understand Jesus and the Bible better. After all, Jesus was Jewish Himself, and all of His Disciples were Jewish. This means that Christianity is rooted in Judaism.

And what many people don't know is that the word, *Jewish*, means to have a Covenant with God. That is what Jewish means. Abraham is considered the first Jew because he was the first person God formed a Covenant with. Judaism explains God's relationship with mankind, and Judaism explains God's Ways.

Now, most Jews don't believe that Jesus is the Messiah. However, there are some Jews who do believe that Jesus is the Messiah, and those Jews are referred to as Messianic Jews. Messianic Jews and Rabbis refer to Jesus as, Yeshua.

This is really the best of both worlds because Messianic Jews know their Jewish history, customs, and celebrations, along with them believing in Jesus, all at the same time! What this means is that if someone is Jewish and wishes to embrace Jesus as the Messiah, but they also wish to remain Jewish, they don't have to stop being Jewish. Instead, they would be a Messianic Jew who accepts Jesus as the Messiah. Therefore, if someone wants to be both Jewish and believe in Christ at the same time, then they could become a Messianic Jew.

Here are some of the major Jewish celebrations that we have all heard of. I feel that we need to see what these Jewish celebrations are all about in order to start to understand what happened 2,000 years ago and to understand God's Ways. I feel the more that we know about these Jewish celebrations, the more that we can see the entire picture. I'm just focusing on the major holidays and celebrations. Here are the major Jewish festivals:

1) Passover, which occurs around March/April. It runs for seven days in Jerusalem because it took seven days for the Israelites to reach the

Red Sea when they left Egypt. Passover runs for eight days everywhere else around the world. And when I say Passover, I mean the first day of the Passover celebration, which is also referred to as Passover Proper.

Passover remembers the sacrificing of the Passover lambs whose blood was needed for the doorposts before the Angel of Death arrived at midnight in 1445 BC. Passover is the preparation for the 10th plague of Egypt in 1445 BC. Passover is also a day of preparation to remove leaven from the household because leaven is equated with sin. This is because a little bit of leaven (which is yeast) spreads throughout all of the dough that it is introduced to. And in this same way, once a little bit sin is introduced into a person's life, it spreads throughout all of their life.

2) The Festival of Unleavened Bread is the day after Passover. It is a celebration that remembers that at midnight, the Angel of Death passed over Egypt in 1445 BC to bring the 10th plague. This caused the Egyptians to free the Israelites from their bondage. This celebration also lasts for seven days. The first day of this celebration is the first day that the Israelites were freed from Egypt. And as they journeyed to the Red Sea, they ate their unleavened bread. This festival is a Sabbath because it celebrates Israelite freedom which resulted from God's Power and Might.

I believe that the most important significance of this unleavened bread is that it has no leaven in it. And this would signify the absence of sin. Now, even though the Israelites left Egypt in such haste that they did not have time to add leaven to their bread and wait for it to make their bread rise, the actual significance of this bread seems to be that it represents the absence of sin. This is my impression.

3) Rosh Hashanah occurs in September/October and runs for ten days. This event reminds everyone that the celebration of Yom

Kippur will be in 10 days. Therefore, Rosh Hashanah is a preparation celebration and allows people to reflect on their obedience to God and their sins over the last 12 months.

4) Yom Kippur is also known as the Day of Atonement. In Jerusalem, this is where the High Priest would enter the Holy of Holies in the Temple and sacrifice a lamb or goat for all of mankind's sins for the last year. Then, the High Priest would sprinkle the goat's blood onto the golden mercy seat of The Ark of the Covenant. This was only done once a year and was only performed by the Temple High Priest. This was meant to atone for mankind's sins over the last 12 months. This was the only day of the year that the High Priest was allowed to enter the Holy of Holies and view the Ark of the Covenant. I wish to stress that The Ark of the Covenant was a real object. It was essentially a golden altar for the High Priest to offer sacrifices and communicate directly with Yahweh. It also housed the stone tablets that had the Ten Commandments written on them.

5) Chanukah/Hanukkah occurs around mid-December and runs for eight days. This celebration remembers that the Jewish Maccabees regained control of Solomon's Temple from invaders. But to their dismay, there was only one day's worth of sacred oil to light the 7-branch menorah in the Temple. It is my understanding that this menorah has seven branches because it took the Israelites seven days to reach the Red Sea. In addition, seven is also the number of, perfection.

It took eight days to secure more holy oil. Meanwhile, the menorah with only one day's oil continued to miraculously burn for the eight days it took to produce more holy oil. As a result, the oil lasted eight times longer than it should have. This was a miracle. And to commemorate this Temple miracle, a new 9-branch menorah was constructed to be lit for eight days in a row to remember this Temple miracle. Each of those eight branches represent each of the days the oil continued to miraculously burn brightly. The middle branch on this 9-branch menorah is used to light the other eight branches. This is why Hanukkah is called the Festival of Lights.

With that background completed, I wish to discuss the year in which Jesus was crucified. I am interested in learning all of the histories that involve Jesus. This is why I find it essential to know when He was crucified. Many Christians believe that it was AD 33. This is probably because the Bible states that the following day was a Sabbath day. And since Saturday was the weekly Sabbath, the year that had a Friday Passover was chosen as the Crucifixion year. And it turns out that AD 33 did have its Passover fall on a Friday.

Here is a list of the Passover days that occurred in the window of time when Jesus was crucified. These are the only years that Jesus could have been crucified.

AD 29 Passover was Saturday -April 16

AD 30 Passover was Wednesday -April 5

AD 31 Passover was Monday -March 26

AD 32 Passover was Monday -April 14

AD 33 Passover was Friday -April 3

However, a significant problem exists with an AD 33 Crucifixion. This is because of what Jesus told the Pharisees would be His Sign that He is indeed the Messiah. Jesus specifically told the wicked Pharisees that he was rebuking in Matthew 12:40 (KJV):

> For as Jonas was three days and three nights in the whale's
>
> belly; so shall the Son of Man be three days and three
>
> nights in the heart of the earth.

Here, Jesus is fiercely rebuking these wicked and hypocritical Pharisees for demanding another sign from Him. Not only did Jesus specifically respond with the example of Jonah's three days and three nights, but Jesus is doing this while he is harshly rebuking the wicked Pharisees.

That makes the story of Jonah crucial because Jesus is using it to prove to this wicked generation that He is indeed the Messiah. In order to fulfill this promised sign, it means Jesus will be in the heart of the earth for three days and three nights. If Jesus goes out of his way to specifically mention Jonah here, this means Jonah's account was real and true. This story is not an allegory. This also means the time Jesus will spend in the heart of the earth will be true. I would like to clarify that Jonas, is the Greek form of the Hebrew name, Jonah.

This was the result of the Pharisees requesting that Jesus display another miracle or sign to prove that He was indeed the Messiah. By rebuking the Pharisees with this specific promise, Jesus was indicating that His Resurrection from death in three days and three nights would prove that he is indeed the Messiah![413] It is a very important point to realize that three days and three nights was in fact, a promise that Jesus was making. And Him keeping that promise would prove that He is indeed the Messiah. This is why this promise cannot be altered in any way.[414]

Now, if Jesus was crucified on a Friday, then he would only be in the heart of the earth for two nights. And the only way to get three days is if you count three hours of Friday as a whole day and less than one hour of Sunday as a whole day. I doubt that anyone 2,000 years ago would count a small fraction of a day as a full day. However, even if they did count partial days and nights as full days and nights, this still does not equal three nights. The result is only two nights!

Why is this so important? Because three days and three nights will be the proving sign that Jesus is indeed the Messiah! This is non-negotiable. And a Friday Crucifixion does not fulfill that proving sign. Some critics are quick to point this out as a failing of our religion because this promise was not fulfilled with a Friday Crucifixion. And If we examine a theoretical Thursday crucifixion, Thursday is not one of the possible days on the Passover year list that Jesus could have been crucified. Therefore, on our list, the latest day of the week for His Crucifixion which would fulfill the promised sign of Jonah would have been the year that Passover occurred on a Wednesday. There is no way around this. Jesus had to have been crucified on a Wednesday and not on a Friday in order to fulfill this promise and demonstrate the proof that He is indeed the Messiah.

A Friday Crucifixion fails to accomplish this promise, while a Wednesday Crucifixion does fulfill this promised sign. Therefore, there is no failure here because Jesus was crucified on a Wednesday. He was not crucified on a Friday. Most people associate the Jewish Sabbath with Saturday, which is true. But that is the weekly Sabbath. The week that Jesus was crucified had two Sabbaths because of Passover. The weekly Sabbath was on Saturday, but the high holy Sabbath of the Festival of Unleavened Bread fell on the Thursday of that week in AD 30. As a consequence, Passover Day, which is the day before the Sabbath festival, fell on Wednesday of that week.

A researcher named Marie Casale, followed a very accurate ancient calendar program for several well-known events. Marie Casale is an expert on dating events in the past, and she wrote an excellent article titled, "The Hebrew Calendar Points to The Year of The Death Of Christ." And in this article, Marie Casale lists a few notable historical occurrences and their exact dates.

One occurrence was the first destruction of Solomon's Temple. We know that occurred on a Saturday and a Sunday around 586 BC.

Marie Casale found these days correlated perfectly with 584 BC, July 25 and 26. Then she looked up the murder of Ananias. Once again, the day of the week that he was killed was used; it was a Saturday. She ran the program and found that it matched AD 67 on September 5. Then Marie Casale ran the program for Jesus' Crucifixion and knew that it had to harmonize with a Wednesday because Jesus said he would be three days and three nights in the heart of the earth. She also used other factors that needed to be harmonized with His Crucifixion and came out with the calendar year of AD 30 to be a perfect fit.[415] I believe this to be accurate.

Many scholars and sources believe that AD 30 is the actual Crucifixion year, and I agree.[416] And by the way, the letters AD stand for Anno Domini, which means, "In the year of our Lord." Because she knew it was Nisan 14 (Passover), which was a Wednesday, Marie Casale was able to pinpoint the exact year as AD 30. This allows Jesus to be dead and in the heart of the earth for a full three days and a full three nights, just as He promised.

I believe the minute this promise was satisfied, was the minute that Jesus was resurrected and woke up from the dead. And this was exactly at 6:00 p.m. on Nisan 18, just as Saturday ended and Sunday began with its night phase. This means that Jesus sat alive in His tomb and prayed to God the Father from 6:00 p.m. until the angel opened His tomb about 12 hours later, just as the day phase of that Sunday was about to begin. As a consequence, the promise of three days and three nights was fulfilled!

With that being said, if Jesus resurrected at any time during that night, let's say at 4:00 a.m., this would still satisfy the promise of three days and three nights. This is because if Jesus resurrected before 6:00 a.m., while it was still dark, that night would not be counted as a complete night. However, because I find God to be logical, methodical, and perfect, this gives me the impression that the very moment the Sign of Jonah was fulfilled, was the precise moment that Jesus resurrected from the dead. This is why I believe the Resurrection occurred at the very beginning of Sunday (night Phase) which was at 6:00 p.m.

Here are the baseline points to remember that are hypercritical: Jesus was crucified on Nisan 14, in AD 30. This was a Wednesday, and it was also the day of Passover Proper. Therefore, Jesus was crucified on Passover Proper, not the day before Passover Proper, and not the day after Passover Proper.

The reason why Jesus was crucified and was dying at the exact time that the Passover lambs were being sacrificed that day, was because He was the perfect sacrificial Lamb that day! This is not a coincidence that Jesus was crucified at the same time the Passover lambs were being sacrificed. God is logical and methodical, and this Crucifixion was intended to occur exactly on Passover Proper. The Passover lambs were sacrificed that day between noon and 3 p.m. This is precisely when the sky fell dark that day. The Crucifixion started at 9 a.m., as the day wore on, Jesus was in the process of physically dying on the cross between noon and 3 p.m. As I have stated, this was not a coincidence.

I must warn you that if what you are reading online does not correlate with what I am stating here, then that is because the people you are reading comments from are either:

1) not using AD 30 as the Crucifixion year

2) not using Wednesday as the day of the week for the Crucifixion

3) not calling Nisan 14 as Passover

4) not calling Nisan 15 the First day of the Festival of Unleavened Bread

If any of the sources you research online are doing any of what I have listed above, they will appear to be saying something different and it will not make any sense. If what you are reading does not make sense, then the source you are reading has made an error. I also wish to state that Nisan 13 (Tuesday in AD 30) was considered the preparation day for Passover Proper (Nisan 14). At the same time, Passover Proper (Wednesday) was considered the preparation day for the first day of the Festival of Unleavened Bread (Nisan 15, Thursday). From what I understand, the removal of leaven from people's homes started on Nisan 13.[417] Then the leaven removal had to be completed by mid-day Nisan 14.[418] Therefore, both Nisan 13 and Nisan 14 were considered, *preparation days*.

In fact, in John 19:42 (KJV):

> There laid they Jesus therefore because of the Jew's preparation day; for the sepulchre was nigh at hand.

This indicates that Jesus was crucified on the preparation day and placed into His tomb in haste since it was nearby. Therefore, Passover Proper (Nisan 14) is the preparation day for the high holy Sabbath of the first day of the Festival of Unleavened Bread (Nisan 15).

There are several listings on the internet for Passover dates between AD 26 and AD 32. Unfortunately, many of them don't agree with each other and they don't agree with the Hebrew Passover calendars from 2,000 years ago. Therefore, beware of what calendar you use. The most accurate ancient Passover dates that I have found were calculated by Marie Casale using the Biblical Holy Day Calendar Calculator of the Christian Biblical Church of God.

At this point, I am going to give a breakdown of the Passover that Jesus was crucified on in AD 30, along with the high Sabbath which was the following day. This breakdown is meant to help you visualize what occurred on that Passover Day.

Wednesday, Nisan 14 of AD 30, in Jerusalem, was the holy day that started right after Tuesday (Nisan 13), which ended at 5:59 p.m. It is now 6:00 p.m.

6:00 p.m. and Wednesday begins as Passover Day (Nisan 14) when the Passover lambs will be sacrificed about 18-21 hours later.

6:30 p.m. (estimate) is when the Disciples Matthew and Mark ask Jesus where He wanted to have His "Passover Meal" that night? The Jews have no name for the meal that night. It is a regular meal. However, since Jesus knows that He will be dead in about 20 hours, He has moved *Passover Meal* up by one day, and this meal becomes what we now call, *The Eucharist*. This is why The Last Supper is the night before the usual Passover Meal. Jesus will be dead by the time of the traditional Jewish Seder Meal, and He knows this.

9:00 p.m. (estimate) - Judas leaves the upper room during dinner to alert the Roman guards, Jewish Temple guards, elders, and the Pharisees.

11:00 p.m. (estimate) After the Last Supper, Jesus goes outside with the Disciples to pray in the garden of Gethsemane. There were droves and droves of people, all dressed in white robes. They were out at all hours of the night because of the Passover celebration. They covered the hillsides just like we see at outdoor concerts.

Midnight (estimate) - Jesus is met by Judas who betrays Him with a kiss. There were so many people milling about wearing the same white cloaks that this 'kiss' signal was necessary to point out Jesus to the guards. Jesus was then arrested.

1:00 a.m.- 7:00 a.m. - Jesus was relentlessly interrogated, tried by the Jews, and sentenced to death.

7:00 a.m. - 8:00 a.m. - Jesus was turned over to Pilate who interrogated Him. Pilate then sent Jesus to Herod who happened to be in Jerusalem at the time (Luke 23:7, KJV). Pontius Pilate was trying to avoid having the blood of Jesus on his hands because he found Jesus innocent of any crime punishable by death. We see this in Luke 23:14 (KJV), where Pilate states:

> Said unto them, Ye have brought this man unto me, as one that perverteth the people: and, behold, I having examined him before you, have found no fault in this man touching those things whereof ye accuse him.

Clearly, Pontius Pilate disagreed with the accusations of the Pharisees. This is why Pilate sent Jesus to Herod. We see that Herod came to the same conclusion Pilate did in the very next verse, Luke 23:15 (KJV):

> No, nor yet Herod: for I sent you to him; and, lo, nothing worthy of death is done unto him.

Because Herod also found Jesus innocent of any crime punishable by death, he sent Jesus back to Pilate. This placed Pilate in the same position that he was in before.

As a result, Pilate tried one last time to allow the crowd to free Jesus, but spies were planted in the crowd by the Pharisees to cause trouble and they shouted for the release of Barabbas instead. In fact, in Luke 23:21 (KJV), we read:

> But they cried, saying, Crucify him, crucify him.

This is when Pontius Pilate demonstrated that he had no choice in this decision. We read of this in Matthew 27:24 (KJV):

> When Pilate saw that he could prevail nothing, but that rather a tumult was made, he took water, and washed his hands before the multitude, saying, I am innocent of the blood of this just person: see ye to it.

The word tumult means, frenzy. When Pilate realized that a riot was about to break out, he gave up trying to save Jesus and washed his hands of His death. I firmly believe that Pilate was so impressed with Jesus during his interrogation of Jesus that he wanted no part in the death of Jesus. And this statement by Pilate makes perfect sense because he was thoroughly setting the record straight and literally washing his hands of as much of this as he could. Therefore, Pilate was forced to execute Jesus.

8:00 a.m. The pre-Crucifixion beating, and flogging begin. Some historians speculate that Pilate may have had Jesus beaten severely to make Him die faster so that He would suffer less on the cross. There have been instances where the victim was beaten so severely that they died before they could be crucified on a cross.

9:00 a.m. - Jesus is being nailed to His cross while the Jews gather their Passover lambs that are to be sacrificed in a few hours.

Noon-3:00 p.m.- The sacrificing of the Passover lambs occurs. The blood is no longer saved because the Angel of Death only came once in 1445 BC. Therefore, applying blood to the doorposts is no longer necessary but the lamb is still saved for the Passover dinner which will be served about 6 hours later. This meal is the Passover Seder and will be eaten during the evening phase that begins the next day.

Between noon and 3 p.m. is also the same time Jesus is dying on His cross. Jesus is crucified as the perfect sacrificial Lamb at the same time the Passover lambs were being sacrificed. This is not a coincidence. Jesus died for our sins as the perfect sacrificial Lamb on Passover Day at the precise time the sacrificial lambs were dying! The sky grew dark from noon onwards. Once again, this special event is named *Passover Day* because this is when the Passover lambs are sacrificed.

3:00 p.m.- The sky had been darkened for three hours when Jesus finally died as the earth shook from an earthquake that occurred.

4:00-5:30 p.m.- Joseph of Arimathea and Nicodemus place Jesus into His tomb and wrap His body in haste. The Sabbath is approaching, and the tomb must be sealed before the Sun goes down.

5:59 p.m.- This Passover Proper Day is about to end. The Sun is going down.

6:00 p.m.- Marks the beginning of Thursday, Nisan 15 of AD 30, Jerusalem. This is the first day of the Festival of Unleavened Bread which is a high holy Sabbath. Applying the lamb's blood to the lintel and doorposts is no longer needed because that was only done once in Egypt in 1445 BC. However, the sacrificed lamb will be eaten later as the Passover Meal, also known as the Passover Seder.

7:00 p.m.- The Jews are eating the roasted lamb that was sacrificed earlier. This is the evening Passover Meal.

7:00 a.m.- (about 12 hours later- after the Sun comes up and Pilate is awake)- Pharisees urgently request to speak with Pilate to get a guard patrol assigned to the tomb of Jesus before the Disciples can steal His body away and claim a resurrection. The Pharisees are afraid the crowd will riot and turn against them if this happens.

8:00 a.m.- (estimate)- In order to prevent a riot, Pilate has Roman guards inspecting and sealing the tomb that they will guard for three days.

5:59 p.m.- Thursday, the 1st day of the Festival of Unleavened Bread is about to end.

We need to realize that throughout Israel's history, events had caused changes in how Passover Day and the first day of the Festival of Unleavened Bread were celebrated. These changes started with the exile of the Israelites into Babylonian captivity which caused traditions to initially be lost.[419] When Israel re-organized itself either by the decree of Hebrew Kings or otherwise, it was then, that the first day of the Festival of Unleavened Bread was merged with Passover Proper. And because of this practice of combining these two celebrations, the first day of the Festival of Unleavened Bread became synonymous with the word, *Passover*.[420]

In addition, the Old Testament contains instructions the Passover lambs are to be sacrificed at people's homes. In this way, the lamb's blood could be applied to the doorposts of their homes. However, this changed to where the lambs were only sacrificed at Temple by the priests. And it turns out that if people did decide to sacrifice at home, it was performed at a different time than the sacrificing performed by the priests at Temple. Anyone familiar with Jewish history is going to know this.[421]

An example of Jewish changes to these celebrations has occurred in our modern time. Jewish people have recently moved the combination of those two days back a day to now fall on Nisan 15. This is because the sacrificing of lambs on Nisan 14, also known as Pesach, is no longer done. Therefore, the only 'relevant' holiday to many Jews today is Nisan 15. This is the first day of the festival of the Unleavened Bread which is also referred to as the holiday of Matzot. As a consequence, "Passover" is now celebrated by many Jews today on Nisan 15, instead of Nisan 14.[422]

I mention this Passover topic because an online critic of Christianity is trying to use it in an attempt to establish that Christianity is a false religion. In response, it is at this point in the chapter I will focus on the topic of Passover as I address criticisms designed to denounce and discredit Christianity. The critic that I am referring to is named Tovia Singer who runs a website where he answers questions and makes comments.[423] I first noticed this website 3 years ago when I read Singer's answer to a question regarding Christianity. Singer has changed his website a bit since 2019 but his response to this question about Christianity is essentially the same with only a few changes. I started writing a rebuttal to Singer's comments in 2019 but I realized it was turning into a book.

With that said, I will be sharing my rebuttal of Singer's Q&A response to a question which is titled, "Did Jesus Rise from the Dead? What is the Evidence for the Resurrection?"[424] This response also includes a Crucifixion/Resurrection Chart section (part 2).[425]

Before I discuss my response to Singer's comments, I wish to state that Tovia Singer is a Rabbi. I hold Rabbis in high regard because they teach their clergy about God through the Jewish Torah which is exactly the same as the Old Testament in the Holy Bible. I have a deep respect for anyone who teaches people that God is real. We must remember that Christianity has its roots in Judaism. That being said, I find the need to thoroughly address Tovia Singer's criticisms of Christianity because I find them to be flawed.

The first thing I wish to mention regarding Singer is his mention that none of the historians in the time of Jesus recorded anything regarding the Resurrection.[426] Singer mentions that the famous philosopher Philo of Alexandria and the famous historian Josephus say nothing about Jesus and His Resurrection. Singer feels this supports the idea that Jesus never resurrected from the dead, otherwise these famous people would have made a record of this. Well, there is one big problem with this assumption.

As I have mentioned regarding Pontius Pilate, the Romans became concerned that Jesus could become a threat to their control and order. Pilate eventually agreed to crucify Jesus because he could see that a riot was about to erupt. It is clear the Romans wished to subdue and mute anyone proclaiming the name of Jesus in order to maintain order and prevent riots. However, it must be noted, the turmoil Pilate witnessed from the crowd was being stirred up by agitators planted by the Pharisees to shout for Barabbas to be freed and for Jesus to be crucified. Even though Pontius Pilate found Jesus to be innocent of any crime punishable by death, Pilate understood the topic of Jesus could incite unrest and riots. Pilate and the Roman Empire sought to obliterate the topic of Jesus because it was the responsibility of Pilate and Roman officials to prevent riots, maintain control, and ensure peace.

Many people are aware the Romans used horrifying techniques to torture Christians.[427] Once Jesus had been crucified, both the Pharisees and the Romans thought their 'Jesus problem' was over. They were wrong. Therefore, with the assistance of the Pharisees, the Romans set out to exterminate the Christians in order to maintain control and order. The Romans arrested anyone speaking of Jesus, interrogated them, tortured them, and then murdered them if they did not recant their claims of seeing Jesus Risen from the dead. The horrific Roman persecutions of early Christians are well known to the world and were implemented in order to silence the Christians.

The Romans would have thought the greatest threat of fanning the flames of rebellion and a riot would have come from spreading the news of Jesus in writing by someone famous. And if the Romans were going to such great lengths to silence and exterminate Christians, you can be very sure the Romans did not allow anyone to make any written mention of Jesus. What historian alive at that time is going to allow themselves to be arrested, tortured, and then murdered? I can assure you the very first people warned and threatened were the historians because they had the ability to spread the news far and wide. The Romans were not going to allow that to happen. And the influential Jewish Pharisees were not going to allow that to happen either.

Therefore, the fact that no historians make any mention of Jesus and His Resurrection only means the Romans were able to completely control anyone capable of inciting a mob to riot. The Christians were merely speaking of Jesus and this resulted in them being tortured and murdered.

What do you think would happen to a famous historian or philosopher who decided to write about Jesus? Perhaps the Romans would have crucified them to set an example in order to silence the rest of them. This is most likely why Josephus' silence is deafening, as Tovia Singer states.[428] Apparently, Philo of Alexandria and Josephus decided, like many who did not believe in Jesus, that they were not going to get persecuted, arrested, tortured, and murdered for documenting anything in reference to Jesus.

In addition to the threat from Rome, since Philo of Alexandria was a Jewish philosopher, and Josephus was a Jewish historian, neither would have mentioned Jesus because this would have severely offended the Pharisees. I'm sure the Pharisees requested both of them to ignore the story of Jesus completely so that no one could read about it. Therefore, Philo of Alexandria and Josephus had two reasons to remain silent about Jesus.

Anything written that could lead to a mob rebellion would have been considered an act of treason by Rome. Therefore, the fact that famous historians make no mention of Jesus and His Resurrection is explained by the Romans exercising complete and total control of their empire. Quite frankly, the world is well aware the Romans exercised brutal control over their subjects. In addition, the anti-Christian campaign of the Pharisees promoted the persecutions and the efforts to erase Jesus from history. History is written by the victors because they control the narrative. And in this case, the Romans and the Pharisees made sure the story of Jesus and His Resurrection was not put into print. Both the Romans and the Pharisees wanted their 'Jesus problem' to go away.

The topic of Jesus was so significant to the ancient Romans that they persecuted and tortured Christians to turn them away from Jesus. Proof that Jesus was a significant historical person in the eyes of ancient Rome is clear to see as the Romans implemented a campaign of persecuting and torturing Christians. Therefore, the mere fact ancient Rome put forth so much effort to eliminate Christians and erase Jesus from history, proves the influence that Jesus had on the entire Roman Empire! The influence of Jesus was so powerful that countless Roman subjects allowed themselves to be tortured and murdered as they refused to turn away from Jesus.

Have you ever wondered why it took the Synoptic Gospel writers 30 years to begin writing their books? Well, as a consequence of these brutal Roman persecutions, I surmise the reason why it took 30 years for the Synoptic Gospels to finally put their books into writing was because they feared their work to establish the early church would be cut short if they got themselves murdered. As a consequence, to keep a lower profile in the early years of the church, they avoided putting anything into print. Everyone probably knew that writing about Jesus would bring immediate and severe consequences. This would explain why it took so long for the Gospel writers to document what they had been discreetly ministering for 30 years.

Singer then proceeds by criticizing the Crucifixion and the Resurrection, because without them, he states, there would be no Christianity.[429] Singer claims the Synoptic Gospel writers contradicted themselves on what day Jesus was crucified. He claims the Gospel writers can't get their stories straight and in 2019 he stated Jesus could not have been crucified more than once, on two different days.[430] In 2019 Singer stated he was approaching Christianity like a legal case. He also indicated that because the Gospel writers contradicted each other on what day Jesus was crucified, this formed the core of his case against Christianity.[431]

Well, it just so happens this exact topic is right in the middle of the historical Hebrew practice of combining the holiday of Passover with the holiday of the first day of the Festival of Unleavened Bread.

Since Singer is criticizing statements made by the Synoptic Gospels regarding the time leading up to the Crucifixion and the subsequent Resurrection, we need to evaluate what the Synoptic Gospels stated. As I see it, there are two components involved here. The first part is the topic regarding the ancient practices of how the Jews referred to Passover (Proper) and the first day of the Festival of Unleavened Bread. The second component involves the Gospel writer's use of the term, "Passover Meal," which I will discuss later. Let's begin by reviewing the Synoptic Gospel verses that refer to the night before Jesus was crucified.[432] In Matthew 26:17 (KJV), we have:

> Now on the first day of the festival of Unleavened Bread,
> the disciples came to Jesus, saying unto Him, 'Where
> wilt thou that we prepare for thee to eat the Passover?'

Here we see the Disciples asking Jesus on "the first day of the festival of Unleavened Bread," where He wants to eat the Passover Meal. Now, at that time in ancient Jerusalem, the common practice was to refer to Passover Day, also known as Passover Proper (Nisan 14), as the first day of the Festival of Unleavened Bread (Nisan 15). In other words, at that time, people would say that it was the first day of the Festival of Unleavened Bread when it was actually the day of Passover Proper. This means Nisan 14 was being referred to as Nisan 15. A non-Jewish person would be confused by this while someone well versed in Jewish practices would already be aware of this.

The second Gospel writer mentioned is Mark 14:12 (KJV):

> And the first day of Unleavened Bread, when they killed
>
> the Passover, His disciples said unto Him, 'Where wilt thou
>
> that we go and prepare that thou mayest eat the Passover?

In Mark, when he mentions the killing of "the Passover," that means the sacrificing of the Passover lambs. This confirms that Mark is referring to Passover day, also known as Passover Proper (Nisan 14). And you will notice that it is being referred to as the first day of the Festival of Unleavened Bread. As I have stated, it was the tradition 2,000 years ago to combine these two celebrations into one day. And just like in the Book of Matthew, the Disciples want to know where Jesus wishes to eat the Passover Meal? The aspect of importance here is that Mark is talking about the day of Passover Proper (sacrificing the lambs) which he is referring to as the first day of the Festival of Unleavened Bread. Because Matthew mentions this as the first day of the Festival of Unleavened Bread, it is clear he combined the two celebrations into one day (Nisan 14).

Next, we essentially have the same statement being made in Luke 22:7-8 (KJV):

Then came the day of Unleavened Bread, when the Passover must be killed. And He sent Peter and John saying,
'Go and prepare us the Passover, that we may eat it.'

We can see that Luke also clarifies that the killing of the lambs on Passover Proper (Nisan 14) is being referred to as the day of Unleavened Bread (Nisan 15).

And lastly, Disciple John is mentioned who states in 19:31 (KJV):
The Jews, therefore, because it was the preparation, that
the bodies should not remain upon the cross on the
Sabbath day, (for that Sabbath day was an high day,)
besought Pilate that their legs might be broken and that
they might be taken away.

John states that the Crucifixion occurred on Passover Proper, also known as the preparation day for the first day of the Festival of Unleavened Bread. This is why John refers to the next day as the (high) Sabbath day. The first day of the Festival of Unleavened Bread is a high Sabbath. And since dead bodies could not be on their crosses once this high Sabbath starts, the legs of anyone still alive would be broken to hasten their death.

Notice how Matthew, Mark, and Luke, use similar references while John's statement is worded in his unique way. Part of the reason for this is that John wrote down his Gospel 30 years after the Synoptic Gospel writers wrote theirs. However, all four of these Apostles are speaking about the same day that Jesus was crucified.

Matthew, Mark, and Luke, record what occurred at the beginning (around 6:30 p.m. of Nisan 14) of that day before they ate supper which was about 14 hours before Jesus was crucified. By contrast, the statement made by John records what occurred about 22 hours later, which would have been around 4:00 p.m. of Nisan 14. This was near the end of that day that Jesus died. Jesus died at 3 p.m. You will notice that because the ancient Jews counted a day as beginning at 6 p.m. and ending at the next 6 p.m. (6:00 p.m.-6:00 p.m.), this means that all the statements made by Matthew, Mark, Luke, and John, referred to events that occurred within the same day (6:30 p.m.-4:00 p.m.). These statements made by Matthew, Mark, Luke, and John, all refer to the same 24-hour day.

These are the verses (posted in 2019) that Singer stated constituted the core of his criticism of Christianity.[433] He claimed the day that Jesus was crucified is being contradicted in these verses. As I have pointed out, it was common practice 2,000 years ago to combine Passover Day with the first day of the Festival of Unleavened Bread and then refer to that day as **the first day of the Festival of Unleavened Bread**. And instead of celebrating these combined celebration days on Nisan 15, this combination day was **celebrated on Nisan 14** which was actually Passover Day (Passover Proper).

By contrast, nowadays, these two celebrations are still combined but are **celebrated on Nisan 15** and referred to as, **Passover**. This is the opposite of what was practiced 2,000 years ago and is confusing to anyone unfamiliar with these Jewish practices. In today's modern era, remembering the slaughtering of the lambs (which is Passover Proper, also known as *Pesach*-Nisan 14), gets a mild amount of attention. While the first day of the Festival of Unleavened Bread, which also known as *The Holiday of Matzot* (Nisan 15), garners the majority of attention because it is the high holy Sabbath. This is the evening when the Passover Meal is eaten, also referred to as the Passover Seder.

The most significant events in 1445 BC, were the application of the lamb's blood to the doorposts, the eating of the Passover Meal, the Angel of Death passing through Egypt delivering the 10th plague, and then the Israelite's Exodus to freedom (probably at sunrise). All of this occurred on Nisan 15. This is why the first day of the Festival of Unleavened Bread is a high holy Sabbath and more sacred than Passover Proper (Nisan 14), which is when the lambs were sacrificed. In our present day, all of this history and celebration is summed up into one word, Passover.

Anyone familiar with Jewish customs and practices would know this. Therefore, we know that the Synoptic Gospels are talking about Passover Proper because Mark and Luke clearly state that it is the day that the Passover lambs are sacrificed. While John, accurately describes Passover Day as the preparation day for the following day's Sabbath (the first day of the Festival of Unleavened Bread), which he refers to as a, "high day" Sabbath.[434] This confirms that the following day, which is about to start at 6 p.m., is the first day of the Festival of Unleavened Bread (Thursday of this year), not the weekly Sabbath (on Saturday).

If someone is not aware of these historical Jewish practices, this topic would be quite confusing. This is why I am going over this as much as I am. We have to be focused and understand. We have to be able to see through the smoke of confusion in order to see the truth and thwart any 'mistaken' comments attempting to discredit Christianity.

To help put this issue with the Synoptic Gospels and Disciple John into perspective, I will spotlight the analysis of Biblical Scholar Bill Fortenberry. First, Bill Fortenberry compares what the Apostle Mark and the Disciple John wrote about the day that Jesus was crucified. This is what scholar Bill Fortenberry had to say after his analysis:

> Jesus died during the Day of Preparation which was after the
> evening of the Passover proper but before the first Feast of

the Passover Week. There is no contradiction between the two accounts. They are simply describing an event which the average Gentile American knows nothing about.[435]

Notice how the Biblical scholar Bill Fortenberry states that there is no contradiction here. And I interpret what Fortenberry states about the average American Gentile knowing nothing about this to mean, if you are not Jewish, you will probably be really confused about this topic and fail to realize that no contradictions exist here.

Therefore, the combining of celebrations and how they are referred to, should not be an issue. The fact that Matthew, Mark, and Luke, all wrote their Gospels under the influence of the local Jewish practices and jargon used in their day cannot be used against them. The practice that causes confusion to Gentiles stems from the Jews creating a combination day, which fuses Passover Proper (Nisan 14) and the first day of the Festival of Unleavened Bread (Nisan 15) into a single day. When, in fact, they are two distinct celebration days. This is confirmed by the fact that one celebration is a high holy Sabbath (Nisan 15), while the other celebration on Nisan 14, is not a Sabbath.

In addition, the celebration of this combination day has been moved back and forth (to either Nisan 14 or Nisan 15). Even the name used to refer to this combination day has changed over time (Passover vs. the first day of the Festival of Unleavened Bread). On top of this, Matthew, Mark, and Luke, are talking about the night phase of Passover Proper before Jesus was crucified. By contrast, John is talking about the day phase of Passover Proper just after Jesus had died. John is also writing his Gospel 30 years after Matthew, Mark, and Luke wrote theirs. These facts serve to explain the different ways in which the Synoptic Gospels and John refer to the day that Jesus was crucified. All of these subtle facts expose the truth that no contradictions exist regarding what day Jesus was crucified.

I wish to clarify that I am not criticizing what the Jews have done with their celebrations. They can combine them, move them back and forth, and change what they call them, all they wish. My intent is to make sure that confusion about these practices does not get utilized as an opportunity to falsely claim Christian contradictions. That would be unfair, flawed, and should never be tolerated.

With all of that being said, there is one more detail that I have briefly mentioned and is the only area that needs explanation. That detail has to do with the meal that Jesus and His Disciples were going to eat later that evening which they refer to as the "Passover." Well, the Passover Meal is not supposed to be eaten that night. Passover Meal is to be eaten the following night. The Jews don't have a name for the meal eaten in the evening that begins Passover Proper (Nisan 14, 6:30-7:30 p.m.). Why, then, are Jesus and His Disciples referring to this night's meal as the *Passover*? This is the only issue of significance I see regarding this particular topic. This seems puzzling at first, but the use of simple logic quickly resolves this perceived issue.

The logical reason why this meal is being called the *Passover,* is that Jesus will not be alive for the official Passover Meal. And Jesus knows this. If you look at Matthew 26:2 (KJV), Jesus said to his disciples:

> Ye know that after two days in the feast of the Passover,
>
> and the Son of man is betrayed to be crucified.

Clearly, Jesus is warning his Disciples two days in advance that he will be crucified on Passover (proper). And because of this, Jesus would have to make adjustments for the *Passover Meal* by moving it one day sooner in order to have His Last Supper with His Disciples. This is why they all moved *Passover Meal* up one day. This does not mean that the Disciples are contradicting each other on what day Jesus was crucified. They were all referring to one single day, Nisan 14, which was Passover Proper.

This fact is confirmed by Mark and Luke who mention the killing of the Passover lambs. Matthew left the killing part out, but because he mentions the Festival of Unleavened Bread, just like Mark and Luke (which was the jargon in their day to refer to Passover Proper), this confirms they are all talking about the same day, Passover Proper (Nisan 14). On that evening of Passover, which Matthew, Mark, and Luke, are referring to, Jesus knows that He will be in the tomb in about 20 hours. Because of this serious fact, Jesus will not be able to attend the official Passover Meal the following day. This explains why they ate their "Passover" a day early.

But having a special meal just before Jesus was set to be crucified is not the only change to the Passover holiday that occurred that evening. This meal was entirely different and brand new because Jesus was the sacrificial Lamb. The Messiah that everyone had been waiting for is now present and about to be sacrificed to cover mankind's sins, once and for all. Jesus knew that changing the name of this meal would confuse His Disciples, and this is why He continued to refer to this new supper as eating the "Passover." It is really as simple as that. This meal becomes what we now celebrate as *The Eucharist*. This is why The Last Supper was the night before the usual Passover Meal. Therefore, it is quite logical why the Synoptic Gospels recorded what they did. There are no contradictions regarding what day the Crucifixion occurred. This is the logical explanation for why the re-scheduled Passover Meal became The Last Supper.

Singer also complains that it does not make sense that Judas Iscariot was asked if he was going to purchase supplies for the holiday

(Passover) Seder as he left their *Passover Meal*.[436] Well, there is a simple explanation. The dinner they ate that night was *The Last Supper* and was scheduled to accommodate Jesus' fast-approaching Crucifixion. Nevertheless, this did not change the plans of the Disciples to still eat the official Passover Meal the next evening. At this early point, they were still going to participate in their traditional Jewish practices. They were still Jewish until Jesus resurrected from the dead. This is why the Disciples were still going to eat the traditional Passover Meal the next evening (on Nisan 15). This explains why Judas was assumed to be going to buy more preparation supplies for that following evening's Passover Meal.

This answers Singer's next question when he asks: why would the Pharisees and Jewish elders be concerned about defilement as they handed Jesus over to Pilate?[437] Since Matthew, Mark, and Luke were **not** referring to Nisan 15 as the Crucifixion day, this activity is occurring on Nisan 14, contrary to what Singer is claiming. And because it is about 7 a.m. on Nisan 14, it is 12 hours *before* the Passover Seder is intended to be eaten, at 7 p.m. Since the new day begins at 6 p.m., the Passover Seder Meal is the beginning of the next day, Nisan 15. Therefore, the Pharisees and Jewish elders must avoid possible defilement when they hand Jesus over because it is Nisan 14, which is 12 hours before they will be eating the Passover Seder Meal on Nisan 15. The Passover Seder Meal is about one hour into the new day.

Many of Singer's complaints revolve around the 'misunderstanding' that the Gospel writers claimed that Jesus was crucified of Nisan 15.[438] The Gospel writers **did not claim this**. As I have stated, Mark and Luke specifically state the Passover lambs were killed that day. In ancient Jerusalem, killing of the lambs only occurred on Nisan 14. In ancient Jerusalem, the lambs were not sacrificed on Nisan 15. This should have indicated to Singer that the Gospel writers were referring to Nisan 14. I stress this fact because once we clear up this 'misunderstanding,' it negates many of these invalid claims against Christianity.

Singer goes on to state, that according to Jewish tradition, at the Last Supper Jesus should have presented a sacrificed lamb to represent his body.[439] But instead, Singer states, Jesus raised the matzo bread. What is being missed here is that *The Last Supper*, which is now celebrated as *The Eucharist*, was breaking away from Jewish tradition. The Old Covenant of the law was being replaced with the New Covenant of Jesus. This had to take place because mankind continued to find new ways to violate the law. Because the New Covenant is between God the Father and His Son, there is no way for mankind to breach this contract. The Old Testament signifies the Old Covenant, while the New Testament signifies the New Covenant.

As a result of there being a New Covenant, the Crucifixion of Jesus put an end to blood sacrifices, once and for all. This is another profound departure from Jewish tradition. This was necessary because the blood of goats and lambs failed to cover the sins of mankind, who continually found new ways to violate the law. Only the blood of a perfect sacrifice was able to cover all of mankind's sins. This is why Yahweh sent His only begotten Son to the earth. This is why Jesus was crucified the day the lambs were killed. As I have stated, this was not a coincidence.

Singer also wondered why priests don't present lamb chops at communion?[440] The simple answer to this question is that the sacrifice and Resurrection of Jesus put an end to blood sacrifices for those who believe that Jesus is the perfect sacrificial Lamb and the Son of God. Priests present bread and wine at communion because this is what Jesus did at *The Last Supper.* We refer to this commemoration as *The Eucharist.* Christians no longer need to present blood sacrifices.

Then Singer states that the Disciple John is the only one who records that the legs of Jesus were not broken because Jesus was lanced in His side.[441] Singer makes an issue out of this because none of the Synoptic Gospel writers record this detail. That said, this is explained by the fact that John was the only male Disciple or Apostle who was present at the Crucifixion. All of the others were busy preparing to slaughter the lambs set to be sacrificed. That was Jewish tradition.[442] And since John's older brother was responsible for that duty, this left John as the only writer who was able to attend the Crucifixion.[443]

And yes, the other gospel writers included many details about the Crucifixion that they did not personally witness. However, John personally witnessed the leg breaking of the other men. This was undoubtedly a disturbing experience for John to witness and caused him to remember it and include it while the other writers did not because they did not see this violent action take place. It should be clear why this statement by Singer is not an issue.

At this point, I will discuss the burial and the Resurrection. One online blogger, who I cannot recall, claimed the reason why Jesus' body was never found was because wild animals probably dragged it off. This is absurd because that was not something that the Jews were ever going to allow to occur on their high holy Sabbath! The bodies had to be removed and buried well. The Jews had strict laws regarding protocol on high Sabbaths. Deuteronomy 21:22-23 (KJV), specifically states of the bodies of crucified men:

> And if a man have committed a sin worthy of death,
>   and he be put to death, and thou hang him on a tree:

His body shall not remain all night upon the tree, but thou shalt in any wise bury him that day; that thy land be not defiled, which the Lord thy God giveth for an inheritance.

Therefore, the idea that wild animals dragged the body of Jesus off somewhere is impossible. The Jews would never have allowed for that possibility. That was strictly against Jewish law.

Now, this next criticism I'm addressing is where Singer claimed contradictions regarding various statements in the Synoptic Gospels regarding the burial preparations for Jesus.[444] Because it was Passover and the day before the high Sabbath, those crucified had to be off of their crosses before sundown. As I have mentioned, Jewish law required that bodies had to be buried before the Sabbath began at 6 p.m. The ancient Jewish day began with the night phase at 6 p.m., then 12 hours later, the day phase began at 6 a.m. We need to get comfortable with this if we want to follow the timeline of what happened without feeling confused. Just remember that the new day starts in the evening (nighttime) at 6 p.m.

That being said, Jesus was deceased by 3 p.m., however, the two criminals on either side of Jesus were not dead yet. This meant there were less than three hours to get them off of their crosses and buried because the high Sabbath would begin in 3 hours. This is why the legs of the criminals were broken so that they would die faster. They had to be off of their crosses soon, well before 6 p.m.

It is well documented in the Bible that Jesus was laid to rest in a tomb. After Jesus' death, he was taken to the tomb of Joseph of Arimathea who was a wealthy man that followed Jesus. He asked Pilate for the rights to the body in order to bury it properly. This is in John 19:38 (KJV):

And after this, Joseph of Arimathea, being a disciple of
Jesus, but secretly for fear of the Jews, besought Pilate
that he might take away the body of Jesus: and Pilate gave
him leave. He came therefore and took the body of Jesus.

Joseph had immense respect for Jesus. Pilate agreed, and Joseph
of Arimathea and Nicodemus put Jesus into the tomb, wrapped
his body, and laid Jesus to rest. Mary Magdalene and other women
were present, watched from a distance, and wept. Then John 19:39
(KJV) states:

And there came also Nicodemus, which at the first came
to Jesus by night, and brought a mixture of myrrh and
aloes, about a hundred-pound weight.

The myrrh and aloes were applied to the body of Jesus. This was
very similar to an embalming process. Nicodemus and Joseph would
have applied these quickly as they wrapped Jesus in burial sheets.

Then Nicodemus and Joseph of Arimathea, who owned the tomb,
finished placing the body of Jesus into the Tomb. The value of the
essential oils used on Jesus has been estimated to be between $150,000
to $200,000 dollars in today's money.[445] Scholar Dr. David Stewart
(as cited in Felts, 2016) states, "This tells us two things: 1) Joseph
and Nicodemus were very wealthy; and 2) their regard and reverence
for their Lord and redeemer were very great, indeed." Scholar Landis
Felts goes on to state that, "only Kings received such extravagance in
burial. They were grieving their King."[446] And because the high holy
Sabbath was approaching, the stone was rolled into place to seal the
tomb. The rest of the burial process had to be completed on Sunday.
There was no time for the entire burial process to be completed that day.

The Pharisees thought about the death of Jesus and discussed it
that night. One of them must have realized that the tomb should be

guarded to prevent the disciples from stealing the body and claiming a resurrection. This could cause a riot and violence against them. This demonstrates to me that they devised this plan while talking that evening. However, it was now too late to ask Pilate to do this that same day. They had to wait until the morning to approach Pilate. They finally realized that if the body of Jesus went missing and was claimed by his Disciples as "resurrected," the crowd may riot against them. If the Pharisees had thought of this before Pilate left the Crucifixion site, they would have asked Pilate right away for an immediate guard detail to secure the tomb. The fact that they had to wait until the next morning to ask Pilate proves the Pharisees realized this urgent threat after everyone had already left the Crucifixion site.

There were about three million people gathered there in Jerusalem for the Passover. The population of Jerusalem at the time was typically about 100,000.[447] This means that Passover caused an influx of three million people that swelled the population to almost 30 times its normal amount. The Pharisees and Pilate knew this could have been a powder keg ready to explode with the right spark. Once the Pharisees thoroughly explained the enormous riot threat to Pontius Pilate, this is when he readily gave them one of his guard units. This all makes perfect logical sense.

Some critics claim that the Pharisees would never have asked for a guard because none of them thought that Jesus would resurrect. And indeed, they did not believe in a resurrection. No one thought Jesus was going to rise from the dead, not even his Disciples. This is evidenced by Mary Magdalene and the other women going on Sunday to finish the burial process of Jesus. The women did not go thinking that he had risen. And, of course, the Pharisees did not believe that Jesus was going to resurrect either. However, I am convinced that the

Pharisees were deathly afraid of a mob attack from the congested Passover crowd. This is why they went to Pontius Pilate the very next day. There are few passages in the Bible where they wanted to move against Jesus and harm Him, but they "feared" the crowd may react against them. This is evidenced in Matthew 21:46 (KJV), where we read:

> But when they sought to lay hands on Him, they feared the multitude, because they took Him for a prophet.

In Matthew 26:3-5 (KJV), we read:

> Then assembled together the chief priests, and the scribes, and the elders of the people, unto the palace of the high priest, who was called Caiaphas. And consulted that they might take Jesus by subtilty, and kill Him. But they said, Not on the feast day, lest there be an uproar among the people.

You could call this a *Passover security concern*. These verses right here explain why the Pharisees insisted on guards at the tomb of Jesus. If the body of Jesus was stolen and the crowd was told by the Disciples that their Messiah had been Resurrected, the congested Passover crowd of three million angry people would have stoned to death the real killers of their Messiah. It's clear to me that the huge congested Passover crowd would have posed a severe threat to the Pharisees.

The whole reason why those 3 million people were there was to worship and wait for the day that their Messiah would come. And the Pharisees were well aware of this explosive threat. This is what the Pharisees were deathly afraid of. And this is why it is logical they would have insisted on a guard detail for the tomb of Jesus for three days and three nights.

The fact that the Pharisees were not stoned to death by the crowds after Jesus did resurrect, is because Jesus was preaching a message of peace and forgiveness. During the forty days that Jesus walked among His Disciples, followers, and others, Jesus would have delivered a message of peace, hope, love, salvation, and forgiveness. Remember that Jesus even asked God His Father to forgive those who had terribly abused Him and nailed Him to the cross. Jesus preached a message of Peace, not war. In addition to this, people would have eventually realized that Jesus dying in the first place, allowed Him to resurrect and demonstrate that He was indeed the Messiah.

Jesus did not appear to everyone. He only chose to reveal himself to about 500 people, not the entire Passover crowd. And I would imagine that one of the reasons why Jesus wished for His Disciples to reunite with Him in Galilee was because the Pharisees would not be there. Jesus kept somewhat of a low profile because he did not want His Disciples and followers to be killed by Pharisees and Roman guards. Jesus needed his followers alive in order to establish His Church. And this is why I suspect Jesus only revealed himself to 500 people. You will notice that the human behaviors and activities that are recorded in the New Testament are logical and make sense.

In scripture, we even see evidence of the fear that the Pharisees had of being stoned just for saying the wrong thing. In Luke 20:5-7 (KJV), we see that Jesus asked the Pharisees if John the Baptist received his authority to baptize from Heaven or was it merely human? We read:

> And they reasoned with themselves, saying, if we shall
> say, from heaven; he will say, Why then believed ye him
> not? But and if we say, of men; all the people will stone
> us: for they be persuaded that John was a prophet. And
> they answered, that they could not tell whence it was.

The Pharisees, religious leaders, and elders would have all been severely afraid of a riot backlash from the Passover crowds. If they thought they could be stoned to death for answering that John the Baptist did not receive his authority from Heaven, then they certainly thought they would be stoned for having the Messiah killed. Can you imagine what fear raced through their minds as they imagined the whole Passover crowd being violently angry at the killers of the real Messiah?

I have no doubt that the Pharisees convinced Pilate to guard the tomb to prevent the theft of the body of Jesus which could have been perceived as a resurrection instead. Therefore, this fear led to the strong motivation of wanting a guard posted. I believe that Pilate agreed and posted a guard the next morning because he agreed with the Pharisees that such a situation could incite profound mob disorder and violence. It was Pilate's duty to keep the peace and prevent riots. Therefore, the posting of Roman guards that following morning on Nisan 15 makes perfect sense.

An online critic blogged that Matthew fabricated his documentation, made the guards in his story the only eyewitnesses to the Resurrection, and then made up a "stupid" testimony for the guards.[448] If Matthew is so stupid, why is the rest of his gospel as coherent and intelligent as it is? Did Matthew decide to get stupid all of a sudden, just on Resurrection Sunday? The reason why Matthew's testimony sounds as it does, is because it is the truth. If Matthew was fabricating a fable, then he was certainly intelligent enough to write a narrative that would make sense to his readers and critics. How do I know this? Because I can see how Matthew was able to document all the intelligent wisdom that is recorded in his Gospel. That's how I know. Therefore, the science of logic suggests that Matthew is telling the truth about the guards.

That being said, I admit that Matthew's issue was that he seems to have forgotten that Mary Magdalene ran back to the tomb with

Peter and John. Matthew wrote his Gospel 30 years after the fact. I strongly believe that Mary was at the tomb twice that day. When this vital detail was left out by Matthew 30 years later, it caused him to struggle as he tried to make all the pieces fit together as they actually unfolded.

Tovia Singer is correct here when he states that everything that Matthew writes could not have been the case. Nevertheless, I believe Matthew's goal was to be truthful in his documentation but struggled with the fact he did not include Mary's second trip to the tomb. Whatever caused this omission prevented Matthew from properly sequencing the events of Resurrection Sunday.

Another online critic, who I cannot recall, claimed in a blog that Disciple Matthew lied about the Resurrection and called Matthew's report "stupid" for saying that the guards showed up the next day. This critic said Matthew was "stupid" for not placing the guards at the tomb immediately.

This critic claims this makes no sense at all. Once again, someone who is going to fabricate a lie like this, **will not** deliberately leave a 15-hour hole in it, now are they? Where is the logic there? If Matthew was lying, then he would have easily completed the lie with an immediate guard detail to prevent the claim that the body of Jesus was merely stolen and not resurrected.

The reason why Matthew records that there was a gap in the coverage of the tomb was because, there was a gap in the coverage of the tomb. This gap occurred because the Pharisees did not realize the threat to their lives until it was too late to ask Pilate that day. As a consequence, they were forced to wait until the next morning.

Matthew's testimony actually lends strong support that he is telling the truth. What Matthew records must have happened, otherwise, we would be reading that a guard detail was posted right away. Why would anyone fabricating a lie like this deliberately put a 15-hour gap into his lie? What would be the point? Why would a liar deliberately place another specific lie into his story that leaves a 15-hour hole in it, allowing his first lie to be undermined? That makes absolutely no sense at all if this is a fabrication. But this makes perfect logical sense if it is the truth. If Mathew is a liar, then putting a 15-hour gap in coverage actually undermines his claim that a Resurrection occurred. A liar is not going to do that.

This is why Matthew must be telling the truth. The insertion of this gap would allow someone the ability to steal the dead body away. What these critics are saying of Matthew is beyond stupid. If Matthew was a liar, then falsely placing a 15-hour gap into his fabrication would not be stupid, it would be insane. Therefore, by utilizing the science of logic, we can ascertain that Matthew is telling the truth. As I have stated, the fact that a 15-hour gap exists demonstrates that the Pharisees did not think about this threat possibility until it was too late to approach Pilate about it that evening.

And another thing, that 15-hour gap was of no consequence because the body of Jesus was not stolen during that period of time. How do I know this? Because when the Roman guards came to the tomb, they inspected the tomb, confirmed the identity of the occupant (Jesus), and then placed official seals on the entrance forbidding entry.[449] The Romans were not stupid. They were not going to guard an empty tomb and then, three days later, be accused of allowing the body to be stolen. That kind of dereliction of duty resulted in a death sentence for the Roman soldiers involved. Therefore, we can be certain Jesus was in His tomb when it was sealed and there was no opportunity for His body to be stolen.

Some critics argue that if there was a guard detail, it would have been the Jewish Temple guard. That being said, if the Pharisees could guard it themselves, then the Pharisees would not have bothered to ask Pilate in the first place. Also, I ask the question, is this even possible on the high Sabbath? Would a Jewish Temple guard assume non-Temple 'work' on the high holy Sabbath of the first day of the Festival of Unleavened Bread? I understand that Temple guards have the strict duty of guarding only the Temple. They don't leave the Temple to guard a tomb somewhere else, especially on a high holy Sabbath day. The Pharisees do have a Temple guard, but I ask: was it proper for Temple guards to 'work' outside of the Temple at a tomb on the high holy Sabbath? There is not supposed to be any 'work' done on the high holy Sabbath. It should be obvious that the only 'work' allowed was at the Temple to ensure necessary security.

This is why in Matthew 27:64 (KJV), the Pharisees said to Pilate:

> Command therefore that the sepulchre be made sure until
> the third day, lest His disciples come by night, and steal
> Him away, and say unto the people, He is risen from
> the dead: so the last error shall be worse than the first.

Here you can see that the Pharisees were gravely concerned for their safety. They were desperately trying to protect themselves.

In Matthew 23:3 (KJV), Jesus tells the crowd and his Disciples:

> All therefore whatsoever they bid you observe, that
> observe and do; but do not ye after their works: for
> they say, and do not.

We see here that because the teachers and Pharisees were the ones teaching the law of Moses to the people, they had to be listened to. But Jesus tells the people not to behave as the teachers and Pharisees did because they do not practice what they teach. These teachers were hypocrites; they only cared about themselves and what they wanted. And it was because of rebukes like this one that the Pharisees wanted Jesus dead.

It is documented that after the Pharisees asked Pilate to guard the tomb in Matthew 27:65 (KJV), Pilate said unto them, "Ye have a watch; go your way, make it as sure as ye can." Many contend that this was Pilate agreeing and ordering a Roman guard detail to guard the tomb to prevent any unrest that could be caused if the body of Jesus went missing and His Disciples and followers claimed a resurrection. When Pilate stated, "Ye have a watch…," this meant, *You have a guard duty now that I've given you one. Now go and use my guards to secure the tomb in a manner that you deem necessary.*

It was the duty of Pilate to keep peace in Jerusalem, especially during a 3 million visitor Passover. As I have mentioned, the normal population of Jerusalem at the time was over 100,000.[450] The influx of 3 million people swelled the population to almost 30 times its normal size. As stated, this was a powder keg ready to explode with the right spark; the Pharisees and Pilate recognized this. Therefore, once the Pharisees fully explained the enormous riot threat to Pontius Pilate, this is when he readily gave them one of his guard units. This all makes perfect logical sense.

This is something to think about, Pilate was the Roman commanding officer of Jerusalem and his duty was to maintain order and peace in Jerusalem, at all costs. If he failed at this task and a huge riot broke out, then Pilate would risk losing his command and possibly even be demoted. The Pharisees already thoroughly explained this threat to Pilate when they made their case for him to provide the Roman guards that would be necessary for this task. They told him all of this because they needed him to supply the guards because they could not do this type of 'work' on the high holy Sabbath. This whole situation caused Pilate to realize that he would be the one held responsible if a riot occurred.

Does anyone really think that Pilate, after realizing the threat of an enormous riot, would then place his future into the hands of the Pharisees? After hearing all of this, does anyone logically think that Pontius Pilate is going to refuse to get involved and instead rely on Pharisees to guard the tomb in an attempt to prevent a huge riot in Jerusalem?? No, he is not. He knows that this is his responsibility, and it would have been a dereliction of duty to depend on Pharisees to prevent a potential riot like this.

In no way, shape, or form, would Pilate have just told the Pharisees to run off and do it themselves. Pilate's future was at risk here. Therefore, he gave them a competent guard unit and told the Pharisees to assist his guards in making sure that a riot did not erupt. The core of this riot prevention plan was Pilate's Roman military guard unit, and the Pharisees were to add another layer of prevention on top of this with their assistance.

I would also like to point out that this is an example of how the Romans and the Pharisees worked together on their shared 'Jesus problem.' Both the Romans and the Pharisees had strong motivations to put a lid on anything related to Jesus. You may notice that all of this behavior makes sense. That is because this is how the real-world works. The fact that the documentation in the New Testament follows a logical progression strongly supports the claims that the New Testament speaks the truth.

It is here that I wish to quickly mention that some scholars in the past had believed that Pontius Pilate was merely a fictional character. In the past, there was no archaeologic evidence at all of Pontius Pilate.

Roman documents are not as readily available as one would hope. Well, this all changed in 1961 when the *Pilate Stone* was found in the ruins of Caesarea. This stone fragment is evidence that declares Pontius Pilate was the prefect of Judea and that he built a temple called a *Tiberium* and dedicated it to Caesar Augustus. Therefore, we do indeed have evidence that is literally written in stone which proves that Pontius Pilate was a real person who was really where the Bible said that he was.[451] All of the critics of Pontius Pilate and the New Testament fell silent in 1961 when this stone was recovered from ruins. For the doubters of Pontius Pilate, they can check out the *Pilate Stone.*

On this same note of proving that people mentioned in the Bible were not fictional characters, the burial box of Caiaphas was found. This limestone burial box is referred to as *The Bone Box of Caiaphas,* who was the Pharisee High Priest that presided over the arrest and trial of Jesus right before Jesus was handed over to Pontius Pilate. This fantastic archaeologic discovery in 1990 proves that Caiaphas was not a fable or a fictional character.[452] Therefore, we have proof of both Pontius Pilate and Caiaphas. And that proof is literally, rock-solid. These people referenced in the New Testament are not made-up fictional characters. The New Testament is real and documents ancient history.

Tovia Singer also criticizes various statements in the Synoptic Gospels regarding the burial preparations for Jesus.[453] He complains that one Gospel states that Nicodemus prepared the body of Jesus. Then another Gospel said Mary Magdalene was preparing after the Sabbath, and yet another Gospel said she was preparing before the Sabbath. Singer is implying that these statements could not all be true and therefore represent contradictions. Despite this claim, it turns out that all of these statements in the New Testament could easily be true. As I have stated earlier, Nicodemus and Joseph of Arimathea retrieved the body of Jesus and then placed Jesus into His tomb. Then Mary Magdalene went to prepare for Sunday's official burial ceremony *before* the sun went down on Wednesday. Luke 23:55-56 (KJV) states:

> And the women also, which came with Him from Galilee followed after, and beheld the sepulchre, and how His body was laid. And they returned, and prepared spices and ointments, and rested the Sabbath day according to the commandment.

This means that right after Jesus was placed into His tomb on Wednesday, is when Mary Magdalene went to prepare spices and ointments *before* the Festival of Unleavened Bread started at 6 p.m. She did this to get supplies to complete the burial process for Jesus on Sunday. This occurred *before* the Thursday high Sabbath officially started. But Mary had not completed her preparations for Sunday. So, Mary went to buy more preparation supplies. In Mark 16:1 (KJV), we read:

> And when the Sabbath was past, Mary Magdalene, and Mary the mother of James, and Salome, had brought sweet spices, that they might come and anoint Him.

This Scripture merely tells us this second trip was at sundown as the Sabbath ended. I believe most people assume it was just after the Saturday weekly Sabbath. That being said, this is twice that Mary prepared for Sunday. In fact, Mary had the opportunity to prepare *before* the Thursday high Sabbath and *after* the Thursday high Sabbath. In addition, Mary also had the opportunity to prepare *before* the Saturday weekly Sabbath and *after* the Saturday weekly Sabbath. As you can plainly see, Mary had the opportunity to prepare four times if she wished. This is because there were two Sabbaths that Passover week. Therefore, all of these burial preparations made by Nicodemus, Joseph of Arimathea, and Mary could most certainly be true. But instead, Singer implies they contradict each other which they do not.

This is another invalid attempt to claim Christian contradictions. Notice how the practice of logical reasoning resolves most of these criticisms leveled against Christianity.

With that being said, I admit there are sequencing related details that don't agree regarding the recording of Resurrection Sunday. I believe those discrepancies are due to the Synoptic Gospel writers leaving out Mary's second trip to the tomb. Somewhere along the line, 30 years later, most of the followers of Jesus forgot about Mary following Peter and John back to the tomb. This resulted in Mary being the only person to witness Jesus alive at the tomb. And by failing to include this single, critical detail, it prevents the proper sequencing of what occurred that day. I feel this explains the sequencing discrepancies that we see in the Synoptic Gospels.

All things considered regarding the minor details, people have to understand that the accounts from the Gospels are not going to be word-for-word carbon copies of one another. If they were, then another critic would be claiming collusion because scholars would expect to see some degree of variability. You are supposed to put these Gospels together in order to add as many details as people could write down. What one Gospel writer leaves unmentioned, is remembered and mentioned by another Gospel writer. This is meant to form a more comprehensive picture, a Gestalt, where the whole is more than the sum of its parts. That is the definition of teamwork.

The next criticism from Singer concerns Resurrection Sunday and also involves Mary which can be found in Mark 16:8 (KJV):

And they went out quickly, and fled from the sepulchre;
for they trembled and were amazed: neither said they any
thing to any man; for they were afraid.

All of the other Gospels have Mary telling all of the followers about the Resurrection, but at this point in Mark's gospel, Singer readily points out that the women said nothing to anyone.[454] Singer is trying to say that Mark contradicts what everyone else states about the women notifying the other followers once they returned to their hiding place.

First of all, let's look at what logically happened as the women were on the road rushing back to return to the Disciples and Apostles. As they were returning on the road, *before they got back* to the other followers, they were afraid to tell anyone they did not trust. The women were not telling anyone they did not know very well about this monumental event. They were waiting until they were received by their brothers and sisters in faith, who were hiding behind locked doors. Then they would tell them everything that had happened. If you are on the road rushing back to your friends with earth-shaking news about Jesus, you are not going to be stopping along the way talking to anyone who could be a friend to the Pharisees. This makes perfect sense and logically explains why the women said nothing to anyone on the road.

Their level of fear was also experienced by the Roman guards who fled from the tomb as Matthew records in Matthew 28:2-4 (KJV), where one angel descended from heaven. His radiance lit up his face and clothing. I would imagine that he lit up the sky over the tomb as well. Matthew records a great earthquake that opened the tomb. Then the angel rolled away the stone and sat upon it. All this commotion greatly frightened the Roman guards, who fled in great haste and abandoned their post. In Matthew 28:11-15 (KJV), we read:

Now when they were going, behold, some of the watch (guards) came into the city, and shewed unto the chief priests all the things that were done. And when they were assembled with the elders, and had taken counsel, they gave large money unto the soldiers, saying, Say ye, His disciples came by night, and stole him away while we slept. And if this come to the governor's ears, we will persuade him, and secure you. So they took the money, and did as they were taught: and this saying is commonly reported among the Jews until this day.

Leaving a guarded post was a grave crime in the Roman military. Since the Jewish elders were involved in this whole tomb guarding process, this explains why the soldiers fled to the leading Jewish priests to immediately report what happened. The Roman guards were afraid of what Pilate would do to them. The religious leaders and the elders told them to lie about what happened and gave them a large bribe to keep them silent, promising to keep them out of trouble if Pilate heard of this.

Pontius Pilate was the Roman governor and commander who gave the order for his troops to guard the tomb of Jesus. The religious leaders were having the Roman guards falsely claim that the Disciples stole the body of Jesus. In this way, the religious leaders were denying that a Resurrection ever took place. I suspect that the Pharisees and religious leaders convinced Pilate not to punish the Roman guards to avoid an enormous riot. If Pilate had severely punished the guards, then the public would have wanted to know, why? Now that the body of Jesus was no longer in the tomb, Pilate and the Pharisees did not want to alert the crowds of this fact. With that being said, I'm sure that an immediate search was ordered by Pilate to find the body of Jesus.

Scholar Anthony Horvath tells us:

> We know that these guards would not have been Temple Guards because the Pharisees would not be telling Temple Guards that they will keep them out of trouble. The Jewish Temple Guards work for the Pharisees and would therefore not get into trouble with the governor. Only Roman Guards would be at risk of getting into trouble with the Roman governor.[455]

Everyone was shaking in great fear that morning and this explains why the women did not say anything to anyone on the road. However, because the Gospel of Mark abruptly cuts off here, critics use this as an opportunity to claim another contradiction amongst the Gospels. This is because, for some reason, the Book of Mark abruptly stops right at verse 8, of Chapter 16. That is the very odd ending of his entire book.

Some historians speculate that Mark may have been killed around this time and was unable to complete his Gospel. Mark's ending seems to be incomplete. Something is missing. Common sense dictates that the women most certainly would have told the followers of Jesus when the women were reunited with them. It appears obvious to many scholars that Mark's documentation in his Gospel was cut short and Mark was unable to complete it for some reason. This may have been the point in time where he could have been pulled out of his room and then tortured to death and Martyred. Mark was murdered (Martyred) in Alexandria in AD 68.[456] The Gospel of Mark was the earliest book written, between AD 64-and 70.[457]

This begs the question: Was the Apostle Mark murdered because it was discovered that he was writing his Gospel about Jesus? Mark was the very first Synoptic Gospel book written. Therefore, it makes logical sense that the very first gospel author was murdered once it was circulated that an Apostle of Jesus was putting Christianity into print. As I have stated, I believe fear of this occurring was the reason why the Gospel writers waited as long as they did to begin writing their books. And sure enough, as soon as the very first book starts getting compiled, the author appears to have been murdered before he could finish it.

During the era of Christian persecution, I'm sure there was a relentless policy of the Romans and Pharisees to quickly react to anyone committing 'Christian acts.' This would explain why the Book of Mark abruptly cuts off. I surmise that while Mark was being tortured for two days, one of his students rescued his Gospel and hid it. I surmise that the people who killed Mark were so consumed by their murderous rampage that they waited until after they were done before they returned to grab Mark's writings. By then, one of Mark's students had already secured the Book of Mark to protect it.

History reveals that shortly after the Gospel of Mark abruptly ended, 'someone' wrote what we now know as Mark 16:9-20. Someone put this ending on Mark's Book. Many believe that it was possibly one of Mark's students who wrote vss. 9-20. I believe this could have been the student who retrieved the Book of Mark while Mark was being tortured. It is my understanding that this student was responsible for the *Short Ending* version and the *Long Ending* version that we now have at the end of Mark where the women are telling the others.

The author who wrote Mark vss. 9-20 knew that Mark had to have known what the women were reporting in order for Mark to have written vss. 1-8, in the first place. The *Shorter Ending* and *Longer Ending* versions were soon added that many believe were not written by Mark. It appears that Tovia Singer is talking about the original Gospel of Mark that seems to not have the short or long version endings attached. And this means that Singer is ignoring Mark vss. 9-20.

There does seem to be some evidence that the *Longer Ending* version with verses 9-20 was written a short time after Mark stopped writing. As stated, the short and long version endings were probably written by a student of Mark, shortly after Mark's death around AD 68. As a consequence, we are compelled to incorporate these endings. The scholar Kyle Pope states that the fourth century historian Eusebius and the fourth-century Biblical Scholar Jerome:

> . . .did not emphatically reject the reliability of vss. 9-20, but did acknowledge the fact that they were disputed in their day." "Overwhelmingly the evidence from the testimony of ancient writers falls in support of the antiquity and originality of the passage. Not only do contemporaries of Jerome and Eusebius use the verses as authoritative but writers which predate Sinaiticus, Vaticanus, and the translations quote the passage!"[458]

Kyle Pope goes on and states that the earliest undisputed example of this is found in the second-century writings of Irenaeus. In his work 'Against Heresies,' he writes:

> ...the end of the Gospel Mark says, 'So then after the Lord Jesus had spoken to them, He was received up into Heaven, and sat at the right hand of God' (III.10.5).

Here, Irenaeus not only quotes verse 19, but he claims that this comes at the end of the Gospel. Pope asks:

> How can we question the antiquity and originality of this text if someone barely a generation after the composition of the New Testament quotes it?[459]

Therefore, we do have an ending to Mark pre-dating AD 180 that has been quoted by famous history scholars. This means that vss. 9-20 (KJV), should be included by us as well. And if Singer had accepted either the *Shorter Ending* or *Longer Ending* version, then he would have no ability to criticize Mark 16:8 (KJV), because both versions indicate the women told everyone who was grieving and weeping about the Resurrection. I believe it is obvious that something abruptly happened to Mark which prevented him from finishing his Gospel. The *Longer Ending* version of Mark (vss. 9-20, KJV) has been associated with the Book of Mark for over 1,000 years. Why then, do some critics seem to ignore this fact?

Singer also criticizes how many angels were seen on Resurrection Sunday.[460] This criticism exists because all of the Synoptic Gospels are not saying the same exact thing about the angels. One Gospel mentions only one angel, another mentions that there were two angels. Were they sitting, were they standing? Remember, none of the Synoptic Gospel authors or John saw these angels in the first place, only Mary and the women did. Mary and the women were very excited and scared. Just look how the Roman guards fled? And those were battle-hardened soldiers who were scared off.

The women were just as scared as the Roman guards, and they ran back to tell everyone what they saw. You can imagine the excitement in the room as they were out of breath from running, with all of them proclaiming what they had seen. There was no way anyone was going to be able to catch and remember every word. And what's worse is that no one believed them. Not one follower of Jesus believed these eyewitnesses. With that said, how many of the insignificant details of what happened 30 years prior for Matthew, Mark, and Luke will be remembered exactly as they happened? And let's not forget that John wrote his Gospel 60 years after the fact.

Disciples and Apostles trying to remember every single detail 30-60 years after the fact, will naturally produce some minor variations in their Gospels. One Gospel says there was only one angel at the tomb but then another Gospel states there were two angels at the tomb, and so on.

All that anyone should care about is that the tomb was empty, the body of Jesus was not stolen, and Jesus has risen from the dead! In the big picture, insignificant 30-60-year-old details about how many angels were present, whether the angels were sitting or standing, are irrelevant. The Gospel writers are human beings, not tape recorders. If the Gospel writers all wrote the same details down, then why would you need four of them? You would only need one. And if they did all write every insignificant detail down as the same, critics would accuse them of colluding. The critics are missing the advantage of having four authors. Instead, critics think this allows them the opportunity to attack the Gospels.

With different authors, there are different perspectives, this builds a more comprehensive picture that builds faith and credibility. Let's also consider and understand that Matthew, Mark, Luke, and John, all have different styles and were writing to different audiences. Matthew writes to the Jewish population. Mark writes to persuade the population of Roman citizens. Luke writes in detail and chronological order.[461] John, by contrast, is a deep thinker in his recounting of Jesus as the Messiah and the Son of God. Different, in no way means defective. This is why putting all the Gospel writings together forms a more comprehensive picture, or Gestalt. This is much better than merely reading the writings of only one of author.

If every word and detail were the same in all of the Gospels, we would not be able to form a comprehensive picture because we would only have one picture, from one perspective. Illuminating and varied perspectives are brought together in the Synoptic Gospels. This Synoptic phenomenon is meant to bring us the most vivid picture possible of what occurred. This is why God's Word is processed through these four particular authors. With that being said, it's just as important to realize that if every word and detail were the same in all four Gospels, then some of the audiences would have been left out. This is because the individual Gospel writers would have all been writing in exactly the same manner to only one audience.

Interestingly, in this particular situation, I believe that I have a perfect explanation for this presumed discrepancy. There was only one angel that initially came down to scare off the guards and open the tomb. We read of this in the testimony from the guards. I believe that we can see indications that Matthew incorporated the testimony of the guards in Matthew 28:2-4 (KJV):

> And, behold, there was a great earthquake: for the angel of the Lord descended from Heaven, and came and rolled back the stone from the door, and sat upon it. His countenance was like lightning, and his raiment white as snow: And for fear of him the keepers did shake, and became as dead men.

The *keepers,* of course, were the Roman guards and could possibly include the Jewish elders as well. They were scared to death and some of them fainted. Only the guards witnessed all of this. We know this because Mark, Luke, and John, all report that when the women arrived at the tomb that morning, the stone had already been rolled away. This means that only the Roman guards, and possibly some Jewish elders, witnessed the first angel descend and watched the angel roll the stone away.

This indicates that Matthew has included the testimony of the Roman guards in his Gospel. This explains why Matthew reports in his Gospel there was only one angel that morning. Matthew recorded one angel because the guards reported seeing one angel. Then in verse 5, Matthew reports this one angel spoke to the women once they arrived. In addition, further evidence that Matthew is including the testimonies of the guards is found in verses 11-15 of Chapter 28, where the guards speak of the bribe they were given in order to silence the truth. Based on what Matthew records, I believe one angel was outside of the tomb in the early phase of Resurrection Sunday. However, from carefully reading the Gospels of Luke and John, I am convinced there were two angels present inside the tomb that greeted the women when they arrived.

After Mary returned from the tomb the first time, she was told by the Disciples that her report of seeing angels was nonsense. As a consequence, when Mary returned to thc tomb the second time, she refused to believe that she was talking to angels and decided they were just men. This is when Jesus had to personally appear in order to finally convince her. This explains why the guards saw one angel, and the women saw two angels. I am convinced that Mary ran back to the tomb with Peter and John, and after they left, this is when she saw the two angels again, and then Jesus.

Now, some people interpret Matthew 28:1-7 (KJV), as indicating the women witnessed the angel descend, roll the stone away, and watched some of the guards faint. And I agree this appears to be how Matthew recorded this event. However, I believe that if the women arrived at the tomb before the angel descended and saw the guards there, the women would have fled immediately to notify the others. In addition, if they were there to witness the angel descend abruptly, some of the women would have fainted just as the guards had.

With that said, let's take a close look at Matthew 28:1-7 (KJV). It is true the women set out and walked toward the tomb early that morning. However, before they arrived at the tomb, the angel came down, opened the tomb, scared off the guards, and then Jesus emerged from the tomb and left. In verse six, the angel tells the women that Jesus is not in the tomb. This means the women arrived after the guards left, otherwise, they would have witnessed Jesus exiting the tomb and the angel would not have to tell them that Jesus was not inside. In addition, if Mary had witnessed Jesus exit the tomb, she would not have been crying at the tomb later when Peter and John left her there by herself. Mary was weeping and filled with sorrow and this would not have been the case if she saw Jesus alive as he emerged from the tomb at the beginning of that glorious morning.

We see evidence of this where Mark 16:4 (KJV), and Luke 24:2 (KJV), state that when the women arrived at the tomb, the stone had already been rolled aside. Likewise, John 20:1 (KJV), states that when Mary arrived early that morning, the stone had already been rolled away from the entrance.

That being said, I feel that it is far more likely that the angel descended and scared off the guards several minutes before the women arrived at the tomb as the new day dawned. This means that a short period of time passed between verse 4 and verse 5 in Matthew Chapter 28. Therefore, the women arrived after the guards had fled the scene. Remember, after Peter and John leave Mary at the tomb all by herself, she is the only one left to witness Jesus. Therefore, the report of only one angel being seen by the guards, two angels being seen by the women, and Jesus only being seen by Mary on her second visit to the tomb, could all be quite possible.

Only by meshing what the Gospel writers document, can we attempt to get the full picture. Witnesses came and went; this is the same issue that existed at the Crucifixion where witnesses came and went at various times during the 6-hour Crucifixion of Jesus. John had to leave to get his mother and later returned with his mother and some of her friends. Because of his absence, he missed Jesus talking about His Kingdom to the repentant thief.[462] It appears that John was the only Disciple present for parts of the Crucifixion. This is most likely because the other Disciples would have been obligated by Jewish law to participate in the custom of the slaughtering of the Passover lambs during the time that Jesus was dying on the cross.[463] John was able to be present for the Crucifixion because his older brother would have been handling the Passover sacrificing duties. This means that the only Disciple present for the Crucifixion was John.[464]

Now, this brings up a very interesting point. Since John was the only Gospel writer present for the Crucifixion, then whatever John records, in my opinion, must be considered first. Any perceived variations in the Gospels need to be explained by first looking at what John records. It is important to also note that John was present at the tomb with Peter, he was present at the Transfiguration, and he was given visions that allowed him the write the Book of Revelation. This is why I focus on what John writes about the Crucifixion and the Resurrection.

I will also add that none of the Gospels disagreed on any of the major pivotal points like the tomb being opened and Jesus not being in it. There was at least one angel present that spoke to the women. And the body of Jesus had not been removed or stolen by anyone because Jesus has Risen! This is universally stated by *all* of the Gospel writers. Those are the most important details. The rest are less important details that were passed down and then remembered 30-60 years later.

Singer also points out that in Mark 15:25 (KJV), the Crucifixion time is the "third hour."[465] That means 9 a.m., because the third hour past 6 a.m., is 9 a.m. This is only the case for the Jews, the Romans count time differently. But then Singer points to John who allegedly stated in his Gospel that the Crucifixion took place around the "sixth hour," which means noon.[466] In John 19:14 (KJV), we read:

> And it was the preparation of the Passover, and about the
>
> sixth hour: and He saith unto the Jews, Behold your King!

Singer claims this serves to discredit Christianity and the Crucifixion because of this contradiction.[467] Many experts have investigated this topic and many scholars believe that a probable transcription error may be the reason that a "3" was changed into a "6."[468] The translation of a Greek "gamma" (for the third hour) could have been substituted with a "digamma" (for the sixth hour). The two symbols look extremely similar and it is speculated that when transcribing the gamma, if a little hook is accidentally formed at the bottom in the process of lifting the writing tool up and away from the document, this could make it look like a digamma.[469]

What should have been John's report of the "3rd" hour, got turned into the "6th" hour because of a transcription error. Also, if a letter below had looped upward, it could have connected with the gamma above it and made it look like a hook was at the bottom when there was not supposed to be one. And this of course turns a gamma (3) into a digamma (6).[470] In the Greek written language, gamma and a digamma look almost identical. They don't look clearly different, like a 3 and a 6 look different to us. Many speculate this is where the 3-hour difference comes from.[471] Scholar Father Bartina S.J. (as cited in Davis, 2013) is quoted (this is a rough translation) as saying:

> Due to of all that has been reasoned before from the context of the Gospels, from textual criticism and from sufficient ancient testimony, it appears clear, it is more probable that John 19:14 originally had the third hour not the sixth.[472]

Singer also mentions the criminals on either side of Jesus, and how they are quoted differently depending upon which Gospel you read.[473] In Matthew 27:44 (KJV), we read:

> The thieves also, which were crucified with Him, cast the same in His teeth.

This means they were shouting insults at Him as the Pharisees did. Then in Luke 23:39-43 (KJV), we have:

> And one of the malefactors which were hanged railed on Him saying, if thou be Christ, save thyself and us. But the other answering rebuked Him, saying, Dost, not thou fear God, seeing thou art in the same condemnation? And we indeed justly; for we receive the due reward of our deeds: but this man hath done nothing amiss. And he said unto Jesus, Lord, remember me when thou comest into thy Kingdom. And Jesus said unto Him, Verily I say unto thee, Today shalt thou be with me in paradise.

We can see that one of the criminals beside Jesus scoffed at Him while the other protested this. So clearly these are two different statements from Matthew and Luke. One passage has both criminals scoffing at Jesus and another passage has only one criminal scoffing at Jesus. And remember, neither Matthew nor Luke were present for the Crucifixion.

In this particular criticism, scholar John Gill discusses his Bible commentary of "Matthew 27:44," where he presents two possible explanations.[474] In the first, Gill feels that the original translation only means that one criminal reviled Jesus, not both. The other possibility, Gill states, is that at first both men did revile Jesus, but then one realized that Jesus was not a criminal after all.[475] We need to remember that these men were hanging next to each other for 6 hours. As I figure this, and I'm sure that John Gill would probably agree, as the day dragged on, these crucified men began to talk to each other.

Initially, the two criminals heard the jeering of Jesus and that he was being called the King of the Jews. In Matthew 27:41-43 (KJV), the leading priests, teachers of religious law, and elders, were jeering Jesus. They told him to save himself and to come off of the cross. They said that he trusted God, so let God save him now. Then they shouted that he claimed to be, "The Son of God." And you know that the Pharisees, religious leaders, and elders, would have started jeering Jesus as soon as he was nailed to the cross and hoisted up. This would have all started around 9:00 a.m. When the other criminals heard this, they probably both joined in and scoffed at Jesus adding to the verbal harassment and insults. This would have occurred between 9:00-9:30 a.m.

Then as time wore on and the Pharisees and elders got tired and then left, I'm guessing that both of these criminals started to talk to Jesus. The crucified men started to talk back and forth to each other. I'm sure the criminals shared why they were being crucified and then asked Jesus why he was being crucified? This is when they both learned that Jesus was not even guilty of a crime. And because they were hanging on their crosses for several hours, they had enough time to hear everything that Jesus had to say. But then something happened. Going back to Matthew 27:44-45 (KJV), we read:

The thieves also, which were crucified with Him, cast the same in His teeth. Now from the sixth hour, there was a darkness over all the land unto the ninth hour.

This indicates that darkness had fallen upon the whole land at noon. This would have been an extremely unusual situation where the whole land became darkened. Notice how one criminal (or both) was ridiculing Jesus, and *then* it got dark. These criminals heard what Jesus had to say for 2-3 hours, then they saw the whole land become darkened. They knew something very special was happening.

After 3 hours, I figure that one of the criminals had become impressed by what he had heard from Jesus and then most likely interpreted the land growing dark to be a sign from God. It was at this point that one criminal realized Jesus was indeed the Son of God. The other criminal just continued to ridicule Jesus. The repentant criminal then asked Jesus to remember Him in His Kingdom. And Jesus replied that today he would be with Jesus in Paradise.

I find it important that the repentant criminal specifically mentions Jesus' "Kingdom." How would this criminal know about a "Kingdom" unless they were talking back and forth, and Jesus told him about His Kingdom? And I believe there may be some other information here as well. You will notice in Matthew 27:44 (KJV), it is mentioned both criminals ridiculed Jesus (there is some debate whether it was one or both). After Matthew states the ridicule, he then mentions in the next verse, "Now from the sixth hour there was a darkness. . . ." What this means to me is that the ridicule from the criminals occurred *before* noon. So sometime after the ridicule, it then became noon and dark.

However, in Luke 23:41-44 (KJV), we see the one criminal repent and ask Jesus to remember him in paradise. Luke specifically states that by this time it was already noon and darkened. Notice that Matthew is stating that the ridicule occurred *before* noon and *before* it got dark, while Luke states that one criminal had repented when it was noon and became dark. I believe this supports the fact that Matthew and Luke are referring to two different points in time during the Crucifixion. Matthew is referring to an earlier time in the morning than Luke is. What this means is that both Synoptic Gospels could be correct and are referring to events that occurred hours apart.

This appears to be yet another claim of a contradiction, when in fact, both statements that are being criticized are either correct or could be correct. But because every single word is not written down by the Gospel authors, critics find another opportunity to criticize.

Another example from Singer criticizes the story of the Roman officer traditionally identified as Longinus.[476] Longinus was the officer who was responsible for conducting the Crucifixion and he was the one who thrust his lance into the side of Jesus to make sure that Jesus was really dead. He also had one blind eye, possibly from a combat-related injury. Just after stabbing Jesus in His side, blood and water flowed out of Jesus and into the eyes of Longinus. When this happened, it restored the vision in his blind eye. In addition to this, Longinus would have witnessed the sky grow dark. He would have also witnessed the earthquake which took place the moment that Jesus died.

It was at this point that Longinus proclaims of Jesus, in Matthew 27:54 (KJV), "…Truly this was the Son of God." And then Mark 15:39 (KJV), "…Truly this man was the Son of God." And finally, in Luke 23:47 (KJV), "…Certainly this was a righteous Man." The critics claim there are two to three different quotes from Longinus and all of the Synoptic Gospels have him saying something different, which implies this is evidence of a fabricated story. However, what is being overlooked is the very strong possibility that officer Longinus could have made more than one statement.[477] And in this instance, it is clear that Matthew and Mark are essentially recording the same statement. Luke's statement is different. Some scholars feel that there is no contradiction here because Longinus probably made both of these statements.[478] I agree because that is logical.

How do we know that Longinus did not say all of this with several statements? It is very possible that Longinus could have said all three of these statements once his blind eye was cured. Longinus could have been so excited that his blind eye was cured, along with everything else that he witnessed, that he kept on making statement after statement after statement. Longinus could have gone on and on with his praise of Jesus for a long time.

Let me give an example. It's like watching an unbelievable play in sports where someone keeps shouting how incredible a play was. The fan could make several statements in a row about how shocking and incredible it was. And every shouted statement could be just a little bit different from the last statement. That would make perfect logical sense. Why is Longinus limited to making just one single statement? It is logical to conclude that Longinus made several similar statements because that is how astonished he was. Once again, basic logic is ignored by the critics.

In Matthew 28:7 (KJV), Jesus tells Mary to remember to remind everyone to meet him in Galilee. But Singer is quick to point out that Jesus instead appears to people on the road to Emmaus, and then He makes a few appearances in Jerusalem.[479] Because Jesus does not make His next appearance in Galilee as He said that he would, Singer claims Jesus said something that was not true.[480] With that, let's look at the facts and the truth of this situation. Jesus did tell his Disciples beforehand to meet Him in Galilee after His Resurrection. Is that what they did? No, it is not, at least not right away. The Disciples did not obey the wishes of Jesus. Did the Disciples believe the women's news from the angels? No, they did not. Did they believe Mary's news from a Resurrected and Risen Jesus? No, they did not.

His followers must have thought that when Jesus stated He would resurrect, that He was talking about the "Resurrection of the Dead" in the future. This is what Martha thought when Jesus told her that Lazarus would rise from the dead. Remember that Martha tells Jesus if he had been there sooner then He could have saved her brother. Jesus tells Martha in John 11:23 (KJV), "Thy brother shall rise again." Martha states in the next verse, "I know that he shall rise again in the Resurrection at the Last Day." She knows that her brother will rise in the Resurrection of the Dead and thinks this is what Jesus is referring to. Then Jesus states in John 11:25 (KJV):

> I am the Resurrection, and the Life: he that believeth in
>
> me, though he were dead, yet shall he live:

We have all of these followers, Apostles, and Disciples, and none of them believed nor understood that Jesus would rise from the dead in 3 days and 3 nights, just as Jesus promised. I believe this is because they were thinking as Martha did. They were thinking that Jesus was referring to the Resurrection of the Dead in the distant future. Even Mary did not believe that Jesus would resurrect in 3 days because she went to prepare his body for the completion of his burial on Sunday. No one went expecting to see Jesus raised from the dead, no one.

The followers of Jesus needed more faith in believing exactly what Jesus told them. They needed faith like Joshua and Caleb had after the Exodus. And because of this lack of belief, no one was going to Galilee as Jesus had requested. They don't believe the women, they don't believe Mary, and this is why they are not going to walk 76 miles to Galilee. This makes it necessary for Jesus to start appearing to his followers in order to prompt them to believe that He is risen, alive, and the Messiah. Jesus still wants the Disciples to go to Galilee to meet with Him. And this is the reason why Jesus has to appear. Thus, the lack of belief on behalf of His followers prompts Jesus to have to start appearing to them.

The first appearance of Jesus was when He spoke to Mary at the tomb. The Disciples did not believe Mary. Then Jesus appeared to two of his followers on the road to Emmaus who eventually realize that Jesus is amongst them once Jesus finally reveals himself. They hurry back to Jerusalem to tell the others. Does anyone believe them? No, they do not. This puts Jesus into an odd situation. No one is going to meet him in Galilee. Jesus wants to meet everyone in Galilee because that is where it all began. He grew up in that area and selected His Disciples from there. Galilee is special to Jesus. Jesus wanted a reunion in Galilee, and no one is going. What is Jesus to do now?

At this point I would like to pause to say that some critics may feel that Jesus should have known all of this was going to happen. And this would have caused Jesus to inform His Disciples and followers beforehand, that He will have to appear to them after the Resurrection before they decide to go to Galilee. Clearly, this is not the case. As stated earlier in this chapter, only God the Father knows everything. In this instance, Jesus is only provided with the information that He needs to accomplish His primary Mission on the earth. This is why I'm under the impression that Jesus was not informed by God the Father this situation would occur.

As a consequence of the unbelief of His followers, this compels Jesus to make more appearances, now in Jerusalem. Jesus appears to Peter and everyone else, except Thomas, who was not there. As a result, everyone is on board with the Galilee reunion except for Thomas because he will only believe if he can put his finger into the holes in Jesus' hands and put his hand into the hole in Jesus' side from the Roman lance.

At this point, everyone else is stuck in Jerusalem because of one guy who is not walking 76 miles each way unless there is a really good reason. This forces Jesus to appear one more time, and this time Thomas is present. Jesus directs Thomas to place his finger into the holes in his hands/wrists and then his hand into his side. In ancient Jerusalem, the wrist was considered a part of the hand. In John 20:27-28 (KJV), Jesus tells Thomas to "…be not faithless, but believing." And when Thomas was sure this was indeed Jesus, he said, "My Lord and my God!" Then Jesus tells Thomas, in John 20:29 (KJV):

> Thomas, because thou hast seen me, thou hast believed:
> blessed are they that have not seen, and yet have believed.

Only then does Thomas believe. This is not good for Thomas because Jesus just told him that those who believe in Him without seeing physical evidence, are blessed. Therefore, this means that Thomas may not be as blessed as someone who believes without demanding the high degree of proof that Thomas just did. This is a message for us to remember. There are a few important points to be seen here. The most important one, of course, is that God values faith and belief more than almost anything else. Jesus was amazed by the great faith of some Gentile followers to the extent that he granted their pleas for healing, like when the Roman Centurion's servant was gravely ill. Because of the great faith and humility of this Gentile Roman, Jesus gave healing and cured his servant. In Matthew 8:13 (KJV), we read:

And Jesus said unto the centurion, 'Go thy way; and as thou hast believed, so be it done unto thee. And his servant was healed in the selfsame hour.'

I would like to say that the reason why Jesus was so amazed by this Gentile Roman, is because God the Father did not tell Jesus this situation would occur. God the Father wanted this to be a pleasant surprise. This is why there are instances where we witness Jesus being astonished and amazed by some of His encounters, especially regarding Gentiles who possess great faith.

With that being said, Thomas finally believed after witnessing the proof that he demanded. Only then are all of the Disciples convinced that Jesus has truly risen. Only now will they travel to Galilee to meet up with Jesus there. Jesus was on the earth and resurrected for 40 days. This gave his followers plenty of time to walk to Galilee to meet him there. Jesus is the great, I Am.

It is disappointing to see that Jesus had to go to such lengths to finally convince everyone. The *common-sense* explanation for this situation is that because no one listened to the order to go to Galilee, Jesus was going to have to convince them to go to Galilee. Hence, the appearances became necessary. This does not prove that Christianity is a false religion. In fact, Matthew 26:32, states, "But after I am risen again, I will go before you into Galilee." Technically, Jesus eventually did go ahead of His followers and He did eventually meet up with them in Galilee. This is what Jesus had planned. His followers just had to be prompted first. Let's not confuse this reunion plan with a stated prophesy or the promised proof that He is the Messiah. This was just a plan for a reunion. That is all that it was. And as simple as that plan was, the Disciples messed it up.

I would also like to point out that all of this skeptical drama is what we encounter in the real world of human behavior. If this story were merely a myth, the writer would not have had the Son of God being forced to make 4 appearances to His followers before they finally all believed and obeyed to meet Him in Galilee. That said, Galilee is perfect because there are no Pharisees or religious leaders to persecute them there. The Disciples are safe. Seventy-six miles is far away. They can be relaxed and happy with their Lord. Remember, Jesus will be walking among them for 40 days.

It is here that I wish to discuss my analysis of Resurrection Sunday and what I perceive the reasons are for the variations seen in the documentation on that glorious day. The various Gospel writers think differently, have different experience levels, and each is writing to their particular audience. As a result, they write differently. With that being said, we can all see there are constants where all four writers report a supernatural event occurred where the tomb was now empty and at least one angel descended, who informed at least one woman that Jesus was alive and risen. The Synoptic Gospels and John all agree on these universal facts.

The more subtle variations between their writings are considered normal and to be expected when you have four different authors. This is why the Gospels need to be used in conjunction with each other in order to see the complete picture. They are all trying to convey the truth to the best of their ability and recollection. All things considered, there are some minor detail differences regarding Resurrection Sunday that I wish to address here. And very interestingly, I believe that most of the minor differences related to the documentation of Resurrection Sunday are all the result of one single factor. To reconcile these accounts with each other, there is one missing critical detail that must be incorporated.

That missing detail concerns the fact that Mary Magdalene was at the tomb twice on Resurrection Sunday. She was initially there with the women who went to the tomb early that morning when they witnessed the empty tomb and were spoken to by angels. Then Mary went back a second time with Peter and John to investigate the empty tomb.

I believe the Gospel differences that exist regarding Resurrection Sunday are caused by not including the fact that Mary was at the tomb twice that day. Leaving out this critical detail causes the events that occurred to be sequenced differently. Each author who is not incorporating Mary's second visit to the tomb will find it challenging to attempt to properly sequence events on Resurrection Sunday. As a result, each author who is unaware or forgets about Mary's second visit to the tomb, will come up with their own unique solution of how events sequenced together on Resurrection Sunday. This will cause some minor differences in what they record. That being said, the variations caused by not incorporating Mary's second visit to the tomb are not intended to mislead anyone. The Gospel writers are doing their best to record events to the best of their abilities and knowledge.

A quick review of what happened that morning was that an angel came down at twilight, just as the dark of the night was slowly receding. This angel lit up the sky and then rolled the stone of the tomb aside with a quake that shook the ground. This scared off the Roman guards and any Jewish Elders that may have been there to supervise. The Elders would have been there to make sure that the body of Jesus did not get stolen away, thus preventing His Disciples from claiming that a resurrection occurred. The Elders were there to protect their lives and the lives of the Pharisees.

Shortly after the guards and the Elders fled the scene, the darkness of the night continued to recede. In the morning twilight before the Sun rises above the horizon, Mary Magdalene and the other women arrived at the tomb. I believe this is what John means in Chapter 20:1 (KJV), when he states that Mary arrived, "…when it was yet dark." I believe there was a bit of light because at the end of that verse, John states that Mary, "…seeth the stone taken away from the Sepulchre." Therefore, John was not saying that it was pitch-black. In other words, it does not have to be pitch-black to be considered, dark.

The women are greeted by two angels who were inside the tomb. They inform the women that Jesus is not there, and that He is Risen! They run back to tell the others. Peter and John run to the tomb to see for themselves, and I'm sure that Mary Magdalene followed them in order to show them that the women were not talking nonsense. Also, she would have wanted to see what they could find out. The other women, the disciples, and the followers remained in hiding to keep a low profile and not draw the attention of the wicked Pharisees. They all waited for Peter, John, and Mary to return. Peter and John witness the empty tomb and leave perplexed. Mary remained at the tomb bewildered and grieving for her Lord.

Because Jesus knows that no one is believing the women's report that they saw two angels and that He is Risen from the dead, Jesus now has to intervene and appear to Mary. The original plan was for Jesus to return to God the Father after His Resurrection and then meet up with His Disciples in Galilee. But that plan needs to be delayed for now because no one is believing that He is alive. Jesus left the tomb once it was opened, this is why He was initially not there. But then Jesus had to return to the tomb grounds in order to convince Mary Magdalene.

Once Peter and John had left the tomb site, it was at this point the two angels appeared to Mary again. However, because the Disciples did not believe the women talked to angels, Mary was filled with doubt and was now convinced they were only men. The angels asked Mary why she was crying, and she stated in John 20:13 (KJV), "… Because they have taken away my Lord, and I know not where they have laid Him." If Mary thought that Jesus was alive, she would not have been crying like this. She thought someone removed His body and was preventing her from properly preparing Jesus for His burial. In John 20:15 (KJV):

> Jesus saith unto her, Woman, why weepest thou? Whom seekest thou? She, supposing Him to be the gardener, saith unto Him, Sir, if thou have borne Him hence, tell me where thou hast laid Him, and I will take Him away.

Mary offered to go and get the body of Jesus if she was told where He was. This means that Mary still did not believe the angel's statement even though this is the second time that Mary has been talked to by the angels. I believe Jesus intended to appear to his followers first in Galilee, but this chaotic situation of unbelief made it necessary for Jesus to appear to Mary while she was at the tomb for the second time.

It is here that I wish to direct attention to John 20:16 (KJV), "Jesus saith unto her, 'Mary,' she turned herself and saith unto Him, 'Rabboni.'" The word, *Rabboni*, means teacher. I mention this verse because of the Da Vinci Code nonsense. If Jesus and Mary had an intimate relationship or were married, then once Mary realized that Jesus was alive, she would have called Him as her husband or some other affectionate name. The fact that Mary's response is to call Jesus as her teacher, demonstrates we have Scripture that clarifies exactly what their relationship was.

At this point, I wish to discuss the differences that each Gospel writer documented for Resurrection Sunday. Matthew writes about one angel and all of the women seeing Jesus. Mark states that there was one angel, but no appearance of Jesus is mentioned. Luke documents two angels, but no appearance of Jesus is mentioned. Then there is John, who records two angels and Jesus speaking only to Mary. These are the differences that I feel can be explained by realizing that three of these authors do not include Mary's second visit to the tomb.

Let's first evaluate Matthew, who knows that Mary Magdalene and the women went to the tomb early that morning. Matthew knows that there was some *running* involved and he knows that Jesus was seen. But unlike the other authors, Matthew begins with what the Roman guards experienced, and this includes the report of only one angel. Now, to incorporate everything that Matthew knows without leaving anything out, he writes that the women were spoken to by the same angel the guards saw. Then because he does not know or has forgotten that Mary ran back to the tomb with Peter and John, he writes that all the women saw Jesus as they were running.

Indeed, there was running, but the most important running involved Mary running back to the tomb with Peter and John. And since Matthew knew that Jesus was seen by a woman, he assumed that all of the women saw Jesus because all the women were supposed to be together. Matthew does not appear to know that only Mary saw Jesus because she was the only woman to run back with Peter and John to investigate the tomb. Mary was at the tomb twice that morning and she was left alone at the tomb by Peter and John when they returned to the others. In my opinion, Matthew does not have all of these facts. As a result, he tried to string together what he did know. This explains Matthew's account.

If you think about this situation, one of the women would have wanted to show Peter and John they were telling the truth and see what they might find out. One of the women would have wanted to run back with Peter and John. I am convinced that Mary Magdalene was that woman. This explains the variation in Matthew's report of Resurrection Sunday. I don't believe that he remembered Mary running back and forth or he was unaware that she ran back with Peter and John. Either way, Matthew is incorrect about the number of angels that talked with the women and he is incorrect when he thinks that all the women saw Jesus.

Now, explaining Mark's version is more dramatic because his account just abruptly cuts off at verse 8. Many scholars believe that he died at this time. Mark was tortured and killed for his beliefs in Jesus and this may have occurred when it did because someone found out that he was talking about writing a Gospel about Jesus. Many scholars feel that the Book of Mark was finished by one of his students. For all we know, if Mark had been allowed to finish his Book, then it could have continued like John 20:2-31 (KJV).

With that being said, in verse 5, Mark records the presence of only one angel, just like Matthew did. This differs from the two angels that Luke and John record. As I have stated earlier, I believe

one angel was present earlier, but then a second angel joined in and greeted the women. The two angels were in the tomb during their discussion. If Mark had lived long enough to complete his Gospel, then he may have also included that Mary saw two angels and Jesus after Peter and John left her at the tomb? I'm convinced the reason why Mark does not mention Jesus is because he died right before he could record that Mary personally talked to Jesus. Mark's Book abruptly cutting off makes perfect sense with an abrupt death.

This bring up a worrisome question: Was Mark murdered in order to stop him from recording in his Gospel that Mary saw Jesus alive? We need to remember that the Book of Mark was the first Gospel written. You will notice that his Gospel cuts off right before Peter, John, and Mary ran back to the tomb. It is a fact that Mark was murdered. The apprentice who wrote the *Longer Ending* of Mark (vss.9-20) reports that Mary was the first person to see Jesus that morning, that she told the Disciples, and that no one believed her. Everything recorded by this author is correct, except he is not indicating that Mary made two trips and saw Jesus the second time she was at the tomb. If this apprentice was aware that Mary made two trips to the tomb that morning, then he decided to only mention the second trip where she saw Jesus. This is what John decided to do.

After Mary's first visit to the tomb, she returned with the women to tell the Disciples what the angels had told them. And after Mary's second visit, when she was left alone at the tomb and saw Jesus, she returned to tell the Disciples that she saw Jesus, along with the two angels again. Mary returned with news twice that day and none of the Disciples believed anything about angels or Jesus being seen.

You will notice that leaving out the one critical detail of Mary's second trip makes it much harder to reconcile what occurred that morning. Leaving out this single detail creates an important gap that causes the Gospel writers, who have forgotten this detail or are unaware, to push the other details together in an attempt to form a reasonable sequence of events. But any strung together sequence that does not incorporate Mary's second visit will form a picture that is not exactly what happened.

Then we have Luke's account. Luke is correct about everything that he includes, but the mention of Mary running back a second time to the tomb and seeing Jesus is not there. If this one detail of Mary running back and forth is not known, then it will prevent Luke from adding this history to the account. I'm guessing that Luke found out that none of the other women actually claimed to have seen or talked to Jesus. The other women only claimed that they saw two angels that talked to them. This would have made Mary the only one who claimed to have seen and talked with Jesus.

If Luke does not realize that Mary ran back with Peter and John and then stayed at the tomb after they left, then Luke won't see that Mary's report makes any sense. How could Mary talk to Jesus if she was with the other women and they did not see Jesus? The Jesus encounter will not make sense if you don't know that Mary went back without the other women and was left at the tomb and then talked to Jesus by herself. If you don't know that Mary went back, then the Jesus encounter becomes confusing. And if something does not make sense to doctor Luke (remember that he was a physician), then he is just going to leave it out. This is the logical reason why Luke makes no mention of Jesus being seen.

The only one who remembers all of the facts is John. That is because John was the only one who was present at the tomb and also wrote a Gospel. John is technically correct in what he has recorded. It is clear to me that he is only focusing on the importance of Mary Magdalene because she was the only one who spoke with Jesus, by herself. None of the other women were present during this second visit to the tomb. Only by combining all of the Gospel writer's documentation, are we able to piece together the complete picture.

When John states that Mary got to the tomb while it was still dark but was able to see that the stone of the tomb was rolled away, this means Mary (and the other women) got there at morning twilight.

This is when Mary and the other women first arrived at the tomb that morning. As I have stated, John does not mention the other women and chooses to focus on Mary because she was the only one to see Jesus.

We know the other women were with Mary on the first trip to the tomb because John includes that Mary states in John 20:2 (KJV), "…They have taken away the Lord out of the Sepulchre, and **we** know not where they have laid him." Notice that Mary used the word, "we." Mary did not say, "I know not," she said, "we know not." This indicates Mary was not alone because the other women were with her. This means that John was well aware that Mary made two trips. With that being said, John only chose to mention the second visit because the Jesus encounter made it the more significant visit.

Also notice this was stated in verse 2. I say this because in verse 3, John is recording that Peter and another Disciple (who was John himself) then started to run to the tomb to investigate. I feel it should be obvious that the "other Disciple whom Jesus loved," is John. Then John records that Peter and the other Disciple left the tomb in verse 10.

This is important, because in verse 11, John mentions Mary standing outside of the tomb. This sequence is correct because John remembered that Mary was left at the tomb as he walked away with Peter to go home. This also explains why John mentions Jesus appearing and speaking with Mary in verses 15-17. Clearly, this was after Peter and John had left the tomb in verse 10. This means that Mary was at the tomb twice that morning because she ran back to the tomb with Peter and John. This is the only way that she is at the tomb after they left for home. Mary remained at the tomb to grieve. This all made sense to John. The events that he chose to include were all written down in the correct order.

As I have stated, because the Disciples did not believe Mary when she reported that all the women were spoken to by angels that they saw on her first trip, Mary became convinced the Disciples were right. This is why she refused to believe these were angels talking to her on her second trip. She thought they were just men and she wanted them to tell her where the body of Jesus was. The man who she thought was the gardener that was standing behind her, turned out to be Jesus once he revealed his identity to her.

I feel this explains the insignificant variations that exist that we can all see regarding what was recorded about Resurrection Sunday. I say this because all of the Gospel writers agree on the major core declarations of what happened on Resurrection Sunday. There was no deception going on here. Each author was doing their best to represent the truth as they saw it and remembered it, some 30-60 years later. The Gospel writers are like filters that process information and then translate that into written form. The overall net effect of including these four authors creates a comprehensive picture that reaches more audiences than any one of them could have accomplished by themselves.

Therefore, in conclusion, in evaluating Resurrection Sunday, I feel that we need to realize that Matthew, Mark, Luke, and John, all include the same core declarations in their documentation:

1) That the tomb had its stone rolled away and it was empty.

2) There was at least one angel present which represents a miraculous event.

3) Mary was talked to by at least one angel and/or Jesus.

4) Jesus was resurrected from the dead and He is alive! His body was not stolen.

All four of these core declarations appear in every single Gospel. We have to realize and take note of this consistency regarding these core points. These 4 points are the take-home message of what happened that day and represent the message that the Gospel writers were passing along as best as they knew how. The Gospel writer's objectives were to project their impression of what had occurred, as truthfully as possible.

This brings me back to Tovia Singer. He stated in his Q&A response regarding the Crucifixion and Resurrection that there is virtually not a single detail the Gospel writers all agree on.[481] By contrast, what we observe by analyzing Resurrection Sunday is that all of the Gospel writers agree on all of the four major points that I have listed.

One of the last criticisms that I will mention concerns the ascension. Singer makes an issue out of Jesus preparing for His Ascension.[482] Jesus' last appearance was to be in Bethany (Day 40) where he ascends into Heaven. Singer states that while Jesus was in Jerusalem, he specifically told all of his followers to remain in Jerusalem and to wait for the Holy Spirit. Singer points out that right after this, Jesus then leads them to Bethany instead. Singer claims that Jesus is contradicting himself here.[483] Jesus indeed told all of his followers in Jerusalem that they needed to remain in Jerusalem after he ascends in order for them to receive the Holy Spirit. In Luke 24:49 (KJV), he writes that Jesus states:

> [49]And, behold, I send the promise of my Father upon you; but tarry ye in the city of Jerusalem, until ye be endued with power from on high.

Jesus let them all know that they will soon, all go to Bethany where He will ascend into Heaven to be with his Father. Then, they are to immediately go back to Jerusalem and wait for the Holy Spirit to fill them with His Power. Luke did not write this instruction down, *word for word*. When Jesus was in Bethany for his Ascension, Mark 16:19 (KJV) states:

So then after the Lord had spoken unto them, he was received up into Heaven and sat on the right hand of God.

This was probably one of Mark's proteges recording the Ascension of Jesus into Heaven from Bethany. We know this took place in Bethany because it's recorded in Luke 24:50-52 (KJV):

> [50]And He led them out as far as to Bethany, and He lifted up His hands and blessed them. And it came to pass, while He blessed them, He was parted from them, and carried up into Heaven. And they worshipped Him, and returned to Jerusalem with great joy.

Here you can see that Jesus' followers did indeed immediately leave Bethany, returned to Jerusalem, and waited there to receive the Holy Spirit, just as Jesus instructed them to. But critics try to take this as yet another opportunity to discredit Christianity because of the way in which Luke records that Jesus told his followers to stay in Jerusalem in verse 49. Then in verse 50, Jesus is leading them to Bethany. Singer claims this is a contradiction.[484] Luke left out the fact that Jesus probably told his followers something like this right after verse 49:

> *However, before you get filled with the power of Heaven by the Holy Spirit here in Jerusalem, you first need to follow me to Bethany where I will ascend into Heaven to join My Father. Then you are to return immediately to Jerusalem and wait to receive the Holy Spirit.*

Common sense dictates that something like this had to have been said by Jesus. Because Luke does not record every single word like a tape recorder, Singer uses this as yet another opportunity to claim another contradiction. Bethany is only 2 miles away from Jerusalem. I believe the use of basic logic demonstrates that many criticisms against Christianity are flawed and 'mistaken.'

And let's not forget that the body of Jesus was never found. According to Paul's testimony in 1 Corinthians 15:6 (KJV), more than 500 eyewitnesses saw the resurrected Jesus. On 12 separate occasions, spread out over 40 days, He talked with them and walked among them. Two of these people were documented to have physically touched Jesus.[485] These eyewitnesses allowed themselves to be persecuted, tortured, and even killed because they refused to recant their testimony of seeing the Risen Jesus.

A former atheist named Lee Strobel formerly worked as the legal editor for the Chicago Tribune.[486] And he set out to prove that all religions were essentially fairy tales. He conducted a thorough and detailed "forensic investigation" into Christianity which focused on Jesus. After 2 years of painstaking work, this former atheist, who is now a Christian scholar, determined that Jesus was real and that he did indeed resurrect from the dead. Lee Strobel stated in his forensic investigation that he found over 500 people admitted to seeing the resurrected Jesus and that some of these people were interrogated by the Romans and tortured in an attempt to make them recant their testimony. But they did not.

Since some of these people allowed themselves to be tortured to death, instead of recanting their eyewitness accounts. Lee Strobel concluded that human beings don't allow someone to harm them in order to protect a lie. All they had to do was admit that they were 'mistaken' and change their testimony in order to save their lives. But instead, people refused to change their testimony that they witnessed Jesus alive. This, in addition to the rest of his investigation, meant to Strobel that Jesus must have resurrected and walked among the people.[487]

Listed below are several major paraphrased points from scholar Adriana Hanson indicating strong support for the Resurrection of Jesus:

1. There were more than 500 people who witnessed the resurrected Jesus, including two important critics of Jesus before He died. One was Jesus' half-brother, later called James the Just. According to the Biblical witness, James never believed Jesus during His ministry on the earth and thought that Jesus was "out of his mind." Most of Jesus' family thought this as well, except for Mary and Joseph. However, after the Resurrection, Jesus appeared to James, who became a leader of the Church in Jerusalem! The Apostle Paul even referred to James as one of the three pillars of the Church (Galatians 2:9). The other critic, of course, was the Pharisee Saul of Tarsus, who became the Apostle Paul.

2. The tomb of Jesus was found empty, and His body was never recovered.

3. After the death of Jesus, His followers all went into hiding, grieving and weeping. Not until Jesus appeared to Peter and the rest, did they finally emerge from hiding with courage and conviction. They were filled with so much courage and conviction that they suffered and died. Their transformation is best explained by a resurrected Jesus!

4. Many Jewish leaders and skeptics converted to Christianity after the Crucifixion and Resurrection of Jesus. This would be hard to imagine happening if there were a Crucifixion alone (and no Resurrection that followed).

5. No physical site was ever dedicated and venerated as the burial site of Jesus. This does not mean that a site was not identified. A resurrected Jesus, and no corpse, best explains why the tomb of Jesus was never venerated as a burial site.

6. The early Church centered its teachings and practices around the supernatural Resurrection instead of the righteous teachings

and sermons of Jesus. It would have been far less controversial for the Church to center itself on the ministry of Jesus. Therefore, a resurrected Jesus best describes this behavior.

7. A Resurrection best explains the rise and expansion of Christianity so soon after the death of Jesus. This is especially true since Jesus was crucified as a political traitor and declared a religious heretic by the Jewish religious leaders. Only a resurrected Jesus could cause such a powerful and forceful reversal of the propaganda and lies surrounding Jesus.[488]

This completes my discussion of the Crucifixion and the Resurrection. I feel that it is now time to answer the question of what year Jesus was born?

Let's begin with John the Baptist who is believed to be the cousin of Jesus. This was the case because John's mother, Elisabeth, was Mother Mary's relative, believed to be a cousin. In Luke 1:36-37 (KJV), we read what the Archangel Gabriel said to Mary:

> And, behold, thy cousin Elisabeth, she hath also conceived
> a son in her old age: and this is the sixth month with
> her, who was called barren.

You will notice that the King James Version states Mary and Elisabeth are cousins, however, the original Greek translation is less specific and only states that Elisabeth is Mary's "kinswoman."[489] With that being said, we are told that Elizabeth's pregnancy is at six months by this point. Then in Luke 1:41-42 (KJV), we see:

> And it came to pass, that when Elisabeth heard the saluta-
> tion of Mary, the babe leaped in her womb: and Elisabeth
> was filled with the Holy Ghost. And she spake out with
> a loud voice, and said, Blessed art thou among women,
> and blessed is the fruit of thy womb.

We see that a few days after Mother Mary finds out that Elisabeth is six months pregnant, Mary visits her. And Elizabeth knows that Mary is now pregnant as well. This means that their pregnancies are six months apart because Mary was just told two days ago that Elizabeth was six months pregnant. And two days prior, would have been when the Holy Spirit caused the Immaculate Conception. Therefore, their pregnancies are indeed six months apart.

Jesus was born six months after his cousin, John the Baptist. And as I have stated, John was born in March. This means that Jesus was probably born in September of the same year. And if you trace back 9 months to Mary's Immaculate Conception, we are in December of the previous year. This means that the traditional Christmas celebration in December may correspond with the Immaculate Conception. In other words, a December Christmas celebration remains constant.

At this point, I wish to briefly discuss the Immaculate Conception. To demonstrate the complexity of this unique situation, let's put ourselves in the position of needing to come up with a solution. Let's say for argument's sake, that we are faced with the challenge of figuring out how to place a Divine messiah on the earth, who is also in the flesh. How can this be done? Well, the only way to solve this significant challenge is to have a Divine male DNA strand combine with a human female DNA strand which causes conception to take place. This is the most logical and intelligent solution to this challenge. With that being said, this is precisely what God the Father had the Holy Spirit do.

Therefore, the Immaculate Conception is not some mysterious story that may cause some people to think is strange. No, the Immaculate Conception was the perfect logical solution to overcome the challenging requirement of placing a Divine messiah on the earth and in the flesh. The Immaculate Conception was brilliant and was the product of pure logic. And just to clarify, Archangel Gabriel was the messenger sent to inform Mary, while the Holy Spirit was the one sent to cause the Immaculate Conception.

Now, let's move on and examine a very important piece of evidence in Luke 3:1 (KJV), where we read of when John the Baptist began his ministry:

> Now in the fifteenth year of the reign of Tiberius Caesar, Pontius Pilate being governor of Judea and Herod being tetrarch of Galilee, and his brother Philip tetrarch of Ituraea and of the region of Trachonitis, and Lysanias the tetrarch of Alilene. Annas and Caiaphas being the high priests, the Word of God came unto John the son of Zacharias in the wilderness. And he came into all the country about Jordan, preaching the baptism of repentance for the remission of sins;

This correlates with when John the Baptist was baptized and started his ministry. Tiberius was appointed as co-regent with Augustus in AD 11, and 15 years later, would be AD 26.[490] Jesus began His Ministry shortly thereafter at approximately the age of thirty (Luke 3:23). Jesus would have been 30 years old in September of AD 26 (if He was born in September of 5 BC). While John the Baptist, would have been exactly 30 years old when he started his ministry because John started six months before Jesus did.

I believe the correct Tiberius calculation is AD 26 for the year that Jesus and John started their ministries. This would put the first Passover of Jesus' ministry at AD 27. This means the ministry of Jesus would have ended on the fourth Passover after His baptism. Many scholars agree that there had to be four Passovers during the ministry of Jesus.[491] These four Passovers are mentioned in: John 2:13; John 5:1; John 6:4; and John 19:14.

We can say with confidence that Jesus and John were both born in either the year of 6 BC or 5 BC based upon the link with the 15th year of Tiberius Caesar's reign. And please be aware that in AD 30, Jesus was crucified in April, so He had not yet had His birthday that year. This is why we have to subtract half a year in this calculation. In order to make this calculation, you have to first take the BC year and subtract one year because there is no "0" year. There is no zero year in the ancient Gregorian calendar. Then you add to that, the number of AD years only if the birthday has been reached, otherwise, you have to subtract half a year. Therefore, in a 5 BC birth year, this equals 4 BC years that get added to the AD years if the birthday has been reached.

Now, an AD 26 baptism around September would equal 26 AD years. Then if we add this to the 4 BC years (based on a 5 BC birth), we have Jesus at 30 years old at His baptism. Once again, there is no "0" year between the transition from BC to AD. And by the time we get to the Passover in AD 30, this puts Jesus at 33 ½ years old. All of this makes perfect sense with what we have all heard as to how long the ministry of Jesus was (3 ½ years) and how old Jesus was when He was crucified (33 ½ years old). You will notice this calculation is based upon the scripture of Luke referring to ancient Roman history. This means the Apostle Luke wanted us to know precisely when in time Jesus started His ministry.

This is important because if Jesus died in AD 33 on a Friday Passover, this would indicate a 2 BC birth year for Jesus. I don't see from this factual Roman history recorded in Luke 3:1, that Jesus could have been born in 2 BC? A 2 BC birth year is off by about three years. Unless we are going to say that the ministry of Jesus lasted 6 ½ years? I don't know anyone who is claiming that His ministry was that long. This is very important because it supports that Jesus must have been crucified in AD 30 which fulfilled the sign of Jonah, proving that He is indeed the Messiah.

This also proves, in particular, that the Gospel of Luke is correct when he stated that Herod the Great was alive when Jesus was born. In addition, this also agrees with Luke's reference to General Quirinius, which I will discuss in great detail in the next chapter.

This brings us to the Star of Bethlehem. As we all have heard, the Three Wise Men followed the Star of Bethlehem to find the newborn King of the Jews. Were they really following a star? Scholar Grant Matthews (as cited in Blackwell, 2016) has figured out what the "Star of Bethlehem" really was. Matthews states, "the Star of Bethlehem was likely not a star but rather a rare, once-in-several-millennia alignment of planets."[492] Matthews states that it occurred in 6 BC and would have only been visible just before dawn, not at night.

This alignment of planets is referred to as a conjunction which is when a few planets are in close alignment. As a result, they reflect a lot more light than a star does, in the same way that a full Moon is brighter than the stars. That's if it is the type of conjunction that can be seen at night.

Scholar Tom Blackwell states that "the magi are believed to have been Zoroastrian priests from Mesopotamia who analyzed astronomical data, assigning various portents to what they observed in the cosmos." This confirms the wise men were astronomers. Matthews states that this ". . .phenomenon would have grabbed the attention of the magi signifying to them that a momentous birth had occurred." Matthews and Blackwell are also saying that only an experienced astronomer would have noticed this particular conjunction because it was subtle and only visible just before dawn.[493] Others state that the wise men seem to have been from the ancient kingdom of Sheba. This would have been on the Arabian Peninsula and would have been controlled by the kingdom of Sheba. This is speculated because the gifts that were brought to the newborn King indicated that they probably came from the Arabian Peninsula.[494] Sheba was the great, great-grandson of Noah.

The wise men clearly believed in God and the coming Messiah. The people who were looking forward to the coming of the Messiah would have made a big deal out of this conjunction. While the people who did not believe in the coming Messiah, would have noted and recorded this conjunction but would have had nothing special to say about it. What is very interesting here is that the Queen of Sheba is mentioned in the Bible to have visited King Solomon at his Temple in Jerusalem. In the Book of 1 Kings 10:1 (KJV), we read:

> And when the Queen of Sheba heard of the fame of
> Solomon concerning the name of the Lord, she came
> to prove him with hard questions.

Sheba was an ancient city in the Ethiopian State which was at the southern tip of the Arabian Peninsula. There is the belief in Ethiopia, that when the Queen of Sheba came back from visiting King Solomon, she bore him a son. This started a Solomonic Dynasty in Ethiopia.[495] This is why there are so many Jews and Christians in Ethiopia today. Therefore, if the Wise Men were from Sheba, this would explain why they traveled to Bethlehem to worship the birth of the Messiah.

With that said, the Wise Men met Herod first who inquired of Jesus' whereabouts. To protect Jesus, they did not return to Herod which made him intensely furious. In Matthew 2:16 (KJV), we read:

Then Herod, when he saw that he was mocked of the wise men, was exceeding wroth, and sent forth, and slew all the children that were in Bethlehem, and in all the coasts thereof, from two years old and under, according to the time which he had diligently inquired of the wise men.

King Herod felt threatened by anyone else who was to be called the King of the Jews. He felt that *he* was the king of the Jews. This is why he set out to kill this new threat. And the reason why Herod chose to kill children two years and under, can be seen in Matthew 2:7 (KJV):

Then Herod, when he had privily called the wise men, enquired of them diligently what time the star appeared?

The wise men told Herod that this *Star of Bethlehem* first appeared about 1-2 years prior. Herod figured if he killed all male children who were two years and younger, then he would make sure to kill this newborn King. This tells us that the conjunction was between 1 and 2 years old by the time the wise men reached Herod. If this 6 BC conjunction is the correct one, then it would indicate a 5 BC birth.

Now, the reason why I dismissed this 6/5 BC conjunction is because I was looking for something visible at night. However, Blackwell and Matthews make the great point that what is not obvious to average people would have been noticeable to astronomy experts like the wise men.[496] This means that Jesus was either born in 6 BC or 5 BC. His birth would still have been in the latter part of the year around September. For me to triangulate the correct answer, I will need to bracket my answer as: "Jesus was born either in September of 6 BC or September of 5 BC." And this is probably why most scholars place the birth of Jesus as, "6/5 BC."

This brings up the question: Isn't Jesus supposed to be born in the year 0? Once again, there was no zero year in the ancient Roman calendar. The calendar went from 1 BC to AD 1. The practice of counting the years since the birth of Jesus was started by Denys the Little who was a theologian and an astronomer.[497] In 533 AD, Denys used information from Clement of Alexandria who declared that Jesus was born in the 28th year of the reign of Caesar Augustus. This is how Denys came up with 1 AD (or AD 1). However, Denys apparently left out the fact that Augustus first reigned under his original name of Octavian, for four years.[498] This is why the birth of Jesus is off by four or five years. If this calculation is off by four years, Jesus was born in early, 4 BC. If this calculation is off by five years (with inclusive reckoning), Jesus was born in late, 5 BC.

The famous astronomer and scientist Johannes Kepler determined in 1603 that a triple conjunction of Jupiter, Saturn, and Mars, occurred in 7 BC. This supports the *Star of Bethlehem* account perfectly as it would have continued into late 6 BC.[499] In addition, David Hughes is quoted as stating that this triple conjunction may very well be the *Star of Bethlehem* and that the Babylonians would have been able to see this bright conjunction in their night sky. Babylonian records do indeed indicate that they also witnessed this 7 BC triple conjunction. However, the Babylonians did not know what the significance of this conjunction was.[500] This confirms that there were multiple witnesses to this triple conjunction. This means there were two conjunctions.

In addition, Chinese astronomers also observed these 7 BC and 6 BC conjunctions.[501] Therefore, these conjunctions are well-established historical facts. This raises the question: Which conjunction was Jesus born under? No one can say for sure.

That said, the birth year of Jesus brings us back to Herod. The account of Herod trying to kill baby Jesus is recorded in the Book of Matthew. In order to establish that Herod was in a position to try to kill Jesus, we need to establish that Herod was still alive when Jesus was born. It turns out that many historians agree that Herod died in 4 BC. This is because Herod's three sons took over his rule in the spring/summer of 4 BC. It seems that Herod the Great was no longer ruler by the summer of 4 BC because his sons went to Rome to contest his will with Caesar Augustus.[502] Why would the sons of Herod contest their father's will with Augustus if Herod was still alive? And why would they be taking over his rule if he were still alive?

There is a highly detailed and complete listing of every event that went on regarding Herod in 4 BC that was written by Mahlon H. Smith, titled, "Uprisings after Herod." I highly recommend that everyone read this online article to get the complete picture of what went on in Jerusalem in 4 BC regarding Herod. In this article, we see that Herod's sons have a dispute over Herod's will, where Antipas and Archelaus both travel to Rome to contest their father's will. This was around April of 4 BC.

In addition, Caesar Augustus sends his treasurer to audit Herod's estate. That *procurator* was Sabinus. As a result, in the spring of 4 BC, we have General Varus and Sabinus in Jerusalem. This audit of Herod's estate in the spring of 4 BC was soon followed by a serious riot in Jerusalem. There are a lot of detailed events in Smith's article that will give you a sharper picture of just what happened in 4 BC regarding Herod.[503]

With Jesus being born in 6/5 BC, this means that Jesus was born while Herod was still alive. This supports the passages in the Bible which tell us of Herod's plot to kill newborn Jesus.[504] This is why we need to reconcile the exact dates for everything as much as possible so that we can see how all of this actual history falls into place and fits together. You will also notice that this actual history does not contradict what is written in the Bible. Therefore, what we can see from all of this analysis regarding Jesus, is that the Bible is not contradicted by history or logic.

With all of that being said, referring back to Denys the Little's calculation, if it is off by four years, Jesus was born in (early) 4 BC. This would work if Herod died in late 4 BC. If Denys calculation is off by five years (with inclusive reckoning), Jesus was born in (late) 5 BC. This would work if Herod died at any time in 4 BC. It is my personal inclination to triangulate the birth of Jesus to probably be around late September of 5 BC.

To close out this pivotal chapter, one more thing needs to be said. With His Resurrection, Jesus proved that He is indeed the Messiah, the Son of God, and that we can be saved through faith in Him. As Romans 8:3-4 says (KJV):

> For what the law could not do, in that it was weak through
> the flesh, God sending his own Son in the likeness of
> sinful flesh, and for sin, condemned sin in the flesh:
> That the righteousness of the law might be fulfilled in
> us, who walk not after the flesh but after the Spirit.

Jesus was the blood sacrifice that put an end to sin's control over us. This is why Jesus died for us. Numerous eyewitnesses of the Risen Jesus provide powerful evidence that this *Good News* is indeed true.

CHAPTER ELEVEN

Paul, Luke, and a Man Named Ramsay

The purpose of this chapter is to spotlight the conversion of the Pharisee, Saul of Tarsus, and the other Jewish men that dedicated themselves to following Jesus. I will also examine criticisms regarding the truthfulness of the New Testament as it pertains to Paul and Luke.

Saul was one of the most highly educated Pharisees of his era. He was a supreme expert in Jewish laws and customs, respected among his fellow Pharisees, religious leaders, and priests. Pharisee Saul from Tarsus was of the tribe of Benjamin. He violently persecuted Christians. He held the cloaks and cheered on those who stoned Stephen to death as the first Christian martyr. Saul relentlessly pulled Christians out of their homes and threw them into prison which led to them facing prosecution, torture, and execution.

In Acts 9:3-5 (KJV), we read that on the road to Damascus to persecute more Christians, Saul was suddenly surrounded by a light that caused him to fall to the ground. The men with him heard sounds but they could not make the words out. What Saul heard was, "Saul,

Saul, why persecutes thou me?" Saul asks, "Who art thou, Lord?" Saul believed in God, of course, and thought he was protecting God and the Jewish laws by persecuting Christians. Saul thought that God's answer would be, *Yes, I am your Lord.* But instead, Saul heard, "I am Jesus whom thou persecutest."

Note that God identified himself as Jesus. This is not what Saul expected at all. I'm sure this shocked him to his core. Saul is blind at this point, afraid, and asks what he must do? This begins Saul's new life where he becomes Jesus' most zealous, vigorous, and tireless missionary.

Can anyone who does not believe in Jesus tell me how the greatest enemy that Christianity has ever known, immediately switched sides and threw absolutely everything that he had ever worked for, away? Who does that? Saul's colleagues went from loving him to hating him. Those who now condemned him included the Pharisees, the Sadducees, and the Jewish Elders. The change was so profound that Saul started going by the name of Paul—meaning, *small.* He wound up being hunted, persecuted, and conspired against for being an open advocate of Jesus.

If that wasn't enough, in 2 Corinthians 11:22-33 (NLT), Paul is attacked by followers in Churches he established who were now complaining against him. We can see in this statement how Paul needed to fiercely rebuke the rivals in the Churches that rejected his authority. This is what Paul exclaims to the congregations, regarding the people in the Churches who are attacking him personally:

> Are they Hebrews? So am I. Are they Israelites? So am
> I. Are they descendants of Abraham? So am I. Are they
> servants of Christ? I know I sound like a madman, but
> I have served Him far more!

I have worked harder, been put in prison more often, been whipped times without number, and faced death again and again. Five different times the Jewish leaders gave me thirty-nine lashes. Three times I was beaten with rods. Once I was stoned (he was left for dead). Three times I was shipwrecked. Once I spent a whole night and a day adrift at sea. I have traveled many long journeys.

I have faced danger from rivers and from robbers. I have faced danger from my own people, the Jews, as well as from the Gentiles. I have faced danger in the cities, in the deserts and on the seas. And I have faced danger from men who claim to be believers but are not.

I have worked hard and long, enduring many sleepless nights. I have been hungry and thirsty and have often gone without food. I have shivered in the cold, without enough clothing to keep me warm. Then besides all this, I have the daily burden of my concern for all the Churches. Who is weak without my feeling that weakness? Who is led astray, and I do not burn with anger?

If I must boast, I would rather boast about the things that show how weak I am. God the Father of our Lord Jesus, who is worthy of eternal praise, knows that I am not lying. When I was in Damascus, the governor under king Aretas, kept guards at the city gates to catch me. I had to be lowered in a basket through a window in the city wall to escape from him.[505]

No one suffered more hardships than Paul did for the sake of God and for the sake of God's Church. Would anyone on the earth as intelligent and highly educated as Paul really put himself through all this for a lie? Does that make any sense? And who is going to share a detailed history of pain and suffering like this without it being true? Who is going to sit down and write all this if he is living a lie? You can clearly hear in his words the authenticity of his testimony. Paul even states that God knows that he tells the truth.

On top of this, Paul is telling these things to people in Corinth who are supposed to be followers of Jesus. Paul knows these people. They know Paul's history. If any of this were a lie, they would have confronted him about it right away. Paul has a painful history with this Church, with some rival elements in it accusing him of being weak and ineffective. If he were making all this up, he would be discredited quickly. Paul has to endure not just sufferings but significant disrespect as well.

I'm sure there are critics that cast doubt upon Paul and claim his experiences to be fabrications. To those people, I ask, who would sit down and make up all this pain, suffering, and horror? What would be the point to fabricating a story like this? Any liar holding up this kind of suffering and turmoil from following Jesus, not to mention experiencing persecution from his fellow Jews, is certainly not going to gain any recruits to a club like this. There is no doubt, that some people in the audience would have questioned what they were getting themselves into? They would ask themselves, "Why would I put myself at risk for this type of maltreatment?" The sufferings that Paul speaks of doesn't have the earmarks of a fraudulent organization trying to sell itself.

Are all these Christian Disciples, Apostles, and followers of Jesus insane, or are they telling the truth? It's either one or the other. Seriously, what are the odds that this many people just go insane all at the same time? And if critics claim that nothing written about Paul ever happened, then ask them why anyone would make up such a horrible story? Paul's accounts would scare many people off. None of this makes any sense unless it's the truth.

What kind of a fraudulent cult is going to try to recruit members with the severe suffering that Paul must endure and tells everyone about? Who is going to sign up to join a club like that? Does that make any sense? No, not unless it is the truth. What fraudulent club is going to present their Lord as being beaten beyond recognition, whipped to the point that so much skin and flesh was torn away that you could probably see His lungs by looking at His back? Then, this Divine Savior gets nailed to a cross until he dies. Crucifixion was a publicly humiliating torture, a grisly spectacle for all who walked by to gawk at. Is this how a new "club" decides to promote itself? There is only one way that any of this makes any sense, and that's if it's the truth. On top of all of this, Paul is ultimately killed for proclaiming Jesus as Lord.

An important point to be seen here, is that if all of these stories about the Disciples and Apostles were being made up as a fairy tale and a lie, then the writers of these accounts would certainly have painted themselves as much more heroic, loyal, and faithful. They would have written that they were all camped outside of the tomb of Jesus for 3 days and 3 nights for Him to emerge. They would have waited there with dutiful preparation for their Lord's triumphant emergence and resurrection from the dead. Maybe only one of them would have had doubt. And of course, that would have been doubting Thomas. But all of the rest would have been faithfully and obediently awaiting the Resurrection of their Lord. They would already be packed up for their reunion trip to Galilee to meet up with their Risen Lord, just as He had instructed them to do.

Is that what happened? Is that how the Synoptic Gospels recorded themselves? Is this how they wrote themselves into eternal history? No, they recorded nothing like that. If this was a fairy tale, then the Disciples would have painted themselves in a completely different light. Instead, they were afraid, grieving, weeping, and filled with unbelief. They were *all* weeping in sorrow and filled with great fear behind locked doors. This was because they had just lost their leader and their Lord.

They were afraid because they feared that they would be killed next just as Jesus had been killed. Peter swore that he would not deny his Lord. However, he denied even knowing Jesus three times because of the fear that he would be grabbed next. These Disciples were afraid for their lives and weeping over their severe loss. Does this sound like any lie that you would make up about yourself? Would you voluntarily write that you abandoned your Lord 3 times in one night, if it was just a lie? And remember, Peter would go on to become the foundation of the Church.

Who on planet Earth really thinks that a bunch of liars are going to write themselves into history like this??? That is completely devoid of logic. Do you really think that a made-up religion is going to paint "The Rock of the Church" as someone who is afraid, and abandons his Lord in his greatest time of need? Just listen to what Jesus tells all of his Disciples as they were walking to the Mount of Olives; in Matthew 26:31 (KJV), Jesus tells them:

> All ye shall be offended because of me this night: for it
> is written, I will smite the shepherd, and the sheep of
> the flock shall be scattered abroad.

This means that *all* of Jesus' Disciples abandoned him, not just Peter!

Do you really think that this would ever be put into print if this whole thing were just a lie? What liar would do that to themselves? That makes absolutely no sense whatsoever. Once again, we have to use our common sense here. These stories were not written by their enemies who would have lied about their behavior. These details are all written by the Disciples themselves.

We have to ask the question: Who is going to want to join a Church with those kinds of issues? I will tell you this, no group of liars is going to put painful lies like this into print for all to read. The only way that anyone would write about themselves like this, is if they were honest enough to put these embarrassing truths into print. If the New Testament is a fabrication based upon lies, then you have to explain why 10 of these original Disciples would go on to be killed in the name of Jesus. How do you explain that? You would have to explain why they preached a lie until they were all murdered for it, instead of just admitting that they were lying.

And another thing, all of these Disciples were Jewish men. What Jewish person is going to denounce his God and his religion so that they can run off and follow a fairy tale?? As a Jewish person, the most important thing in their life was their eternal soul returning to God. Can someone please tell me why 12 Jewish men, and the Pharisee Saul from Tarsus, would just, all of a sudden, throw their eternal souls away? They have been working their entire lives on returning their eternal souls to their Creator. Did all of these men go out of their minds at the same time?? What are the odds of that? No, Jewish men and women are not going to throw their eternal inheritance and their anointing away for a lie. These followers believed that they were indeed, in the presence of the Messiah.

Now, getting back to Paul, we see that he had the task of travelling as a missionary to establish and sustain the Churches throughout the Mediterranean, Galatia, and Asia Minor. In addition, we observe in 2 Corinthians 11:28, that Paul also had the daily burden of being the Church's daily administrator. His burdens could not have been greater. And to assist Paul on his journeys, he had a companion named Luke who was a physician. Luke's main task was to support Paul's missionary work and to document their countless journeys together.

This brings us to Sir William Mitchell Ramsay who was a professor at Oxford University and was appointed Regius Professor of Humanity at Aberdeen. The only way to become a Regius Professor is to be appointed by a King or a Queen. He is considered to be a brilliant mind that was the foremost authority on Asia Minor, and he has been described as the "New Testament scholar without peer."[506] In addition, William Ramsay was knighted by the British crown for his work in archaeology.[507]

With that being said, the reason why William Ramsay is being mentioned here with Apostle Paul and Dr. Luke, is because Ramsay set out to prove that the writings of Luke, especially the Book of Acts, were false. We need to realize that William Ramsay's father was an atheist. And William Ramsay was such a staunch atheist himself that he specifically traveled to the Holy Land in order to prove that the Bible was filled with fables conjured up by monks. Ramsay was an outspoken atheist who was determined to expose the New Testament as a fraud. So, he packed up, set out, and traveled to the Holy Land to do this in person.

Ramsay focused his investigation on the stories of Paul and Luke as traveling missionaries. Ramsay believed the travel routes and ports of call that were recorded in the New Testament would be easy to disprove if they were false.[508] This is how Ramsay became committed to spending the next 15 years of his life in the tireless pursuit of the truth regarding Paul and Luke. After 15 years of intensive and relentless research to prove that the New Testament was a fraud, Ramsay concludes:

> The present writer takes the view that Luke's history is unsurpassed in respect of its trustworthiness. At this point, we are describing what reasons and arguments changed the mind of the one who began under the impression that the history was written long after the events and that it was untrustworthy as a whole (*The Bearing of Recent Discovery of the Trustworthiness of the New Testament*, 1915).[509]

I believe it is clear that William Ramsay changed his mind and now believes Apostle Luke's writings are trustworthy.

Here is another source that provides a revealing quote from Ramsay that is pertinent. The editing author states that Ramsay, a famed archaeologist, began a study of Asia Minor with little regard for the Book of Acts. Ramsay later wrote:

> I may fairly claim to have entered on this investigation without prejudice in favor of the conclusion which I shall now seek to justify to the reader. On the contrary, I began with a mind unfavorable to it. . . . It did not then lie in my line of life to investigate the subject minutely; but more recently I found myself brought into contact with the Book of Acts as an authority for the topography, antiquities and the society of Asia Minor. It was gradually borne upon me that in various details the narrative showed marvelous truth.[510]

We can see from this quote that Ramsay admits that at the start he was unfavorable to the Book of Acts as he did not think it contained the truth. But then as he progressed in his research, he found it to be incredibly accurate.

In the beginning, Ramsay sought to disprove the Book of Acts and history remembers him as a very important historical scholar. Ramsay has been honored with doctorates from nine universities and was knighted for his contributions to modern scholarship.[511] Disproving the Book of Acts and the Bible was Ramsay's sole purpose for investigating the Holy Land. Ramsay spent over 15 years on this quest, but at the end of his investigation and archaeological research he stated:

> Luke is a historian of the first rank; not merely are his statements of fact trustworthy'. . .'this author should be placed along with the very greatest of historians'. . .'Luke's history is unsurpassed in respect of its trustworthiness.'[512]

It turns out that Luke names 32 countries, 54 cities, and nine islands without error. As the great scholar A. N. Sherwin-White states:

> For Acts (Book of Acts) the confirmation of historicity is overwhelming. Any attempt to reject its basic historicity must now appear absurd. Roman historians have long taken it for granted.[513]

Most of the arguments against the New Testament turn out to be either from a lack of detailed historical knowledge of the ancient Roman world, or from a misreading of the New Testament documents which have been proven over and over to be trustworthy accounts.

After finding all of this out, Ramsay then spends the next 20 years investigating the rest of the New Testament. In total, 35 years of his life was spent trying to doggedly disprove the New Testament. In the end, this resulted in Sir William Mitchell Ramsay becoming a Christian because he was absolutely convinced by the evidence that he examined in the New Testament.[514]

This reminds me of what Napoleon Bonaparte is quoted as telling General Charles de Montholon:

The Bible is no mere book, but a Living Creature, with a power that conquers all that oppose it.[515]

Clearly Napoleon believed in God for him to make such a definitive statement about the Holy Bible. I would like to point out that this wonderful statement comes from the military genius who is deemed by many military experts to be the greatest tactical general of all time.[516] This quote from Napoleon demonstrates that the greatest tactical general in history, admits that the Holy Bible conquers all who oppose it!

In getting back to the discussion of the accuracy of the Apostle Luke, this brings up the topic of a very serious accusation leveled against him and the entire New Testament. I refer to this accusation as, *The Inquisition of Luke.* Some critics claim that Luke makes several false statements in his Gospel. These accusations of alleged falsehoods reside in Chapter 2, verses 1-4. Some critics even claim they reject the entire New Testament just because they believe some of these verses are false.

In defense of the entire New Testament and Apostle Luke, I am going to examine this very serious accusation and then present the facts. As I have stated, Ramsay found that Luke and the New Testament document the truth. Therefore, what I am going to present now is the actual research from William Ramsay's 15-year extensive investigation. Ramsay conducted a tremendous amount of hard work and I believe we should examine what he uncovered. Therefore, the extensive presentation that follows is the exhaustive research accumulated by William Ramsay that uncovered the truth regarding the New Testament and Luke's documentation.

The four verses in question refer to the time just before the birth of Jesus. Let's now examine the Gospel of Luke, Chapter 2:1-4 (KJV):

> *Verse 1:* "And it came to pass in those days, that there went out a decree from Caesar Augustus that all the world should be taxed."
>
> *Verse 2:* "(And this taxing was first made when Cyrenius [Quirinius] was governor of Syria."
>
> *Verse 3:* "And all went to be taxed, every one into his own city."
>
> *Verse 4:* "And, Joseph also went up from Galilee, out of the city of Nazareth, into Judea, unto the city of David, which is called Bethlehem; (because he was of the house and lineage of David:)."

Critics claim many serious errors involving these 4 verses. Some claim that the census did not involve the whole world. Some claim there was no such census and tax ordered by Augustus. Some claim that Quirinius was not governor of Syria until AD 6 which is nowhere near when Jesus was born. (Please note that Quirinius is also known as Cyrenius because the ancient Greeks did not use the letter Q). And finally, some claim that no one had to register in their hometown for a census as Joseph is claimed to have done in Bethlehem.

To start the examination of what Apostle Luke documented here, I will address the first verse by stating, when we read that Caesar Augustus published a decree ordering a tax of "…all the world," this meant, of course, the whole Roman world which was part of his Empire. Therefore, this verse only refers to the Roman Empire, not the entire world.[517]

With that said, in order to process people for a tax, the Romans first needed to conduct a census. Some scholars, such as William Ramsay refer to this administrative event as an *enrollment*.[518] Ramsay even specifies this event as the *First Enrollment*, while the *Great Enrollment* took place later, between AD 6 to AD 9.[519] Therefore, be prepared to see this administrative decree referred to as a tax, a census, a registration, or an enrollment.

Next, I will discuss verse 2 of Chapter 2 in Luke's Gospel which mentions general Quirinius. Before I discuss this verse in-depth, you will notice this verse is in parentheses. This tells me that I need to present the original Greek for this verse. The original Greek of verse 2 translates into: "This registration first took place [when] Quirinius was governing Syria."[520] However, this situation is more complicated than it appears. General Quirinius did hold governing powers in Syria in the BC era, but Quirinius was not the primary domestic governor at that time. To shed more light on this situation, I once again present the esteemed scholar Sir William Mitchell Ramsay who investigated these very verses in his famous book, *Was Christ Born At Bethlehem?*

Ramsay points out that general Quirinius was based in Syria where he conducted a war in the Taurus mountains. The Taurus mountains were in the southern part of Galatia in present-day Turkey. General Quirinius would have conducted this war as a distinct official. Ramsay describes such a distinct official as a "*Dux.*" Therefore, Ramsay states that Quirinius was sent to Syria as a *Dux* at the same time that Syria was being ruled by its regular Roman domestic governor, who is officially referred to as the Primary Imperial Legate.[521]

A *Dux* is a Roman general who is sent into a province on special missions to conduct a war or to address special external affairs at the same time the Primary Imperial Legate is governing domestic affairs in that same province. While in Syria during these BC years, General Quirinius was a Lieutenant of Caesar Augustus (a *Dux*), who possessed the same technical rank as the Primary Imperial Legate.[522]

The official office that General Quirinius held as a *Dux*, was that of Legatus Augusti pro praetore, which translates as, Imperial Legate (Second Imperial Legate). There is a distinction between the added Second Imperial Legate officer (War governor) and the Primary Imperial Legate officer (Domestic governor), but their powers were equal.[523]

In a nutshell, the Primary Imperial Legate was the regular governor conducting internal affairs, while the Second Imperial Legate (*Dux*) was usually a waring governor conducting wars and special external affairs.

This means that General Quirinius held the same level of power as the Primary Imperial Legates that occupied Syria while Quirinius was stationed there for the Homonadenses War.[524] This explains why the Apostle Luke was able to select Quirinius and mention him in his Gospel. Luke was impressed with Quirinius as a Roman officer who was successful in commanding Rome's armies, directing Rome's foreign policies, and acting as a leader in Syria at that time.[525]

Therefore, for at least 5 years as the BC era was drawing to a close, Syria had two Roman officials at the same time with equal governing powers. One official was the Primary Imperial Legate, and as I have mentioned, the other distinct official was a *Dux*. The *Dux* was also an Imperial Legate but was not the Primary Imperial Legate. And in this case, the *Dux* was General Quirinius. Ramsay indicates that Quirinius (also known as Cyrenius) was in Syria for the first time, around 7 BC.[526] Ramsay also states that 3 BC is the latest that Quirinius could have completed this Syrian command.[527]

To demonstrate how careful Luke was in referring to General Quirinius, Ramsay tells us that:

> Luke, does not specify exactly what was the Roman office which Quirinius held at the time when the first enroll-ment was made. The Greek word which he uses occurs

elsewhere in his history, indicating the office of procurator; and the noun connected with it is even used to indicate the supreme authority exercised by the reigning Emperor of a province.[528]

In the original Greek, Luke described Quirinius as, "holding the Hegemonia of Syria." This means holding governing powers of Syria. A Hegemon is a Roman official that holds imperial governing powers granted by Caesar Augustus.[529] This does not necessarily mean the official is the Primary Imperial Legate (also known as the Resident Domestic governor). What all of this means is that Luke did not make a mistake in his Gospel when he mentioned General Quirinius held governing powers in Syria at the time Jesus was born.

The original Greek translation of Luke 2:2, is:

> This registration first took place [when] Cyrenius (Quirinius) was governing Syria.[530]

As Ramsay points out, the Greek word used describes Cyrenius (Quirinius) as holding the Hegemonia.[531] A *Hegemon* is not necessarily the domestic governor. Hegemon can also be used to describe someone as a commander, like a military commander.[532] More specifically, Luke used the verb *hegemoneuo* in reference to Quirinius. This word means Quirinius was exerting his authority in some way without necessarily holding the title of governor.[533]

I feel that now is a good time to review the duties of the two Roman officials who were based in Syria at the same time, around 7 BC.

1) General Publius Quinctilius Varus was the Primary Imperial Legate of Syria conducting domestic affairs. His duties also included keeping the peace in vassal kingdoms like Judea.[534]

2) General Publius Sulpicius Quirinius was a "Consul" with Imperial Legate powers in Syria to conduct the war effort in

present-day Turkey and to handle certain external affairs. And as such, Quirinius was a directly appointed representative of Caesar Augustus who was commanded to carry out the Imperial orders of the special mission of leading a war in Turkey against the Homonadenses.[535]

Ramsay specifically references the esteemed ancient Greek historian Strabo who stated the distinct official that was sent into Syria as a *Dux* in the BC era was indeed General Quirinius.[536] Strabo was also a world-famous geographer, philosopher and scholar.[537] According to Ramsay, Strabo documents that General Quirinius was stationed in Syria in 7 BC at the same time General Varus was serving in Syria as the domestic governor. Therefore, if anyone wishes to deny the fact that General Quirinius held governing powers in Syria between 6 BC and 5 BC (when Jesus was born), then you would be contradicting the highly esteemed and famous Greek historian Strabo.

It turns out that historian Strabo was born in 64 BCE and died after 21 CE.[538] This means that Strabo actually lived during both times in history when General Quirinius held governing powers in Syria (BC era and AD era). As a result, Strabo had the best vantage point to accurately describe exactly what happened at these points in history because he watched all of this history unfold. That being said, please take note that the ancient Greek historian Strabo is not to be confused with General Gnaeus Pompeius Strabo who was a Roman general and politician.

If critics wish to challenge and contradict the great Greek historian Strabo, they would be contradicting clearly documented historical facts. Strabo was there, the critics were not. These historical facts prove that General Quirinius did indeed hold governing powers in Syria during the period that the Apostle Luke said that he did as recorded in Luke 2:2 (KJV).

Because of its supreme importance, I'm going to clarify this one more time, as a result of Rome's war declaration against the Homonadenses in present-day Turkey, Rome sent a distinct Lieutenant of Caesar Augustus with supreme Imperial powers to execute the Emperor's direct orders to conduct this war. It was because of this war effort that Syria had both a Primary Imperial Legate and a Second Imperial Legate (referred to as a *Dux*). They were both in Syria at the same time and possessed the same technical rank and title of Imperial Legates. This means their power and authority were on the same level.[539]

This is how Syria possessed two governors at the same time.[540] This continued to be the case for almost ten years because the war lasted that long. The confusion that exists here, revolves around the fact that many historians question why Quirinius would be in Syria, if Syria already had a Primary Legatus? A Primary Legatus (Primary Imperial Legate) is also referred to as a Resident Legatus (Resident Legate). The researchers asking this question don't see the timeline where Quirinius could fit in-between the other governors. The explanation for this is that Quirinius was not in-between them, he was there in addition to them.[541] Quirinius was not considered the "Primary" Legatus or the "Primary" Imperial Legate governor. Quirinius was a *Dux*. He was sent to Syria specifically for the war effort.

People need to understand this part of Roman history. Quirinius later became the Primary Legatus when he governed Syria in AD 6 (a.k.a. Resident Imperial Legate). This is the well-known Syrian governing command of Quirinius that modern-day historians recognize and refer to. Nevertheless, that is a separate command that came about 9 years after Quirinius won the war against the Homonadenses when he governed that war from Syria. The Homonadenses War was the **first time** that General Quirinius was dispatched to Syria.

Therefore, the AD 6 Syrian Primary Imperial Legate governor post of Quirinius, was indeed Quirinius' first Resident Imperial Legate command (he was no longer a "Dux"), however, this was the second time Quirinius possessed governing powers in Syria.[542]

As stated, the reason why all of this is so important is that some critics attempt to discredit Luke and the entire New Testament because they claim that Luke made false statements in Luke 2:1-4. An online critic said that he rejects the entire New Testament because of Luke 2:1-4. He specifically used the AD 6 command of Quirinius as his reason to discredit Luke and the New Testament. If this person knew the complete Roman history instead of only a part of it, then he would have a very different opinion. These critics are the ones in error; Apostle Luke is not the one in error. I am heavily concentrating on this topic because the stakes are very high, and the historical truths need to be known.

That being said, if people like this critic still have an issue with Luke regarding these verses, then the real issue resides with them contradicting the highly esteemed Greek historian Strabo. Strabo was alive when Quirinius was alive; these present-day critics weren't. Are we going to believe critics who weren't even alive when Quirinius lived, or are we going to believe the ancient Greek historian Strabo? The logical choice is obvious. And once we place our trust in the esteemed historian Strabo, this allows us to place our trust in the Apostle Luke.

Scholar William Mitchell Ramsay points out that Strabo specifically names Quirinius as the distinct official that conducted the war that conquered the Homonadenses and revenged the death of Amyntas. Ramsay states that he figures that Augustus had Quirinius in Syria in 7/6 BC for this war when Varus came to govern Syria. This places Quirinius in Syria between 6 BC and 5 BC, right where Luke said that he was. And the famous ancient Greek historian Strabo confirms Quirinius by name as being the distinct extra official that Rome sent to Syria to defeat the Homonadenses and revenge the death of Amyntas.[543] Ramsay states that Caesar Augustus sent Quirinius to Syria to start the Homonadenses War. And Ramsay states that he believes Quirinius fought that war from 7 BC to at least 5 BC[544] However, Ramsay also admits that Quirinius could have been in Syria waging this war as late as 3 BC.[545]

History suggests this war lasted longer than 2-3 years. This was not a normal command, so it was not going to only last the traditional 2-3 years that a typical Legate command would require. This war duty assignment was going to last as long as it took to win this war. That said, Quirinius was going to stay there until it was won. There are modern-day historians who indicate that Quirinius started fighting this war in 12 BC.[546] As stated, Ramsay believes the latest Quirinius could have remained in Syria for this war was 3 BC.[547] Taking all of this into consideration, it appears this war lasted a long time and places Quirinius was in Syria for about 10 years, not 2 to 3 years. And since many scholars strongly believe that Jesus was born in either 6 BC or 5 BC, even Ramsay's shorter timeline for the duration of this Homonadenses War, still works to validate what the Apostle Luke has documented. That said, based on modern research, I believe Quirinius was stationed in Syria for the first time as a commander for about 10 years.

I wish to stress that a game-changing historic revelation has been uncovered by Ramsay once he confirmed that historian Strabo identified Quirinius by name. There is "no doubt" as to who the distinct official was that was sent to Syria to defeat the Homonadenses and revenge the death of Amyntas.[548] Strabo definitely places Quirinius in Syria in the BC years when Quirinius used the Roman military base in Syria from which to fight the Homonadenses War.

As mentioned, General Varus was the Primary Imperial Legate of Syria during this period. In fact, General Varus became notably involved in history in 4 BC regarding Herod. In the spring of 4 BC, Caesar Augustus gave imperial orders for Sabinus, who was a "Procurator," to audit Herod's Estate.[549] However, Sabinus causes a riot with his aggressive actions in Jerusalem. Varus was not in Jerusalem because he had left for Antioch on business. This gave Sabinus, who was sent to settle Herod's estate, the opportunity to cause a serious riot and revolt in Jerusalem that included him taking 400 talents of gold from the Jewish Temple.[550] Varus finally took control and had 2,000 Jews crucified for the revolt in the summer of 4 BC.[551] This reinforces that Herod probably died in the spring of 4 BC. I just can't imagine that Sabinus would loot the Temple's gold like that if Herod was still alive. It seems that Herod's death provided a temporary power vacuum where Sabinus thought that he could exploit the situation and plunder the Temple's gold.

Now, to clarify the duty responsibilities in Syria, I will give a breakdown of what the various duties were from my research:

1) General Titius was the Primary Imperial Legate governor of Syria from 13/12 BC to 10/9 BC.[552]

2) General Saturninus was the Primary Imperial Legate governor of Syria from 9 BC to 7 BC.[553] He was supposed to have conducted the 8 BC enrollment/census of Syria. The famous ancient author Tertullian claimed that Saturninus made the first periodic enrollment of Syria in 8/7 BC.[554] It makes sense that Saturninus would have conducted an enrollment in Syria because a Syrian enrollment is classified as an internal affair.

However, Ramsay does state that Tertullian's hasty assumption that Saturninus also conducted the enrollment in Palestine in 6 BC, was incorrect. This is because the command of Saturninus had come to an end and he was no longer stationed in Syria by 6 BC.[555]

3) Recent research indicates that General Quirinius was dispatched to Syria by Rome to conduct a war against the Homonadenses Tribes in 12 BC.[556] The Homonadenses were troublesome tribes that occupied present-day Turkey. Remember, Ramsay's earlier research led him to believe that Quirinius arrived in Syria in 7 BC.[557] According to Ramsay, Quirinius was sent to Syria as a war general (*Dux*) and remained there as late as 3 BC.[558] With that being said, modern-day scholars Holden and Geisler agree that the Homonadenses War commanded by General Quirinius was conducted between 12 BC and 2 BC (2013, as cited by Windle, 2019).[559] This research establishes that all of the mentioned scholars agree that Quirinius was in Syria between 7 BC and 3 BC. In addition to his war duties, he was also responsible for governing the administration of foreign *external affairs* outside of Syria.[560]

4) General Varus was the Primary Imperial Legate governor of Syria from 7 BC to 4 BC.[561] His duties extended outside of Syria only to keep the peace in the associated vassal kingdoms like Judea. This is why Varus was the one to put down the riots in Jerusalem in 4 BC.[562]

The Roman Empire practiced a logical method of rule. This is why we read from Ramsay that Rome had, on occasion, a history of dispatching an additional *Dux* Imperial Legate to wage war so that the Primary Imperial Legate would not be distracted from his domestic governing. Everyone had their duty. The *domestic affairs* Legates (Titius, Saturninus, and Varus) had different duties compared to the military and *external affairs* Legate (Quirinius).[563] Once again, everyone had their duty. Rome was very organized and disciplined in its imperial structure. This is what made them so successful, and this appears to be the way that ancient Rome delegated the various duties mentioned above.

I mention this because it may answer the question that some may have as to why Quirinius did not assist Varus in putting down the civilian uprising in Jerusalem? This may even make some people question whether Quirinius was still in Syria in 4 BC? As mentioned, Varus was the primary governor of Syria who started in 7 BC and served until 4 BC. This is why Varus had to march from Syria into Jerusalem to put down the revolt in 4 BC. And this explains why Quirinius had nothing to do with that uprising. Maintaining peace in Jerusalem was the responsibility of Varus. Quirinius had a war to win in Galatia and was focused on those orders. Quirinius was not going to split his forces, distract his troops, or distract himself with Varus' *civilian issues*. Varus was the general responsible for maintaining peace in the outside vassal kingdom provinces like Palestine and Judea.[564]

This means that the situations were different for Quirinius and Varus regarding their use of military force. Quirinius used his powers to wage war against military combatants, while Varus was called upon to put down a civilian uprising. There is a big difference between these two duties as one duty falls under the jurisdiction of a Dux war general while the other falls under the jurisdiction of the Primary Imperial Legate.

The fact that Quirinius is not helping Varus should not cause us to believe that Quirinius has already left Syria. This war was so difficult to win that Rome had to embark on special military construction projects in 6 BC which included the building of 5 garrison cities with imperial roads to connect them.[565] If Rome was initiating all of this military construction in 6 BC in this rugged mountainous campaign in Turkey just to win this war, it means this war was not even close to being over. The construction of the fortresses alone would take 6-12 months because of the rugged terrain. Therefore, based on these significant war construction projects, it seems reasonable to conclude this war took another 3 years to bring to an end.

This was a decade-long war that stretched from 12 BC to 3 BC. The ultimate resolution of this long and drawn-out war explains why Quirinius received not one but two prestigious Supplicationes, and the Ornamenta Triumphalia processions for this victory.[566] This war was so difficult to finally win that Rome decided to give General Quirinius two parades instead of just one. That war dragged on for more than 2-3 years, and we see support of this when Ramsay states:

> Now, his (Quirinius) Syrian administration was earlier,
> and therefore 4 BC to 3 BC is the latest that he can have
> spent in Syria.[567]

Here we can see Ramsay admitting that Quirinius may have been in Syria fighting this war until 3 BC.

To reinforce that Luke's documentation of Quirinius is correct, I will now present the illustrious career of General Quirinius so that we can follow along and get a clearer picture of his military career. This allows us to see where he was, what he was doing, and when he was doing it. I will list the accomplishments in the order that I perceive them to have occurred. The career of Publius Sulpicius Quirinius is as follows:

1) In 15 BC, Quirinius appears to have been proconsul of Crete and Cyrene where he led a successful campaign against the North

African Marmaridae Tribe. This war seems to have lasted from 15 BC to 12 BC.[568]

2) Because Quirinius secured these victories in North Africa in 12 BC, Caesar Augustus awarded Quirinius with the prestigious title of "Consul" in 12 BC and then dispatched Quirinius to Syria to put down the Homonadenses Tribes in the mountains of Cilicia (Turkey).[569] The arrival of Quirinius in Syria in 12 BC is supported by scholars Holden and Geisler (2013, as cited by Windle, 2019).[570]

3) Consul Quirinius was dispatched to put down the plundering Homonadensian Tribes in the mountains of Cilicia (Turkey) which is next to Syria. Quirinius officially possessed the title of "Consulship" when he was sent to Syria as a war general. Syria was a large Roman base with several legions stationed there. Syria was used as a launching point by Rome which had as many as four legions garrisoned in Syria at any given time.[571] It appears that Quirinius spent the next decade leading military campaigns from Syria to ultimately defeat the Homonadenses. Therefore, Quirinius was "governing" the war from Syria during the time of the "census" mentioned in Luke 2:2 (6 BC or 5 BC, when Jesus was born).

4) Quirinius finally secures a very hard-fought and drawn-out victory by 3 BC. The war was finally over.

5) It is at this point that Quirinius is ready for another assignment. Ramsay believes it is very possible the latest that Quirinius received his "Proconsulship" in Asia was 3 BC.[572] I fully agree with this conclusion. Quirinius ended the Homonadenses War in 3 BC and this is when he was awarded his Proconsulship in Asia. That command lasted one year from 3 BC to 2 BC.[573]

6) Then after serving in Asia, Quirinius appears to have been sent to command in Armenia in 2 BC. This command seems to have also

included the duties of starting the mentoring process of the prodigy Gaius Caesar. Then after the completion of that one-year command, Quirinius leaves Armenia and Lollius was sent in 1 BC to take over the mentoring of Gaius Caesar.[574]

7) Rome honors General Quirinius with two Supplicationes, and the Ornamenta Triumphalia processions in AD 2. This was a huge celebration that is very similar to a ticker-tape parade and Quirinius received two of them! Ramsay also mentions a fragment of marble that attests to this event that was found near Tibur (Tivoli) in AD 1764. Ramsay states all scholars agree and acknowledge this marble fragment is describing General Quirinius. Ramsay states that all of the highest authorities are in agreement, including Mommsen, Borghesi, de Rossi, Henzen, Dassau, and many others.[575] This archaeologic piece is now referred to as the *Fragment of the Sepulchral Inscription of Quirinius*.[576]

This marble fragment states that the recipient of these honors became Proconsul of Asia and twice governed Syria as Legatus of Caesar Augustus. This marble fragment also states that the Roman officer honored on this fragment was still alive at the time of the death of Caesar Augustus in AD 14. All of this perfectly describes the most important part of General Quirinius' career. There is no debate amongst serious scholars about this marble fragment referring to anyone else. The name is missing but every notable scholar has attributed this glorious career to General Quirinius.[577]

This marble tombstone acknowledged Quirinius' successful career and his dutiful service to Rome. The significance of this discovery involves this marble fragment stating the person being honored on it, had served two tours of duty in Syria. And as Ramsay states, all serious scholars attribute this honoring marble fragment to the career of General Quirinius. This confirms that Quirinius served two tours of duty in Syria. His first tour of duty in Syria was during BC years while his second tour of duty in Syria occurred during AD years.

One online critic tried to attribute this celebration marble fragment to Varus. That is impossible because Varus died five years before the death of Augustus. This marble fragment indicates that the officer honored on it was still alive when Caesar Augustus died.[578] In addition, Varus caused Rome's worse military failure in history by losing 18,000 soldiers in Germania which means he was not going to be honored for anything. More importantly, because Varus never served as proconsul of Asia, he could not possibly be the officer referred to on this stone. Varus served as proconsul in Africa, not Asia[579] As Ramsay states, there is no debate amongst the highest authorities, and they are all in agreement that this marble fragment is describing the illustrious career of General Quirinius.

This very thoroughly addresses the critics who accuse Luke of falsehoods in verse 2, of Chapter 2 of his Gospel. Quirinius most certainly was in Syria during the first enrollment which finally reached Palestine in 6 BC.[580] As a consequence, General Quirinius most certainly had governing powers as a *Dux* Imperial Legate when Luke said that he did.[581]

It is also worth mentioning here, that if the Syrian enrollment of 8 BC took until June/July of 6 BC to finally reach Palestine, and it then took another 2-3 months to get to Bethlehem from there, then Jesus was born in 6 BC. However, if it took 14-15 months to get from Palestine to Bethlehem, then Jesus was born in 5 BC. Once we figure out how long it took to get to Bethlehem, then we will know the exact birth year of Jesus.

8) Quirinius also seems to get married somewhere around AD 2. My guess from what Ramsay states is that Quirinius gets married

at the end of AD 2. This could have taken place after his parade processions.[582]

9) Lollius died in AD 2 and this caused General Quirinius to be sent back to Armenia to take command and continue the tutoring of Gaius Caesar. Ramsay thinks Quirinius was in Armenia with Gaius Caesar from AD 2 until the very end of AD 3.[583] It seems clear that Quirinius was stationed in Armenia twice. Despite this, the prodigy prince Gaius Caesar tragically gets wounded in battle and died in AD 4.

10) Quirinius is granted the title of Resident (Primary) Imperial Legate of Syria in AD 6. This is his second governing command in Syria. Quirinius holds this office from AD 6 to AD 9.[584] This is the governing command in Syria that most people think about regarding General Quirinius.

11) Quirinius effectively retires in AD 9.

For those of you wondering why Luke would mention Quirinius instead of Varus in his Gospel, I have an explanation. As mentioned, Varus entered the vassal territory of Jerusalem in 4 BC when he went there to put down the civilian revolt. Varus had 2,000 Jews crucified in 4 BC.[585] I will add that Varus had at least 2,000 Jews crucified in 4 BC. I say this because there are some scholars who state that Varus had this done to more than 2,000 Jews. As a consequence, Varus would have clearly been reviled by the Jews for this. Therefore, perhaps Luke chose to only mention Quirinius in order to be sensitive to the Jewish readers of the Gospels. In addition to the crucifixions of 2,000 Jews, it is also possible that because Sabinus was a colleague of Varus, the Jews may have suspected that Varus wound up with some of their Temple's gold which was looted by Sabinus. I'm sure that none of the Jews wanted to hear or read anything mentioning Varus.

Another reason to avoid mention of Varus would be rooted in the fact that he caused Rome's worst military defeat in its history by losing 18,000 Roman soldiers in Germania. If any Romans were reading the Gospels, they did not want to hear the name of Varus mentioned ever again. Rome was so devastated by Varus' defeat that Augustus would say for years, "Quinctilius Varus, give me back my Legions!"[586] Remember, by the time that Luke wrote his Gospel it was around AD 70. That was after Varus lost those 3 Roman Legions, which eventually caused Varus to commit suicide. That being said, Luke only needed to mention one of the two people with governing powers in Syria when Jesus was born, and Luke wisely chose to mention Quirinius. It's easy for me to see why Varus would go unmentioned; it would have been politically incorrect to talk about Varus.

It's at this point that I will move on to Luke 2, verse 3. Now, as far as the enrollments are concerned, William Ramsay discusses the Syrian 8/7 BC enrollment. The first thing that I wish to point out is that Luke does not state that Quirinius was the one who actually "conducted" the enrollment. Luke merely states that Quirinius had governing powers in Syria when this census was conducted which was also when Jesus was born. We see evidence from Ramsay that Saturninus started the first periodic enrollment of Syria in 8/7 BC. The reason why this enrollment occurred is because 8 BC marked a special year in the administration of the Roman Empire.

Augustus was engineering a new Rome, and this involved establishing a new era of organization in 8 BC. Thus, a 14-year enrollment cycle was established in 8 BC.[587] This also pertains to verse 1 in Chapter 2 of the Gospel of Luke. There most certainly was a census/enrollment that occurred in 8 BC. This was part of the infrastructure that Caesar Augustus was now engineering to organize and modernize the Roman

Empire.[588] As a result, it appears that Saturninus conducted the first periodic enrollment of Syria in 8/7 BC. With that being said, the 8/7 BC enrollment in Judea appears to have been the responsibility of Herod who asked Saturninus for a time extension in conducting this enrollment.[589] We know from Ramsay that the enrollment of Palestine was delayed by Herod until the late summer or autumn of 6 BC.[590] Herod governed Judea because he was the king of the Jews.

This means we know the 8 BC Syrian enrollment had reached Palestine by around June of 6 BC. Once again, if it took 3 months for this enrollment to progress from Palestine to Bethlehem, then Jesus was born in 6 BC. But, if it took 15 months, then Jesus was born in 5 BC. This is the closest we can get to being able to pin-point the exact year Jesus was born.

We see further supporting evidence for this BC enrollment where Ramsay states:

> Tertullian's procedure was probably this: he knew that an enrollment period fell in 9 BC, which was the first enrollment; and Roman authorities either official documents or historians, showed him that Sentius Saturninus was governor of Syria at that time. The only other alternative seems to be that he investigated Roman documents and found evidence that a census of Syria had been held by Saturninus. In the former case he was aware of the Fourteen-Year's-Cycle; in the latter case he knew of a census of Syria about 9-7 BC; and in either case he is an important yet independent witness in favour of Luke, so far as concerns the reality of a Syrian enrollment about 9-7 BC.[591]

Ramsay specifically states that Tertullian is an important and independent witness in favor of Luke, so far as regarding the reality of a Syrian enrollment around 9-7 BC. Tertullian was a prominent Christian theologian and author who is regarded as the Father of Latin Theology. I agree with Ramsay, by Tertullian stating this, he acknowledged that an enrollment did occur around 8 BC.[592]

I might also add that I have witnessed several scholars debating whether Quirinius could have been the person who conducted this enrollment. Personally, I am not claiming that Quirinius conducted the enrollment that occurred during the time Jesus was born. From what I read in the Gospel of Luke, 2:1-4 (KJV), I don't see anything that claims Quirinius was the Roman officer who conducted this enrollment. What I read in these verses is that Caesar Augustus ordered a registration/enrollment. Then, we are told General Quirinius held governing powers of some sort in Syria when this registration first occurred. Here is the translation of the original Greek of the first three verses in the Book of Luke:

> It came to pass then in those days, a decree went out from Caesar Augustus, to register all the world (verse 1). This registration first took place (when) Quirinius was governing Syria (verse 2). And all were going to be registered each to the city of themselves (verse 3).[593]

As mentioned, verse 2 can be even more accurately translated to read, "This registration first took place (when) Quirinius was holding the Hegemonia of Syria."[594] This means that Quirinius held governing power or military commanding power in Syria. Ramsay states that Luke was very careful mentioning Quirinius because Luke does not specify exactly what Roman office Quirinius held in Syria when this first enrollment occurred.[595] To hold military governing power is not the same as being the domestic governor, especially in the case of a *Dux*. Therefore, Caesar's enrollment registration, and Quirinius commanding military forces in Syria, represent two different historical facts that were being used to mark the timeframe when Jesus was about to be born. Essentially, these two facts were being used by Luke to triangulate when Jesus was born. In Luke's testimony, I don't read that Quirinius is being claimed to have been the person who conducted this enrollment.

That said, let's remember, this 8 BC registration was the first initiation of Rome's new organized municipal administrative census enumeration plan which was also referred to as the "First Enrollment."[596] This event is not to be confused with the AD 6 registration which was referred to as "The Great Census" or "The Great Enrollment."[597] Therefore, it seems reasonable to figure Luke intended to draw attention to when this special registration *first* took place because it correlated with when Jesus was born. At that same time, the birth of Jesus also happened to correlate with when Quirinius was the military commander in Syria. As explained, it would have been *unpopular* for Luke to have mentioned Varus in his Gospel. Since Luke was able to choose between mentioning either Quirinius or Varus to mark the birth of Jesus, Luke logically chose to only mention Quirinius.

With all of this being said, I don't see any indication from Luke that Quirinius was being claimed to be the person who conducted this first enrollment. Possibly, this assumption has been made because the governor of Syria should be the person conducting this enrollment in territories controlled by Syria. But this assumption is flawed regarding Quirinius because he was a *Dux*.[598] Quirinius was not the Primary (domestic) Imperial Legate. That person was General Varus. Therefore, I feel efforts are being wasted debating whether Quirinius was the officer who conducted this enrollment. As a Christian, I am not claiming Quirinius conducted this enrollment. I am, however, claiming that at the time when Jesus was born, this Roman enrollment was advancing through Judea at the same time General Quirinius held governing powers as a *Dux* in Syria, while prosecuting a war against the Homonadenses Tribes.[599]

As I have mentioned, you will notice that Ramsay believes Quirinius was in Syria for the first time with the earliest date being in 7 BC while the latest he could have left that command was in 3 BC.[600] However, modern scholars now believe the beginning of this range extends back to around 12 BC.[601] By adding all of this data together, we can see that the Homonadensian War probably lasted about 10 years.

At this point, let's move on to Herod's involvement regarding this enrollment. Ramsay speculates that Herod's involvement in this enrollment may have included "Tribal Numbering."[602] This would be the requirement to return to your ancestor's village and register if you were Jewish, like Joseph was. Ramsay goes through the possibility that the *Tribal Numbering* was Herod's technique to obscure from his population that he recently lost his title as "Caesar's Friend" and had been demoted. Apparently, Herod had conducted a war against the Arabians without the approval of Caesar Augustus.[603] This is why Herod was demoted and lost his status as, "Caesar's Friend." This was humiliating for Herod. Before this demotion, the Jewish population under Herod pledged their allegiance to him. And then he pledged their allegiance and his allegiance to Caesar. This prevented the Jews from having to pledge allegiance directly to Caesar.

However, once Herod was demoted by Caesar Augustus, all of Herod's subjects now had to register and pledge their allegiance directly to Caesar himself. In order to hide his demotion, Ramsay speculates Herod may have thought up the idea of *Tribal Numbering* as an excuse to give to people, instead of telling them they were now required to pledge their allegiance directly to Caesar.

Ramsay essentially states that *Tribal Numbering* was the concept that everyone under Herod's ruling influence would be expected to return to their hometowns and register a declaration of whether they were a real Jew or not? Since Herod was considered the king of the Jews, his subjects would have believed what he was telling them. This would have made the real Jews excited to return to their hometowns in order to assert that they were indeed true Jews. In this way, none of Herod's Jewish enemies would know he had been demoted by Caesar.[604] Herod's subjects would not have realized they were now agreeing to swear subordination to Caesar.

We are not just talking about the Roman 8 BC enrollment here, there is the additional requirement that all of Herod's subjects had to now pledge their allegiance directly to Caesar. This is something that the Jews under Herod never had to do while Herod was "Caesar's Friend." Herod could very well have been trying to hide this new allegiance requirement with a *Tribal Numbering* scheme. Therefore, Herod's *Tribal Numbering* is one of the speculated reasons why Jews like Joseph were required to return to their ancestor's hometown. King David is the ancestor of Joseph, and Bethlehem was King David's hometown. If Herod did attempt to mask his demotion with a *Tribal Numbering* smokescreen, this would explain why Joseph was required to return to Bethlehem for this enrollment.

Ramsay points out the time of the year for such registration would have been in the months before it got cold because it requires people to travel back to their hometowns.[605] Ramsay believes this would have been between August and October which agrees with the impression that Jesus was born in September and not December, as many scholars believe.

Ramsay also mentions another reason for a possible requirement for Joseph to return to Bethlehem to enroll. Ramsay states this enrollment is similar to the periodic enrollments by households in Egypt. It seems that Egypt required registration of inhabitants, property, and values. This required that people return to their hometowns. Ramsay states that if Caesar Augustus had instituted a periodic enrollment system in Egypt like this, then Augustus would have also ordered a similar system for the entire empire. What we see carried out in Syria should demonstrate that.[606] Ramsay states that in all probability, Augustus inaugurated a series of enrollments in Egypt.[607] Ramsay states that Augustus was extremely fond of Egypt and favored Egypt. I'm under the impression that Ramsay is stating that Augustus started these enrollments in Egypt first, then implemented them throughout the rest of the Roman empire in 8 BC.

Scholars explain that an Egyptian papyrus from AD 104 confirms the necessity of returning to one's homeland for a census. This is what was ordered:

> Because of the approaching census, it is necessary that all those residing for any cause away from their homes should at once prepare to return to their own governments in order that they may complete the family registration of the enrollment and that the titled lands may retain those belonging to them.[608]

What we see here are a few examples of legitimate historical reasons why the 8 BC Syrian Enrollment, which did not reach Bethlehem until 6/5 BC, may have indeed required citizens to return to their place of birth.

The story of Sir William Mitchell Ramsay is a wonderful one, because his life started out with him being an atheist who set out to prove that Luke and the New Testament were both fraudulent. And because of Ramsay's extreme efforts to disprove the writings of Luke and the New Testament, he winds up becoming the first person to discover that Luke's documentation in Chapter 2, verses 1-4, are historically accurate. Because of all of this extensive research by Sir William Mitchell Ramsay, we can see he was correct when he stated that the Apostle Luke was a fine historian of the first rank.

Not only did Sir William Mitchell Ramsay's tireless research exonerate the Apostle Luke and the New Testament, but just as important, these truths are what transformed this outspoken and stubborn atheist into a Christian! And that, my friends, is a wonderful story, of a wonderful life!

CHAPTER TWELVE

Fulfilled Prophecies

Dr. Peter Stoner is the chairman of the Department of Mathematics and Astronomy at Pasadena College. Stoner has identified 55 Old Testament prophecies that he says have been fulfilled by Jesus as the Messiah. To grasp the significance of this, consider that Stoner states the mathematical probability of Jesus fulfilling just eight of these prophecies is less than 1 in 10 to the 17th power (that's one in 100,000,000,000,000,000). This number is incomprehensible. If you placed 100 quadrillion silver dollars over the state of Texas, they would not only completely cover the Lone Star State, they would do so in stacks two feet high! The odds of finding one specific coin out of 100 quadrillion silver dollars are truly astronomical.[609]

Let's examine one of these astonishing prophecies. Around 605 BC a devout Hebrew named Daniel was taken into captivity by Babylon. Daniel began to prophesy around 540-537 BC. He was such an accurate dream interpreter and prophet that he continually received high positions in the government even though he was a member of a captive people.

- Nebuchadnezzar promoted Daniel to one of the highest governing positions possible after an accurate dream interpretation.
- Belteshazzar promoted Daniel to one of the highest governing positions possible after Daniel read and interpreted mysterious handwriting on a wall.
- Darius promoted Daniel to one of the highest positions in the kingdom.[610]

Then Daniel is visited by the Archangel Gabriel in Daniel 9:21-27 (KJV), who gives him a vision of the future:

> Yea, whiles I was speaking in prayer, even the man Gabriel, whom I had seen in the vision at the beginning, being caused to fly swiftly, touched me about the time of the evening oblation.
>
> And he informed me, and talked with me, and said, O Daniel, I am now come forth to give thee skill and understanding.
>
> At the beginning of thy supplications the commandment came forth, and I am come to shew thee; for thou art greatly beloved: therefore, understand the matter, and consider the vision.
>
> Seventy weeks are determined upon thy people and upon thy holy city, to finish the transgression, and to make an end of sins, and to make reconciliation for iniquity, and to bring in everlasting righteousness, and to seal up the vision and prophecy, and to anoint the most Holy.
>
> Know therefore and understand, that from the going forth of the commandment to restore and to build Jerusalem unto the Messiah the Prince shall be seven weeks,

and threescore and two weeks: the street shall be built again, and the wall, even in troublous times.

And after threescore and two weeks shall Messiah be cut off, but not for himself: and the people of the prince that shall come shall destroy the city and the sanctuary; and the end thereof shall be with a flood, and unto the end of the war desolations are determined.

Let's analyze this intricate and amazing prophecy. The first thing to note is there are 70 "weeks" in total. Clearly, each "week" is not a standard Sunday through Saturday cycle of 168 hours. If these were standard weeks of 24-hour days, all the events involving this prophecy would be occurring in just under a year and a half. It hardly seems likely the momentous events described could be squeezed into such a short timeframe. And if they were, this prophecy would not wind up anywhere near the life of Jesus. Instead, as I have mentioned before, we should understand that each "week" is a grouping of seven years and the angel is using language that constitutes symbolic "apocalyptic literature."[611]

That being said, the first seven "weeks" are 7 X 7 = 49 years. Then the next 62 "weeks" come out to 62 X 7 = 434 years. Adding 49 + 434 = 483 years.[612] This needs to be converted to modern years which comes out to 470 modern years. The Hebrew calendar was 12 months, each with 30 days, for a total of 360 days. Our calendar, of course, is 365 days. However, the question we must ask is: when does this prophetic clock start ticking? According to the prophecy, "the issuing of the decree to restore and rebuild Jerusalem" marks the beginning of the 70 weeks. Historians know that this happened in 444 BC, when king Artaxerxes sent Nehemiah, a trusted Jewish official in the Persian Empire, to lead in the rebuilding of the walls of Jerusalem, which at that time lay in ruins.[613]

Now, if we advance 470 years from 444 BC this brings us to the last "week" of the Messiah's ministry, during which the Anointed One will be "cut off. . . ." Note that the Greek word, *Christ*, means, *Anointed One*, which is the same as the Hebrew word, *Messiah*. At the end of this prophecy, the Anointed One will "confirm a Covenant" for one week which is seven years long. But in the middle of this last "week" he will put an end to sacrifice and offering. This only happens because he is "cut off." The middle of seven years is three and a half years—which is how long Jesus' ministry lasted before he was "cut off."[614]

Jesus' Crucifixion ended blood sacrifices as a sin offering because *He* was the final and most perfect sacrifice. Jesus' Crucifixion started the New Covenant where sacrifice and offering were no longer necessary because He came to die for our sins once and for all. Jesus was the last sacrifice. Putting all the figures together, we find the prophecy's last week begins in AD 26—precisely what we have discovered through other means—and ends three and a half years later. Since we know Jesus was crucified in AD 30[615] This means the prophesy's last week started in AD 26. Jesus started His ministry in late AD 26. This means that by Passover of AD 30 (which was in April), the ministry of Jesus lasted 3½ years. This agrees with the timeframe associated with Daniel's prophecy.

According to Daniel, the Messiah had to die as a sacrifice around AD 30. In addition, Jesus had to arrive before AD 70 when Jerusalem was destroyed by the Romans. How much more accurate can you reasonably be?[616] In summary, we have the first seven "weeks," the next 62 "weeks," and then we go halfway through the last "week." This prophecy seems to fit perfectly with when His ministry was to begin, how long it was to last, and when His death was to occur.

While some critics of the Bible have claimed the Book of Daniel was written much later, during the Exile, and by someone other than the prophet Daniel, no one has ever been able to prove this. In addition, no one has ever asserted it was written at the time of Jesus Christ. This means this prophecy was written long before Jesus came to the earth. The astounding accuracy of Daniel's prophecy of the "70 weeks," written centuries before Jesus, proves that the Bible is of Divine origin.

Now let's look at just one more powerful but brief prophecy about Jesus. The prophet Micah, who lived in southern Judah from approximately 750-700 BC, foretold of the Messiah being born in Bethlehem. As Micah 5:2 (KJV) predicts:

> But thou, Bethlehem Ephratah, though thou be little among the thousands of Judah, yet out of thee shall he come forth unto me that is to be ruler in Israel; whose goings forth have been from of old, from everlasting.

Clearly the Messiah's birthplace was predicted more than 700 years before his birth. This was no Christian invention. Even the Jerusalem Talmud Berakoth 5a. states, "The King Messiah . . . from where does he come forth? From the royal city of Bethlehem in Judah."[617] Luke 2:4 informs us that Jesus was born in this small Judean town, which was also the hometown of King David a thousand years before. As Luke 2:4 (KJV) informs us, "And Joseph also went up from Galilee, out of the city of Nazareth, into Judaea, unto the city of David, which is called Bethlehem; (because he was of the house and lineage of David:)." It is a seemingly small detail to pinpoint the birthplace of Jesus, but it is not so small when you consider all the other places where He could have been born.

Peter Stoner considered 55 prophecies fulfilled by Jesus. We have looked at two of them. Whether we study dozens or only two, the fact remains, only Jesus has the Messianic credentials predicted by the Hebrew Scriptures. He alone is the Messiah and worthy of our trust.

Jesus was not only born in Bethlehem, but Jesus was also to be immaculately conceived with Mother Mary because Jesus had to be Divine. In this way, He would not be fully man. This conflicts with what people in ancient Jerusalem were waiting for. They were expecting the Messiah to be fully man because the Messiah's father had to be of the proper Jewish pedigree. Many people know that Joseph was a descendent of King David. Joseph descended from King David through one of his sons, King Solomon. I mention this because many people are under the impression that the Messiah was supposed to be of the lineage of King David through Solomon. However, Joseph was not the biological father of Jesus. It is also a fact that Mother Mary was also descended from King David. Mary was related to King David's other son, Nathan. Nathan and Solomon were brothers. Nathan was Mary's legal ancestor.

As mentioned, many people are under the impression that scripture prophecies the Messiah had to be a blood descendant of King David through King Solomon. However, I have witnessed at least one scholar online who states there is no requirement in writing that mandates the Messiah had to be a direct descendant of King Solomon. With that being said, the Messiah did have to be a descendant of King David.

What is very interesting in this case, it turns out that a prophecy spoke of the offspring of Nathan's wife Hephzibah being the mother of the Messiah. The Messiah would be her descendant. This explanation is found in: Zohar III:173b, Parashat Shlach Lecha 45:298, Zohar.com.[618] I found this in an article by scholar Ben Burton who states that Nathan was married to Hephzibah, and apparently Nathan died before he could have any children.[619] This resulted in Nathan's brother, Solomon, legally marrying his wife, Hephzibah. This serves to carry on the legacy of Nathan's name. As a result, King Solomon bore her a son. Legally this son belongs to Nathan, however, this means Nathan's line is really Solomon's bloodline. All of the descendants of Nathan are really Solomon's offspring! As a consequence, Mary was a legal descendant of Nathan, but she was in fact a blood descendant of Solomon and Hephzibah.[620]

This means that Jesus was indeed a blood descendant of King David through Solomon. Mary's mother, St. Anna, was barren for most of her life. As a consequence, Mother Mary was a miracle blessing from God which explains why Mary was an only child. And because Mary was an only child, she inherited all the birthrights from her father.

Now, it is stated in John 19:25 (KJV), that at the Crucifixion, standing next to Mother Mary was her sister, Mary, the wife of Cleophas. That being said, scholars point out that Mary's parents are not going to name two of their daughters with the same name of Miriam (Mary). Therefore, the wife of Cleophas was probably Mother Mary's sister-in-law.[621] This is because Cleophas was the brother of Joseph, Mother Mary's husband. Therefore, if the wife of Cleophas is named Mary, then Mother Mary would have a sister-in-law named Mary.

As a side note, if by any chance Mother Mary did have any sisters, with Mary being the first-born daughter, she would have held the birthrights of a first-born son. I mention this because once Mary became the wife of Joseph, all of her legal rights were passed over to her husband. This means that legally, all of Mary's bloodline birthrights were passed to Joseph. Since Joseph was Jesus' legally adopted father, all of Mary's legal rights from the blood of Solomon were transferred legally to Jesus through Joseph's adoption. In this way, the lineage goes through the father just like Jewish law requires for the Messiah. This is how Jesus was blood related to Solomon and legally related to Nathan. All these rights were legally passed onto Jesus through his adopted father who married into this lineage. And, of course, Mary giving birth to Jesus physically passed the blood of King David and King Solomon onto Jesus. This is how the prophesy came to be fulfilled.

Burton is saying that Jesus was of the Davidic line physically through Solomon's descendant, Mary, while Jesus had legal rights of inheritance to be the Messiah that were passed onto him through his adopted father, Joseph. The Immaculate Conception birth of Jesus caused one parent to be left out in order to make Him Divine and the Son of God.

By contrast, the Jewish population in ancient Jerusalem was looking for a Messiah that was 100% human because of their requirement of a bloodline passed down through the biological father. Instead, Jesus satisfied this requirement legally in order to be born Divine, as the Son of God. Jesus has the best Father possible! This is the perfect trade off. Give up the biological father because God is your Father, while still satisfying all the legal requirements that were passed down from the adopted father.[622] Remember that Mary's pedigree birthrights from King David, King Solomon, and Nathan were all transferred to Joseph once they were married. As a consequence, all of these rights were then legally passed to Jesus from Joseph.

This is how the lineage situation is explained in the article by Ben Burton:

> Miriam is a direct physical descendant from Solomon, although it is *legally counted* to Nathan. Yeshua descends not only *legally* from David and Solomon through Joseph, but also *physically*. Yeshua is indeed the Branch of David

who will wear the crown and restore Israel and the world to perfect peace. In the Siddur, the following prayer is part of the Shemoneh Esrei, the Eighteen Benedictions. And of course, Miriam is Mary.[623]

It is plain to see that Jesus was indeed born of the house of David. This is why Jesus was often called "Son of David" by the people who called out for Him to heal them. To my knowledge, this is all true and fulfilled prophesy. If God can create the universe, the genetic code, and all life on Earth from nothing, then God is perfectly capable to cause His Son to be born, by an immaculate conception. This was not a problem for the Creator of the two-trillion-galaxy Universe.

CHAPTER THIRTEEN

The Miracles of Jesus

Skeptics have long scoffed at Christian claims of the miraculous, saying that such things are scientifically impossible because nothing can suspend or evade physical laws. Of course, such reasoning is circular because at the outset it denies the possibility of God who alone decides what happens in the universe.

At first glance, some people may say that miracles don't occur because there is no God to cause them. As mentioned, these people would also claim that miracles don't occur because they violate the laws of physics. However, what these people think has a fatal flaw. A person who does not believe in the existence of miracles and God, is living in a fantasy world. Let me give an example. People who don't believe in God, believe they live in a universe that can create itself from absolutely nothing in the absence of time. This, of course, violates the laws of physics because nothing physical existed in the absence of time!

That said, common sense dictates that if something does not exist, then it cannot bring itself into existence, before it existed. Anyone who believes this happened, not only lives in a fantasy world (a fantasy universe) but they most definitely believe in miracles. I say this because, a universe creating itself from nothing in the absence of time, before it existed, would most definitely qualify as being a miracle! That would be a miracle that violates hard science. A self-creating universe without any time to do so, violates the laws of physics and the ways in which the universe functions. As a consequence, anyone claiming this happened naturally would be claiming that a miracle occurred that evaded the laws of physics. Therefore, people who believe the universe just made itself, are believers in wild miracles.

Let me give another example. People who don't believe in God, believe they live in a universe that can create life from protons, neutrons, electrons and the lifeless molecules that they form. We saw this in a previous chapter where a famous scientist refused to believe in a universe with a God, but then he had no problem believing in a universe that could make living creatures from dead molecules and lifeless atoms. If he is correct, this would mean we live in a godly universe that has the power to create life from dead things. This would most certainly qualify as being a miracle! However, this is another example of a miracle that would evade the constraints of hard science because dead atoms and molecules can't bring themselves to life, before they are alive. This belief clearly violates common sense. And more importantly, the hard science of what atoms and molecules do, tells us that atoms and molecules CAN'T WRITE GENETIC CODE!

As a consequence, skeptics who don't believe in God and His miracles are instead believing in fantastic self-creating miracles. Regardless, these self-creating miracles contradict what hard science demonstrates that it can do. As you can see, anyone who thinks they don't believe in God and miracles is mistaken about what they believe. They don't realize that skeptics who do not believe in God, must believe in self-creation miracles that disobey the construct of hard science.

The point of this discussion is to establish that EVERYONE believes in miracles! If you believe in God, you believe that He can do anything, which sometimes includes causing miracles to occur.

And if you don't believe in God, then you believe in miracles of self-creation that violate what is scientifically possible. Notice how there are only two possibilities here. This is exactly what Professor George Wald stated in a previous chapter (remember that he won the Nobel Prize in Biology). This is just like a coin because there are only two sides. However, in this case we have a very special coin which I refer to as the, *miracle coin*. This is a *miracle coin* because no matter which side comes up, a miracle has occurred. The *miracle coin* has a 'Heads' side for God as the Creator, while the 'Tails' side is for self-creation.

Now that we have established that **everyone believes in miracles**, either 'Heads' miracles or 'Tails' miracles, I will state that because there is a God capable of the miraculous, we should not be surprised if they happen—at least sometimes. For the most part, I believe God does not micromanage Earth. He set the universe in motion a long time ago and allows His created physics to operate within the confines of its designed construct. With that being said, sometimes He finds it absolutely necessary to step in, intervene, and cause a miracle. Miracles are more than the mere suspension of physical laws—such as when the laws of decay and death are overturned by Resurrection. Some theologians say miracles are more like signposts that point us to an ultimate reality when decay and death are no more in the new Heaven and new Earth. This is certainly the case with the miracles that Jesus performed while on the earth.

Now that you have heard the argument for why everyone on Earth believes in miracles, let's explore documented miracles in the Bible by taking a look at the list of the miracles that Jesus performed while here on the earth.

The Miracles

1. Jesus heals a Roman official's son about to die (John 4:46-54)
2. Jesus heals the demoniac in the synagogue (Mark 1:23-26; Luke 4:33-36)
3. Jesus heals Simon's mother in-law (Matthew 8:14-15; Mark 1:29-31; Luke 4:38-39)
4. Jesus heals diseases in Galilee (Matthew 4:23-24; Mark 1:34)
5. Jesus' miracles in Jerusalem (John 2:23)
6. Jesus cleanses the leper (Matthew 8:1-4; Mark 1:40-45; Luke 5:12-16)
7. Jesus heals the paralytic (Matthew 9:1-8; Mark 2:1-12; Luke 5:17-26)
8. Jesus heals the lame man (John 5:1-16)
9. Jesus restores the withered hand (Matthew 12:9-13; Mark 3:1-5; Luke 6:6-11)
10. Jesus heals multitudes in Judah, Jerusalem, and the coasts of Tyre and Sidon (Luke 6:17-19)
11. Jesus saves from death the centurion's servant (Matthew 8:5-13; Luke 7:1-10)
12. Jesus heals demoniacs (Matthew 8:16-17; Luke 14:40-41)
13. Jesus resurrects the widow's son from the dead (Luke 7:11-16)
14. Jesus heals again in Galilee (Luke 7:21-22)
15. Jesus heals another demoniac (Matthew 12:22-37; Mark 3:19-30; Luke 11:14-15; Luke 11:17-23)

16. Jesus heals the diseased in Gennesaret (Matthew 14:34-36)

17. Jesus heals demoniacs Gadara (Matthew 8:28-34; Mark 5:1-20; Luke 8:26-39)

18. Jesus resurrects Jairus's daughter from the dead (Matthew 9:18-19: Matthew 9:23-26; Mark 5:22-24; Mark 5:35-43; Luke 8:41-42; Luke 8:49-56)

19. Jesus heals the bleeding woman (Matthew 9:20-22; Mark 5:25-34; Luke 8:43-48)

20. Jesus restores the sight of two blind men (Matthew 9:27-31)

21. Jesus casts out the devil in one man and restores the speech of another (Matthew 9:32-33)

22. Jesus heals the sick in Galilee (Matthew 14:14)

23. Jesus heals the daughter of the Syrophoenician (Matthew 15:21-28; Mark 7:24-30)

24. Jesus heals the lame, blind, and maimed near the Sea of Galilee (Matthew 15:30)

25. Jesus restores speech and hearing (Mark 7:31-37)

26. Jesus cures a blind man (Mark 8:22-36)

27. Jesus heals boy with an unclean spirit (Matthew 7:14-21; Mark 9:14-29; Luke 9:37-43)

28. Jesus cures 10 lepers (Luke 17:11-19)

29. Jesus gives vision in a man born blind (John 9:1-41)

30. Jesus resurrects Lazarus from the dead after four days, astounding and infuriating the Pharisees to the point that they seek to kill both Jesus and Lazarus (John 11:1-54)

31. Jesus heals a woman crippled by a spirit for 18 years, then points out the hypocrisy of certain religious leaders (Luke 13:10-17)

32. Jesus heals the abnormal swelling of a man's body on the Sabbath in front of a prominent Pharisee (Luke 14:1-6)

33. Jesus restores the sight of two blind men near Jericho (Matthew 20:29-34; Luke 18:35-43)

34. Jesus heals blind Bartimaeus (Mark 10:46)

35. Jesus heals Malchus's ear (Luke 22:49-51)

36. Jesus gives numerous healings (Matthew 4:23-24; Matthew 14:14; Matthew 15:30; Mark 1:34; Luke 6:17-19; Luke 7:21-22; John 2:23; and John 3:2)

37. Jesus feeds 5,000 people from five loaves of bread two fish (John 6:10; Mark 6:41)

38. Jesus walks on the water (John 6:16)

39. Jesus turns water into wine at a wedding (John 2:1-11)

40. Jesus feeds 4,000 people with seven loaves of bread and a few fish (Matthew 15:32-39; Mark 8:1-10)

Let me touch on the significance of just a few of His miracles to show how they demonstrate the truth of the New Testament. Keep in mind that in His day, Jesus' harshest critics didn't deny His miracles; they simply attributed them to the Devil. Modern scholars today frequently acknowledge that Jesus was a miracle worker. The question is *why*? I personally believe that Jesus healed people out of His compassion and love for them. Jesus proved His Love for us by dying on the cross for our sins! I also believe that His healings were meant to convince people that He was indeed the Messiah.

All things considered, I'm going to start with #39, (John 2:1-11), where Jesus turns water into wine at a wedding in Cana. I'm starting here because this is the very first miracle that Jesus performed.

Turning water into wine, in John 2:3-4 (KJV), we read:

And when they wanted wine, the mother of Jesus saith
unto Him, they have no wine. Jesus saith unto her,
Woman, what have I to do with thee? Mine hour is not
yet come.

Because the wine ran out in the middle of the wedding, this was
very embarrassing for the bride and groom. Mother Mary wanted
Jesus to help. But notice that Jesus tells Mary that His time has not
yet come. What this means is that Jesus was sent by God the Father to
perform certain miracles while He was on the earth. The request for
this miracle from Mary came before the time that Jesus was to start
His miracles. This tells us that there was a prescribed time when Jesus
was to start performing miracles. Considering that God the Father
gave Jesus a list of miracles to perform when the time was right, I can
assure you that turning water into wine was not on the original list.

Nevertheless, this did not deter Mary who instructed the servants,
"Do whatever He tells you." At this point the wedding servants are
standing there in front of Jesus waiting for His orders. As a result,
Jesus finds Himself in the position of either ignoring Mary's request
to save the day, or not waiting for His prescribed time for starting
miracles. Jesus has just been put on the spot. I'm sure that Jesus first
looked up to His Father to ask for permission before granting Mary
her wish. Jesus loved Mary very much and this is the reason why the
very first miracle to be performed by Jesus was Him turning water
into wine. It was done out of His Love for Mary.

All of the miracles that Jesus performed were done out if His Love
for His people, and the very first miracle is no exception. However,
it is clear this first miracle was not initially intended to take place.

I would also like to point out one more important realization here.
If this were a mere myth being made up as a fable, then why would

a myth writer have the Son of God put on the spot by Mary? Jesus was indicating to Mary that He was not going to do this because His time for miracles had not yet come. Did Mary listen to this? No, she did not. Mother Mary was not taking, No, as an answer. What we see here is the real-life drama of Mother Mary standing her ground in trying to get Jesus to save the day for this bride and groom.

No one is going to make this kind of drama up if this was not true. Why? The main reason is that it would make no sense to the reader. A reader is not going to understand what is meant by, "Mine hour is not yet come." In my opinion, it just makes no logical sense to fabricate this kind of drama and conflict in order to start off a miracle story of water being turned into wine. If this were indeed a made-up tale, when Mary asked Jesus for help, Jesus would have simply stepped forward to save the day by turning water into wine. A fable writer would not have Jesus initially reject this request only to then have Jesus change His mind. It just seems confused and illogical for a myth writer to have conjured up this kind of drama. However, all of this makes perfect sense if we are dealing with real life human drama.

As stated, I believe the reason why Jesus yielded to Mary's request was because of His Love for her. With that being said, I feel the reason why this passage was included in the Gospels, was to document the very first miracle that Jesus performed. Now let's look at more of Jesus' miracles.

Walking on the Water. In Matthew 14 (KJV), Jesus is walking on the water toward the disciples who were in a boat amid a great storm. Peter called to Him, "Lord, if it be thou, bid me come unto thee on the water" (v. 28). Jesus told him to come, so Peter got out of the boat and walked toward Jesus. But he became frightened and began to sink. Jesus reached out immediately and grabbed him, saying, "O thou of little faith, wherefore didst thou doubt?" (v. 31).

One of the early leaders of the Christian faith is rebuked for his doubt. Yet Peter was going to become the rock and foundation of Jesus' Church. Jesus stated in Matthew 16:18 (KJV):

> And I say also unto thee, That thou art Peter, and upon this rock I will build my Church; and the gates of hell shall not prevail against it.

Here we see that someone who has little faith is still chosen to serve, despite his failures. What man speaks like this and can walk on water? And what liar is going to write this as a fairy tale about a fellow Disciple and portray Peter as weak and filled with doubt? If this were a lie, then Matthew would have written that Peter had stood firm in his faith and walked upon the water triumphantly with Jesus. Matthew would have made the future rock and foundation of the Christian Church look like a brave, and strong hero. What kind of 'club' is going to advertise itself with a sinking failure as its earthly leader?

In Matthew 16:23 (KJV), Jesus even rebuked Peter as a tool of Satan. The only way this makes any sense is if it is the truth. Liars don't say negative things like this about themselves. The Gospel writers would never have fabricated a story where the future Rock of their Church is rebuked by Jesus as a tool of Satan! Liars don't do that to themselves.

What I also appreciate about Peter is the fact that no matter how much he fails, Jesus is not giving up on him and still has a very important use for him! Jesus in not going to fire Peter. This is a lesson for all of us. No matter what failures or sins we have experienced in life, God is not giving up on us. God still has an important use for each and every one of us, no matter how much we feel that we are beyond redemption, and no matter how much we feel useless to God. We need to stop concerning ourselves with how we *feel* and start focusing on doing the *work* that God created us to do. We need to focus on how much that God Loves us. We must never forget that God the Father sent his only begotten Son to die for us!

Next, we have the miracle of *Healing the daughter of the Syrophoenician*. In Matthew 15:24-28 (KJV), a Gentile woman comes to Jesus and pleads for Him to heal her daughter, who is possessed by a demon. Jesus at first ignored her; however, the woman persisted. Then Jesus said to her, "I am not sent but unto the lost sheep of the house of Israel" (v, 24). The woman pleaded, "Lord, help me" (v. 25). Jesus responded, "It is not meet to take the children's bread, and to cast it to dogs" (v. 26). Then the woman replied, "Truth, Lord: yet the dogs eat of the crumbs which fall from their masters' table" (v. 27). Jesus then said, "O woman, great is thy faith: be it unto thee even as thou wilt" (v. 28). And her daughter was instantly healed.

This incident is extremely interesting to say the least. The focus of the story turns out not so much to be Jesus' miraculous powers, but this Gentile woman's great faith. In this, the account rings true, loaded with the kinds of details no embellisher could make up. That's because it really happened.

The Gentiles did not know God's ways, did not believe in God, and were not "His people," as the Jews were. This reminds us that Jesus was sent to the earth with one mission, and that was to die as the perfect sacrificial Lamb, whose precious blood would effectively cover the sins of "His people." That being said, because this Gentile woman had total faith in Jesus and believed that He could heal her daughter, and refused to give up despite being strongly rebuked, Jesus had mercy on her and her daughter. What we see here is that Jesus values faith more than almost anything else. This woman and her daughter suddenly gained favor in God's eyes because of their strong faith in His Son! She even called Jesus as her Lord.

Feeding the multitudes. As we have seen, Jesus fed massive crowds on two occasions, according to the witness of the New Testament. However, these were not merely acknowledged to be acts of physical compassion, though of course they certainly were that. In addition, they were object lessons, not only of Jesus' power and Divinity, but also calls to faith for the Disciples—and us. As Mark 8:17-21 (KJV) states:

> And when Jesus knew it, he saith unto them, Why reason ye, because ye have no bread? perceive ye not yet, neither understand? have ye your heart yet hardened?
>
> Having eyes, see ye not? and having ears, hear ye not? and do ye not remember?
>
> When I brake the five loaves among five thousand, how many baskets full of fragments took ye up? They say unto him, Twelve.
>
> And when the seven (loaves of bread) among four thousand, how many baskets full of fragments took ye up? And they said, Seven.
>
> And he said unto them, How is it that ye do not understand?

Despite Jesus demonstrating on two prior occasions that He can feed the multitudes, His disciples have lost their faith and are arguing. Apparently, they had not learned from what they saw during these two prior events. They were being called to have complete and total faith in Jesus all the time, and for everything. If these accounts were merely lies generated by Matthew, Mark, Luke, and John, why would they show a watching world what failures they are? Who does that? If you are going to make up a fairy tale involving yourself and your friends, you are not going to state that everyone was a foolish failure, lacked proper faith, and got rebuked by their Lord. Only if this testimony were the truth would it ever be put into writing like this.

The Resurrection: Of course, Jesus' physical Resurrection from death is the greatest miracle of all. Once the despondent Disciples saw Him Risen with their own eyes on Resurrection Sunday, everything changed. Instead of cowering in fear, they boldly stepped out and proclaimed the Risen Messiah—even while being threatened with death. It was at that point the Apostles and followers truly became *Christians*. It was only then, that they finally understood everything.

This so because they had seen Jesus Risen from the dead! All the sufferings that would come along with being an early Christian are incomparable with the joy and excitement the Disciples and followers experienced seeing their Lord Risen from the grave! The Disciples were willing to tell the truth despite the consequences because they knew that if Jesus rose from the dead, then He will raise them from the dead and give them everlasting life. If Jesus kept His promise to rise from the dead, this proves He meant everything He said to the Disciples. They realized that Jesus was not a fairy tale.

Ten of the Disciples would go on to be murdered (martyred) for their beliefs and ministering to others. Mark and Paul faced the same end. Church tradition says that the former Roman officer Longinus and two of his fellow soldiers were hunted down and murdered for their ministry about Jesus in Cappadocia. All these and more, were willing to suffer and die for God's Son, Jesus Christ. John is the only Disciple who died of old age, dying in exile. This brings to mind Tovia Singer pointing out that none of the historians in the time of

Jesus recorded anything regarding the Resurrection.[624] That's because it was lethal to do so.

Let's not forget that the body of Jesus was never found. After His Resurrection, Jesus made 12 appearances. On one occasion, He appeared to 500 people at once. Two of these people physically touched Jesus.[625] The former atheist Lee Strobel, who is now is a Christian scholar, conducted a thorough and detailed "forensic investigation" into Christianity. After two years of painstaking work, Strobel determined that Jesus was real and did indeed resurrect from the dead. Strobel stated in his forensic investigation that some of these eyewitnesses were interrogated by the Romans and tortured in an attempt to make them recant their testimony. Despite this, they stood firm to their declarations.[626]

Lee Strobel came to the obvious conclusion that people are not going to allow this kind of maltreatment to themselves in order to perpetuate a lie.

CHAPTER FOURTEEN

In the End

In order to demonstrate how the book of science and the Holy Bible can be brought into agreement, this book needed to introduce to the reader many critical scientific facts that most people are completely unaware of. Most people have never had their attention drawn to these facts before. No one ever pointed these facts out to me which is why my doubt increased over time. Knowing all of these scientific facts is necessary for the people who are working on establishing their belief structures. In effect, this book was written for those who have the pressing question: Is there a God, or isn't there?

This book was also written for the many people who are under the false impression that hard science is based on observation and reason, while religion is only based on authority and faith. Many people have been misled into believing there is a battle being waged where they must choose between these two sides. They believe this is a battle between the facts of hard science vs. the miracles of mystic religions. As a result, many people have chosen one over the other, whether they realize it or not.

In the process of establishing their belief structures many people may have asked themselves the question: Doesn't hard science win this battle every single time? I can assure you, for the people who have been misled into thinking this way, many of them have become skeptics. These people would have asked themselves why they would believe in a God who cannot be proven when they can put their trust in science which can be proven. People are going to base their belief structures on something they feel that they can depend on. This is why science is trusted to be the source that people can rely on for solid answers. I know some people think this way because I used to think this way.

However, once I learned the universe really did have a beginning and that it cannot create itself from nothing in the absence of time, this was surprising news to me. This is why countless physicists around the world became believers in God as soon as the Big Bang was proven to be a fact. For most of my life, I did not know any of this. When I found this out, it pointed to the existence of a Creator.

When I learned that Darwinian evolution has already been found to be a false theory because there are no evolutionary mutated skeletons in the Fossil Record, this was news to me. You can't have a mutant process without any mutants! We know that Darwin clearly understood this by reading one of his quotes which is presented earlier in this book where he admits this is an obvious problem that allows for grave objections to be raised against his theory.[627] For most of my life, I did not know any of this. And I must say, when I learned what Charles Darwin had stated about his own theory, I was shocked. When I finally realized all of this, it pointed to the existence of a Creator.

When I learned the stories in the Bible are not recycled Mesopotamian myths because the first oral Hebrew stories existed thousands of years before the first Mesopotamian myth was ever written, this was game-changing news to me. For most of my life I did not know this. No one ever drew my attention to this important fact. The only fact my attention was drawn to, was that the Hebrew Bible stories were very similar to many Mesopotamian myths that were written before the Hebrew Bible was written. This left me with the profound impression that the Hebrew Bible stories were copies of myths from other cultures. However, once I realized the oral Hebrew histories of creation and the Great Flood existed thousands of years before the myths were written, it was only then that I realized I had been under the wrong impression for my entire life.

When I found this out, I realized there was no legitimate way that anyone could claim the Bible was merely a collection of recycled myths from other cultures. This is the case because there is no way to prove the Hebrews were not the original source of these stories because of the simple fact that oral histories existed before the written word was invented. Once this false stigma of plagiarism was removed, it finally provided me the opportunity to study the Holy Bible as an authentic and credible collection of historic documents.

Once I learned these three core facts, I knew that God must exist, and the Holy Bible was authentic and not a recycling of myths from other cultures. Being in possession of all of this information was a complete game-changer for me. My belief structure has completely changed once I was given all of the facts!

What we see from the evidence presented in this book is that people have grown up with the wrong impression about God and religion because they have not been given all of the scientific and historic facts.

When people are not given all of the scientific facts, I refer to this as, pseudoscience (sort-of-science). People will be led to the wrong conclusions if they are only in possession of some of the facts. While on the other hand, when people are given ALL of the scientific facts, I refer to this as, sound science. People will be led to the correct conclusions if they are in possession of all of the facts. This observation is supported by common sense. That being said, I realize people are entitled to come to whatever conclusions they wish. With that being said, I advocate that people are entitled to do this while in possession of ALL the facts, not some of the facts. This allows people to make an informed consent decision when formulating their belief structures. People are entitled to know the entire truth, not some of the truth.

As stated, incomplete information leads people to incorrect conclusions about God and religion. And if that wasn't bad enough, incomplete information causes one more big problem. Because most people have not been given all of the scientific facts, they also wind up with the wrong impression about science. **This is why many people are misled into believing science can do things that it cannot. Science cannot create itself from nothing, and science doesn't possess godly powers to create living organisms from dead things.** Therefore, this is not a battle between the cold-hard facts of science vs. the mystic fairy tales of religion. No, instead, it should be clear this is a matter of science fiction fantasies vs. the miracles of a Creator. And that is an entirely different match-up from which to choose.

At the beginning of the last chapter, it was discussed that skeptics scoff at Christian claims of Divine miracles because such events are scientifically impossible. They believe that nothing can suspend or evade physical laws. Nevertheless, what these skeptics propose instead, whether they realize it or not, is that the universe created itself through some unknown physical phenomenon. The fatal flaw of this idea, is that before a universe and time existed, there was no physical universe platform or time for any such physical phenomenon to have existed in. This means that whatever these skeptics are claiming to be the cause of our universe, that cause had to suspend and evade the constraints imposed on physical entities and physical realities, just like Christian miracles are claimed to.

You may ask: Why is that? Essentially, whatever skeptics claim brought the universe into existence, had to evade the physical realities that require the presence of a universe platform, which in turn, requires the existence of time. In other words, these skeptics are not dealing with physical reality; they are not dealing with the reality of how the real world and the real universe works. Before the universe existed 14 billion years ago, time did not exist. It's this absence of time that prevented any kind of physical phenomenon from existing in the first place. On top of this, as discussed in Chapter Three, the absence of time prevents any kind of *Work* from being allowed to take place. Regarding physical laws, *Work* cannot be done without the *Time* to do the *Work*. In addition, *Work* cannot be done outside of the construct of our space-time universe.

Therefore, what skeptics propose actually constitutes a miraculous event that completely evades physical laws, physical requirements, and physical reality. You see, God can create a universe from nothing in the absence of time, but hard science can't do that! This is quite simple. God has powers that hard science simply does not possess on its own.

This is the case because *"science without a God"* cannot explain how our universe created itself from nothing in the absence of time. This means their proposal qualifies as a supernatural event. Remember that a supernatural event is anything that cannot be explained by science. This is also the case for the first life created by God. Since the physical requirements for an evolutionary process were impossible to be satisfied by dead clumps of atoms floating around in the water, this means the idea of abiogenesis would constitute a miraculous event that is beyond the explanation of science. As a result, the proposal of abiogenesis also qualifies as a supernatural event.

In addition to this, since dead molecules are incapable of writing sophisticated genetic code as an intricate operating system (mindless molecules don't have the reputation of being code writers), just considering the existence of the code itself would qualify as yet another miraculous and supernatural event. This leads us to the realization that skeptics believe in miracles that are far more fantastic than people who believe in God. This is true whether the skeptics realize this or not. You see, hard science cannot step outside of the constraints of its well-defined order, structure, and function, in order to do miraculous things that it cannot do.

Hard science does not have the reputation for being a magical fountain of miracles. Hard science is known for its reliability in being an agent of physical realities, not fantastic miracles that defy scientific explanation and defy the physical realities of the framework that they exist in. Hard science is restricted to its functional role inside the construct of a universe which clearly defines what hard science can and cannot do. As a result, miraculous events are not listed in the skillset of what hard science is capable of.

As I have stated before, this is not a matter of the facts of hard science vs. the miracles of a Divine Creator. No, this is a matter of science fiction miracles vs. Divine miracles of a Creator. As a consequence, both skeptics and Believers alike, embrace miracles. Hence, everyone believes in miracles, whether we realize it or not.

Do you remember the Nobel Prize winner Dr. George Wald? He believed that the universe had the power to create life. This means

George Wald believed the universe has godly creative powers. That would be miraculous. And this begs the logical question: If the universe has godly creation powers, then why can't a God exist that has creation powers? If someone believes in a magical universe, then why can't they believe in a magical God that created the universe??? It is far more logical to believe that the universe has a Wizard (God) that performs the magic, than it is to believe in magic that performs itself. Simple logic dictates that if someone believes in a magical universe where life creates itself, then that person should also leave open the possibility there may be a God that is creating the life. Hence, we either live in a magical universe or there is a magical God.

If the decision is made by someone to continue to refuse to believe that God may exist, I am convinced that decision has nothing to do with logic, observation, reasoning, or scientific facts. I believe Dr. George Wald is a perfect example of this. Do you recall his quote in Chapter One regarding spontaneous generation where he chose to believe what he knew was scientifically impossible?[628]

One may argue, that if the skeptics should be leaving the possibility open that a Creator may exist, then the religious folks should leave open the possibility that the universe and life could have created themselves without a God. However, this argument is flawed because hard science exists inside of a construct that constrains what it is capable of doing. The capabilities and behaviors of the universe (described as the laws of physics) have limitations that are clearly defined by countless physics equations. In other words, we know what 'science' can do and the performing of supernatural miracles is NOT what a universe does. There are no physics equations in existence for creation miracles. We know the limitations of what science can do, while on the other hand, God is unlimited in what He can do. In other words, "*science without a God*" has scientific limits, while "*science with a God*" does not have limits. With that being said, what really defeats the arguments for "*science without a God*" is that they don't pass the Scientific Method of proving.

When we analyze the situation very carefully from a scientific standpoint, we come to four very specific realizations:

1) The claim that the universe created itself, **does not pass the Scientific Method**. The Scientific Method of proving does not support the idea that a universe can create itself from nothing in the absence of time.

2) The claim that the first living cell created itself, **does not pass the Scientific Method**. The Scientific Method of proving does not support the idea that the first living organism made itself come into existence from dead clumps of atoms and molecules. In addition, the Scientific Method of proving does not support the idea that dead molecules started writing intelligent instructional genetic code. Code writing is not what atoms and molecules do.

3) The claim that an error-based mutant process created all of the species on the earth, **does not pass the Scientific Method**. The Scientific Method of proving does not support the idea that all of the species that have ever lived on the earth, created themselves through a random process of mutation errors. In addition, the Scientific Method of proving does not support the idea that all of the species that have ever lived on the earth, created themselves through a random process that is guided by Natural Selection.

4) The claim that Hebrew scribes embellished Mesopotamian myths simply because the Mesopotamian myths were put into

print first, **does not pass the Scientific Method of proving.** Since history is a social science, it can also be analyzed with the Scientific Method. It is an historic fact that oral traditions existed before written ones. This means there is no way to prove the Hebrews were not the originators of the stories found in the Holy Bible. I would argue that common sense dictates that it is far more likely that oral Hebrew stories were adopted and adapted into Mesopotamian myths by Sumerian scribes. Sumerian scribes were able to create written stories first because they invented the written word.

All four of these "science without a God" ideas fail to pass the Scientific Method which means the skeptics don't have a scientific case for their rejection of God. And when the skeptics don't have a scientific case, they don't have any case at all for their rejection of a Creator.

In a nutshell, the scientific evidence demonstrates that our universe could not have created itself. The scientific evidence demonstrates that all of the species on the earth did not create themselves through Darwinian evolution, this includes neo-Darwinian evolution. The fact that human history demonstrates oral Hebrew traditions existed before writing was invented, provides common sense support that the stories in the Holy Bible could very well be the authentic originals. They were impressive enough to inspire other cultures to adopt and adapt them into fanciful myths.

If any of you are ever in a debate with skeptics about the existence of God, I recommend bringing up these four main points.

The skeptic's position has been scientifically proven to be false, while the existence of God has not been proven to be false. This automatically proves the existence of a Creator. If 'Tails' is false, then 'Heads' must be true. When one side is proven to be false, this proves that the other side must be the truth. Do you remember the Sherlock Holmes quote?

> When you have excluded the impossible, whatever remains, however improbable, must be the truth.[629]

It is here that I would like to spotlight another quote that I presented in Chapter Four. This is the quote from chemist Paul Higgs from the chapter on abiogenesis where he makes a statement about chemical evolution:

> Here, I argue that chemical evolution, although Darwinian, does not quite constitute life, and a good place to put the conceptual boundary between non-life and life is between chemical and biological evolution.[630]

You will recall that the highly esteemed Dr. Raup abandoned Darwinian evolution. He instead spent the remainder of his career looking for a *non-Darwinian* evolution. He went looking for another explanation for why species are different today.[631] Dr. Raup went looking for 'another kind of evolution,' but he never found a non-Darwinian model for evolution.

This brings us to the significant conclusion that science presently has no working model for the theory of evolution. It should also be realized that if chemical evolution is Darwinian as Dr. Higgs states, and Dr. Raup has abandoned Darwinian evolution, then the hypothesis of chemical evolution should also be abandoned. Of course, this includes abandoning the hypothesis of abiogenesis as well. This is the case because, not only is the idea of abiogenesis also Darwinian, but chemical evolution is speculated to be a critical intermediate step in the alleged hypothetical process of abiogenesis. The fact that Dr. Raup has demonstrated the need to find a non-Darwinian model for the theory of evolution, hence, discarding the Darwinian model

(Raup, Conflicts, 1979, p. 26), effectively negates this statement made by Paul Higgs.

As I have stated in Chapter Four, one of my main objections to chemical evolution and abiogenesis is that the phenomenon of natural selection cannot be experienced by lifeless objects. Natural selection is a core requirement for an evolutionary process to occur. This is why the ideas of chemical evolution and abiogenesis don't satisfy the necessary physical requirements of an evolutionary process. As a consequence, if chemical evolution and abiogenesis are still being seriously considered by anyone, then both of these ideas would qualify as being miracles because they are both contradicted by sound science.

Let's not forget that Dr. Raup found no evidence natural selection had anything to do with the theory of macroevolution. As a result, Dr. Raup abandoned natural selection as the mechanism responsible for the appearance of species found in the Fossil Record. Remember that Dr. Raup had this to say regarding the Fossil Record:

> Data appears to be much more complex and much less gradualistic. . . Darwin's problem has not been alleviated in the last 120 years and we still have a record which *does* show change but one that can hardly be looked upon as the most reasonable consequence of natural selection.[632]

This is one of the reasons why the esteemed Dr. Raup went looking for a non-Darwinian evolution.

Since natural selection has no support for being the guidance system in evolution, how can natural selection be assumed to have played a role in abiogenesis? It defies logic to assume that natural selection was the driving force behind the creation of the first living cellular machine, while at the same time, it has been established that natural selection should be abandoned as the guidance system responsible for the creation of all the other species on planet Earth.

Once the death of natural selection was established regarding macroevolution, it spelled the death of chemical evolution, abiogenesis, and Darwinian macroevolution. This resulted from the thorough scientific analysis of the Fossil Record. Therefore, the collapse of chemical evolution, abiogenesis, and Darwinian macroevolution, spells the death of all evolutionary theories and hypotheses which claim to spawn new species through the propagation of errors guided by natural selection.

Evolutionary theories claim errors occur that are then positively directed by a guidance system. Without a guidance system, progressive improvement is not possible. For example, it's like NASA having a rocket program where new experimental fuels (discovered through errors) are placed into rockets that don't have a guidance system. Without a guidance system, those rockets are not going to progress in a positive direction. A rocket program without a guidance system is not a rocket program at all. In this same way, because the theory of evolution has no guidance system (no natural selection) it's not a workable theory at all. Evolution theory crashes and burns just like rockets that don't have a guidance system.

And speaking of the death of evolution, in addition to Dr. Raup's findings, let's not forget the findings of Dr. Stephen Jay Gould, and the Wistar Institute Symposium held in Philadelphia in 1966. As we can see, Dr. Ebifegha's book, *The Death of Evolution*, has the perfect title. In addition, you will recall that Dr. Gould stated that species appeared 'fully formed' (Gould, 1977). This means there is no fossil evidence of them transitioning from something else. If species were slowly introduced 'fully formed' through a *creation seeds* strategy, as I suggest, this would explain why there is no evidence of species transformations.

It is clear that species could not have made themselves through evolution. Once evolution was eliminated, there is only one possibility left. The biggest problem with life creating itself relates to the absolute need for complex genetic instructional code. Instructional code does not write itself, and mindless atoms and molecules do not write genetic code either. As a consequence, logic dictates that the same brilliant Creator who engineered every DNA profile on planet Earth must also be the genius who engineered our high precision universe. To get to the truth, all we have to do is follow the science and follow logic.

What all of this boils down to is that *"science without a God"* vs. *"science with a God"* is not a case of hard scientific facts vs. religious beliefs and miracles. Instead, this is a matter of science fiction fantasies that do not pass the Scientific Method vs. a Divine Creator's miracles. Once we realize that **these** are the two opponents in this battle for the truth, it's a complete game-changer. Because *"science without a God"* does not pass the Scientific Method, it does not hold the higher ground in this battle! This is a fact that I wish for people to fully realize and remember.

Whether we realize it or not, we all believe in the magical. And there are two magical camps of belief. One camp believes in *"science without a God"* miracles, while the other camp believes in

"science with a God" miracles. It's either one or the other. The *"science without a God"* camp includes a universe that can make itself appear from nothing at all, like a magic trick without a magician and with no time to do it. This camp also promotes the claim that the ultra-complex DNA molecule perfectly assembled itself and then

wrote tens of millions of lines of intricate code as an ultra-sophisticated operating system.

On top of this, the fantasy epic continues with error-based mutants producing all of the species on the earth that managed to magically hide all of their tens of millions of fossilized mutated skeletal remains. This is just an estimate of the total number of mutants that should wind up fossilized. Even Charles Darwin admitted he should have found these mutant fossils everywhere, but none were to be found.[633] The absence of mutant intermediates in the Fossil Record proves Darwinian evolution to be pure Sci-Fi fantasy that completely defies reality. This is in contrast to the Divine miracle camp which includes the accounts that are listed in God's History Book.

Whether we realize it or not, we all believe in the miraculous. One way for us to find the truth when nothing else has worked is to turn to science, history, logic, and problem-solving. And when I mention science here, I mean sound science, not pseudoscience. Blessed are those who have faith and believe. But for people who are like doubting Thomas, we have to follow the science in order to see the truth. Once again, follow the science!

In the introduction of this book, I related my personal experiences with trying to figure out what to believe. I am convinced that many people in the world have had a similar experience when it comes to believing what they have always been told about *science* and its alleged superiority and independence from religion. And when I say religion, I am talking about God. With that being said, perhaps when we think of the word, religion, it may be more accurate to think about the word, relationship. This is less about religious denominations and more about forming a relationship with God. Therefore, when I mention the word, religion, I'm referring to the relationship we have with God coupled with our understanding of God.

I believe many people have the perception that science does not need a God and is superior to religious faith. We saw this from Stephen Hawking:

> There is a fundamental difference between religion, which is based on authority, and science, which is based on observation and reason. Science will win because it works. [634]

However, I feel the scientific facts that comprise the research in this book allow me to make up my own quote:

> There is a fundamental difference between religion, which is based on observation and reason, as compared to pseudoscience, which is based on authority and only half of the facts. God wins because He works.

Another quote that I mentioned previously from Hawking states:

> One can't prove that God doesn't exist, but science makes God unnecessary. [635]

The reason why this is false is because the self-creating *science* Hawking speaks of does not pass the Scientific Method. This means that *science* has not demonstrated God to be unnecessary. In fact, because the science of self-creation does not pass the Scientific Method, it has not demonstrated anything at all. This is the case because skeptics claim to base their arguments on *science.*

When it comes right down to it, we have to ask ourselves some hard questions, like: *Do I believe science is based on facts while religion is not based on facts but instead is solely based on faith and authority? Do I believe science and religion are like oil and water and do not mix? Do I believe science seems to be independently powerful and completely self-sufficient? Do I believe science battles religion and contradicts what is written in the Bible? Do I believe that hard science is the master of the universe and superior to religion?* And this last question may be the most important one: *When I hear that the stories found in the Bible were first written as epic Mesopotamian myths, does this make me believe the Bible is merely a collection of fables from other cultures?*

As I have mentioned, this is exactly what I believed once I heard people imply this conclusion. This embellishment misconception is entirely the result of realizing ancient cultures put their stories into print first, but then at the same time, not realizing that pre-existing oral Hebrew traditions existed first and were the original source. This embellishment misconception is the result of not being told about the pre-existing Oral Abrahamic-Hebrew stories.

The dramatic effect this had on me from that point forward, was that it caused me to only read the Bible for the morals of the stories. I became convinced the Bible stories were not even Hebrew in origin. At that point, I no longer wondered if they were true because I stopped trying to believe the stories in the Bible. When this occurs, it is spiritually lethal. What happens next is that some of us come to the conclusion that religion is based upon human superstitions and the stories in the Bible are just epic fairy tales.

There are many nonbelievers who reject the Scriptural argument for the existence of God. I believe the main reason for this is because these people have been convinced earlier in their life that the Bible stories have their origins in the myths of other cultures. This represents a significant reason why a purely Scriptural argument does not work on these skeptical individuals. The truth of the matter is that the first Oral Abrahamic-Hebrew stories were passed down by word -of-mouth, from generation-to-generation, thousands of years before the Sumerians invented the first written language which they used to write their epic myths.

This is the reason why I stress the scientific argument (Scientific Apologetics) as much as I do. I believe that in order to reach the skeptical people who reject a purely Scriptural argument, these people also need to be presented with all of the scientific facts. Only then, do these people have all of the facts that are necessary to properly formulate their belief structures. I believe the result is overwhelmingly impressive once all of the scientific facts are assembled and combined with Scripture.

Have you ever asked yourself: Do I believe it when *"science without a God"* claims the universe created itself and there was "No God Needed"? Do I believe it when I hear from *"science without a God"* that it is impossible for God to exist? Do I believe the claim that the first living cell created itself from the "soup of life" and then evolved itself into every single species on Earth? Do I believe that *"science without a God"* is the truth and has won its battle for supremacy over mystic religion?

In the absence of all the facts, these are reasonable questions that many of us probably have. This book has been compiled to answer these questions. You will notice that almost all of this book is based on the various disciplines in science. There is the science of physics and its space science, biology, chemistry, biochemistry, genetics, geology, paleontology, archaeology, anthropology, philosophy, logic, history, and human psychology. Therefore, this book is not based upon fairy tales; it is based on the sound disciplines in science.

I hoped that God was real for most of my life, but deep down, I figured that He did not actually exist. Here is my old checklist, as to why I became someone who was effectively operating as a nonbeliever:

1) In order to produce the Bible, I thought the Hebrews copied ancient myths from other cultures.
2) No God was needed for the existence of the universe.
3) No God was needed for life to emerge from the "soup of life" which initiated a self-driven evolution.
4) I only believed in facts that passed the Scientific Method and I was under the impression that evolution did pass the Scientific Method (which it does not).

Once I became convinced the Bible stories were not true, combined with evolution and my inability to prove the existence of God using the Scientific Method, I effectively stopped believing in the existence of God. I didn't even realize this belief structure formulation process had occurred. I didn't realize that somewhere along the line I went from trying to believe in God, to barely hoping that maybe God was somehow real.

I never thought deeply enough about any of this to get to the realization that there is a huge difference between weakly hoping in something and truly believing in it. In fact, I was a nonbeliever to the extent that I would have been extremely surprised if it was ever proven to me that God actually existed. And this is precisely what happened. I now realize that a universe cannot create itself from nothing. I now realize that evolution theory does not pass the Scientific Method and is contradicted by the Fossil Record. And to top it all off, I now realize the oral Hebrew stories existed way before other cultures started writing their myths.

If anyone else has a list like this one, this book is meant to thoroughly address these concerns. This is the list that I used to establish my belief structure. Once I established my belief structure, I found myself subconsciously adding whatever agreed with, while I subconsciously rejected whatever conflicted with it. My belief structure was much like a first impression; once it was formulated, I would not stray from it.

People possess vast amounts of general and scientific knowledge that we have learned throughout our lives. This information is what we use to formulate our belief structures. However, this book introduces some factual information that many of us did not previously possess. This added information allows us to see what we could not see before. This added knowledge allows us to see that the question of whether there is a God or not, is not a case of hard science vs. religious miracles. This message comes from implementing the Scientific Method and applying it directly to *"science without a God."* Once this is done, it can be clearly seen that *"science without a God"* does not pass the Scientific Method of proving.

All things considered, I don't wish to give the wrong impression about Charles Darwin. On the whole, Charles Darwin had several good ideas. He was correct about survival of the fittest, natural selection, and microevolution. Darwin also confirmed and championed support for environmental adaptation. Charles Darwin was clearly a brilliant scientist. With that being said, Darwin's idea regarding macroevolution is not correct. He clearly suspected this when he admitted as much in his famous, "…most obvious and gravest objection…" quote regarding his macroevolution theory.[636]

God is many wonderous things. God is love; God is forgiveness; God is grand, and God is also the Master Scientist. Since we know that all of this science did not come from itself, it means that God is the Father of science, which He bends to His Will when necessary.

The purpose of reconciling the book of science with the Book of God is to demonstrate how compatible these two books are and how they both come from the same source. This agreement demonstrates that they do *not* battle each other for supremacy. There is no battle between science and God; there never was. The only battle that ever existed was in our own minds because we could not see how the book of science and the Word of God were compatible.

The method I used to find how the book of science and the Book of God were compatible, was to imagine the possible bridges that could connect these two books, in every regard. And if those bridges were possible, then those were the answers. In other words, whatever possible scenario allowed both books to be true, must be the way that things actually happened. Once bridging solutions were identified, I immediately accepted them because I knew that these two books must in fact reconcile with each other.

The book of science and the Book of God *can* be brought into agreement by mainly looking at one topic, the topic of time. We need to realize that mankind's time did not start until Adam was created at the very end of Day Six of *Creation Week*. This means that all of the rest of *Creation Week*, which occurred before Adam, was created in God's Time. Mankind's version of time did not exist before mankind existed. Once we wrap our heads around this reality, we can then see how the timeline in the Fossil Record is true and finds agreement with the Book of Genesis, especially if we consider that *Creation Week* probably had two phases.

The *creation seed* is a bridging concept because it represents a way to connect the Fossil Record with what is written in the Bible. The idea that the Creator planted *seeds* that would germinate and bring forth the various species at their predetermined times brings the Fossil Record into perfect alignment with the Word of God. This *creation seed* concept is the solution to the problem that Dr. Raup spent much of his career looking for. Dr. Raup pointed out that the species witnessed today are obviously different compared to the species that existed in the past. He knew that an explanation had to be found to account for this. Without this explanation, there is no working model for evolution. *Creation seeds* explain how species became different over time; they were replaced.

I am convinced that God decided upon a system that introduced various species to the earth who prepared it for the species that would follow. When their job was completed, the earlier species were designed to go extinct. The Fossil Record documents the story of this Divine timeline for these designed inceptions and extinctions. This is why Dr. Raup never found a self-driven, hard science explanation for how species are different today. Dr. Raup was looking in the wrong place because he was searching for a *"science without a God"* explanation.

While on the other hand, the *"science with a God" creation seeds* explanation works as long as we admit that the concept of time may be more complex than we now understand it to be. If we can accept that God's Time is different from mankind's time, we can begin to see how this may indeed be an old Earth that we live on and how the dates in the Fossil Record make sense.

And let's not forget about all of the famous scientists who believe in God. Highly esteemed professionals like those mentioned in this book don't believe in fairy tales. One of these famous scientists is Verner Heisenberg. As mentioned, he is considered the father of quantum mechanics and he received the Nobel Prize for this work. Some present-day scientists try to use Heisenberg's Uncertainty Principle to claim that quantum gravity fluctuations could have existed and possibly brought the universe into existence, by itself. Nevertheless, Heisenberg strongly believed in God and since the uncertainty principle was discovered by him, it clearly did not suggest to him that the universe could create itself or did create itself. This should tell us something.

As mentioned, the uncertainty principle, along with quantum gravity and quantum fluctuations, could only exist within the construct of an already established universe platform. As a consequence, before the universe existed, there was no platform for gravity, quantum gravity, quantum fluctuations, or the uncertainty principle to have existed in, in the first place. Without time, nothing in the physical realm exists, nothing.

If the majority of this book seems to have little to do with Scripture and more to do with science, data, logic, and history, you would be correct. This book takes a fresh perspective approach. It is a scientific analysis of the Bible and its relationship to history and science. As a result of comprehensive analysis, I believe solutions have been found that bridge the gaps between science and the Bible. This book is meant to empower people with all of the facts as I understand them, with the intention that people will make the best, informed consent decision possible when they formulate their belief structures.

Don't feel odd if you struggle in your faith, many people do. Just look at the Disciples and followers of Jesus who did not believe that Jesus would rise from the dead in three days and three nights. His followers did not believe what Mary Magdalene and the women told them happened at the tomb. Even Mary herself lost faith and finally decided to not believe what the angels were telling her about Jesus. Only after Jesus appeared to Mary did she finally believe. Only when Jesus appeared to all of the others, did they finally believe. Each one of them had to see for themselves.

In reality, they were all like doubting Thomas on Resurrection Sunday. Thomas was not the only one with doubt that morning, and

I am no different. And I'm pretty sure that I am not alone. This is why I feel the need to share what it took to make a true believer out of someone who used to be a skeptical doubting Thomas. This book is for anyone who seeks the truth and has serious questions.

This reminds me of a question that I noticed posted online, which asked: "Why do I get the impression that Christianity is a scam?" Well, this is what the atheist Sir William Mitchell Ramsay thought when he set out to the Holy Land to prove that the Apostle Paul, the Apostle Luke, and the entire New Testament were all frauds. As a result, he spent 35 years of his life as a skeptical archaeologist who doggedly tried to prove the New Testament and Christianity to be false. Ramsay conducted a professional 35-year intensive investigation to research the authenticity and validity of Christianity and the New Testament. This is why Ramsay is referred to as the New Testament scholar "without peer."[637] William Ramsay is the ultimate New Testament scholar and considered to be the world's best authority on the New Testament and Asia Minor. As a consequence, no skeptic on planet Earth has ever put forth the effort, the time, and the expertise to prove that the New Testament and Christianity were a fraud, like Ramsay did.

And what became of that intensive and exhaustive 35-year investigation??? Sir William Mitchell Ramsay became a Christian! He clearly believed everything that had been written which he scrutinized with a fine-tooth comb. He followed the evidence, and it led him to the truth. You could say that Sir William Ramsay finally got to the "bottom of the glass," and once there, found God waiting for him. Therefore, for anyone who wonders if Christianity is a fraud, my suggestion is for them to research Sir William Mitchell Ramsay. This highly esteemed and former atheist has already done all of the hard work for you in answering that question!

Do you see how ALL of this makes perfect sense? We have the existence of our high precision universe that could not make itself from nothing in the absence of time. We have the DNA profiles of billions of species over the course of Earth's lifespan that could not have created themselves through Darwinian evolution and molecules that could not have written genetic code for themselves. We have the archaeological accuracy of what is listed in the Holy Bible. And finally, we have the logic that Jesus came to the earth to die as the perfect sacrificial Lamb on Passover because of the need for a perfect blood sacrifice. The blood of lambs and goats was not strong enough to cover the sins of mankind.

John 3:16-17 (KJV):

> For God so loved the world, that He gave His only begotten Son, that whosoever believeth in Him should not perish, but have everlasting life. For God sent **not** His Son into the world to condemn the world, but that the world through Him might be saved.

I believe the story of Jesus Christ exemplifies a story of love, forgiveness, and perfection of logic. I believe this because everything makes sense. Do you see the absolute perfection of love here and how everything precisely connects together? The sacrifice of Jesus was absolutely necessary in order to cover mankind's sins with the blood of the perfect sacrificial Lamb who was crucified at the exact time the Jewish Passover lambs were being sacrificed. This was not a coincidence. This was all planned out ahead of time and executed right on schedule. This type of scheduling precision is also responsible for when all of the species appeared on the earth at their predetermined times. The earlier species paved the way for the more complex species that followed. This all makes perfect logical sense. As I have stated several times, God is logical and methodical. God's Science, God's History, and God's Son, all demonstrate this perfection.

At the end of the day, we all have to ask ourselves: Did this perfect universe and the elegance of the DNA molecule along with its precisely coded operating system, all just happen on its own? Here is Stephen Hawking's answer to this question regarding the universe:

> It is said that there's no such thing as a free lunch. But the universe is the ultimate free lunch.[638]

That would be two trillion galaxies of free lunches! In addition, the billions of species that have existed on the earth would all be free lunches as well. All of these free lunches fall into the category of science fiction fantasy. The one thing that I believe most of us can agree on is that there is no such thing as a free lunch. I argue that the dignity of hard science should not be contaminated with the folly of "free lunches." I don't believe hard science should be watered down to the point that "free lunches" are used as 'scientific' explanations. This reminds me of how Oxford Professor John Lennox openly criticized Hawking in a YouTube video and called Hawking, "Triply Ridiculous."[639]

I feel that some people think that if God existed, He would just snap His fingers and things would happen. But this is not how God usually chooses to operate. Instead, God has created His Science to logically and methodically carry out His Will. And because God designed His Science to carry out most of the day-to-day operations of the earth, it gives the impression that *science* is self-driven and has the power to create life. This mindset has convinced some people that the universe has godly powers, where chemistry creates life. I insist that it just seems this way because of how efficiently God has engineered the universe and life to function. God is logical and methodical, and this is why His Universe behaves in a logical and methodical fashion.

Let me give an example. Imagine that a scientific research team wants to conduct research in a rainforest. They build a solar powered plant that produces electricity in the middle of a remote tropical jungle. This plant was also built as a water well pump station. Its function is to pump fresh water to the surface and supply electricity to their shelters once they return to build them. Because it's solar powered, this power plant will practically run itself for a very long time.

Despite this plan, the researchers never return because their funding was cancelled. Now, let's say that native tribes start to move into the area of this small power plant. And let's say these native tribes have never had any contact with the modern world before. The natives can hear a constant humming sound coming from this structure and they can see this building has a bright light inside that is always on. The natives can also see a turbine wheel that is constantly spinning in this electrical room which constantly pumps fresh water into a fountain in the middle of this room. Since they have never seen another human enter or leave this structure, they believe this phenomenon to be supernatural and self-driven.

This small building is perceived to have great powers because it makes sound, spins a wheel, lights up the night with its electric bulb, and constantly provides clean water. As a result of how perfectly this small building functions all on its own, they perceive all of this to be miraculous and they start to worship this structure as having godly powers. They soon come to the conclusion that the surrounding jungle has godly powers which caused this life-sustaining source of fresh water to come into existence.

Now, we all know this solar powered plant and water pump station didn't engineer and build itself. We all know this structure is not the product of a "free lunch." Everyone knows this power plant does not have godly powers even though it creates sound, energy, light, and reliably provides fresh water. With all of that being said, this is not what the locals think. The locals have been collecting their clean water from this plant for many years. It is clear to them that this magical fountain is self-sufficient and will last forever. They believe it was brought into existence by the natural powers of the rainforest, as part of the order of nature.

Does this sound familiar? Why does this remind me of what George Wald declared? Because of how perfectly the universe and living organisms have been engineered and function, some people are under the false impression this perfection just made itself. I can assure you that the universe and the first living cellular machine are infinitely more complex than a solar powered electrical plant and water pump station. None of these things could have just made themselves!

In the introduction, I stated this book was like a box of puzzle pieces. Now, as this book is about to draw to a close, you will notice how all of the pieces in this book fit logically and seamlessly together to form one comprehensive picture. This is not a coincidence. And it is this comprehensive picture that allows us to see how the book of science and the Book of God can be brought into agreement. I know that some people think that God and the Bible are fairy tales. I used to think the same thing. However, the *science* that most of us think we understand is only half of the truth. Most of us are not in possession of all the scientific facts. This is why many of the facts listed in this book will come as a surprise to many of the people reading about them here. The consequence of not being in possession of all the facts, is that we wind up believing in a *science* that turns out to be a Sci-Fi myth.

In reality, we are confronted with a coin flip where only one side can be true. The result can only be 'Heads' or 'Tails.' And from the scientific data, we not only know that *"science without a God"* does not pass the Scientific Method, but *"science without a God"* also contradicts sound science. This relates directly to one of our main goals in life which I am convinced, must include having a personal central core of belief. In my opinion, the ideal foundation for our core belief structure would be based upon Scripture and how it is supported by sound science. Scripture will lead us to the truth, and when necessary, sound science can be incorporated as support. Having sound science available when extra support would be helpful, is like having an extra tool in the toolbox. When we seek the truth, what will lead us in the right direction is the guidance of Scripture complimented by sound science.

And speaking of sound science, regarding the theory of evolution, sound science requires that a mutant process must produce countless numbers of mutants. Instead, sound science demonstrates that this is not the case. As a consequence, Darwinian macroevolution has been proven false by the absence of evolution mutants in the Fossil Record. In addition, sound science dictates that the natural selection-driven idea of Darwinian macroevolution has been proven false by the characteristics of the Fossil Record. The characteristics of the Fossil Record serve as evidence that Darwinian natural selection is not responsible for the appearance of the multitude of species found in the Fossil Record. When we take all of this into consideration, it leads us to the obvious and definitive conclusion that the Fossil Record evidence wipes Darwinian macroevolution right off the table.

What's more, sound science requires that a universe cannot create itself before it even existed. Sound science requires that a universe cannot create itself without any time to do so, and before it even existed. And lastly, sound social science dictates that provenance (the original source) is not established by the culture that puts a story into print first. Sound science dictates that provenance is established by the culture who first communicates the historical account.

As a side note, I would also like to say that I believe the rich diversity of life on the earth has convinced some people to accept the error-based idea of evolution. I believe that some people just can't imagine why a God would deliberately make strange animal species like porcupines, the platypus, or the flounder? With that being said, I believe that every species we witness here on the earth demonstrates the infinite creativity and imagination of God. In addition, and in some manner that we probably don't realize, each species somehow contributes to the entire ecosystem of the earth. Earth's ecosystem embodies a continuum where the present relies on the past and the future relies on the present. Therefore, the bizarre species that we see here are not the product of some wild, unpredictable, and random process. They are here by design.

Along these same lines, some people may wonder, if mankind and the earth are God's sole intention, then why are there two trillion galaxies in our universe? I personally believe this is a demonstration by God of how Big He is! God is putting on a galactic show to demonstrate just how magnificent and all powerful that He really is. Since He created the two-trillion-galaxy universe with all of its vast energy, stars, and planets, the universe shows us that God is even more powerful and larger than this. God is a Big God!

You will recall in the introduction of this book that I mentioned the great detective Sherlock Holmes who is quoted as stating:

> When you have excluded the impossible, whatever remains, however improbable, must be the truth.[640]

Sherlock Holmes is designed to be a brilliant fictional character. As a result, I believe we can all see how intelligent and true this statement is. With all of this being said, if we were to ask the great Sherlock Holmes for his analysis and diagnosis of whether God exists or not, he would undoubtedly reply, "It is elementary."

As this book draws to a close, I wish for people to really remember that the skeptics base their argument on science. However, hard science (sound science) states that it CAN'T DO what the skeptics claim that it can! It's a false claim to hear from a skeptic that their position is based on science. This is false because hard science has its limits and rules. What skeptics believe, actually violates the laws of physics and the ways that hard science operates. This means the skeptics do not have a scientific argument. The skeptic's argument presents incomplete *science* as their defense (pseudoscience), and this means they don't have a legitimate argument at all. The skeptic's position withholds certain scientific facts in order to make their case. Those facts are all clearly presented throughout this book. This makes the skeptic's position in this battle for the truth, indefensible.

By contrast, the person who believes in God has their argument supported by the realities of sound science along with the fact that God exists and functions outside of the construct of physics and time.

Therefore, God has to be the correct conclusion because He can exist and function outside of the construct of physics, hard science, and time. By contrast, the skeptic's argument falls woefully short because their *scientific* argument cannot exist and function outside of the construct of physics, hard science, and time.

Finally, regarding the topic of evolution, when it comes to the billions of people who think that the science of evolution makes a God unnecessary, I am going to repeat what I stated in Chapter Five regarding the scientific findings of highly esteemed experts in the field of evolutionary biology.

The scientists who really know their evolutionary biology are well aware that Darwinian evolution is a failed theory. Everyone else on planet Earth, who is not well versed in evolutionary biology, is under the false impression that Darwinian evolution is a sound scientific explanation for how all of the species appeared on the earth.

I firmly believe that many people are under the false impression that Darwin's theory of evolution must be correct because of its wide acceptance and because of his other good ideas. As stated, Darwin was correct about survival of the fittest, he was correct about natural selection, and he was correct about microevolution. He was also correct to support the phenomenon of environmental adaptation.

You will recall that microevolution represents minor improvements resulting from mutations. The COVID virus is a perfect example where variants are produced through mutations causing microevolutionary improvements. However, as we can all plainly see, this does not cause the genesis of a brand-new species, only variants of the same COVID species. The four billion people on planet Earth who believe that evolution makes God unnecessary are not talking about microevolution. These people believe in macroevolution which is the claim that brand-new species can make themselves without a God. Most of those people don't know that Darwin was correct about survival of the fittest, natural selection, and microevolution, but that he was completely wrong about macroevolution. This is because most people who believe in evolution don't really know what it is. For example, here are some basic questions to ask someone who claims to believe in evolution:

1) Is evolution a scientific fact or only a theory?

2) What are the two requirements for an evolutionary process?

3) What is microevolution and how is it different from macroevolution?

4) Have mutant fossils that prove evolution been found to exist in the Fossil Record?

5) How can you have a mutant process without any mutants???

6) Are you aware that the characteristics of the Fossil Record absolutely contradict the involvement of natural selection?

7) The Fossil Record has no mutants, and no signs of natural selection, so how do you have an evolutionary process without these two necessary requirements???

8) Are you aware of the Charles Darwin quote where he admits that his macroevolution theory has an obvious problem that allows for grave objections to be urged against it?

If people are unaware of the answers to these questions, then they really don't understand the topic of evolution. In essence, billions of people believe in something that they don't even understand! This is why it makes perfect sense these people don't understand that the Fossil Record findings have already proven Darwin's theory of evolution to be false. Most people are not in possession of all the facts. Everyone is entitled to know. This is a grave problem for four billion people because their eternal souls are in dire straits as a result of them putting all their faith into an idea that they really don't understand which has already been proven false by the Fossil Record.

This brings us full-circle as to how this book began where I mentioned a very, very interesting story. The fascinating story of Dr. Anthony Flew is one of intrigue because of the fact that the world's most notorious and outspoken atheist in modern history changed his mind and became a believer. He became a believer because of the richness and complexity of the genetic code found in every living organism that has ever lived on Earth. You will recall that Microsoft genius Bill Gates describes the genetic code on DNA to be very similar to the code that makes up a Microsoft Windows operating system. As mentioned previously, this is what Bill Gates stated about DNA:

DNA is like a software program, only much more complex than anything we've ever devised.[641]

In the same way that your computer needs millions and millions of lines of intelligent instructional code, so does your DNA. Remember that your DNA is like a computer's hard drive and the intelligent instructional code on the DNA is like a Microsoft Windows operating system. Do you remember how many lines of very specific instructional code make up a Microsoft Windows operating system? These operating systems have 50 million lines of code on them! Your computer needs 50 million lines of very specific instructional code that was meticulously engineered to tell it precisely what to do.[642]

Because a Microsoft Windows operating system has 50 million lines of specific instructional code, and since the operating system on our code is much more complex than 50 million lines of Microsoft code, this means that we have tens of millions of lines of intelligent instructional code on our DNA. This reality brings us to the ultimate question that we have to ask ourselves: Do we really believe that atoms and molecules floating around in the water wrote tens of millions of lines of intelligent instructional code that is more complex than a Microsoft Windows operating system???

Does that really make sense to anyone? Well, it didn't make any sense to the world's most notorious and most outspoken atheist in modern history. The obvious answer to this pivotal question is what ultimately changed the mind of Professor Anthony Flew. Anyone who believes that atoms and molecules floating around in the water invented a more complex and ingenious operating system than a Microsoft Windows software program, is not dealing with reality. This is not how the real-world works.

Skeptics may attempt to mention natural selection as a defense, but natural selection is not the magic fairy dust that saves the day for their indefensible position. As pointed out in Chapter Four, the phenomenon of natural selection cannot be experienced by dead things. In addition, recall that Dr. Raup found that the Fossil Record cannot be found as the most reasonable consequence of natural selection (Raup, Conflicts, p. 25). In other words, natural selection cannot be claimed to be the mechanism responsible for the appearance of all the living creatures that have ever lived on the earth. Because natural selection cannot be claimed to be responsible for the appearance of all the species on the earth, it makes no sense whatsoever to claim that natural selection was responsible for the appearance of the very first life on Earth. This truly spells the death of the theory of Darwinian evolution, neo-Darwinian evolution, and the hypothesis of abiogenesis.

It is also important to remember that natural selection does not write code. When an organism has been naturally selected to survive better, it's because of positive errors in DNA replication. As a consequence, DNA code has to already exist. Natural selection does not cause DNA to exist and natural selection does not cause the DNA errors to occur. The DNA code that already exists must experience errors during replication that gives the organism an advantage in surviving, only then has the organism been, 'naturally selected.' In other words, natural selection is not the cause for the biological improvements. Natural selection is the increase in survival that results from code errors that happen to cause biological improvements.

Based upon the facts of what natural selection actually is, and what it does regarding microevolution, it can be understood that natural selection is not a code writer. Writing code is not what natural selection does. The writing of intelligent instructional genetic code is not what an atom does, it is not what a molecule does, and it is not what natural selection does. None of these three things can write genetic code, let alone, tens of millions of lines of intelligent instructional code that is far more complex than a Microsoft Windows operating system! Therefore, the ingenious instructional code found on our DNA, which is more complex than a Microsoft Windows operating system, had to have come from a truly brilliant source that is capable of writing intelligent and magnificent genetic code.

This brings us back to the response that Professor Anthony Flew gave when asked why he changed his mind? Anthony Flew stated:

> No, I did not hear a voice. It was the evidence itself that led me to this conclusion.[643]

The evidence Anthony Flew is speaking about is the richness and complexity of DNA's genetic code. The realities and evidence that I have drawn your attention to, bring us to the same conclusion that was ultimately reached by the world's most notorious and most outspoken atheist in modern history. To get to the truth, all we have to do is follow the science.

In conclusion, science presents us with three core facts:

1) A universe cannot create itself from nothing in the absence of time.

2) Before it even existed, the first living organism that ever lived could not have written its own genetic code, and then designed and assembled itself from dead things floating around in the water.

3) Darwinian evolution is not how all of the species appeared on the earth. This is why present-day evolutionary biologists are quietly looking for a **non-Darwinian** evolution. When we examine Darwin's "most obvious and gravest objection" quote, it tells us everything we need to know regarding how the theory of evolution breaks down.[644]

Therefore, it should be clear from the evidence that self-creation is scientifically impossible. As a consequence, this most certainly makes God a necessary reality. The ultimate intended purpose for compiling this book is to reinforce the faith and knowledge of believers and to convert the unconverted.

In closing, I wish to remind people that God created the universe and the earth to support His most prized and most loved creation, mankind. God made humanity because He wished to have a family to share His Love. God wanted a family to join Him in His Kingdom, forever. This is why we were created with a part of us that is immortal, our soul. The souls who choose to live for God will ascend to their Maker upon their death. But the other souls, who choose to live for themselves in their self-centered nonbelief, will spend eternity in that other place.

God is many things. God is Love; God is merciful, and God is righteous because He always does the right thing for the right reason! None of us can claim that everything we do is for the right reason. In this book's exploration of God, you will notice the consistent presence of logic. This is because God is logical and methodical. And if that wasn't enough, God is also a brilliant scientist and a masterful engineer who just happens to love all of us very much and wishes for us to join Him in His Kingdom!

Endnotes

1   Benjamin Wiker, "How the World's Most Notorious Atheist Changed His Mind," Strange Notions, May 15, 2013, https://strangenotions.com/flew/.

2   Ibid.

3   Merriam-Webster, "Science," n.d., https://www.merriam-webster.com/dictionary/science.

4   Khan Academy, "The Scientific Method," n.d.,

5   Bonnie Sala, "The Difference Between A Non-Believer And An Unbeliever," June 30, 2020, https://www.guidelines.org/sermons/the-difference-between-a-non-believer-and-an-unbeliever/.

6   Brandon Specktor, "Stephen Hawking's Final Book Says There's 'No Possibility' of God in Our Universe", October 17, 2018, https://www.livescience.com/63854-stephen-hawking-says-no-god.html#:~:text=Stephen%20Hawking%27s%20Final%20Book%20Says%20There%27s%20%27No%20Possibility%27,in%20March%2C%20wrote%20that%20it%20is%20impossible%20. [cited from: Stephen Hawking (2018) *Brief Answers to the Big Questions,* U.S.: Hodder & Stoughton (hardcover) and Bantam Books (paperback)].

7   Philip K. Wilson, editor for Britannica.com, "Sherlock Holmes," n.d., https://www.britannica.com/topic/Sherlock-Holmes.

8   Catherine Giordano, "Here's Why Stephen Hawking Says There Is No God," October 25, 2018, https://owlcation.com/humanities/Stephen-Hawking-Says-There-Is-No-God-Heres-Why#:~:text=Science%2C%20philosophy%2C%20politics%2C%20

and%20religion%20are%20frequent%20topics,that%20it%20
has%20nothing%20to%20do%20with%20God.

9 Erin Kee, "Opinion: Evolution Shouldn't Be Taught as A
Fact," Scot Scoop, April 21, 2020, https://scotscoop.com/
opinion-evolution-shouldnt-be-taught-as-a-fact/.

10 Khan Academy, "The Scientific Method," n.d., https://www.
khanacademy.org/science/high-school-biology/hs-biology-foundations/
hs-biology-and-the-scientific-method/a/the-science-of-biology.

11 Brandon Specktor, "Stephen Hawking's Final Book…

12 Michael Ebifegha, *The Death Of Evolution*, (Xulon Press, 2007), p. 68.
(cited from: The Declaration of Students of the Natural and Physical
Sciences, by the Royal College of Surgeons of England. (PDF) p.2.
https://archive.org/details/b22371382/page/n1/mode/2up.

13 Kyle Butt M.A., "Syncretism and the Age of the Earth," Reason and
Revelation, August 2011, vol. 31, no. 8., (section: The Age of the
Earth and the Universe, 3rd paragraph). https://apologeticspress.
org/syncretism-and-the-age-of-the-earth-4081/. (cited from: Frances
Crick (1988), *What a Mad Pursuit: A Personal View of Scientific
Discovery* (New York: Basicbooks).

14 The Christian Contender, "The Scientific View Is To Believe In A
Creatior God," January 25, 2014, http://www.thechristiancontender.
org.uk/2014/01/1021/. (cited from George Wald, 1954. The Origin
of Life. *Scientific American* August: pp. 44-53).

15 The Harvard Crimson, "Wald Revives Spontaneous Birth Theory:
'Rejected' Concept Gets New Backing," January 7, 1957, https://
www.thecrimson.com/article/1957/1/7/wald-revives-spontaneous-
birth-theory-pthe/. (cited from: not listed)

16 Biology online.com Editor, "Spontaneous Generation," n.d., https://
www.biologyonline.com/dictionary/spontaneous-generation.

17 Kara Rogers for Britannica-Science&Tech, "Abiogenesis," Section
titled: Modern Concepts of Abiogenesis, Last Update October 12,
2023, https://www.britannica.com/science/abiogenesis.

18 The Harvard Crimson, "Wald Revives… (cited from: not listed)

19 "Spontaneous Generation," Lumen Learning, https://courses.
lumenlearning.com/microbiology/chapter/spontaneous-generation/.

20 The Christian Contender, "The Scientific View Is To Believe In A Creatior God,"

21 The Harvard Crimson, "Wald Revives… (cited from: not listed)

22 Ibid. (cited from: George Wald 1954. The Origin of Life. Scientific American August: pp. 44-53.

23 Chelsea Gohd for Space.com, "Astronomers Reevaluate the Age of the Universe," January, 08, 2021, https://www.space.com/universe-age-14-billion-years-old.

24 Miss Gina for LanguageTool.org, "What Is a Proverb," n.d., https://languagetool.org/insights/post/what-is-a-proverb/.

25 Tereza Pultarova for Space.com, "What If the Big Bang Wasn't the Beginning? New Study Proposes Alternative," December 5, 2017, https://www.space.com/38982-no-big-bang-bouncing-cosmology-theory.html.

26 Nine Planets Editor, "How Many Galaxies Are There in the Universe?" September 29, 2020, https://nineplanets.org/questions/how-many-galaxies-are-there-in-the-universe/.

27 Chelsea Gohd for Space.com, "Astronomers Reevaluate… (original referenced text not listed)

28 American Museum of Natural History editor, "Revolution: Time," Part of the Einstein exhibition, n.d., https://www.amnh.org/exhibitions/einstein/time/revolution-time.

29 Gilead.org Editor, "What is Einstein's Theory of Time?" n.d., http://co.gilead.org.il/what is einsteins theory of time.

30 Justin Taylor, (Blogs) "Biblical Reasons to Doubt the Creation Days Were 24-Hour Periods," January 28, 2015, https://www.thegospelcoalition.org/blogs/justin-taylor/biblical-reasons-to-doubt-the-creation-days-were-24-hour-periods/. (original referenced text not listed)

31 Oxford Dictionaries, "Time," n.d., https://www.bing.com/search?q=definition+of+time&qs=HS&pq=defi&sc=8-4&cvid=48C2980FC1414C47A3F5B8EBA2F933E7&FORM=QBRE&sp=1.

32 Cambridge Dictionary, "Clock," n.d., https://dictionary.cambridge.org/dictionary/english/clock.

33 Fiona MacDonald, "Earth Is Made Up of Two Planets Fused Together, New Research Suggests," February 02, 2016, https://www.sciencealert.

com/earth-is-made-up-of-two-planets-fused-together-by-a-head-on-collision-new-research-suggests.

34   John Ankerberg, The John Ankerberg Show, "What Scientific Evidence Proves God Created and Designed the Universe?" Program 1 and Program 2, 2009 with Dr. Hugh Ross, https://jashow.org/articles/what-scientific-evidence-proves-god-created-and-designed-the-universeprogram-1/. https://jashow.org/articles/what-scientific-evidence-proves-god-created-and-designed-the-universeprogram-2/.

35   Ibid.

36   Oldest.org Editor, "8 Oldest Fossils in the World," n.d., https://www.oldest.org/animals/fossils/.

37   Pew Research Center, "The Evolution of Pew Research Center's Survey Questions About the Origins and Development of Life on Earth," February 6, 2019, https://www.pewforum.org/2019/02/06/the-evolution-of-pew-research-centers-survey-questions-about-the-origins-and-development-of-life-on-earth/.

38   Wikipedia, "Level of Support for Evolution," n.d., https://en.wikipedia.org/wiki/Level_of_support_for_evolution.

39   Biology Dictionary Editors, "Fossil Record," January 7, 2018, https://biologydictionary.net/fossil-record/.

40   Lunar and Planetary Institute (LPI) Editor, "About Day and Night," n.d., https://www.lpi.usra.edu/education/skytellers/day_night/.

41   John Calvin, Genesis, The Crossway Classic Commentaries, Alister McGrath and J.I. Packer, eds. (Wheaton: Crossway, 2001.), n.p. (https://www.christianbook.com/genesis-the-crossway-classic-commentaries/john-calvin/9781581343014/pd/43019) Also found: Christianity.com, John Calvin's Bible Commentary, Genesis 1, https://www.christianity.com/bible/commentary/john-calvin/genesis/1,

42   Ibid.

43   Ibid. (original referenced text not listed)

44   Ibid. (original referenced text not listed)

45   Tereza Pultarova for Space.com, "What If the Big Bang Wasn't the Beginning? New Study Proposes Alternative," December 5, 2017, https://www.space.com/38982-no-big-bang-bouncing-cosmology-theory.html.

46 Ibid.

47 "The early universe," CERN, https://home.cern/science/physics/
early-universe.

48 Mike Austin, "God and the Good Life," September 13, 2010, https://
godandthegoodlife.blogspot.com/2010/09/aristotle.html.

49 Brandon Specktor, "Stephen Hawking's Final Book Says There's
'No Possibility' of God in Our Universe," October 17, 2018,
https://www.livescience.com/63854-stephen-hawking-says-no-god.
html#:~:text=Stephen%20Hawking%27s%20Final%20Book%20
Says%20There%27s%20%27No%20Possibility%27,in%20
March%2C%20wrote%20that%20it%20is%20impossible%20.
(cited from: Stephen Hawking, *Brief Answers to Big Questions*, October
16, 2018, (eBook) https://www.amazon.com/dp/B07D6BBGKL/
ref=dbs_p_ebk_dam.

50 Adam Mann, "What Is Space-Time?" *LiveScience*, December 19,
2019, https://www.livescience.com/space-time.html.

51 Ethan Siegel, "Ask Ethan: Is Spacetime Really A Fabric?"
Forbes, August 11, 2018, https://www.forbes.com/sites/
startswithabang/2018/08/11/ask-ethan-is-spacetime-really-
a-fabric/?sh=5e20f03c97fc#:~:text=Remember%2C%20
it%20isn%27t%20actually%20a%20fabric%2C%20but%20
rather,Universe%20away%20that%20we%27re%20capable%20
of%20taking%20away.

52 Ibid.

53 Oxford Dictionaries, "Gravity," n.d., https://www.bing.com/search?q=
gravity+dcfinition&qs=LS&pq=gravity+def&sc=8-11&cvid=D6B46C
6D8823444F9166CD0F9C4FA1F9&FORM=QBRE&sp=1.

54 Derek Muller of Veritasium on YouTube, "Why Gravity is
NOT a Force," October 9, 2020, https://www.youtube.com/
watch?v=XRr1kaXKBsU.

55 Ibid.

56 Ibid.

57 John Ankerberg, The John Ankerberg Show, "What Scientific
Evidence Proves God Created and Designed the Universe?"
Program 1 and Program 2, 2009 with Dr. Hugh Ross, https://
jashow.org/articles/what-scientific-evidence-proves-god-created-

and-designed-the-universeprogram-1/. https://jashow.org/articles/ what-scientific-evidence-proves-god-created-and-designed-the-universeprogram-2/.

58   Ethan Siegel, Ph.D., "Ask Ethan: How Does the CMB Prove the Big Bang?" September 20, 2022, https://bigthink.com/starts-with-a-bang/ cmb-prove-big-bang/.

59   John Ankerberg, The John Ankerberg Show, "What Scientific Evidence Proves God…

60   Ibid.

61   The Nobel Prize-Roger Penrose Nobel Lecture, "Black Holes, Cosmology, and Space-Time Singularities," March 4, 2021, https:// www.nobelprize.org/prizes/physics/2020/penrose/lecture/.

62   The Rational Zealot editor, "Roger Penrose on Entropy: How Did He Calculate That?" March 16, 2014, https://therationalzealot.blogspot. com/2014/03/roger-penrose-on-entropy-how-did-he.html.

63   All About Philosophy.org editing author, Q&A: "Teleological Argument and Entropy," n.d., https://www.allaboutphilosophy.org/ teleological-argument-and-entropy-faq.htm.

64   Scott Youngren, for God Evidence.com, "OK…I Want Numbers. What is the Probability the Universe is the Result of Chance?" December 01, 2010, https://godevidence.com/2010/12/ok-i-want-numbers-what-is-the-probability-the-universe-is-the-result-of-chance/. (cited from: Roger Penrose, *The Emperor's New Mind*, in the chapter entitled, "Cosmology and the Arrow of Time," p. 344.

65   Oxford Dictionaries, "Entropy" n.d., https://www.bing.com/search?q= entropy+definition&qs=LS&pq=entropy&sk=AS1&sc=8-7&cvid=DA 5E5556D95649019CC5A53705FA403C&FORM=QBRE&sp=2.

66   Unknown internet source

67   Surfguppy Editor, "Entropy," (Section: Entropy and Disorder), n.d., https://surfguppy.com/thermodynamics/ entropy-chemical-thermodynamics/.

68   The Rational Zealot editor, "Roger Penrose on Entropy,,,

69   Difference Between.Com, posted by Madhu, "Difference Between Atoms and Particles," June 5, 2019, https://www.differencebetween. com/difference-between-atoms-and-particles/#:~:text=The%20 key%20difference%20between%20atoms%20and%20particles%20

is,exists%20and%20we%20cannot%20break%20it%20down%20
further.

70   Definitions.net, "Phase Space," n.d., https://www.definitions.net/
definition/Phase%20Space.

71   The Rational Zealot editor, "Roger Penrose on Entropy: How Did He
Calculate That?" March 16, 2014, https://therationalzealot.blogspot.
com/2014/03/roger-penrose-on-entropy-how-did-he.html.

72   Ibid.

73   Ibid.

74   Scott Youngren, for God Evidence.com, "OK…I Want Numbers…

75   The Rational Zealot editor, "Roger Penrose on Entropy: How Did He
Calculate That?"

76   John Ankerberg, The John Ankerberg Show, "What Scientific
Evidence Proves…

77   Youngren, "OK…I Want Numbers…"

78   All About Philosophy.org editing author, "Teleological Argument
and Entropy," n.d., https://www.allaboutphilosophy.org/teleological-
argument-and-entropy-faq.htm.

79   Youngren, "OK…I Want Numbers…."

80   Brandon Specktor, "Stephen Hawking's Final Book Says There's
'No Possibility' of God in Our Universe," Live Science, October 17,
2018, https://www.livescience.com/63854-stephen-hawking-says-
no-god.html#:~:text=Stephen%20Hawking%27s%20Final%20
Book%20Says%20There%27s%20%27No%20Possibility%27,in%20
March%2C%20wrote%20that%20it%20is%20impossible%20.

81   Ibid.

82   Ibid.

83   Brandon Specktor, "Stephen Hawking's Final Book Says There's 'No
Possibility' of God in Our Universe,"

84   Catherine Giordano, "Here's Why Stephen Hawking Says
There Is No God," October 25, 2018, https://owlcation.com/
humanities/Stephen-Hawking-Says-There-Is-No-God-Heres-
Why#:~:text=Science%2C%20philosophy%2C%20politics%2C%20
and%20religion%20are%20frequent%20topics,that%20it%20
has%20nothing%20to%20do%20with%20God.

85   Ibid (section: Did ALS Influence Hawking's Religious Beliefs?).

86   Ibid.

87   YouTube video posted by MrEpistemologist1, "Sir Roger
     Penrose's critical reaction to 'The Grand Design,' by Stephen
     Hawking," November 1, 2012, https://www.youtube.com/
     watch?v=b2kVPnussGo.

88   Ibid.

89   Ibid.

90   Ibid.

91   Youngren, "OK…I Want Numbers…"

92   YouTube video, "STEPHEN HAWKING'S argument DESTROYED
     BY John Lennox," https://YouTube.com, 2018, https://www.youtube.
     com/watch?v=FaYtAQFXWFg.

93   Ibid.

94   Ibid.

95   Nine Planets Editor, "How Many Galaxies Are There in the
     Universe?" September 29, 2020, https://nineplanets.org/questions/
     how-many-galaxies-are-there-in-the-universe/.

96   John Ankerberg, The John Ankerberg Show, "What Scientific
     Evidence…"

97   Nick Watt for NBC News, "Stephen Hawking: 'Science Makes God
     Unnecessary,'" September 6, 2010, https://abcnews.go.com/GMA/
     stephen-hawking-science-makes-god-unnecessary/story?id=11571150.

98   Matt Strassler, "Quantum Fluctuations and Their Energy,"
     August 29, 2013, https://profmattstrassler.com/articles-and-posts/
     particle-physics-basics/quantum-fluctuations-and-their-energy/.

99   Ibid.

100 Alastair Wilson, "How Did the Big Bang Arise Out of
     Nothing?" January 04, 2022, https://www.sciencealert.com/
     how-did-the-big-bang-explode-out-of-nothing-this-could-be-the-way.

101 Ibid.

102 Brandon Specktor, "Stephen Hawking's Final Book Says There's
     'No Possibility' of God in Our Universe," Live Science, October 17,
     2018, https://www.livescience.com/63854-stephen-hawking-says-
     no-god.html#:~:text=Stephen%20Hawking%27s%20Final%20
     Book%20Says%20There%27s%20%27No%20Possibility%27,in%20
     March%2C%20wrote%20that%20it%20is%20impossible%20.

103 Encyclopedia Britannica Editor, "Uncertainty Principle," last updated April 27, 2025, https://www.britannica.com/science/uncertainty-principle.

104 Tihomir Dimitrov, submitted by 2012daily.com administrator, "Nobel Laureate Werner Heisenberg: GOD Is Waiting at the Bottom of the Glass," 11/03/2011, https://2012daily.com/?q=node/52.

105 Ibid.

106 Nicolas Burk, "Did the Universe Come From Nothing?" June 03, 2019, https://www.freethoughtforum.org/blog/did-the-universe-come-from-nothing. This website appears to be expired now. This endnote was referencing a conversation on this blog site between Nicolas Burk and a member named Simon. Simon was the one who put forth the argument that science will never be able to establish an underpinning foundation that is the cause of it all.

107 AZ Quotes Editing Author, "Roger Penrose Quotes," n.d., https://www.azquotes.com/author/23942-Roger_Penrose.

108 PNAS Lucie Laplane, et al., "Why Science Needs Philosophy," March 5, 2019, https://www.pnas.org/content/116/10/3948.

109 Khan Academy, "The Scientific Method," n.d., https://www.khanacademy.org/science/high-school-biology/hs-biology-foundations/hs-biology-and-the-scientific-method/a/the-science-of-biology.

110 Merriam-Webster, "Empiricism," n.d., https://www.merriam-webster.com/dictionary/empiricism.

111 Christianity Today Editor, "Francis Bacon-Philosopher of Science," (section: Years of Achievement) n.d., https://www.christianitytoday.com/history/people/scholarsandscientists/francis-bacon.html.

112 Francis Bacon on West Egg.com, "Of Atheism," n.d., https://www.westegg.com/bacon/atheism.html.

113 Christianity Today Editor, "Francis Bacon…

114 National Space Society Editor, "National Space Society Governor Robert Jastrow Biography," n.d., https://space.nss.org/national-space-society-governor-robert-jastrow-biography/.

115 Ibid.

116 Specktor, "Stephen Hawking's Final Book Says There's 'No Possibility' of God…"

117 Dennis D. Chamberlain, The Chamberlain Story 2017, "E-6 Sir Isaac Newton: The Athanasian Creed and Bible Prophecy," 2017, (section: Was Isaac Newton an Arian?) http://www.thechamberlainstory. com/2018/01/19/isaac-newton-bible-prophecy/.

118 Ibid.

119 Baxter Dmitry for News Punch.com, "World Famous Physicist Says He's Found Evidence That God Exists," December 28, 2018, https:// newspunch.com/world-physicist-evidence-god/

120 Ibid.

121 Paul Sutter for Live Science.com, "What If the Universe Had No Beginning?", October 11, 2021, https://www.livescience.com/ universe-had-no-beginning-time.

122 The video of this interview is now posted on YouTube under the title, "Sir Roger Penrose's critical reaction to 'The Grand Design,' by Stephen Hawking," https://www.youtube.com/ watch?v=b2kVPnussGo.

123 Ibid.

124 Sutter, "What If the Universe Had No Beginning?"

125 Spector, "Stephen Hawking's Final Book…"

126 The Rational Zealot editor, "Roger Penrose on Entropy:…"

127 Akash Peshin for Science ABC, "What Existed Before The Big Bang?" (in Multiverse section), Jan 26, 2022, https://www.scienceabc.com/ nature/universe/what-existed-before-the-big-bang.html.

128 Sutter, "What If the Universe Had No Beginning?"

129 The video of this interview is now posted on YouTube under the title, "Sir Roger Penrose's critical reaction to 'The Grand Design,' by Stephen Hawking," https://www.youtube.com/ watch?v=b2kVPnussGo.

130 Peshin on Science ABC, "What Existed Before…"

131 Tereza Pultarova for Space.com-Astronomy, "What If the Big Bang Wasn't the Beginning? New Study Proposes Alternative," December 5, 2017, https://www.space.com/38982-no-big-bang-bouncing- cosmology-theory.html.

132 Ibid.

133 Ibid.

134 Robert Sanders for Berkeley News, "How Fast Is the Universe Expanding? Galaxies Provide One Answer," March 8, 2021, https://news.berkeley.edu/2021/03/08/how-fast-is-the-universe-expanding-galaxies-provide-one-answer/.

135 Ibid.

136 Jacqueline Mitchell for Now Tufts.edu, "In the Beginning Was the Beginning," May 29, 2012, https://now.tufts.edu/articles/beginning-was-beginning.

137 Merriam-Webster, "Natural Selection," n.d., https://www.merriam-webster.com/dictionary/natural%20selection.

138 Dictionary.com, "Natural Selection," n.d., https://www.dictionary.com/browse/natural-selection.

139 Oxford Dictionaries, "Microevolution," n.d., https://www.bing.com/search?q=microevolution&qs=SC&pq=micro-evolution&sk=SC3&sc=8-15&cvid=4C1CEB88B4144191AE64763B6736BC3E&FORM=QBRE&sp=4.

140 Oxford Dictionaries, "Macroevolution," n.d., https://www.bing.com/search?q=macroevolution+definition&qs=LS&pq=macroevolution+def&sc=8-18&cvid=F07415D8DBFC46F09A3B19B4DE363A75&FORM=QBRE&sp=1.

141 Austin Cline, "Abiogenesis and Evolution," LearnReligions.com, updated June 25, 2019, https://www.learnreligions.com/abiogenesis-and-evolution-249875.

142 Ibid.

143 "Abiogenesis," Oxford Dictionaries, n.d., https://www.bing.com/search?q=abiogenesis+define&qs=AS&pq=abiogenesis&sk=HS1&sc=8-11&cvid=014BCFBD984740BF9E03FA4A7ABEB574&FORM=QBRE&sp=2.

144 Difference Between, posted by Dr. Samanthi, "Difference Between Chemical and Organic Evolution," August 31, 2018, https://www.differencebetween.com/difference-between-chemical-and-organic-evolution/.

145 PG Higgs (Paul G. Higgs), "Chemical Evolution and the Evolutionary Definition of Life," *PubMed*, June 29, 2017, https://pubmed.ncbi.nlm.nih.gov/28664404/.

146 Code.org editor, "How Many Lines of Code?" n.d., https://code.org/loc.

147 Mario Seiglie, "The Tiny Code That's Toppling Evolution," United Church of God, May 21, 2005 (section: DNA contains a genetic language), https://www.ucg.org/the-good-news/dna-the-tiny-code-thats-toppling-evolution.

148 Oldest.org Editor, "8 Oldest Fossils in the World," n.d., https://www.oldest.org/animals/fossils/.

149 Britannica, "Deoxyribonucleic Acid (DNA)," n.d., https://www.britannica.com/science/nucleic-acid/Deoxyribonucleic-acid-DNA.

150 Michael Graham Richard, "How Many Atoms Encode the Human Genome?" Posted April 6, 2008, https://michaelgr.wordpress.com/2008/04/06/how-many-atoms-to-encode-the-human-genome/.

151 Henry Morris, Ph.D., "Probability and Order Versus Evolution," Institute for Creation Research, July 1, 1979, https://www.icr.org/article/probability-order-versus-evolution/. (cited from: Frank B. Salisbury, "Doubts about the Modern Synthetic Theory of Evolution," *American Biology Teacher*, September 1971, p. 336.)

152 Henry Morris, Ph.D., "Probability And Order Versus Evolution," Institute for Creation Research, July 1, 1979, https://www.icr.org/article/probability-order-versus-evolution/. (cited from: Marcel Golay, "Reflections of a Communications Engineer," *Analytical Chemistry*, V. 33, June 1961, p. 23.)

153 Amoeba Sisters on YouTube, "DNA Replication (updated)", 2020, https://www.youtube.com/watch?v=Qqe4thU-os8.

154 MooMooMath and Science on YouTube, "Decode from DNA to mRNA to tRNA to Amino Acids," 2019, https://www.youtube.com/watch?v=0SM1YEBrOyI.

155 David Warmflash and Nathan Lents for Vision Learning.com, Under **Evolutionary Biology**, "Origins of Life I: Early Ideas and Experiments (section: Moving To A DNA World), Vision learning Vol. BIO-4 (6), 2016, https://www.visionlearning.com/en/library/Biology/2/Origins-of-Life-I/226.

156 Ibid.

157 Ibid.

158 Ibid.

159 Ibid.

160 Katrina Kramer for Chemistry World.com, "Self-Replicating Molecules Show Signs of Metabolism For the First Time," (section: Life As We Don't Know It), July 29, 2020, https://www. chemistryworld.com/news/self-replicating-molecules-show-signs-of-metabolism-for-the-first-time/4012152.article.

161 Mario Seiglie, "The Tiny Code That's Toppling Evolution" (section: Amazing revelations about DNA), United Church of God, May 21, 2005, https://www.ucg.org/the-good-news/dna-the-tiny-code-thats-toppling-evolution. (cited from: Evolution: A Theory in Crisis, 1996, p. 334).

162 Benjamin Wiker, "How the World's Most Notorious Atheist Changed His Mind," Strange Notions, May 15, 2013, https://strangenotions. com/flew/.

163 Ibid.

164 Ibid.

165 Ibid.

166 Sarah Knapp for BiologyDictionary.net, "Artificial Selection," last update October 27, 2020, https://biologydictionary.net/ artificial-selection/.

167 Ibid.

168 Ibid.

169 Marcel P. Schutzenberger, "Algorithms and the Neo-Darwonian Theory of Evolution," *Mathematical Challenges to the Neo-Darwinian Interpretation of Evolution* (Philadelphia, Wistar Institute Press, 1967). P. 75., https://www.ncbi.nlm.nih.gov/ nlmcatalog/122541#:~:text=Title%20%28s%29%3A%20 Mathematical%20challenges%20to%20the%20neo-Darwinian%20 interpretation,United%20States%20Publisher%3A%20 Philadelphia%2C%20Wistar%20Institute%20Press%2C%201967.

170 Murray Eden, "Inadequacies of Neo-Darwinian Evolution as a Scientific Theory," *Mathematical Challenges to the Neo-Darwinian Interpretation of Evolution* (Philadelphia, Wistar Institute Press, 1967). P. 109., https://www.ncbi.nlm.nih.gov/ nlmcatalog/122541#:~:text=Title%20%28s%29%3A%20 Mathematical%20challenges%20to%20the%20neo-Darwinian%20

interpretation,United%20States%20Publisher%3A%20 Philadelphia%2C%20Wistar%20Institute%20Press%2C%201967.

171 Alan McDougall on Science Forums.net blog, "What Are The Odds Of Life Evolving By Chance Alone?" *Evolution, Morphology and Exobioogy*, posted on July 22, 2012, https://www.scienceforums.net/ topic/67884-what-are-the-odds-of-life-evolving-by-chance-alone/.

172 Alan McDougall on Science Forums.net blog, "What Are The Odds Of Life Evolving By Chance Alone?" *Evolution, Morphology and Exobioogy*, posted on July 22, 2012, https://www.scienceforums.net/ topic/67884-what-are-the-odds-of-life-evolving-by-chance-alone/. (cited from: [Fred Hoyle and N. Chandra Wickramasinghe, *Evolution From Space*, (Aldine House, 33 Welback Street, London W1M 8LX: J.M. Dent & Sons, 1981), p. 148, 24, 150, 30, 31 (emphasis added).]

173 Ibid.

174 Bridgett Payseur, Ph.D., and Allison Denny, "What is Molecular Evolution," n.d., https://study.com/academy/lesson/what-is-molecular-evolution.html.

175 Dan Hogan, "Family Genetic Research Reveals the Speed of Human Mutation," ScienceDaily, June 13, 2011, https://www.sciencedaily. com/releases/2011/06/110613012749.htm.

176 J. Flegr, "III.6 Mutations Can Be Differentiated As Positive, Negative and Selectively Neutral On the Basis of their Effect On The Biological Fitness Of The Organism," Academia Prague, 2009 (second paragraph), https://www.frozenevolution.com/ iii6-mutations-can-be-differentiated-positive-negative-and-selectively-neutral-basis-their-effect-bi. (cited from: *Draft translation from: Evoluční biologie, 2. vydání (Evolutionary biology, 2nd edition), J. Flegr, Academia Prague 2009.*

177 Young Genome.org Editor, "Evolution of Modern Humans," Young Genome, n.d., https://www.yourgenome.org/stories/ evolution-of-modern-humans.

178 Flegr, "III.6 Mutations Can Be Differentiated As Positive…"

179 Dennis O'Neil, "Homo Erectus," 2013, https://www2.palomar.edu/ anthro/homo/homo_2.htm.

180 Ibid.

181 Susan C. Anton, Hannah G. Taboada, Emily R. Middleton, Christopher W. Rainwater, Andrea B. Taylor, Trudy R. Turner, Jean E. Turnquist, Karen J. Weinstein, and Scott A. Williams, for the National Center for Biotechnology Information, "Morphological Variation in Homo erectus and the Origins of Developmental Plasticity," (Table 1), https://www.ncbi.nlm.nih.gov/pmc/articles/PMC4920293/.

182 CDC.gov Editor, "Data and Statistics on Birth Defects," https://www.cdc.gov/birth-defects/data-research/facts-stats/index.html#:~:text=About%20one%20in%20every%2033%20babies,is%20born%20with%20a%20birth%20defect.

183 Raup, *Extinction: Bad Genes or Bad Luck?* p. 10-11.

184 Ibid.

185 Molly Campbell for Technology Networks.com, "Genotype vs. Phenotype: Examples and Definitions," December 18, 2020-last updated: September 12, 2022, https://www.technologynetworks.com/genomics/articles/genotype-vs-phenotype-examples-and-definitions-318446.

186 Ibid.

187 Jon Perry narrates YouTube video by *Stated Clearly*, (Arabic CC by Mustafa Farqad and Mohammed Baset), "What Is A Chromosome?" July 26, 2017, https://www.youtube.com/watch?v=IePMXxQ-KWY.

188 Emmanuel Kingsley for AZ-Animals.com, "African Wild Dog vs. Wolf: Key Differences," (section: Habitat and Distribution), September 8, 2022, https://a-z-animals.com/blog/african-wild-dog-vs-wolf-key-differences/.

189 Michael Ebifegha, *The Death Of Evolution* (Xulon Press, 2007), viewed on http://books.google.com. (1864, as cited in Ebifegha 2007).

190 Charles Darwin, *On the Origins of Species by Means of Natural Selection, or Preservation of Favored Races in the Struggler for Life,* (London: John Murray, 1859), p. 292.

191 David M. Raup, *Extinction: Bad Genes or Bad Luck?* (W.W. Norton & Company, Inc., New York, N.Y., 1992), p. 3.

192 Charles Darwin, *On the Origins of Species by Means of Natural Selection, or Preservation of Favored Races in the Struggler for Life,* (London:John Murray, 1859), p. 292.

193 David M. Raup, "Conflicts Between Darwin and Paleontology," Bulletin of the Field Museum of Natural History (of Chicago). V. 50, January 1979, p. 22-23. (end of p. 22 and beginning of p. 23). https://ia800702.us.archive.org/0/items/cbarchive_35806_conflictsbetweendarwinandpaleo1930/conflictsbetweendarwinandpaleo1930.pdf.

194 Art Battson, evaluates "Conflicts Between Darwin and Paleontology," n.d., http://www.veritas-ucsb.org/library/battson/stasis/2.html. (Darwin, 1859, p. 219)

195 Michael Foote for PNAS (Proceedings of the National Academy of Sciences of the United States of America) , "David M. Raup, 1933-2015," November 24, 2015, https://www.pnas.org/content/112/49/15002.

196 Steve Koppes, "David Raup, Paleontologist Who Transformed His Discipline, 1933-2015," July 14, 2015, https://news.uchicago.edu/story/david-raup-paleontologist-who-transformed-his-discipline-1933-2015.

197 Ibid.

198 Morris, "Probability And Order Versus Evolution," [cited from: "Conflicts Between Darwin and Paleontology," Bulletin of the Field Museum of Natural History (of Chicago). V. 50, January 1979]. https://ia800702.us.archive.org/0/items/cbarchive_35806_conflictsbetweendarwinandpaleo1930/conflictsbetweendarwinandpaleo1930.pdf.

199 Darwin, *On the Origins of Species by Means of Natural Selection, or Preservation of Favored Races in the Struggler for Life*, (London:John Murray, 1859), p. 292.

200 Raup, "Conflicts Between Darwin and Paleontology," p. 23, (top left column)

201 Danita Brandt for EBSCO.com, "Fossil Record," 2024, https://www.ebsco.com/research-starters/earth-and-atmospheric-sciences/fossil-record.

202 Raup, "Conflicts Between Darwin and Paleontology," p. 23, (top left column, 5th line down)

203 Henry Morris, Ph.D., "Probability And Order Versus Evolution," July 01, 1979, https://www.icr.org/article/

probability-order-versus-evolution/. (citing David M. Raup, "Conflicts Between Darwin and Paleontology," Bulletin of the Field Museum of Natural History (of Chicago). V. 50, January 1979, p. 23. and 26.) https://ia800702.us.archive.org/0/items/cbarchive_35806_conflictsbetweendarwinandpaleo1930/conflictsbetweendarwinandpaleo1930.pdf.

204 Ibid. p. 24, (bottom of right column)

205 David M. Raup, "Conflicts Between Darwin and Paleontology," Bulletin of the Field Museum of Natural History (of Chicago). V. 50, January 1979, p. 25. (middle of first full paragraph in left column) https://ia800702.us.archive.org/0/items/cbarchive_35806_conflictsbetweendarwinandpaleo1930/conflictsbetweendarwinandpaleo1930.pdf.

206 Ibid. p. 25. (middle of first full paragraph in left column)

207 Ibid. p. 25. (middle of first full paragraph in left column)

208 Ibid. p. 23. (left column, second paragraph and p. 25. First full paragraph)

209 Raup, "Conflicts Between Darwin and Paleontology," p. 25. (left column, near end of first full paragraph) https://ia800702.us.archive.org/0/items/cbarchive_35806_conflictsbetweendarwinandpaleo1930/conflictsbetweendarwinandpaleo1930.pdf.

210 Ibid. p. 23. (left column, first and second paragraphs)

211 Ibid. p. 23. and 26.

212 Ibid. p. 25. (left column, near end of first full paragraph)

213 Ibid. p. 26 (last paragraph)

214 Ibid. p. 26. (left column, near end of first full paragraph)

215 Ibid. p. 26. (left column, last paragraph)

216 Foote, for PNAS (Proceedings of the National Academy of Sciences of the United States of America) , "David M. Raup, 1933-2015,"

217 Encyclopedia Of Creation Science Editor, "Wistar Institute Symposium (1966)," n.d., https://mail.creationwiki.org/Wistar_Institute_Symposium_(1966)#:~:text=The%20conference%20was%20chaired%20by%20Nobel%20Laureate%20Sir,whether%20the%20neo-Darwinian%20theory%20is%20mathematically%20feasible.%20.

218 Ibid.

219 Raup, "Conflicts Between Darwin and Paleontology," p. 25. (middle of first full paragraph in left column)

220 Raup, "Conflicts Between Darwin and Paleontology," p. 25. (left column, last paragraph) https://ia800702.us.archive.org/0/items/cbarchive_35806_conflictsbetweendarwinandpaleo1930/conflictsbetweendarwinandpaleo1930.pdf.

221 Ibid. p. 23. (left column, last paragraph)

222 Ibid. p. 24. (left column, last paragraph)

223 Ibid. p. 24. (right column)

224 Ibid. p. 26. (left column, 6th line down)

225 Ibid. p. 26. (left column, lines 23-30)

226 Ibid. p. 26. (left column, lines 4-6)

227 Ibid. p. 24 (right column)

228 Ibid. p. 25. (left column, near end of first full paragraph)

229 Ibid. p. 26. (left column, first full paragraph)

230 Ibid.

231 Ibid. p. 25. (left column, near end of first full paragraph)

232 Raup, "Conflicts Between Darwin and Paleontology," p. 26. (right column, last paragraph)

233 Ibid. pp. 22-27.

234 Ibid. p. 25 (bottom of page)

235 Russell Levine and Chris Evers, "The Slow Death of Spontaneous Generation (1668-1859), https://webprojects.oit.ncsu.edu/project/bio183de/Black/cellintro/cellintro_reading/Spontaneous_Generation.html#:~:text=The%20theory%20of%20spontaneous%20generation%20was%20finally%20laid,variation%20of%20the%20methods%20of%20Needham%20and%20Spallanzani.

236 Oxford Dictionaries, "Microevolution," n.d., https://www.bing.com/search?q=microevolution&qs=SC&pq=micro-evolution&sk=SC3&sc=8-15&cvid=4C1CEB88B4144191AE64763B6736BC3E&FORM=QBRE&sp=4.

237 Oxford Dictionaries, "Macroevolution," n.d., https://www.bing.com/search?q=macroevolution+definition&qs=LS&pq=macroevolution+def&sc=8-18&cvid=F07415D8DBFC46F09A3B19B4DE363A75&FORM=QBRE&sp=1.

238 Raup, "Conflicts Between Darwin and Paleontology," p. 25. (left column, near end of first full paragraph)

239 Morris, "Probability And Order Versus Evolution," [cited from: "Conflicts Between Darwin and Paleontology," Bulletin of the Field Museum of Natural History (of Chicago). V. 50, January 1979] p. 23.

240 Darwin, "*On the Origins of Species…*" (Chapter 6-On the Absence Or Rarity of Transitional Varieties, top of second paragraph) and (Chapter 9-On the Imperfection of the Geological Record, end of second paragraph, p.292).

241 Art Battson, evaluates "Conflicts Between Darwin and Paleontology," n.d., http://www.veritas-ucsb.org/library/battson/stasis/2.html. (cited from: Gould, S.J. (1977), "Evolution's Erratic Pace." Natural History, vol. 86, May. (also cited from: David M. Raup Ph.D., "Conflicts Between Darwin and Paleontology," *Field Museum of Natural History Bulletin,* 1979, vol. 50 (1): (pp. 22-29) https://archive.org/details/cbarchive_121465_conflictsbetweendarwinandpaleo1930/mode/2up.

242 Art Battson, evaluates "Conflicts Between Darwin and Paleontology," n.d., http://www.veritas-ucsb.org/library/battson/stasis/2.html. (cited from: Gould, S. J. (1980), "Is a new and general theory of evolution emerging?" *Paleobiology,* 6(1), p. 120, (PDF),https://www.jstor.org/stable/2400240.

243 Art Battson, evaluates "Conflicts Between Darwin and Paleontology," n.d., http://www.veritas-ucsb.org/library/battson/stasis/2.html. (cited from: Gould, S.J. (1977), "Evolution's Erratic Pace." Natural History, vol. 86, May.

244 Charles Darwin, *On the Origins of Species by Means of Natural Selection, or Preservation of Favored Races in the Struggler for Life,* (London: John Murray, 1859), p. 292.

245 Raup, "Conflicts Between Darwin and Paleontology," p. 25, (left column, 24th line from the top)

246 Art Battson, evaluates "Conflicts Between Darwin and Paleontology," n.d., http://www.veritas-ucsb.org/library/battson/stasis/2.html. (cited from: Gould, S. J. (1980), "Is a new and general theory of evolution emerging?" *Paleobiology,* 6(1), p. 120, (PDF),https://www.jstor.org/stable/2400240.

247   Philip K. Wilson, editor for Britannica.com, "Sherlock Holmes," n.d., https://www.britannica.com/topic/Sherlock-Holmes.

248   Art Battson, evaluates "Conflicts Between Darwin and Paleontology," n.d., http://www.veritas-ucsb.org/library/battson/stasis/2.html.

249   Goodreads.com, "Benjamin Franklin Quotes," https://www.goodreads.com/quotes/11227350-you-will-observe-with-concern-how-long-a-useful-truth#:~:text=Benjamin%20Franklin%20—%20'You%20will%20observe%20with%20concern,before%20it%20is%20generally%20received%20and%20practiced%20on.'

250   Stephanie Hertzenberg, "The Faith of 5 Founding Fathers," copyright 2024, https://www.beliefnet.com/news/politics/the-faith-of-5-founding-fathers.aspx.

251   John Fuller for How Stuff Works.com, "What Did Benjamin Franklin Invent? Much More Than Bifocals," Update October 20, 2023, https://science.howstuffworks.com/innovation/famous-inventors/10-ben-franklin-inventions.htm.

252   Ibid.

253   POE editor, "How Did Benjamin Franklin Successfully Gain France's Support During the American Revolution?" Updated May 4, 2024, https://poe.com/p/How-did-Benjamin-Franklin-successfully-gain-Frances-support-during-the-American-Revolution.

254   Stoyan Zaimov, Christian Post Reporter, "Pat Robertson Says Dinosaurs Prove Young Earth Creationists Are Wrong," November 28, 2012, https://www.christianpost.com/news/pat-robertson-says-dinosaurs-prove-young-earth-creationists-are-wrong.html.

255   Unknown author

256   Oxford Dictionaries, "Nuclear Fusion," n.d., https://www.bing.com/search?q=nuclear+fusion+definition&qs=LS&pq=nuclear+fusion+definition&sc=8-25&cvid=8EF5757043BE459F803CC327EAEB234B&FORM=QBRE&sp=1.

257   Science Daily Editor, "Stellar Nucleosynthesis," n.d., https://www.sciencedaily.com/terms/stellar_nucleosynthesis.htm.

258   Jennifer Chu for the MIT News Office, "Neutron Star Collisions Are A 'Goldmine' Of Heavy Elements, Study Finds…." October 25, 2021, https://news.mit.edu/2021/neutron-star-collisions-goldmine-heavy-elements-1025.

259 Oldest.org Editor, "8 Oldest Fossils in the World," n.d., https://www.oldest.org/animals/fossils/.

260 Liz Thompson, "Unlocking The Secrets of Earth's Early Atmosphere," April 27, 2021, https://www.anl.gov/article/unlocking-the-secrets-of-earths-early-atmosphere#:~:text=A%20long%20time%20ago%2C%20as%20our%20solar%20system,collided%20with%20a%20planet%20the%20size%20of%20Mars.

261 Matthew Ward Agius for Cosmos Magazine.com, "Without This Moon-Sized Hunk Of Iron We Wouldn't Exist," July 27, 2022, https://cosmosmagazine.com/earth/inner-core-saved-earths-magnetic-field/.

262 Shannon Hall for Scientific American, "Earth's Tectonic Activity May Be Crucial for Life—And Rare in Our Galaxy," July 20, 2017, https://www.scientificamerican.com/article/earths-tectonic-activity-may-be-crucial-for-life-and-rare-in-our-galaxy/.

263 Brian Molinari, Life Verse.com (Space), "10 Changes The Earth Would Suffer If It Had No Moon," April 23, 2019, https://listverse.com/2019/04/23/10-changes-the-earth-would-suffer-if-it-had-no-moon/.

264 Ibid.

265 Oldest.org Editor, "8 Oldest Fossils in the World," n.d., https://www.oldest.org/animals/fossils/.

266 Elise Kjorstad, "These Small Bacteria Eat Huge Amounts of Methane. How Will They Respond to Climate Change?" February 4, 2023, https://www.sciencenorway.no/bacteria-climate-methane/these-small-bacteria-eat-huge-amounts-of-methane-how-will-they-respond-to-climate-change/2150152.

267 Fossils-Facts-And-Finds.com Editor, "Stromatolites-Cyanobacteria and Oxygen," n.d., https://www.fossils-facts-and-finds.com/stromatolites.html.

268 Fossils-Facts-And-Finds.com Editor, "Stromatolites…

269 Ibid.

270 Anusuya Willis on TED-Ed, "How a Single-Celled Organism Almost Wiped Out Life On Earth," August 11, 2016, https://www.youtube.com/watch?v=dO2xx-aeZ4w.

271   Jatan Mehta, "Can We Make Mars Earth-Like Through Terraforming?"(Breathing on Mars section), April 19, 2021, https://www.planetary.org/articles/can-we-make-mars-earth-like-through-terraforming#:~:text=%20Can%20We%20Make%20Mars%20Earth-Like%20Through%20Terraforming%3F,somehow%20managed%20to%20introduce%20enough%20carbon...%20More%20.

272   Lucas J Stal, "Nitrogen Fixation In Cyanobacteria," first published December 23, 2015, https://onlinelibrary.wiley.com/doi/abs/10.1002/9780470015902.a0021159.pub2.

273   Lisbdnet.com editor,"What Period Did Plants First Appear?" January 02, 2022, https://lisbdnet.com/what-period-did-plants-first-appear/#:~:text=All%20the%20analyses%20indicate%20that%20land%20plants%20first,took%20off.%20What%20period%20were%20the%20first%20plants%3F.

274   Stephanie Rose, "Do Plants Need Oxygen? Busting A Plant Myth," January 6, 2024, https://gardentherapy.ca/do-plants-need-oxygen/.

275   Timothy Halasnik, "When Did Sharks First Appear on the Planet Earth?" n.d., https://timothysawesomebioproject.weebly.com/when-did-they-first-appear.html?c=mkt_w_chnl:aff_geo:all_prtnr:sas_subprtnr:1538097_camp:brand_adtype:txtlnk_ag:weebly_lptype:hp_var:358504&sscid=31k6_y72oh.

276   World Atlas Editor, "Which Was the First Dinosaur to Walk Earth?" n.d., https://www.worldatlas.com/articles/which-was-the-first-dinosaur-to-walk-the-earth.html.

277   Charles Q. Choi for Live Science, "Asteroid Impact That Killed the Dinosaurs: New Evidence," February 07, 2013, https://www.livescience.com/26933-chicxulub-cosmic-impact-dinosaurs.html.

278   "K.T. Meteorite," BBC, n.d., https://bbcplanetdinosaur.fandom.com/wiki/K-T_Meteorite.

279   Smithsonian Editor-Ocean Find Your Blue, "What Are Fossil Fuels," n.d., https://ocean.si.edu/conservation/gulf-oil-spill/what-are-fossil-fuels.

280   Ashley May, "Strange Ancient Animal Fossil is the Oldest on Record, Scientists Say," September 21,

2018, https://www.usatoday.com/story/news/nation-now/2018/09/21/oldest-known-animal-fossil-dickinsonia-revealed-scientists/1377436002/.

281　World Atlas Editor, "Which Was the First Dinosaur To Walk Earth?" n.d., https://www.worldatlas.com/articles/which-was-the-first-dinosaur-to-walk-the-earth.html.

282　American Museum of Natural History Editor, "The Evolution of Horses," n.d., https://www.amnh.org/exhibitions/horse/the-evolution-of-horses.

283　American Museum of Natural History Editor, "Researchers Discover Oldest Primate Fossil Skeleton on Record," June 5, 2013, https://www.amnh.org/explore/news-blogs/research-posts/researchers-discover-oldest-primate-fossil-skeleton-on-record.

284　American Museum of Natural History Editor, "Fossil Femur Shows Apes, Old World Monkeys Move Differently Than Ancestor," November 8, 2019, https://www.amnh.org/explore/news-blogs/research-posts/fossil-femur-primate-evolution.

285　Editing author, "Chimpanzees-Chimpanzees Evolution," n.d., https://chimpanzeesss.weebly.com/chimps-evolution.html.

286　Charles Choi, "World's Oldest Tiger Species Discovered," LiveScience, December 01, 2011, https://www.livescience.com/17252-oldest-tiger-species-discovered.html.

287　Exploratorium, "Tracing Fossil Finds: A Hominid Timeline," n.d., http://annex.exploratorium.edu/evidence/lowbandwidth/INT hominid_timeline.html.

288　Ibid.

289　History Editor, "Neanderthals," October 17, 2017, updated September 18, 2019, https://www.history.com/topics/pre-history/neanderthals.

290　Exploratorium, "Tracing Fossil Finds: A Hominid Timeline."

291　Tia Ghose for Live Science, "Genetic 'Adam and Eve' Uncovered," LiveScience, August 1, 2013, https://www.livescience.com/38613-genetic-adam-and-eve-uncovered.html.

292　Colin Schultz, "Homo Sapiens Family Tree May Be Less Complicated Than We Thought," *Smithsonian*, October 18, 2013, https://www.smithsonianmag.com/smart-news/

homo-sapiens-family-tree-may-be-less-complicated-than-we-thought-2819218/.

293 Morris, "Probability and Order…(citing from: David M. Raup, "Conflicts Between Darwin and Paleontology,")

294 Ibid.

295 Ibid.

296 Tia Ghose for Live Science, "Genetic 'Adam and Eve' Uncovered," LiveScience, August 1, 2013, https://www.livescience.com/38613-genetic-adam-and-eve-uncovered.html.

297 Ibid.

298 Ibid.

299 Shanna Johnson for U.S. Catholic, "All Animals Go to Heaven," February 11, 2016, https://uscatholic.org/blog/a-heaven-for-all/#:~:text=In%201990%20he%20is%20reported%20to%20have%20said,souls%2C%20as%20they%20were%20"created%20by%20God's%20breath."

300 Ibid.

301 Ed Anderson, Ph.D., "Animals In Near Death Experience (NDE)," March 13, 2020, https://evidenceofanimalafterlife.com/evidence-of-animal-afterlife-in-ndes/.

302 Ibid.

303 Art Battson, evaluates "Conflicts Between Darwin and Paleontology,"

304 Mike Smith for National Human Genome Research Institute, "Genetic Engineering," last updated July 21, 2022, https://www.genome.gov/genetics-glossary/Genetic-Engineering.

305 Hugh Henry and Daniel J. Dyke for *Reasons to* Believe.org, "The Origin of Human Chromosome 2: Another Look," December 6, 2018, https://reasons.org/explore/blogs/voices/the-origin-of-human-chromosome-2-another-look.

306 Ibid. (6th paragraph)

307 Ibid. (12th paragraph)

308 Tia Ghose for Live Science, "Genetic 'Adam and Eve' Uncovered,"

309 Human Origin Project.com Editor, "The Younger Dryas Event and the Prehistoric Period Extinction," n.d., https://humanoriginproject.com/younger-dryas-event-extinction-prehistoric-period/.

310 Judith Welikala for Time Magazine, "Study: Humans and Neanderthals Didn't Interbreed As Much As We Feared/Hoped," August 15, 2012, https://newsfeed.time.com/2012/08/15/study-humans-and-neanderthals-didnt-interbreed-as-much-as-we-fearedhoped/.

311 Ibid.

312 Raup, "Conflicts Between Darwin and Paleontology," p. 23. (left column, last paragraph)

313 Ibid. p. 26 (left column, second paragraph)

314 Benjamin Wiker, "How the World's Most Notorious Atheist Changed His Mind," Strange Notions,

May 15, 2013, https://strangenotions.com/flew/.

315 Ibid.

316 Ibid.

317 Editor for Courses.lumenlearning.com, Earth Science, "The Sea Floor," section: Features of the Seafloor, n.d., https://courses.lumenlearning.com/suny-earthscience/chapter/the-seafloor/#:~:text=Before%20scientists%20invented.

318 Diva Amon and Deborah Glickson, "Hydrothermal Vents," 2016 Deepwater Exploration of the Marianas, https://oceanexplorer.noaa.gov/okeanos/explorations/ex1605/background/vents/welcome.html.

319 Ibid.

320 Steven A. Austin, Ph.D., "Springs of the Ocean," Institute for Creation Research, August 1, 1981, https://www.icr.org/article/springs-ocean/.

321 Ibid.

322 Ibid.

323 Ibid.

324 James Vincent for Independent, "Earth's 'Underground Oceans' Could Have Three Times More Water Than the Surface," June 13, 2014, https://www.independent.co.uk/news/science/earth-s-underground-oceans-could-have-three-times-more-water-than-the-surface-9534266.html.

325 NASA.gov editing author, "Scientists Confirm Historic Massive Flood in Climate Change," February 28, 2006, https://www.nasa.gov/vision/earth/lookingatearth/abrupt_change.html.

326 Owen Omid Borville, "Flood Stories From Around The World," Creationist.com, November 7, 2018, https://www.creationest.com/flood-stories-world.html.

327 Bible Ask Team, "Who Wrote the Book of Job and When?" December 29, 2021, last update: February 16, 2024, https://bibleask.org/wrote-book-job/.

328 Ibid.

329 John Osgood, "Job? Who Was Job, When Did He Live, and Where Did He Live?" July 20, 2014, https://askjohnmackay.com/job-who-was-job-when-did-he-live-and-where-did-he-live/.

330 Eric Lyons, "When Did Job Live?" 2008, https://apologeticspress.org/when-did-job-live-2516/.

331 Ibid.

332 Khan Academy, "Cuneiform," n.d., https://www.khanacademy.org/humanities/ancient-art-civilizations/ancient-near-east1/the-ancient-near-east-an-introduction/a/cuneiform.

333 Joshua Mark, "Cuneiform," (found in the section: Cuneiform Literature-8th paragraph) March 15, 2018, https://www.ancient.eu/cuneiform/.

334 David Damrosch, "Epic Hero-How A Self-Taught British Genius Rediscovered the Mesopotamian Saga of Gilgamesh After 2,500 Years," May 2007, https://www.smithsonianmag.com/history/epic-hero-153362976/.

335 Mark, "Cuneiform,"

336 Ibid. (found in the section: Cuneiform Literature-3rd paragraph)

337 Ibid. (found in the section: Cuneiform Literature-end of 5th paragraph)

338 Joshua Mark, "The Ludlul-Bel-Nimeqi- Not Merely a Babylonian Job," (found at top of the second paragraph) March 06, 2011, https://www.ancient.eu/article/226/the-ludlul-bel-nimeqi---not-merely-a-babylonian-jo/.

339 Ibid. (found in the first paragraph)

340 Stewart, "When Did Moses Write, Or Compile, The Book Of Genesis?"

341 Mark, "Cuneiform," (found in the section: Cuneiform Literature-end of 3rd paragraph)

342 Osgood, "Job? Who Was Job,…"

343 Mark, "The Ludlul-Bel-Nimeqi- Not Merely a Babylonian Job," (found in the first paragraph).

344 Lyons, "When Did Job Live?"

345 Joshua Mark, "Enuma Elish-The Babalonian Epic of Creation," May 04, 2018, https://www.worldhistory.org/article/225/enuma-elish---the-babylonian-epic-of-creation---fu/ (Commentary Section-first paragraph)

346 Stefan Stenudd, "Enuma Elish3,-The Babylonian Creation Myth," The Enuma Elish Source (section: Enuma Elish tablets), 2007, https://www.creationmyths.org/enumaelish-babylonian-creation/enumaelish-babylonian-creation-3.htm.

347 James M Rochford, "(Gen. 1:1) Did The Jews Steal Their Creation and Flood Story From the Enuma Elish?" n.d., http://www.evidenceunseen.com/bible-difficulties-2/ot-difficulties/genesis-deuteronomy/gen-11-did-the-jews-steal-their-creation-and-flood-story-from-the-enuma-elish/. (cited from: James Hoffmeier see footnote [2])

348 Ibid. (cited from: Kenneth Kitchen see footnote [14] in last paragraph)

349 Ibid. (last sentence of the Ninth point)

350 Ibid. (last paragraph)

351 Ibid.

352 Mark, "The Ludlul-Bel-Nimeqi- Not Merely a Babylonian Job," (found in the first paragraph near the end)

353 Ibid. (found in the first paragraph)

354 Owen Omid Borville, "Flood Stories From Around The World," Creationist.com, November 7, 2018, https://www.creationest.com/flood-stories-world.html.

355 Ibid.

356 Ibid.

357 Wolf Carnahan, translated by Maureen Gallery Kovacs, "The Epic of Gilgamesh-Tablet XI The Story of the Flood." 1998, http://www.ancienttexts.org/library/mesopotamian/gilgamesh/tab11.htm.

358 Ibid.

359 Boating Geeks Editor, "Boat Beam-What Is It and Its Purpose?" (found in the section: Typical Boat Beam Measurements), n.d., https://boatinggeeks.com/boat-beam/#:~:text=Beam%20%3D%20 LOA2%2F3%20%2B%201%20Wherein%20LOA%20is,2%20 as%20the%20denominator%29.%20Here%20is%20an%20 example%3A.

360 Daniel for Maritime Manual, "Ship Sizes: Classification of Ships by Sizes," updated July 2, 2021, https://www.maritimemanual.com/ ship-sizes-classification-of-ships-by-sizes/.

361 Rochford, "(Gen. 1:1) Did The Jews Steal…" (cited from: Kenneth Kitchen see footnote [14])

362 Elaina Zachos for National Geographic, "Why A Giant Green Lake Turned Blood-Red," August 1, 2016, https://www.nationalgeographic. com/science/article/why-giant-green-lake-turned-blood-red-iran-algae.

363 Live Science Staff, "The Science of the 10 Plagues," LiveScience, April 11, 2017, https://www.livescience.com/58638-science-of-the-10-plagues.html.

364 Ibid.

365 Ibid.

366 Kris Permentier, Steven Vercammen, Sylvia Soetaert, and Christian Schellemans, "Carbon Monoxide Poisoning: A Literature Review Of An Often Forgotten Cause Of Intoxication In the Emergency Department," April 4, 2017, Int J Emerg Med. 2017; 10: 14., https:// www.ncbi.nlm.nih.gov/pmc/articles/PMC5380556/.

367 Carl Drews and Weiqing Han, "Dynamics of Wind Stedown at Suez and the Eastern Nile Delta," August 30, 2010, https://journals.plos. org/plosone/article?id=10.1371/journal.pone.0012481.

368 Ibid.

369 Brick Architecture, "The History of Bricks and Brickmaking," (second paragraph), 2017, https://brickarchitecture.com/about-brick/ why-brick/the-history-of-bricks-brickmaking.

370 Kim Phillips for Tyndalehouse.com, "The Rekhmire Tomb Scenes," December 7, 2021, https://tyndalehouse.com/explore/articles/ the-rekhmire-tomb-scenes/.

371 Gary Baxter, Ph.D., "Brick Making In Egypt By Hebrew Slaves," n.d., https://www.adefenceofthebible.com/2020/04/13/brick-making-in-egypt-by-hebrew-slaves/.

372 Ibid.

373 Kim Phillips for Tyndalehouse.com, "The Rekhmire Tomb Scenes,"

374 Bryan Windle, "Biblical Sites: Three Discoveries at Jericho," May 25, 2019, https://biblearchaeologyreport.com/2019/05/25/biblical-sites-three-discoveries-at-jericho/

375 NASA.gov editing author, "Scientists Confirm Historic Massive Flood in Climate Change," February 28, 2006, https://www.nasa.gov/vision/earth/lookingatearth/abrupt_change.html.

376 Julia O'Brien, "Nineveh," *Bible Odyssey*, n.d., https://www.bibleodyssey.org/places/main-articles/nineveh.

377 David P. Livingston, Ph.D., "Who Was Nimrod?" *Ancient Days*, n.d., http://www.davelivingston.com/nimrod.htm.

378 Mark Miller for Ancient Origins, "Ancient Babylonian Tablet Provides Compelling Evidence that the Tower of Babel DID Exist," May 8, 2017, https://www.ancient-origins.net/news-history-archaeology/ancient-babylonian-tablet-provides-compelling-evidence-tower-babel-did-021378.

379 Ibid.

380 Ibid.

381 Ibid.

382 Ibid.

383 Matthew Cullinan Hoffman, "Archeologists: Sodom and Gomorrah Literally Destroyed by Fire and Brimstone Falling From the Sky," LifeSite News, December 11, 2018, https://www.lifesitenews.com/news/archeologists-sodom-and-gomorrah-literally-destroyed-by-fire-and-brimstone/.

384 Ibid.

385 Thomas M. Bolin of Bible Odyssey, "Nineveh as Sin City," updated/cited March 9, 2021, https://www.bibleodyssey.org/places/related-articles/nineveh-as-sin-city#:~:text=Nineveh%20is%20one%20of%20the%20most%20prominent%20foreign,neo-Assyrian%20empire%20in%20the%20late%20seventh%20century%20B.C.E.

386   Malcolm Gladwell on YouTube, "The Unheard Story of David and
       Goliath." September 30, 2013, https://www4.bing.com/videos/search?
       q=Malcolm+Gladwell+on+YouTube%2c+"The+Unheard+Story+of+D
       avid+and+Goliath&view=detail&mid=773D67EC6DA25F2AE6E27
       73D67EC6DA25F2AE6E2&FORM=VIRE.

387   Ibid.

388   Ibid.

389   Steven M. Collins, "Was David's Sling VS. Goliath As Powerful
       As A Bullet?" May 28, 2017, https://stevenmcollins.com/
       was-davids-sling-vs-goliath-as-powerful-as-a-bullet/.

390   Gladwell on YouTube, "The Unheard Story of David…"

391   Clare Fitzgerald, guest author for War History Online., "How Sling
       Weaponry Revolutionized Warfare in The Ancient World," June 29,
       2021, https://www.warhistoryonline.com/war-articles/sling-weaponry-
       ancient-warfare.html?safari=1.

392   Ibid.

393   Bible History.com, Biblical Archaeology-Fallen Empires,
       Archaeological Discoveries and the Bible, (section: Biblical
       Archaeology at end of article in blue print), n.d., https://www.bible-
       history.com/archaeology/#:~:text=The%20Bible%20mentions%20
       many%20things%20about%20people%2C%20places,of%20its%20
       text%20in%20matters%20of%20historical%20fact.

394   Britannica Editor, "Know Why Karl Marx Called Religion
       'The Opium of the People' and His Dream of a Communist
       Revolution," n.d., https://www.britannica.com/video/186414/
       opposition-religion-Karl-Marx.

395   Peter Fenwick MD on Youtube.com, "What Really Happens
       When You Die / End-of-life Phenomenon: At Home with
       Peter Fenwick." May 02, 2018, https://www.youtube.com/
       watch?v=78SkTuk8Zd4&t=2450s.

396   Ibid.

397   Ibid.

398   Ibid.

399   Great Falls Tribune, "Lloyd Rudy Jr. Obituary," April 26-27, 2012,
       https://www.legacy.com/us/obituaries/greatfallstribune/name/
       lloyd-rudy-obituary?id=12553967.

400 Lloyd Rudy MD on YouTube.com, "Famous Cardiac Surgeon's Stories of Near-Death Experiences in Surgery," July 27, 2011, https://www.youtube.com/watch?v=JL1oDuvQR08.

401 Ibid.

402 Ibid.

403 Ibid.

404 Tony Cicoria MD on YouTube.com, "Doctor Struck By Lightning; Learns The Secret Of Creation And Consciousness (NDE)," April, 2023, https://www.youtube.com/watch?v=delYrzd3UGU.

405 Ibid.

406 Scripture4all.org, Hebrew Interlinear Bible (OT) Genesis 1:26, n.d., https://scripture4all.org/OnlineInterlinear/Hebrew_Index.htm.

407 Scripture4all.org, Hebrew Interlinear Bible (OT) Genesis 1:26, n.d., https://scripture4all.org/OnlineInterlinear/OTpdf/gen1.pdf.

408 Marc Zvi Brettler and Amy-Jill Levine, "Is Atonement Possible Without Blood? A Jewish-Christian Divide," n.d., https://www.thetorah.com/article/is-atonement-possible-without-blood-a-jewish-christian-divide.

409 Got Questions Ministries Editing Author, "Why Did God Accept Abel's Offering But Reject Cain's Offering?" Last Updated December 5, 2022, https://www.gotquestions.org/Cain-and-Abel.html.

410 History Channel, "Crucifixion," March 23, 2008, https://www.youtube.com/watch?v=AkGi9-Mb-r0.

411 J. Warner Wallace, "What Was the Shape of Jesus' Cross?" January 8, 2018, https://www.coldcasechristianity.com.

412 Don Stewart, "When Did Moses Write, Or Compile, The Book Of Genesis?" n.d., https://www.blueletterbible.org/faq/don_stewart/don_stewart_678.cfm.

413 Rapture Christ, "Sign of the Messiah," n.d., http://www.rapturechrist.com/sign_of_the_messiah.htm#:~:text=The%20sign%20of%20Jonah%20%28staying%20inside%20the%20belly,would%20believe%20that%20He%20truly%20was%20the%20Messiah

414 Bible Study, "Was Jesus Dead For Three Days and Three Nights?" n.d., https://www.biblestudy.org/basicart/was-jesus-in-the-grave-for-three-days-and-nights.html#:~:text=Our%20Savior%20was%20dead%20and,that%20he%20is%20our%20Messiah.

415 Marie Casale, "The Hebrew Calendar Points To The Year Of The Death Of Christ." Copyright 2011, http://www.marieslibrary.com/PDF_Articles/JesusDiedHebrewCalendar.pdf.

416 Bible Info, "When Was Jesus Born?" n.d., https://www.bibleinfo.com/en/questions/when-was-jesus-born.

417 BibleHub.com editor, "The Thirteenth Day of the First Month," n.d., section: Passover Preparations, https://biblehub.com/topical/t/the_thirteenth_day_of_the_first_month.htm.

418 Chabad.org editor, "Friday, 13 Nissan, 5785," April 11, 2025, section: Burn Chametz, https://www.chabad.org/calendar/view/day.asp?hdate=1/13&mode=j.

419 David C. Grabbe, "Is Passover on the First Day of Unleavened Bread? (Part One)," March 6, 2015, https://www.cgg.org/index.cfm/library/weekly/id/741/is-passover-on-first-day-unleavened-bread-part-one.htm#:~:text=While%20God%20intended%20the%20Passover%20and%20Feast%20of,Passover%20ceremony%20and%20the%20Feast%20of%20Unleavened%20Bread.

420 David C. Grabbe, "Is Passover on the First Day of Unleavened Bread? (Part Two)," March 13, 2015, https://www.cgg.org/index.cfm/library/weekly/id/742/is-passover-on-first-day-unleavened-bread-part-two.htm

421 Ibid.

422 Ask The Rabbi, "Pasover-14th or 15th?" n.d., https://www.aish.com/atr/Passover-14th-or-15th.html

423 Tovia Singer Q&A response on Outreach Judaism.org, "Did Jesus Rise from the Dead? What is the Evidence for the Resurrection?" (part 1) n.d., https://outreachjudaism.org/resurrection-evidence/. Along with Singer's "Crucifixion/Resurrection Chart" (part 2) n.d., https://outreachjudaism.org/crucifixion-resurrection-chart/.

424 Ibid.

425 Ibid.

426 Singer, "Did Jesus Rise from the Dead?/Crucifixion/Resurrection Chart"

427 Listverse.com by FlameHorse, "10 Horrifying Tortures Of Early Christians," September 24, 2013, https://listverse.com/2013/09/24/10-horrifying-tortures-of-early-christians/.

428 Singer, "Did Jesus Rise from the Dead?/Crucifixion/Resurrection Chart"

429 Ibid.

430 Ibid.

431 Ibid.

432 Ibid.

433 Ibid.

434 Biblehub.com Interlinear Bible, Greek Translator of John 19:31, https://biblehub.com/interlinear/john/19.htm.

435 Bill Fortenberry, "Bible contradiction: Did Jesus Die before or After the Passover?" 2/20/14, http://www.increasinglearning.com/blog/bible-contradiction-did-jesus-die-before-or-after-the-passover.

436 Singer, "Did Jesus Rise from the Dead?..." (section-The Crucifixion Date: On Which Day Was Jesus Crucified? - 9th paragraph)

437 Ibid. (section-The Crucifixion Date: On Which Day Was Jesus Crucified? – 10th paragraph)

438 Ibid. (section-The Crucifixion Date: On Which Day Was Jesus Crucified? – 11th paragraph)

439 Ibid. (section-The Crucifixion Date: On Which Day Was Jesus Crucified? – 16th paragraph)

440 Ibid. (section-The Crucifixion Date: On Which Day Was Jesus Crucified? – 16th paragraph)

441 Ibid. (section-The Crucifixion Date: On Which Day Was Jesus Crucified? – 17th paragraph)

442 Mike Haynes, Quora Blogger, "What Disciples Were at the Crucifixion? What Was Their Role During That Event?" Jan 11, 2018, https://www.quora.com/What-disciples-were-at-the-crucifixion-What-was-their-role-during-that-event.

443 Ibid.

444 Singer, "Did Jesus Rise from the Dead?/Crucifixion/Resurrection Chart"

445 Landis Felts, "Essential Oils for Jesus' Burial and the Grieving," June 10, 2016, http://www.reviveseven.com/essential-oils-for-jesus-burial-and-the-grieving/.

446 Ibid.

447   Bible History, "Jerusalem At Passover," n.d., https://www.bible-history.com/backd2/jerusalem.html.

448   Jonathan MS Pearce quoting FTB blogger Alethian Worldview, "Matthew And The Guards At The Tomb," Jan 15, 2013, https://skepticink.com/tippling/2013/01/15/matthew-and-the-guards-at-the-tomb/.

449   Johnny Ova, "The Roman Guard | Evidence For The Resurrection," April 28, 2020, https://www.soh.church/the-roman-guard-evidence-for-the-resurrection/#:~:text=So%20with%20that%20request%2C%20about%2030%20of%20the,himself%2C%20which%20was%20the%20official%20Roman%20wax%20seal.

450   Bible History, "Jerusalem At Passover," n.d., https://www.bible-history.com/backd2/jerusalem.html.

451   Daniel Peterson, "The 'Pilate Stone' in Israel's Caesarea-by-the-Sea," May 3, 2018, https://www.deseret.com/2018/5/3/20644446/the-pilate-stone-in-israel-s-caesarea-by-the-sea#a-stone-with-a-latin-dedicatory-inscription-of-pontius-pilate-was-part-of-an-exhibit-of-holy-land-artifacts-at-emory-universitys-michael-c-carlos-museum-in-atlanta-in-june-2007-ap-photo-john-bazemore.

452   Great Archaeology, "The Caiaphas Ossuary," copyright 2017, https://www.greatarchaeology.com/Caiaphas_ossuary.php#:~:text=Archaeology%20Review%20»%20Archaeological%20Discoveries,man%20about%2060years%20of%20age.

453   Singer, "Did Jesus Rise from the Dead?/Crucifixion/Resurrection Chart"

454   Ibid.

455   Anthony Horvath, "Guards at the Tomb: Were they Roman Guards or Jewish Guards?" StJohnny.com, March 8, 2013, https://sntjohnny.com/front/guards-at-the-tomb-were-they-roman-guards-or-jewish-guards/2203.html.

456   Taylor Marshall, "The Gruesome Death of Saint Mark the Evangelist," n.d., https://taylormarshall.com/2012/04/gruesome-death-of-saint-mark-evangelist.html.

457   Bible Scripture Editor, "The Gospel According To Mark," n.d., https://biblescripture.net/Mark.html.

458 Kyle Pope, "Is Mark 16:9-20 Inspired?" *La Vista Church of Christ*, via *Biblical Insights*, August 2009, http://lavistachurchofchrist.org/LVarticles/IsMark16920Inspired.html.

459 Ibid.

460 Ibid.

461 Quora blogger Boomy Tokan, Pastor at NICC, "What are the Differences Between Synoptic Gospel? October 7, 2018, https://www.quora.com/What-are-the-differences-between-synoptic-gospel.

462 Truth book Editor, "Jesus Asks That His Mother Be Taken From The Scene," n.d., https://truthbook.com/jesus/illustrated-stories/jesus-asks-that-his-mother-be-taken-from-the-crucifixion.

463 Mike Haynes, Quora Blogger, "What Disciples Were at the Crucifixion? What Was Their Role During That Event?" Jan 11, 2018, https://www.quora.com/What-disciples-were-at-the-crucifixion-What-was-their-role-during-that-event.

464 Ibid.

465 Singer, "Did Jesus Rise from the Dead?/Crucifixion/Resurrection Chart"

466 Ibid.

467 Ibid.

468 James Davis, "The Time of Jesus' Death and Inerrancy: Is Harmonization Plausible?" "Ignotum Episemon Gabex," 37., Davis footnotes Bartina, S.J., in section: ***Proposed Views of Harmonization***-*citing Bartina*, November 25, 2013, https://bible.org/article/time-jesus-death-and-inerrancy-harmonization-plausible.

469 Ibid.

470 Ibid.

471 Ibid.

472 Ibid.

473 Singer, "Did Jesus Rise from the Dead?/Crucifixion/Resurrection Chart"

474 John Gill, "Matthew 27:44," in an Exposition of the Bible Commentary, n.d., https://www.biblestudytools.com/commentaries/gills-exposition-of-the-bible/matthew-27-44.html.

475 Ibid.

476 Singer, "Did Jesus Rise from the Dead?/Crucifixion/Resurrection Chart"

477 Christianity Editor, (*Adapted from* The Crises of the Christ, *Book V, Chapter XXIV, by G. Campbell Morgan*, "Who Was Present At The Cross?" September 13, 2010, https://www.christianity.com/jesus/death-and-resurrection/the-crucifixion/who-was-present-at-the-cross.html.

478 Ibid.

479 Singer, "Did Jesus Rise from the Dead?/Crucifixion/Resurrection Chart"

480 Ibid.

481 Ibid.

482 Ibid.

483 Ibid.

484 Ibid.

485 Andrina G. Hanson, "The Witnesses-Who and How Many People Saw Jesus Alive After His Crucifixion." 2013, http://factsandfaith.com/the-witnesses-who-and-how-many-people-saw-jesus-alive-after-his-crucifixion/.

486 John Ankerberg, The John Ankerberg Show with Lee Strobel, "The Evidence for Jesus' Resurrection/Program 2," 2007, https://jashow.org/articles/the-evidence-for-jesus-resurrectionprogram-2/.

487 Ibid.

488 Hanson, "The Witnesses…"

489 Abarim Publications Interlinear Greek/English Translation, "Luke 1:36." N.d., https://www.abarim-publications.com/Interlinear-New-Testament/Luke/Luke-1-parsed.html.

490 Got Questions Editor, "How Long Was Jesus' Ministry?" n.d., https://www.gotquestions.org/length-Jesus-ministry.html.

491 La Vista Church of Christ Editor, "How Many Passovers Did Jesus Attend During His Ministry?" January 6, 2011, https://www.lavistachurchofchrist.org/cms/how-many-passovers-did-jesus-attend-during-his-ministry/.

492 Tom Blackwell, "The Star of Bethlehem Was No Star. 'Wise Men' May Have Followed A Rare Alignment of Plants: Astrophysicist," December 2, 2016, https://nationalpost.com/news/world/

the-star-of-bethlehem-wasnt-a-star-three-wise-men-followed-rare-alignment-of-planets-to-jesus-astrophysicist.

493 Ibid.

494 FR. Dwight Longenecker, "Where Did the Wise Men Come From?" January 5, 2014, https://www.patheos.com/blogs/standingonmyhead/2014/01/where-did-the-wise-men-come-from.html.

495 Jack Kelley, "King Solomon and the Queen of Sheba," December 01, 2012, https://gracethrufaith.com/ask-a-bible-teacher/king-solomon-and-the-queen-of-sheba/.

496 Blackwell, "The Star of Bethlehem Was No Star. . ."

497 L. E. Armfield, "The Star of Bethlehem-Can the Star of Bethlehem Be Explained Astronomically?" 1958, https://milwaukeeastro.org/archive/star_bethlehem.asp.

498 Ibid.

499 Observadores-Cometas Editor, "Possible Explanations of the Star of Bethlehem," n.d., (search in Bing for Possible Explanations of the Star of Bethlehem, then look in the section: Triple Conjunction) http://www.observadores-cometas.com/Star_of_Bethlehem/English/Possible.htm#:~:text=The%20are%20many%20possible%20explanations%20of%20the%20Star,seriously%2C%20is%20the%20idea%20of%20a%20planetary%20occultation.

500 Ibid.

501 Observadores-Cometas Editor, "Chinese and Babylonian Observations," n.d., http://www.observadores-cometas.com/Star_of_Bethlehem/English/Chinese.htm

502 Ray Vander Laan, "Herod's Family," last updated 2020, https://www.thattheworldmayknow.com/herods-family.

503 Mahlon H. Smith, "Uprisings after Herod" n.d., https://virtualreligion.net/iho/uprising.html. (Copyright 1999-2020).

504 Matthew 2:13-15.

505 New Believer's Bible (New Testament), New Living Translation (NLT), copyright C1996, 2004, 2015 Tyndale House Foundation., 2 Corinthians 11:22-33 (NLT).

506 Stephen Nichols, Ph.D., "Sir William Ramsay" January 29, 2020, https://www.5minutesinchurchhistory.com/sir-william-ramsay/.

507   David Cloud, "Men Who Were Converted Trying to Disprove the Bible-Part 2 of 3," *Way of Life Literature*, April 5, 2017, https://www.wayoflife.org/reports/men-who-were-converted-disprove-bible-pt2.php.

508   Ibid.

509   Ibid.

510   Prove the Bible Editor, "Does Archaeology Confirm," in the section titled: *Concerning New Testament Persons And Practices*, n.d., http://www.provethebible.net/T2-Verac/C-0401.htm.

511   Christian Trumpet Sounding Editor, "Archaeology Verifies the Bible as God's Word," *Sir William Ramsay Defends the New Testament-Chapter 2*, n.d., http://christiantrumpetsounding.com/Archaeology/Archaeology%20Bklt/Archaeology%20Verifies%20Bible%20Ch2.htm.

512   Ibid.

513   Ibid.

514   David Cloud, "Men Who Were Converted..."

515   Bill Federer-American Minute with Bill Federer in *Self-Educated American*, March 29, 2021, "Napoleon in Exile-The Bible is No Mere Book," August 15, 2010, https://selfeducatedamerican.com/2010/08/15/napoleon-in-exile-the-bible-is-no-mere-book/#:~:text=Napoleon%20stated%3A%20.

516   Coffee Or Die.com Editor, citing Blake Stilwell's original article published on *We Are The Mighty*, "These Are The 10 Best Generals Of All Time, According To Statistics," January 17, 2021, https://coffeeordie.com/greatest-generals-statistics.

517   William Mitchell Ramsay, *Was Christ Born At Bethlehem?* p. 118. (London: Hodder and Stoughton, 27, Paternoster Row, 1898), 178-179. (This PDF can be found on https://biblicalstudies.org.uk/pdf/e-books/ramsay/was-christ-born-in-bethlehem_ramsay.pdf.

518   Ibid. p. 117.

519   Ibid. p. 227.

520   Bible Hub.com interlinear Bible translator, n.d., https://biblehub.com/interlinear/luke/2.htm.

521   Ramsay, "*Was Christ Born At Bethlehem?*" pp. 239-240.

522 Ibid. p. 239.

523 Ramsay, "*Was Christ Born At Bethlehem?*" pp. 245, 244.

524 Ramsay, "*Was Christ Born At Bethlehem?*" p. 230. (last three lines)

525 Ibid. p. 244.

526 Ibid. p. 243.

527 Ibid. p. 233.

528 Ibid. p. 229.

529 Ibid. p. 245.

530 Bible Hub.com interlinear Bible translator of Luke 2:2; https://biblehub.com/interlinear/luke/2.htm.

531 Ramsay, "*Was Christ Born At Bethlehem?*" p. 245.

532 Bible Hub.com interlinear Greek translator, "2232. Hegemon," n.d., https://biblehub.com/greek/2232.htm.

(see- Strong's Concordance, under "usage")

533 Bryan Windle for Bible Archaeology Report, "Quirinius: An Archaeological Biography," December 19, 2019, (section: Proposed Solutions- 4th paragraph), https://biblearchaeologyreport.com/2019/12/19/quirinius-an-archaeological-biography/#:~:text=Luke%20uses%20the%20verb%20ἡγεμονεύω%20%28hēgemoneuō%29%2C%20which%20means,was%20sent%20into%20Syria%20to%20settle%20his%20estate.

534 Livius.org editor, "Publius Quinctilius Varus," under '*Articles on Ancient History*,' page created 2003, last updated 11 October 2020, (section: Governorships-3rd and 4th paragraphs), https://www.livius.org/articles/person/quinctilius-varus/.

535 Ramsay, "*Was Christ Born At Bethlehem?*" p. 243.

536 Ibid.

537 Philip Chrysopoulos for Greek Reporter, "Strabo: The Ancient Greek Geographer Who Mapped the World," February 14, 2025, https://greekreporter.com/2025/02/14/strabo-ancient-greek-geographer-mapped-ancient-world/.

538 Francois Lasserre, "Strabo-Greek Geographer And Historian," n.d., https://www.britannica.com/biography/Strabo.

539 Ramsay, "*Was Christ Born At Bethlehem?*" p. 239-243.

540 Ramsay, "*Was Christ Born At Bethlehem?*" p. 243.

541   Ibid.

542   Ibid. p. 231-247.

543   Ibid. p. 243-244.

544   Ibid. p. 244.

545   Ibid. p. 233.

546   Ronald Syme and Barbara Levick for Oxford Classical Dictionary, "Sulpicius Quirinius, Publius," (Article Extract) March 07, 2016, https://oxfordre.com/classics/display/10.1093/acrefore/9780199381135.001.0001/acrefore-9780199381135-e-6138;jsessionid=CE5616EB8AD007846014A0040 53FD508.

547   Ramsay, "*Was Christ Born At Bethlehem?*" p. 233.

548   Ramsay, "*Was Christ Born At Bethlehem?*" p. 243-244.

549   Mahlon H. Smith, "Uprisings after Herod" n.d., https:// virtualreligion.net/iho/uprising.html. (Copyright 1999-2020).

550   Study Light, "Sabinus," '*Bible Encyclopedias; The 1901 Jewish Encyclopedia*,' n.d., https://www.studylight.org/encyclopedias/tje/s/sabinus.html.

551   Smith, "Uprisings after Herod"

552   LiquiSearch.com Editor, "List of Roman Governors of Syria-Propraetorial Imperial Legates of Roman Syria (27 BC To 135 AD)., copyright 2023, https://www.liquisearch.com/list_of_roman_governors_of_syria/propraetorial_imperial_legates_of_roman_syria_27_bc_to_135_ad.

553   Ramsay, "*Was Christ Born At Bethlehem?*" p. 237.

554   Ibid. p. 244.

555   Ibid.

556   Ronald Syme and Barbara Levick for Oxford Classical Dictionary, "Sulpicius Quirinius, Publius," (Article Extract) March 07, 2016, https://oxfordre.com/classics/display/10.1093/acrefore/9780199381135.001.0001/acrefore-9780199381135-e-6138;jsessionid=CE5616EB8AD007846014A0040 53FD508.

557   Ramsay, "*Was Christ Born At Bethlehem?*" p. 243.

558   Ibid. p. 233.

559 Bryan Windle for Bible Archaeology Report, "Quirinius: An Archaeological Biography," section: Proposed Solutions, December 19, 2019, https://biblearchaeologyreport.com/2019/12/19/quirinius-an-archaeological-biography/.

560 Ibid. p. 244.

561 Ibid. pp. 238-244.

562 Livius Editor, "Publius Quinctilius Varus," under '*Articles on Ancient History*,' section: "Governorships" (3rd paragraph), n.d., https://www.livius.org/articles/person/quinctilius-varus/.

563 Ramsay, "*Was Christ Born At Bethlehem?*" p. 244.

564 Ibid.

565 Ibid. pp. 242-243.

566 Ibid. pp. 227-228, 231.

567 Ibid. p. 233.

568 Ronald Syme and Barbara Levick for Oxford Classical Dictionary, "Sulpicius Quirinius, Publius,"

569 Ibid.

570 Bryan Windle for Bible Archaeology Report, "Quirinius: An Archaeological Biography," section: Proposed Solutions,

571 UNRV, "Syria," (last paragraph) n.d., https://www.unrv.com/provinces/syria.php.

572 Ramsay, "*Was Christ Born At Bethlehem?*" p. 233.

573 Ibid. pp. 231-233.

574 Ibid. p. 233.

575 Ibid. pp. 227-228.

576 Vatican Museum Editor, "Fragment of the Sepulchral Inscription of Quirinius," n.d., https://www.museivaticani.va/content/museivaticani/en/collezioni/musei/lapidario-cristiano/abercio/frammento-dell-iscrizione-sepolcrale-di-quirinius.html.

577 Ramsay, "*Was Christ Born At Bethlehem?*" pp. 227-228.

578 Ibid.

579 Britannica Editors, "Publius Quinctilius Varus," n.d., https://www.britannica.com/biography/Publius-Quinctilius-Varus.

580 Ramsay, "*Was Christ Born At Bethlehem?*" p. 244

581 Ibid. pp. 239-240.

582 Ibid. p. 234.

583 Ibid. p. 233.

584 Ibid. p. 159.

585 Smith, "Uprisings after Herod"

586 Greg Beyer, "The Battle of Teutoburg Forest: Give Me Back My Legions," April 10, 2023, https://www.thecollector.com/battle-of-teutoburg-forest-quinctilius-varus/.

587 Ramsay, "*Was Christ Born At Bethlehem?*" pp. 158-159.

588 Ibid. p. 138. (top paragraph)

589 Ibid. pp. 183-184.

590 Ibid. p. 244.

591 Ibid. pp. 155-156.

592 Ibid. pp. 155-158.

593 Bible Hub.com, "Luke 2," Interlinear Bible (Greek translator), https://biblehub.com/interlinear/luke/2.htm.

594 Ramsay, "*Was Christ Born At Bethlehem?*" p. 245.

595 Ibid. p. 229.

596 Ibid. pp. 158-159.

597 Ibid. p. 159.

598 Ibid. p. 239.

599 Ibid. pp. 230-244.

600 Ibid. p. 243. and p. 233.

601 Joseph M. Holden and Norman Geisler, *The Popular Handbook of Archaeology and the Bible: Discoveries That Confirm the Reliability of the Scriptures,* (Eugene, Oregon: Harvest House Publishers, 2013) p. 154 (section: Quirinius's Reign-3rd paragraph),

602 Ramsay, "*Was Christ Born At Bethlehem?*" pp. 186-187.

603 Ibid. pp. 178-196.

604 Joseph M. Holden and Norman Geisler, *The Popular Handbook of Archaeology and the Bible:* pp. 185-186.

605 Ibid. p. 192.

606 Ramsay, "*Was Christ Born At Bethlehem?*" pp. 167-170.

607 Ibid. pp. 136-137, 148-149.

608 Prove the Bible Editor, "Does Archaeology Confirm or Deny the Claims of the Bible?" in the section titled: *Concerning New Testament Persons And Practices,* n.d., http://www.provethebible.net/T2-Verac/C-0401.htm.

609 Dr. Peter Stoner, "55 Old Testament Prophecies About Jesus," 'Jesus Film Project,' January 4, 2018, https://www.jesusfilm.org/blog-and-stories/old-testament-prophecies.html.

610 Arnold Fruchtenbaum, "The Messianic Time Table According to Daniel the Prophet," Jews for Jesus, April 20, 2018, https://jewsforjesus.org/publications/issues/issues-v05-n01/the-messianic-time-table-according-to-daniel-the-prophet/.

611 Michael Horton for Core Christianity.com, "How to Understand the End-Times Prophecies in Daniel," January 16, 2019, https://corechristianity.com/resources/articles/how-to-understand-the-end-times-prophecies-in-daniel.

612 Fruchtenbaum, "The Messianic Time Table According to Daniel the Prophet,"

613 Ibid.

614 Ibid.

615 Ibid.

616 Ibid.

617 About Bible Prophecy Editor, "The Messiah Would Be Born In Bethlehem," n.d., http://www.aboutbibleprophecy.com/micah_5_2.htm.

618 Ben Burton for Ladder Of Jacob.com, "Toldot Mashiach, Part 1: Is Yeshua a Descendant of King Solomon?" October 5, 2014, https://www.ladderofjacob.com/post/son-of-solomon#:~:text=According%20to%20Luke%2C%20Yeshua%20descends%20from,Nathan%2C%20the%20son%20of%20David%2C%20not%20Solomon.

619 Ibid.

620 Ibid.

621 Christopher Y Wong, "Mary of Cleophas," copyright 2024, https://www.ewtn.com/catholicism/library/mary-of-cleophas-1080#:~:text=The%20short%20answer%20is%20that%20Mary%20of%20Cleophas,had%20one%20husband%20%28Joseph%29%20and%20remained%20a%20virgin..

622 Ibid.

623 Ibid.

624 Singer, "Did Jesus Rise from the Dead?/Crucifixion/Resurrection Chart"

625   Andrina G. Hanson, "The Witnesses-Who and How Many People Saw Jesus Alive After His Crucifixion." 2013, http://factsandfaith.com/the-witnesses-who-and-how-many-people-saw-jesus-alive-after-his-crucifixion/.

626   John Ankerberg, The John Ankerberg Show with Lee Strobel, "The Evidence for Jesus' Resurrection/Program 2," 2007, https://jashow.org/articles/the-evidence-for-jesus-resurrectionprogram-2/.

627   Charles Darwin, *On the Origins of Species by Means of Natural Selection, or Preservation of Favored Races in the Struggler for Life*, (London:John Murray, 1859), p. 292.

628   The Christian Contender, "The Scientific View…

629   Philip K. Wilson, editor for Britannica.com, "Sherlock Holmes," n.d., https://www.britannica.com/topic/Sherlock-Holmes.

630   Higgs, (Paul G. Higgs) "Chemical Evolution

631   David M. Raup, Ph.D., "Conflicts Between Darwin…" (p. 26)

632   Raup, "Conflicts Between Darwin and Paleontology," p. 25. (left column, near end of first full paragraph) https://ia800702.us.archive.org/0/items/cbarchive_35806_conflictsbetweendarwinandpaleo1930/conflictsbetweendarwinandpaleo1930.pdf.

633   Charles Darwin, *On the Origins of Species*

634   Giordano, "Here's Why Stephen Hawking Says There Is No God,"

635   Watt for NBC News, "Stephen Hawking: 'Science Makes God Unnecessary,'"

636   Charles Darwin, *On the Origins of Species…* (p. 292)

637   Nichols, "Sir William Ramsay"

638   Quote Fancy.com Editor, "Stephen Hawking Quotes," n.d., https://quotefancy.com/quote/910080/Stephen-Hawking-It-is-said-that-there-s-no-such-thing-as-a-free-lunch-But-the-universe-is.

639   YouTube, "STEPHEN HAWKING'S argument DESTROYED BY John Lennox,"

640   Philip K. Wilson, editor for Britannica.com, "Sherlock Holmes," n.d., https://www.britannica.com/topic/Sherlock-Holmes.

641   Mario Seiglie, "The Tiny Code That's Toppling Evolution," United Church of God, May 21, 2005 (section: DNA contains a genetic language), https://www.ucg.org/the-good-news/dna-the-tiny-code-thats-toppling-evolution.

642 Code.org editor, "How Many Lines of Code?" n.d., https://code.org/loc.

643 Ibid.

644 Charles Darwin, *On the Origins of Species…*